10/12

THE ANATOMY OF INFLUENCE

Yale UNIVERSITY PRESS NEW HAVEN AND LONDON

Harold Bloom

The Anatomy
of Influence

Literature as a Way of Life

Yale University Press books may be purchased in quantity for educational, business, or promotional use. For information, please e-mail sales.press@yale.edu (U.S. office) or sales@yaleup.co.uk (U.K. office).

Designed by Nancy Ovedovitz and set in Emigre Filosofia type by Duke & Company, Devon, Pennsylvania. Printed in the United States of America.

Library of Congress Cataloging-in-Publication Data
Bloom, Harold.
The anatomy of influence : literature as a way of life / Harold Bloom.
p. cm.
Includes bibliographical references and index.
ISBN 978-0-300-16760-3 (alk. paper)
1. Literature—Appreciation. 2. Literature—Philosophy. 3. Authors and readers. 4. Influence (Literary, artistic, etc.). 5. Bloom, Harold. I. Title.
PN81.B5449 2011
801'.3—dc22   2010042456

A catalogue record for this book is available from the British Library.
This paper meets the requirements of ANSI/NISO Z39.48-1992 (Permanence of Paper).

10 9 8 7 6 5 4 3 2 1

For John Hollander

For art *criticism* we need people who would show the senselessness of looking for ideas in a work of art, but who instead would continually guide readers in that endless labyrinth of linkages that makes up the stuff of art, and bring them to the laws that serve as the foundation for those linkages.

LEV TOLSTOY, *letter to Nikolai Strakhov*

CONTENTS

PRAELUDIUM

When I began writing this book, in the summer of 2004, I intended an even more baroque work than it has become. My model was to be Robert Burton's *Anatomy of Melancholy* (1621), a thousand-page labyrinth that has dazzled me since I was young. My hero and mentor Dr. Samuel Johnson read Burton to pieces, as did my late friend Anthony Burgess and a living friend, Angus Fletcher, who is my critical guide and conscience.

But Burton was my undoing. Even before a debilitating series of mishaps and illnesses, I could not sustain the challenge. Traces of Burton's marvelous madness abide in this book, and yet it may be that all I share with Burton is an obsessiveness somewhat parallel to his own. Burton's melancholy emanated from his fantastic learning: he wrote to cure his own learnedness. My book isolates literary melancholy as the agon of influence, and perhaps I write to cure my own sense of having been overinfluenced since childhood by the greatest Western authors.

In this, my final reflection upon the influence process, I offer commentary on some thirty writers, half of them British, more than a third American, and a few continental. They do not seem to me arbitrary choices: I have written about all of them before, in widely scattered books and essays, but I strive here to render my appreciations fresh and not reliant upon earlier formulations.

Five of these chapters are centered on Shakespeare, and since he is a presence throughout, probably a third of the book is given to him. There are three chapters on Walt Whitman, but he also is widely present in many more, so that another considerable segment is his. What I have to say about both poets has little to do with any currently fashionable accounts of them. Shakespeare plainly is the writer of writers, and his influence upon himself has become my obsessive concern. Walt Whitman, in the four centuries of New World literature in any Western language—Spanish, English, Portuguese, French, Yiddish—is the strongest and most original writer of the Evening Land, as D. H. Lawrence first recognized. His inner solitude echoes Shakespeare's Edgar and has companions in Dr. Johnson, Lord Byron, and such Lucretian disciples as Percy Bysshe Shelley, Walter Pater, Giacomo Leopardi, and Wallace Stevens. Solitaries in this book also include Ralph Waldo Emerson, James Joyce, Lawrence, the occult seers W. B. Yeats and James Merrill—who ultimately lived only from within—and my personal hero of American poetry, the Orphic Hart Crane.

Fifty-five years of teaching imaginative literature at Yale have taught me better than I myself am capable of teaching others. That saddens me, but I will go on teaching as long as I can because it seems to me a three in one with reading and writing. I had great teachers: M. H. Abrams among the living, Frederick A. Pottle among those departed. I have learned from talking to poets, some of whom are discussed here and some who are not. In one's eightieth year, it is difficult to separate learning from teaching, writing from reading.

Literary criticism, as I learned from Walter Pater, ought to consist of acts of appreciation. This book primarily is an appreciation, on a scale I will not again attempt. In his conclusion to *The Anatomy of Melancholy*, Burton urges: "Be not solitary, be not idle." Samuel Johnson says the same. We all fear loneliness, madness, dying. Shakespeare and Walt Whitman, Leopardi and Hart Crane will not cure those fears. And yet these poets bring us fire and light.

New Haven, Connecticut
July 31, 2010

The Point of View for
My Work as a Critic

LITERARY LOVE

When I was very young, freedom beckoned through the poets I first loved: Hart Crane, William Blake, Percy Bysshe Shelley, Wallace Stevens, Walt Whitman, William Butler Yeats, John Milton, and above all William Shakespeare in *Hamlet, Othello, King Lear, Macbeth,* and *Antony and Cleopatra*. The sense of freedom they conferred liberated me into a primal exuberance. If women and men initially become poets by a second birth, my own sense of being twice-born made me an incipient critic.

I do not recall reading any literary criticism, as opposed to literary biography, until I was an undergraduate. At seventeen I purchased Northrop Frye's study of William Blake, *Fearful Symmetry,* soon after its publication. What Hart Crane was to me at ten, Frye became at seventeen: an overwhelming experience. Frye's influence on me lasted twenty years but came to an abrupt halt on my thirty-seventh birthday, July 11, 1967, when I awakened from a nightmare and then passed the entire day in composing a dithyramb, "The Covering Cherub; or, Poetic Influence." Six years later that had evolved into *The Anxiety of Influence,* a book Frye rightly rejected from his Christian Platonist stance. Now, in my eightieth year, I would not have the patience to reread anything by Frye, but I possess almost all of Hart Crane by memory, recite much of it daily, and continue to teach him. I came to value other contemporary critics—William Empson and Kenneth Burke particularly—but have now dispensed with reading them also. Samuel Johnson, William Hazlitt, Walter Pater, Ralph Waldo Emerson, Oscar Wilde I go on reading as I do the poets.

Literary criticism, as I attempt to practice it, is in the first place *literary*, which is to say personal and passionate. It is not philosophy, politics, or institutionalized religion. At its strongest—Johnson, Hazlitt, Charles Augustin Sainte-Beuve, and Paul Valéry, among others—it is a kind of wisdom literature, and so a meditation upon life. Yet any distinction between literature and life is misleading. Literature for me is not merely the best part of life; it is itself the form of life, which has no other form.

This book returns me to the question of influence. As a child, I was overcome by the immediacy of the poets I first loved. At ten to twelve years of age, I read for the lustres, in Emerson's phrase. These seemed to memorize themselves in me. Hosts of poets have followed, and the pleasures of possession by memory have sustained me for many decades.

If you carry the major British and American poets around with you by internalization, after some years their complex relations to one another begin to form enigmatic patterns. I was a graduate student writing a doctoral dissertation on Shelley before I began to realize that influence was the inevitable problem for me to solve if I could. Existing accounts of influence seemed to me mere source study, and I became puzzled that nearly every critic I encountered assumed idealistically that literary influence was a benign process. Possibly I overreacted to this, as I was a very emotional young man. It took me from 1953 until the summer of 1967 before my meditation clarified. It was then that I awoke in my state of metaphysical terror and after a dazed breakfast with my wife began to write the dithyramb that eventually became *The Anxiety of Influence*. It took about three days to complete, and it baffled me as I brooded. What was it? I could recognize that I had been thinking it a long time, not always consciously.

It is a banal truism that the cultural present both derives from and reacts against anteriority. Twenty-first-century America is in a state of decline. It is scary to reread the final volume of Gibbon these days because the fate of the Roman Empire seems an outline that the imperial presidency of George W. Bush retraced and that continues even now. We have approached bankruptcy, fought wars we cannot pay for, and defrauded our urban and rural poor. Our troops include felons, and mercenaries of many nations are among our "contractors," fighting on their own rules or none at all. Dark influences from the American past congregate among us still. If we are a democracy, what are we to make of the palpable elements of plutocracy, oligarchy, and mounting theocracy that rule our state? How do we address the self-inflicted catastrophes that devastate our natural environment? So large is our malaise that no single writer can encompass it. We have no Emerson or Whitman among us. An institutionalized counterculture condemns individuality as archaic and depreciates intellectual values, even in the universities.

These observations serve only as speculative foreground to the belated realization that my curious revelations about influence came in the summer of 1967 and then guided me in a stand against the great awakening of the late sixties and early seventies. *The Anxiety of Influence,* published in January 1973, is a brief, gnomic theory of poetry as poetry, free of all history except literary biography. It is a hard read, even for me, because it is tense with anxious expectations, prompted by signs of the times, which it avoids mentioning. Faith in the aesthetic, in the tradition of Walter Pater and Oscar Wilde, is the little book's credo, but there is an undersong of foreboding, informed by the influence of Kierkegaard, Nietzsche, and Freud. I did not consciously realize this then, but my meditation upon poetic influence now seems to me also an attempt to forge a weapon against the gathering storm of ideology that soon would sweep away many of my students.

Yet *The Anxiety of Influence* was more than that for me, and evidently for many others worldwide these past forty-five years. Translated into languages I cannot read as well as those I can, it stays in print abroad and at home. This may be because it is a last-ditch defense of poetry, and a cry against being subsumed by any ideology. Opponents accuse me of espousing an "aesthetic ideology," but I follow Kant in believing that the aesthetic demands deep subjectivity and is beyond the reach of ideology.

Creative misreading was the prime subject of *The Anxiety of Influence,* and is no less the issue of *The Anatomy of Influence.* But more than forty years of wandering in the critical wilderness have tempered the anxious vision that descended upon me in 1967. The influence process always is at work in all the arts and sciences, as well as in the law, politics, popular culture, the media, and education. This book will be long enough without addressing the nonliterary arts, even if I were more versed in music, dance, and the visual arts than I am. Obsessed with imaginative literature, I trust my insights with regard to it, but know little of the law or of the public sphere. Even in the university I am isolated, except for my own students, since I am a department of one.

I have looked backward once already, in the preface to the second edition of *The Anxiety of Influence*, which centers upon Shakespeare and his relation to Marlowe. There I acknowledged Shakespeare's Sonnet 87, "Farewell, thou art too dear for my possession," for giving me what have become critical keywords: *misprision, swerving,* and *mistaking.* Sonnet 87 is an exquisitely modulated lament for the loss of homoerotic love but fits extraordinarily well the situation of our belatedness in culture.

The Anatomy of Influence offers a different look back. Spanning an abundance of authors, eras, and genres, it brings together my phase of thinking and writing about influence (mostly from 1967 through 1982) with my more public reflections of the first decade of the twenty-first century. I strive here for a subtler language that will construe my earlier commentary for the general reader and reflect changes in my thinking about influence. Some of these changes have been prompted by shifts in the general climate of criticism and some by the clarity that comes from a long life lived with and through the great works of the Western canon.

Influence anxiety, in literature, need not be an affect in the writer who arrives late in a tradition. It always is an anxiety *achieved* in a literary work, whether or not its author ever felt it. Richard Ellmann, the preeminent Joyce scholar and a dear friend I continue to miss, asserted that Joyce suffered no anxiety of influence, even in regard to Shakespeare and Dante, but I recall telling Ellmann that Joyce's personal lack of such anxiety was, to me, not the issue. *Ulysses* and *Finnegans Wake* manifest considerable belatedness, more in relation to Shakespeare than to Dante. Influence anxiety exists between poems and not between persons. Temperament and circumstances determine whether a later poet *feels* anxiety at whatever level of consciousness. All that matters for interpretation is the revisionary relationship between poems, as manifested in tropes, images, diction, syntax, grammar, metric, poetic stance.

Northrop Frye insisted that great literature emancipated us from anxiety. That idealization is untrue: greatness ensues from giving inevitable expression to a fresh anxiety. Longinus, critical formulator of the sublime, said that "beautiful words are in very truth the peculiar light of thought." But what is the origin of that light in a poem, play, story, novel? It is *outside* the writer, and stems from a precursor, who can be a composite figure. In regard to the precursor, creative freedom can be evasion but not flight. There must be agon, a struggle for supremacy, or at least for holding off imaginative death.

For many years before and after *The Anxiety of Influence* was first published,

literary scholars and critics were reluctant to see art as a contest for the foremost place. They seemed to forget that competition is a central fact of our cultural tradition. Athletes and politicians, of course, know no other enterprise,
yet our heritage, insofar as it is Greek, enforces this condition for all of culture
and society. Jakob Burckhardt and Friedrich Nietzsche inaugurated the modern
recovery of Greek agon, and it is now accepted by classical scholars as a guiding
principle of Greek civilization. Norman Austin, commenting upon Sophocles
in *Arion* (2006), observes that "ancient poetry was dominated by an agonistic
spirit that has hardly ever seen its equal. Athlete competed with athlete; rhapsode with rhapsode; dramatist with dramatist, with all the competitions held
as great public festivals." Western culture remains essentially Greek, since the
rival Hebrew component has vanished into Christianity, itself indebted to the
Greek genius. Plato and the Athenian dramatists had to confront Homer as
their precursor, which is to take on the unvanquishable, even if you are Aeschylus. Our Homer is Shakespeare, who is unavoidable yet is better avoided
by dramatists. George Bernard Shaw learned that wisdom rather slowly, and
most dramatists attempt to evade the author of *King Lear.*

My emphasis on agon as a central feature of literary relationships nevertheless encountered considerable resistance. Much seemed to depend on the
idea of literary influence as a seamless and friendly mode of transmission, a
gift graciously bestowed and gratefully received. *The Anxiety of Influence* also
inspired certain marginalized groups to assert their moral superiority. For decades, I was informed that women and homosexual writers entered no contest
but cooperated in a community of love. Frequently I was assured that black,
Hispanic, and Asian literary artists too rose above mere competition. Agon was
apparently a pathology confined to white heterosexual males.

Yet now, in the first decade of the twenty-first century, the pendulum has
swung to the other extreme. In the wake of French theorists of culture like the
historian Michel Foucault and the sociologist Pierre Bourdieu, the world of
letters is most often portrayed as a Hobbesian realm of pure strategy and strife.
Bourdieu reduces Flaubert's literary achievement to the great novelist's almost
martial ability to assess his literary competitors' weaknesses and strengths and
position himself accordingly.

Bourdieu's now fashionable account of literary relationships, with its emphasis on conflict and competition, has an affinity with my theory of influence and its emphasis on agon. But there are fundamental differences as well.
I do *not* believe that literary relationships can be reduced to a naked quest

for worldly power, though they may in some cases include such ambitions. The stakes in these struggles, for strong poets, are always *literary*. Threatened by the prospect of imaginative death, of being entirely possessed by a precursor, they suffer a distinctively literary form of crisis. A strong poet seeks not simply to vanquish the rival but to assert the integrity of his or her own writing self.

The rise of what I shall call the New Cynicism (a cluster of critical tendencies which are rooted in French theories of culture and encompass the New Historicism and its ilk) causes me to revisit my previous account of influence. In this, my final statement on the subject, I define influence simply as *literary love, tempered by defense*. The defenses vary from poet to poet. But the overwhelming presence of love is vital to understanding how great literature works.

The Anatomy of Influence reflects on a wide range of influence relationships. Shakespeare is the Founder, and I start with him, moving from Marlowe's influence on Shakespeare to Shakespeare's influence on writers from John Milton to James Joyce. Poets writing in English after Milton tended to struggle with him, but the High Romantics always had to make a truce with Shakespeare as well. Wordsworth, Shelley, and Keats in very different ways had to work out a relationship in their poetry between Shakespeare and Milton. As we shall see, Milton's defense against Shakespeare is highly selective repression while Joyce's is total appropriation.

I keep returning to Shakespeare in the chapters that follow not because I am a Bardolator (I am) but because he is inescapable for all who came after, in all nations of the world except France, where Stendhal and Victor Hugo went against their country's neoclassical rejection of what was regarded as dramatic "barbarism." Shakespeare is now the truly global writer, acclaimed, acted, and read in Bulgaria and Indonesia, China and Japan, Russia and where you will. The plays survive translation, paraphrase, and transmemberment because their characters are alive and universally relevant. That makes Shakespeare a special case for the study of influence: his effects are too large to be coherently analyzed. Emerson said that Shakespeare wrote the text of modern life, which prompted me to the widely misunderstood assertion that Shakespeare invented us. We would have been here anyway, of course, but without Shakespeare we would not have seen ourselves as what we are.

Throughout this book I frequently contrast Shakespeare's presence with that of Walt Whitman, the Evening Land's answer to Old Europe and Shakespeare.

Whitman, except for the egregious Edgar Allan Poe, is the only American poet who has a worldwide influence. To have engendered the poetry of D. H. Lawrence and Pablo Neruda, of Jorge Luis Borges and Vladimir Mayakovsky is to be a figure of rare variety, quite unlike the one found in weak readings of our national bard. I identify strong influences on Whitman—Lucretius, Shakespeare, and Emerson among them. And I go on to chart Whitman's influence on later writers, beginning with Stevens, Lawrence, and Crane, and culminating in poets of my own generation: James Wright, Amy Clampitt, A. R. Ammons, Mark Strand, W. S. Merwin, Charles Wright, John Ashbery, and others.

The large contours of this book are chronological: its four sections proceed from the sixteenth to the twenty-first century. But there are multiple crossings over time and space as well. Shelley appears in several chapters as a strong influence on Yeats, Browning, and Stevens, and as a somewhat reluctant skeptic too. Whitman, who appears in many chapters, comes in at least two key guises. He is *the* poet of the American Sublime, but he is an important representative of the Skeptical Sublime, and as such he appears alongside Shelley, Leopardi, Pater, Stevens, and the more covert Lucretians John Dryden, Samuel Johnson, Milton, and Tennyson. The structure of literary influence is labyrinthine, not linear. In the spirit of the passage from Tolstoy that serves as an epigraph to this book, I seek here to guide readers though some of the "endless labyrinth of linkages that makes up the stuff of art."

As *The Anatomy of Influence* is my virtual swan song, my desire is to say in one place most of what I have learned to think about how influence works in imaginative literature, particularly in English but also in a handful of writers in other tongues. Sometimes in the long nights I experience as I recover slowly from my various mishaps and illnesses, I ask myself why I have always been so obsessed with problems of influence. My own subjectivity from the age of ten on was formed by reading poetry, and at some now forgotten time I began to puzzle at influences. The first I recall included William Blake on Hart Crane, Milton and Wordsworth on Shelley, Walt Whitman on T. S. Eliot and Wallace Stevens, Keats on Tennyson. Gradually I realized how to transcend echoes and allusions, and to find the more crucial matter of the transmission of poetic stances and vision. Yeats was a particular problem for me since his relation to Shelley and Blake was palpable but his deepest longings were so contrary to theirs.

My ways of writing about literary influence have been widely regarded as relying upon Freud's Oedipus complex. But that is just wrong, as I have explained before, to little avail. Freud's Hamlet complex is far closer, or even better, your Hamlet complex and mine. Hamlet's deepest struggles are with Shakespeare and with the Ghost, who was played by the dramatist. The agon between Hamlet and his creator was the subject of a brief book I published in 2003, *Hamlet: Poem Unlimited.* There my concern was the hidden combat with the father's spirit for the prize of the name Hamlet. When Hamlet, returning from the sea, grapples with Laertes at Ophelia's grave, he exultantly cries out that he is "Hamlet the Dane."

To unname the precursor while earning one's own name is the quest of strong or severe poets. The transmutation of Walter Whitman, Jr., into Walt was accompanied by the American bard's ambivalent discipleship to Emerson. Never a transcendentalist, Whitman indeed was an Epicurean materialist: "The what is unknowable." Emerson, the Sage of Concord, declared himself free of precursors: "That which I can gain from another is never tuition but only provocation," fit motto for a prophet rather than a poet. Magpie that he was, Shakespeare voids any distinction between tuition and provocation, and loots where he chooses. Whitman tends to limit his sources because his self-presentation demands that he become his own supreme authority.

My students often ask me why great writers cannot start out fresh, without any past at their backs. I can only tell them that it just does not work that way since in practice inspiration means influence, as it did in Shakespeare's vocabulary. To be influenced is to be taught, and a young writer reads to seek instruction, even as Milton read Shakespeare, or Crane Whitman, or Merrill Yeats. More than half a century as a teacher has shown me that I am best as a provocation for my students, a realization that has carried over into my writing. That stance alienates some readers in the media and in the academy, but they are not my audience. Gertrude Stein remarked that one writes for oneself and for strangers, which I translate as speaking both to myself (which is what great poetry teaches us how to do) and to those dissident readers around the world who in solitude instinctually reach out for quality in literature, disdaining the lemmings who devour J. K. Rowling and Stephen King as they race down the cliffs to intellectual suicide in the gray ocean of the Internet.

The ephebe, as Athenians termed the young future citizen, is my word for the young deep reader who dwells in the solitude where she or he goes apart to encounter the imagination of Shakespeare. I still recall the initial impact of Shakespeare when I read *Macbeth* at thirteen. Copiousness of a kind I had never known was bestowed upon me. I did not comprehend how I was to accept the total identification with Macbeth's fierce inwardness that Shakespeare seemed to be imposing upon me. Now it seems to me that Macbeth's proleptic imagination is in some sense Shakespeare's own, even as Hamlet's cognitive quickness and Falstaff's vitalism also may reflect their creator's attributes. So unknowable is Shakespeare to us that these can be wrongheaded surmises, except that I mean Shakespeare as the poet-in-a-poet, a formulation I must adumbrate.

Forty years and more into my explication of influence, I still had not clarified my idea of the poet-in-a-poet. But I think I can manage it now, galvanized in part by the New Cynicism's reductio of all literary relationships to base self-interest. When I think of W. B. Yeats as a personality I am haunted by his images of himself, from the aesthetic 1890s of Lionel Johnson, Ernest Dowson, and Arthur Symons on to the histrionic old man of *On the Boiler,* preaching a fascist eugenics. That is not the *poet* Yeats, probably the major living poet of the Western world up to his death in 1939. When we recite "The Second Coming" or "Leda and the Swan" it is difficult not to yield to the incantatory violence, though you can teach yourself to question it. That addiction to a powerful pride of antithetical annunciations is crucial to Yeats, but it is not what I would call the *poet-in-a-poet,* the deepest Yeats. "Cuchulain Comforted," Yeats's truest death poem, fuses heroism and cowardice into a single song: "They had changed their throats and had the throats of birds." That is the voice of the poet-in-a-poet, free of all ideologies, including the occult kinds Yeats largely made up for himself, relying on Mrs. Yeats as medium for the spooks.

What I mean by the poet-in-a-poet is that which, even in the greatest of poems—*King Lear* or *Paradise Lost*—is poetry itself and not something else. I do not mean what my late friend Robert Penn Warren called "pure poetry," more a French than an American quest. The eighteenth-century poet of sensibility William Collins wrote a rugged "Ode on the Poetical Character," the spirit of which is carried on in Coleridge's extraordinary fragment "Kubla Khan," whose effect upon me is akin to that of Hart Crane's "Voyages II." Ecstatic cognitive music—in Collins, Coleridge, Crane—communicates what cannot be discursively conveyed. The poet-in-a-poet secularizes the sacred, and so one looks for explanatory analogues. Daimon or genius returns us to ancient Greek formulations, and ultimately will bring us forward to Walt Whitman's "real me" or "me myself," the Whitmanian persona's "dusky demon and brother."

E. R. Dodds, whose classic study *The Greek and the Irrational* I have reread literally to pieces, distinguishes the psyche from the daimon, relying first on

Empedocles and then on what is most mysterious in Socrates. The psyche is the empirical self or rational soul, while the divine daimon is an occult self or nonrational soul. From Hellenistic times through Goethe, the daimon has been the poet's genius. In speaking of the poet-in-a-poet, I mean precisely his daimon, his potential immortality as a poet, and so in effect his divinity. It is fitting that a new perspective on Homer is opened up by considering the daimon, since the psyche in the *Iliad* and the *Odyssey* is both breath and double. Before Shakespeare, Homer was *the* poet proper. By choosing the daimon against the psyche as the inward poet, my intent is purely pragmatic. The question is, Why is poetry *poetry* and not something else, be it history, ideology, politics, or psychology? Influence, which figures everywhere in life, becomes intensified in poetry. It is the only true context for the strong poem because it is the element in which authentic poetry dwells.

Influence stalks us all as influenza and we can suffer an anguish of contamination whether we are partakers of influence or victims of influenza. What remains free in us is the daimon. I am not a poet, but I can speak of the reader-in-the-reader and also as a daimon who deserves to be appeased. In our age of the screen—computer, television, movie—the new generations grow up seemingly bereft of their daimons. I fear that they will develop new versions of the daimonic, and that a visual culture will end imaginative literature.

In *A Defence of Poetry,* Shelley set a pattern for thinking about influence that I have consciously followed from *The Anxiety of Influence* through *The Anatomy of Influence.* What does Shelley mean by *influence* in this famous passage?

> For the mind in creation is as a fading coal, which some invisible influence, like an inconstant wind, awakens to transitory brightness: this power arises from within, like the colour of a flower which fades and changes as it is developed, and the conscious portions of our natures are unprophetic either of its approach or its departure. Could this influence be durable in its original purity and force, it is impossible to predict the greatness of the results.

Like Shakespeare, by *influence* Shelley means inspiration. In the penultimate sentence of the *Defence,* poets are made identical with "the influence which is moved not, but moves." Shelley was the most idealistic of the major poets in the language, yet he knew from experience the double nature of influence: love for the poetry of Wordsworth and a strong ambivalence toward a poem like "Ode: Intimations of Immortality." From *Alastor* on to *The Triumph of Life,*

Shelley struggled with his own strong misreading of Wordsworth, a highly creative mistaking that gave us the "Ode to the West Wind" and other supreme lyrics.

But why "misreading"? I recall many cavils during the 1970s and since that accused me of favoring dyslexia, as it were. Silly seasons always are with us. There are strong misreadings and weak misreadings, but correct readings are not possible if a literary work is sublime enough. A correct reading merely would repeat the text, while asserting that it speaks for itself. It does not. The more powerful a literary artifice, the more it relies upon figurative language. That is the cornerstone of *The Anatomy of Influence,* as of all my other ventures into criticism. Imaginative literature *is* figurative or metaphoric. And in talking or writing about a poem or novel, we ourselves resort to figuration.

For many years my late friend and colleague Paul de Man and I would argue as we walked together. More often than not the dispute turned upon de Man's conviction that he had found the truth about criticism, which was that it must take up an epistemological or ironic stance in regard to literature. I answered that *any* perspective we adopted toward figurations would itself have to be figurative, as his philosophical mode clearly was. To practice criticism, properly so-called, is to think poetically about poetic thinking.

The glory and danger of highly figurative language is that we never can be certain how to confine either its possible meanings or its effects upon us. When my personal favorite and first love among the poets, Hart Crane, gives us "peonies with pony manes" ("Virginia" in *The Bridge*) we are initially delighted by the accurate wit, though we might then wonder at the elevation of a flower into an animal. This upward metamorphosis on the scale of being is a feature of the Blakean apocalypse, and the influence of William Blake felt here is throughout Crane. Crane was a far more intelligent person than generally he is taken to be, and he had a mystical and occult side, hence his readings in P. D. Ouspensky's *Tertium Organum* and his deep interest in myths of Plato's lost Atlantis. *The Bridge* reads very differently if its true models are Blake's visionary epics. Crane had immersed himself in Blake, and also in S. Foster Damon's *William Blake: His Philosophy and Symbols,* which he obtained from Damon's brother-in-law, the wonderful poet John Brooks Wheelwright. Brooklyn Bridge itself, the founding emblem of Crane's brief epic, takes on a different aura in a Blakean context. The Blakean relationship does not limit its meaning but rather charts one path through the literary labyrinth.

*   *   *

No one writing about anxiety, even if it is more textual than human, can evade Sigmund Freud, though I have spent a lifetime trying. I prefer the philosopher Søren Kierkegaard on anxiety to Freud, but Anna Freud mapped the mechanisms of defense, and my accounts of influence are indebted to her. Anna's father defined anxiety as *angst vor etwas,* or "anxious expectations."

Freud's theory of the mind or soul, after a century or so, is alive and valuable while his scientism is quite dead. I urge us to regard him as the Montaigne or Emerson of the twentieth century. The best-informed history of psychoanalysis is George Makari's *Revolution in Mind,* just published as I write these pages. Makari concludes by rightly judging psychoanalysis as the leading modern theory of the mind, citing its ideas of defense and inner conflict. Since I define influence here as literary love tempered by defense, Freud is an inevitable presence in this book; yet he is only one presence among many.

Defense (*Abwehr*) is an agonistic concept in psychoanalysis, but it is a dialectical one as well and thus a splendid fit for any theories of influence. We fall in love, and for a time we have no defenses, but after a while we develop an arsenal of apotropaic gestures. We are animated by a drive that wants us to return to the ego's narcissistic investment in itself. So too with poets. Possessed by all the ambivalence of Eros, the new but potentially strong writer struggles to ward off any totalizing attachments. Most powerful of the Freudian defenses is repression, seen as evolving from a social concern (incest taboo) to become part of biological endowment. That of course is a figuration, and even Freud at times could literalize one of his own metaphors.

This book charts varieties of defense, from repression to appropriation, through many different literary relationships, from John Milton through James Merrill. It is preoccupied throughout with our two towering precursors, Shakespeare and Whitman—with both the defenses they employed and those they engendered in others. But between Shakespeare and Whitman there are many paths, some of which will be familiar, some not. Shakespeare's unprecedented triumph over Marlowe; Milton's humbling defeat by Hamlet; the Epicurean skeptic Lucretius's uncanny power over generations of faithful and faithless poets alike; James Merrill's lifelong agon with Yeats; Whitman's still scarcely credited impact on the American anglophiles Henry James and T. S. Eliot; Giacomo Leopardi's miraculous possession of Dante and Petrarch, and on to John Ashbery's noble return to Whitman.

There are many candidates for Freud's best book, yet I favor his 1926 revision of his earlier theory of anxiety, *Inhibitions, Symptoms and Anxiety.* Here

Freud gets free of his weird contention that all anxiety ensues from repressed desire and substitutes the fecund notion that anxiety is a signal of danger, related to the infant's terror at its own helplessness.

A potentially strong poet is hardly helpless, and she may never receive a signal of anxiety in regard to the literary past; but her poems will tally them.

SUBLIME STRANGENESS

I vividly recall, with mingled affection and amusement, my first essay written for William K. Wimsatt, Jr., returned to me with the ringing comment, "You are a Longinian critic, which I abhor!" Much later, gossip reached me that my fierce former teacher had abstained from voting on my tenure, telling his colleagues, "He is an eighteen-inch naval gun, with tremendous firepower but always missing the cognitive target."

The single treatise we have from the more properly named Pseudo-Longinus properly should be translated "On the Heights." But by now we are unable to do without *On the Sublime,* even though *sublime* as a word remains bad currency. So too is *aesthetic,* which Pater (after its popularization by Wilde) wanted to restore to its ancient Greek sense of "perceptive."

To be a Longinian critic is to celebrate the sublime as the supreme aesthetic virtue and to associate it with a certain affective and cognitive response. A sublime poem transports and elevates, allowing the author's "nobility" of mind to enlarge its reader as well. To be a Longinian critic, for Wimsatt, however, was to flout a key tenet of the New Criticism, the tradition of which he was himself a fierce proponent.

The New Criticism was the reigning orthodoxy when I was a graduate student at Yale, and for many years after. Its messiah was that push me–pull you the Pound/Eliot, and its defining feature was a commitment to formalism. The meaning of the so-called "critical object" was to be found only within the object itself; information about the life of its author or the reactions of its readers was deemed merely misleading. Wimsatt's own contribution to the New Critical canon includes two highly influential essays, "The Affective Fallacy" and "The Intentional Fallacy," both co-written with the philosopher of art Monroe Beardsley. First published in 1949, "The Affective Fallacy" launched a major assault on the then pervasive belief that the meaning and value of a literary work could be apprehended by "its results in the mind of its audience." Wimsatt attributed this so-called affective fallacy to two of my own critical precursors, the sublime Longinus and Samuel Johnson.

The New Criticism has now long since ceased to dominate literary studies. Yet the countless critical fashions that have succeeded it have been scarcely more receptive to Longinians. In this respect, the New Critics and the New Cynics are unlikely partners in crime. In the long Age of Resentment, intense literary experience is merely "cultural capital," a means to power and glory within the parallel "economy" that Bourdieu labels the literary field. Literary love is a social strategy, more affectation than affect. But strong critics and strong readers know we cannot understand literature, *great* literature, if we deny authentic literary love to writers or readers. Sublime literature demands an emotional not an economic investment.

Shrugging off descriptions of me as "'sublime' theorist," I cheerfully affirm a passion for the difficult pleasures of the sublime, from Shakespeare, Milton, and Shelley on to Yeats, Stevens, and Crane. If "theory" had not become a mere shibboleth in literary studies, I might have accepted being described as a theorist of the American Sublime, the tradition which Emerson invented, Whitman brought to celebratory glory, and Stevens both mocked and exemplified.

I happily plead guilty also to charges that I am an "incessant canonizer." There can be no living literary tradition without secular canonization, and judgments of literary value have no significance if not rendered explicit. Yet aesthetic evaluation has been viewed with suspicion by academic critics since at least the early part of the twentieth century. The New Critics deemed it too messy an undertaking for the professional scholar-critic. Northrop Frye said that evaluation should be implicit, and that was one of the disagreements between us from 1967 on. But the New Cynicism's roots in the social sciences have produced a more clinical posture still. To speak of the *art* of literature is viewed as a breach of professional responsibility. Any literary academic who issues a judgment of aesthetic value—-better, worse than, equal to—risks being summarily dismissed as a rank amateur. Thus, the literary professoriat censures what common sense affirms and even its most hardened members acknowledge at least in private: there *is* such a thing as great literature, and it is both possible and important to name it.

For more than half a century I have tried to confront greatness directly, hardly a fashionable stance, but I see no other justification for literary criticism in the shadows of our Evening Land. Over time the strong poets settle these matters for themselves, and precursors remain alive in their progeny. Readers in our flooded landscape use their own perceptiveness. But an advance can be of some help. If you believe that the canon in time will select itself, you still can follow a critical impulse to hasten the process, as I did with the later Stevens, Ashbery, Ammons, and, more recently, Henri Cole.

As an aged critic I go on reading and teaching because it is no sin for a man to labor in his vocation. My hero of criticism Samuel Johnson said that only a blockhead would write for anything except money, but that is now only a secondary motivation. I continue to write because of the Stevensian hope that the voice that is great within us will rise up to answer the voice of Walt Whitman or the hundreds of voices invented by Shakespeare. To my students and the readers I will never meet I keep urging the work of the reader's sublime: confront only the writers who are capable of giving you a sense of something ever more about to be.

Longinus's treatise tells us that sublime literature transports and enlarges its readers. Reading a sublime poet, such as Pindar or Sappho, we experience something akin to authorship: "We come to believe we have created what we have only heard." Samuel Johnson invoked precisely this illusion of authorship when he praised Shakespeare's power to convince us that we already knew what he in fact taught us. Freud identified this aspect of the sublime in the uncanny, which returns from the flight of repression as "something familiar and old-established in the mind."

We are still not entirely certain who wrote *On the Sublime* or when; most likely the surviving fragments were composed in the first or third century C.E. But Longinus's theory achieved widespread influence only after the publication of Nicolas Boileau's French translation in 1674. William Smith's English translation followed in 1739, culminating in what Wimsatt lamented as "the Longinian bias" of "the whole eighteenth century."

Longinus's treatise exalts the sublime yet implies ambivalence as well: "what is wonderful always goes together with a sense of dismay." But that ambivalence is muted in comparison to the full-blown paradoxes of Longinus's modern heirs. From Edmund Burke to Immanuel Kant, William Wordsworth to Percy Bysshe Shelley, the sublime is at once magnificent and fraught. Burke's "Philosophical Enquiry into the Origin of Our Ideas of the Sublime and Beautiful" (1757) explains that the greatness of the sublime object induces both delight and terror: "Infinity has a tendency to fill the mind with that sort of delightful horror, which is the most genuine effect, and truest test of the sublime." Sublime experience is a paradoxical coupling of pain and pleasure. For Shelley, the sublime is a "difficult pleasure," an overwhelming experience whereby we forsake simple pleasures for ones that are almost painful.

The late-nineteenth-century critic Walter Pater contributed to theories of the sublime in his pithy description of Romanticism as the adding of strangeness to beauty. "Strangeness" for me is *the* canonical quality, the mark of sublime literature. Your dictionary will give you assurance that the word *extraneous,* still in common use, is also the Latin origin of *strange:* "foreign," "outside," "out of doors." Strangeness is uncanniness: the estrangement of the homelike or commonplace. This estrangement is likely to manifest itself differently in writers and readers. But in both cases strangeness renders the deep relation between sublimity and influence palpable.

In the case of the strong reader, strangeness often assumes a temporal guise. In his wonderful essay "Kafka and His Precursors," Jorge Luis Borges evokes the uncanny process by which the novelist and essayist Franz Kafka seems to have influenced the poet Robert Browning, his precursor by many decades. What is most *strange* in such Borgesian moments is not that the prior poet appears to have written the new poem. It is that the new poet appears to have written the prior poet's poem. Examples of this kind of chronological reordering, in which a strong poet appears miraculously to have preceded his or her precursors, abound in the pages that follow.

Freud's influence on our idea of the sublime is one example of this Borgesian reversal. The sublime from Longinus to Romanticism and beyond is subsumed by Freud's bold apprehension of *das Unheimliche* (from Friedrich Schelling), such that the Sage of Vienna becomes the parental fount to which "the Uncanny" returns. Whether Freud triumphs over literary critical tradition here or is subsumed by it is ambiguous to me. But you cannot reformulate the sublime in the twentieth century, or now in the twenty-first, without wrestling Sigmund, whose Hebrew name, Solomon, suited him far better since he was not at all Wagnerian and very much a part of Hebraic wisdom, "Weisheit the rabbi" as Stevens hinted at naming him. "Freud's eye was the microscope of potency," Stevens said with memorable grimness, and the magnificent last stand of the American Sublime in *The Auroras of Autumn* is as Freudian as it is Emersonian-Whitmanian. Longinus, Kant, Burke, and Nietzsche are all Freud's heirs.

For a strong writer, strangeness *is* the anxiety of influence. The inescapable condition of sublime or high literature is agon: Pindar, the Athenian tragedians, and Plato struggled with Homer, who always wins. The height of literature commences again with Dante, and goes on through Shakespeare, Cervantes, Milton, and Pope. Implicit in Longinus's famous celebration of the sublime—"Filled with delight and pride we believe we have created what we have heard"—is influence anxiety. What is my creation and what is merely heard? This anxiety is a matter of both personal and literary identity. What is the me and the not-me? Where do other voices end and my own begin? The sublime conveys imaginative power and weakness at once. It transports us beyond ourselves, provoking the uncanny recognition that one is never fully the author of one's work or one's self.

More than half a century ago, I lunched occasionally in London with the learned Owen Barfield—solicitor, historian of consciousness, literary critic, visionary, and author of two permanent books, *Poetic Diction* (1928) and *Saving the Appearances* (1957). Though both of us accepted Pater's definition of Romanticism as the adding of strangeness to beauty, I am forever indebted to Barfield for his codicil to Pater: "It must be a strangeness of *meaning.*" This in turn led Barfield to a useful distinction: "It is not correlative with wonder; for wonder is our reaction to things which we are conscious of not quite understanding, or at any rate of understanding less than we had thought. The element of strangeness in beauty has the contrary effect. It arises from contact with a different kind of *consciousness* from our own, different, yet not so remote that we cannot partly share it, as indeed, in such a connection, the mere word 'contact' implies. Strangeness, in fact, arouses wonder when we do not understand: aesthetic imagination when we do."

Shakespeare, when you give yourself completely to reading him, surprises you by the strangeness which I take to be his salient quality. We *feel* the consciousness of Hamlet or Iago, and our own consciousness strangely expands. The difference between reading Shakespeare and reading nearly any other writer is that greater widening of our consciousness into what initially must seem a strangeness of woe or wonder. As we go out to meet a larger consciousness, we metamorphose into a provisional acceptance that sets aside moral judgment, while wonder transmutes into a more imaginative understanding.

Kant defined the sublime as that which defies representation. To which I would add that the turbulence of the sublime needs representation lest it overwhelm us. I began this book by speculating that the author of *The Anatomy of Melancholy* wrote to cure his own learnedness and that I too write to cure a sense of having been overly influenced since childhood by the great works of the Western canon. My critical forerunner Samuel Johnson also viewed writing as a defense against melancholy. The most experiential of poets, Johnson feared "the hunger of the imagination" and yet yielded to it when he read the poetry he loved best. Preternaturally active, his mind courted depressiveness whenever indolent and required labor to achieve freedom. That is quite unlike the many-minded Shakespeare, the remorseless Milton, or the genial Pope. Among poets, Johnson's temperament most resembled that of Lucretius, the Epicurean materialist of whom the Christian moralist disapproved, or Leopardi, a visionary of the abyss who would have filled the great English classicist with dread.

Pater was for me the most important critic after Johnson, and like Johnson he wrote and thought about literature in a literary way. Pater's aesthetic, essentially also my own, is Lucretian through and through; it is deeply concerned with the effects of the work upon its reader: "What is this song or picture, this engaging personality presented in life or in a book, to *me*? What effect does it really produce on me? Does it give me pleasure? and if so, what sort or degree of pleasure? How is my nature modified by its presence, and under its influence?" Pater freed the word *aesthetic* from German philosophy, restoring the ancient Greek meaning of *aesthetes*, "one who perceives." Perception and "sensation" are the governing terms of Pater's criticism. Seeing is thinking for Pater the Epicurean, which accounts for his "privileged moments," which Joyce's Stephen Dedalus named "epiphanies."

Death, hardly the mother of beauty in Lucretius—who in his *De rerum natura* urged us not to bother about death since we will never experience it—is something like that for Pater, self-quarried as he was out of the odes of John Keats, and out of his favorite Shakespearean play, the be-absolute-for-death *Measure for Measure*. He quotes Victor Hugo's "Men are all condemned to death with indefinite reprieves," and this observation moves him to his most notorious eloquence:

We have an interval, and then our place knows us no more. Some
spend this interval in listlessness, some in high passions, the wisest,
at least among "the children of this world," in art and song. For our
one chance lies in expanding that interval, in getting as many pulsa-
tions as possible into the given time. Great passions may give us this
quickened sense of life, ecstasy and sorrow of love, the various forms
of enthusiastic activity, disinterested or otherwise, which come naturally to many of us. Only be sure it is passion—that it does yield you
this fruit of a quickened, multiplied consciousness. Of such wisdom,
the poetic passion, the desire of beauty, the love of art for art's sake,
has most. For art comes to you proposing frankly to give nothing
but the highest quality to your moments as they pass, and simply for
those moments' sake.

["Conclusion," *The Renaissance: Studies in Art and Poetry* (1868)]

Pater silently steals "art for art's sake" from Swinburne's 1862 review of Baudelaire. Yet like most of Pater, this motto has been largely weakly misread from
1873 to the present. Anything misunderstood through four generations has its
own sanction, though I would point out that both Wilde's witty "nature imitates
art" and Lawrence's moralizing "Art for Life's sake" are vulgarizations of the
subtle aesthetic critic. What Pater analyzes is the *love* of art for the sake only of
quickening and enhancing consciousness. We live by and in moments raised in
quality by aesthetic apprehension, and they have no teleology, no transcendent
value. Epicureanism scarcely could be purer.

My reflections on influence from the 1970s on have focused on writers of
imaginative literature, especially poets. *The Anatomy of Influence* will do the
same. But influence anxiety, an anxiety in expectation of being flooded, is of
course not confined to poets, novelists, and playwrights—or to teachers or cob-
blers or whom you will. It is a problem for critics as well. When I first addressed
these issues, I nonetheless confined my remarks to readers and poets: "Every
good reader properly *desires* to drown, but if the poet drowns, he will become
only a reader." Decades later I am acutely aware that for the critic as for the
poet, representation may be the only defense. Poetry and criticism each in its
own way involves coming to terms with the overwhelming flood of images and
sensations that Pater called phantasmagoria. Both Johnson and Pater experi-
mented with different genres of writing, but both made their mark primarily
as critics. For each, literature was not merely an object of study but a way of life.

In my own judgment Johnson remains the major literary critic in all of Western tradition. Even a glance at a good comprehensive collection of his writings shows the variety of the genres he attempted: poetry, brief biographies, essays of all kinds, book reviews, lexicons, sermons, political tracts, travel accounts, diaries, letters, prayers, and an invention of his own, the bio-critiques in *The Lives of the English Poets*. Add the drama *Irene* (a failure) and the novella *Rasselas* (a grand success), and something of Johnson's restless, rather dangerous energies can be intuited.

Johnson should have been the great poet after the death of Pope until the advent of Blake, but an authentic awe of Pope inhibited him. Johnson abandoned his poethood, praising Alexander Pope as perfect in judgment, invention, and verbal style. And yet Johnson knew better, so far as judgment and invention were concerned: Homer, Shakespeare, Milton . . . It is not that Johnson was a Pope idolator; he justly destroyed the *Essay on Man:* "Never was penury of knowledge and vulgarity of sentiment so happily disguised."

But a complex guilt prevented Johnson from the stance of the strong poet that his gifts merited and demanded. Doubtless the human guilt was filial, however unmerited. Michael Johnson, his father, was fifty-two when Samuel, his first child, was born. The father kept a bookshop in the town of Lichfield. A melancholy man, and a failure at all things, during his final months he asked his son, himself given to "vile melancholy," to attend his bookstall for him in a nearby town. Johnson's pride prevented him and he refused his father, who died soon after. Exactly fifty years later, the formidable critic went to Lichfield and took "a postchaise to Uttoxeter, and going into the market at the time of high business, uncovered my head, and stood with it bare an hour before the stall which my father had formerly used, exposed to the sneers of the standers-by and the inclemency of the weather."

The human sorrow and complexity of Samuel Johnson are caught in that bare hour, open to the elements and public mockery. All of us know, to some degree, the guilt of origins. My own memories of my father, a taciturn and restrained man, begin with his bringing me a toy scissors for my third birthday in 1933, when the Depression had left him, like many other garment workers, unemployed. I wept then at the pathos of the gift and am close to tears again as I write this. Having loved Dr. Johnson since I was sixteen when I first read Boswell and started to read the critic, invariably I fell into trying to understand him through my love, and in any case to know myself better by his example.

I regard Johnson as my critical forerunner, since my life's work from *The*

Anxiety of Influence until now seems to me more Johnsonian than Freudian or Nietzschean, a following of the great critic in his quest to understand literary imitation. I turn to Johnson on Shakespeare and Milton, Dryden and Pope, and he induces me to reflect freshly upon them and has the knack of making all four later and himself earlier, as though they were influenced by him. That particular imaginative displacement does not mark the critical work of Dryden and Coleridge, Hazlitt and Ruskin, yet enters again with Pater and his Aesthetic school: Wilde and Yeats, Virginia Woolf and Wallace Stevens.

The living critic who most nurtures my mind is Angus Fletcher, a blessed role he has filled for me since we first we met in September 1951. I nominate Fletcher as the canonical critic of my generation because he teaches what it is to think poetically about poetic thinking. Thoughts, he always emphasizes, are *partial* recognitions: absolute recognition ends even the most powerful of literary works, since how can fictions continue when truth overwhelms? *Don Quixote* seems the grand exception, but then the Knight magnificently refuses any final self-recognition until his defeat, when he falls out of his persona into the death of piety.

I read Fletcher and experience what I wish were my own thoughts coming back to me "with a certain alienated majesty," as Emerson put it. That is the critic's sublime or partial recognition.

What can be the function of literary criticism in a Disinformation Age? I see aspects of the function but only by glimpses. Appreciation subsequent to overt evaluation is vital. For me Shakespeare is the Law, Milton the Teaching, Blake and Whitman the Prophets. Being a Jew and not a Christian, I need not displace the Gospels. What could a literary messiah be? When I was young, I was baffled by modernist or New Critics. So unreal now are their polemics that I cannot recapture my fervor against them. Turning eighty had an odd effect upon me that seventy-nine did not. I will no longer strive with Resenters and other lemmings. We will be folded together in our common dust.

Read, reread, describe, evaluate, appreciate: that is the art of literary criticism for the present time. I remind myself that my stance always has been Longinian rather than philosophical, in the modes of either Plato or Aristotle.

THE INFLUENCE OF A MIND ON ITSELF

P aul Valéry, the major French poet-critic of the twentieth century, always spoke of Stéphane Mallarmé as his master. Meditations upon his relation, both personal and literary, to his forerunner inspired Valéry to the most fecund thoughts concerning influence produced in the twentieth century with the possible exception of Borges's "Kafka and His Precursors." Sadly, Borges idealized his account of literary influence by rejecting any idea of rivalry or competition in regard to precursors. Shelley once grandly remarked that all imaginative literature formed one comprehensive cyclic poem; Borges went further by amalgamating all writers into one, a Here Comes Everybody Shakespeare-Homer, James Joyce's composite before it became Borges's.

Valéry, in the Cartesian tradition, more realistically admitted ambivalences into his loving worship of Mallarmé:

> A mixture of hate and love, a merciless intimacy—with an increasing mutual divination, or closeness, a fury to go faster and deeper into the dear enemy which in itself is like combat, like a race between two only—like coitus.
>   A close game of chess can serve as a model.
>   Rules of the game
>   Proof of man's existence.
>   . . .

If I *adored* Mallarmé, it was precisely my hatred of literature and the sign of that hatred, which was still unconscious.

> [*Leonardo. Poe. Mallarmé,* trans. Malcolm Cowley and
> James R. Lawler (1972)]

This led Valéry to a further reflection:

> We say that an author is *original* when we cannot trace the hidden transformations that others underwent in his mind; we mean to say that the dependence of *what he does* on *what others have done* is excessively complex and irregular. There are works in the likeness of others, and works that are the reverse of others, but there are also works of which the relation with earlier productions is so intricate that we become confused and attribute them to the direct intervention of the gods.
>
> (To go deeper into the subject, we should also have to discuss the influence of a mind on itself and of a work on its author. But this is not the place.)

The mind's defenses are of the essence here since how one poet resists the influence of another is indistinguishable from aesthetic intelligence. To struggle with the influence of Mallarmé became a wrestling with the Angel of Death in order to win the new name: Valéry. Mallarmé, like Leonardo da Vinci, became a name for the power of mind. Over what?

In the Anglo-American tradition, the Miltonic-Wordsworthian poet asserts the power of mind over a universe of death. Valéry, like the French Poe and Mallarmé, desires the power of his mind only over the mind itself, a Cartesian quest rather than a Shakespearean one. The central man in French literature is not Rabelais, Montaigne, or Molière, nor is he Racine, Victor Hugo, Balzac, Baudelaire, Flaubert, or Proust. He is Descartes, who occupies in France the place reserved in other nations for Shakespeare, Dante, Cervantes, Goethe, Tolstoy, or Emerson. Call it the place of the Founder. Literary influence in Britain, Italy, Spain, Germany, Russia, and the United States is not radically different from country to country. But because a philosopher was the Founder, they order these matters differently in France. Thus, Valéry finds the sublime to be "a beauty entirely deductive—Cartesian." Oddly, he is describing Poe's *The Domain of Arnheim,* a work greatly improved (as is all of Poe) by French translation.

Valéry for a time was estranged from writing his poetry, perhaps the finest in the French language since Victor Hugo. Lovers of Baudelaire, Rimbaud, and Mallarmé would dispute my comparison, but not Valéry himself, who accurately observed that Hugo "attained in his illustrious old age the pinnacle of poetic power." Sparse and selective as Valéry was, at his strongest he comes close to Hugo's magnificence. Yet he underwent a phase, just before Mallarmé became his mentor, when poetry was replaced by "self-awareness pursued for its own sake." To clarify that awareness, which Valéry conceded had originated in literature, the poet-critic had to estrange himself from poetry.

Self-awareness sought entirely for its own sake is a significant journey into the interior if you happen to be Hamlet or Paul Valéry, but it is likely to collapse into solipsism for most of us. Those who now prate about either separating literature and life or yoking them together become bureaucrats of the spirit, professors of Resentment and Cynicism. Valéry, supremely intelligent, ended his great poem about the marine cemetery with the monitory outcry that the wind was rising and one should try to live.

"The influence of a mind on itself and of a work on its author" is central to Valéry's speculations upon literature. But how shall we learn to study the influence of Shakespeare's mind on itself and of *Hamlet* on its dramatist? By what procedure can we contemplate Walt Whitman's relationship in "Crossing Brooklyn Ferry" and the three superb elegies ("Out of the Cradle," "As I Ebb'd," "Lilacs") to the original 1855 *Leaves of Grass,* the volume containing what were later to be titled "Song of Myself" and "The Sleepers"? One immediate observation might be that self-influence ought to concern us only in the strongest writers. The effect of *Ulysses* upon the *Wake* is a vital matter; the influence of earlier upon later Updike is of possible interest only to those who esteem him.

Henry James, the master of self-conscious creation, is a proper subject for Valérian investigation, as are Leopardi, Eugenio Montale, Hart Crane, and Wallace Stevens, all of whom unfolded in relation to their prior imaginings. Goethe, that monster of self-awareness, made a celebrated passage from a poetry of self-denial to one of renunciation, though I remain somewhat skeptical as to what, if anything, he ever renounced. By the time he reached his major phase, Freud's precursor was his earlier self.

Shakespeare, as what W. H. Auden facetiously termed "top bard," has to be the paradigm for self-influence. A beautiful weariness is entertained by Shakespeare after his extraordinary *Antony and Cleopatra. Coriolanus* and *Timon of Athens* are in flight from high tragedy, and the so-called late romances (they are tragicomedies) intimate a withdrawal of the daimon. *Cymbeline* is an anthology of self-parody, and even *The Winter's Tale* and *The Tempest* tone down earlier intensities. How did the creator of Falstaff and Hamlet become the artificer who gave us Iago and Cleopatra? There is a curious quality they share, once accepted as a commonplace though now discarded by Shakespearean criticism. I cannot imagine Lear or Macbeth apart from their plays, but Falstaff, Hamlet, Iago, and Cleopatra have an independent existence in our consciousness. Shakespeare's art of foregrounding character is such that we delight in transposing his men and women to other contexts, speculating as to how they might fare in other plays or alongside other characters. How can that be? Each of these fourfold is made up out of words and inhabits a fixed space. Yet the illusion of vitalism is nonetheless particularly strong in them, even though it goes against my deep-est conviction to employ the word *illusion*. If Falstaff and Hamlet are illusive, then what are you and I?

Traumatized by a severe injury some years back, I found myself recovered in body but not in mind. Lying awake at night I tried to reassure myself that I after all was in my own bedroom and stared at the bookshelves, knowing what was and was not there. My sense of my own reality was wavering and needed labor to restore it. Yet no one need labor to bring literature and life together, as generations of historicists and sociologists have endeavored to do, for when could they have been apart? We cannot know where Shakespeare himself dwells in his plays and poems, but we can teach ourselves, by deep rereadings and prolonged thought, the influence on his later writings of his earlier ones. To seek the writer Shakespeare in his work is a vain quest, but to seek the work in the writer can be a rich enterprise.

What could a poet-dramatist do after writing *King Lear*? Bewilderingly, Shakespeare added *Macbeth, Antony and Cleopatra, Coriolanus, The Winter's Tale,* and *The Tempest,* among others. Shakespeare, like his protagonists, over-heard himself, and like them he overheard "Shakespeare." Like them again, he changed. Stevens, walking the beach in *The Auroras of Autumn*, observed how the Northern Lights are always enlarging the change. The movement from *Hamlet* through *Othello* on to *King Lear* and beyond enlarged the change in ways previously unknown to imaginative literature in the West.

Valéry, so far as I know, never found the right time and place to "discuss the influence of a mind on itself and of a work on its author." This book is my time and place to do so. Self-influence is a Valérian concept, and *The Anatomy of Influence* is partly a Valérian investigation, an exploration of how certain strong writers, especially Shakespeare and Whitman, were possessed by and then possessed their precursors in turn. Both Shakespeare and Whitman subsumed a vast array of strong influences in order to emerge as *the* strong influences on future generations. Shakespeare's influence is so pervasive that we all too easily lose sight of his giant art. Whitman is the most consistent influence in post-Whitmanian American poetry. He is and always will be not just the most American of poets but American poetry proper, our apotropaic champion against European culture. Yet the power of Shakespeare and Whitman is palpable not only in their long line of literary heirs but also in their self-possession: the way each exhausted his precursors to unfold finally in relation to his own prior work.

Shakespeare and Whitman are not the only writers who merit this type of Valérian investigation. I have nominated other worthy candidates already: James, Leopardi, Montale, Crane, Stevens. Sigmund Freud is another. But I choose to focus on Shakespeare and Whitman as two exemplars of the phenomenon Valéry identifies. Self-influence as I use the term is not self-reflection or self-reference, nor does it suggest either narcissism or solipsism. It is a sublime form of self-possession. That these two sublime writers came to inhabit a world of their own making reflects not weakness but strength. The worlds they made made us.

Valérian investigation follows from my lifelong interest in literary influence. To understand what makes poetry poetry and not something else one must locate the poem in relation to its precursors. These relations are the element in which true poetry dwells. And in rare instances they lead us back to the poet's own work. My friend and mentor Kenneth Burke once said that a critic must ask what a writer intended to do for himself or herself by creating a specific work. But I would amend Burke's law: the critic must ask not simply what the writer intended to accomplish as a person but what he or she intended to accomplish *as a writer.*

Inevitably, *The Anatomy of Influence* maps my own copious anxieties of influence: Johnson, Pater, Jewish traditions, Freud, Gershom Scholem, Kafka, Kierkegaard, Nietzsche, Emerson, Kenneth Burke, Frye, and above all the poets. As my last reflection on influence, the question that has preoccupied me for more than fifty years, it unfolds in relation to my previous commentary on this topic, perhaps especially *The Anxiety of Influence,* which remains my major statement to date. In that sense *The Anatomy of Influence* too is a Valérian investigation, mapping the influence of a mind on itself and of works on their author.

More than any other I have written, this book is a critical self-portrait, a sustained meditation on the writings and readings that have shaped me as a person and a critic. Now in my eightieth year, I remain gripped by particular questions. Why has influence been my obsessive concern? How have my own reading experiences shaped my thinking? Why have some poets found me and not others? What is the end of a literary life?

Recently I stared unhappily at parts of a DVD my wife brought home, an ambivalent movie called *The Good Shepherd,* directed and scripted out of a Yale that I would have said never was had I not been a marginal graduate student and faculty instructor in the early and mid-fifties. No favorite of that quasi-university centered on the undergraduates of Skull and Bones, and loathing what it represented, I survived by subduing my gentle nature and teaching my barbarous students with an initial aggressivity and hostility that I now scarcely can credit, so contrary was it to my mild and shy *Yiddishkeit* (what other term could be appropriate?). Well beyond a half-century later, I encounter certain remnants of my earliest Yale students, and sometimes warily exchange memories. When I tell them they were unteachable, a number affirm they might have learned more had I manifested even an iota of affection. Dimly I recall wishing that many of them could have been sold to the Barbary pirates, who might have instructed them more appropriately.

When I was twenty-four or thereabouts, this cohort among my students seemed the enemy, if only because they assumed *they* were the United States and Yale, while I was a visitor. After nearly six decades, I regard myself as a perpetual visitor at Yale but begin to believe everyone, alas, is also.

I try to teach in what I take to be the spirit of the sages—Akiba, Ishmael, Tarphon—but realize that they would have regarded me as another of the *minim,* like my hero Elisha ben Abuya, proscribed as the Stranger, *Acher,* or the Other, a Gnostic heretic. But we are now a remnant. Between the United States, Israel, and Europe, there are not twelve million of us remaining who affirm a Jewish identity.

My vocation as a teacher was Jewish in its origin, and in old age becomes more so. I have tried to build a hedge around the secular Western canon, my Torah, one that includes Tanakh but yields to Shakespeare's aesthetic and cognitive primacy. The answer to the Hebraic "Where shall wisdom be found?" is multiform, yet most universal in Falstaff, Rosalind, Hamlet, Cleopatra, and Lear's godson Edgar.

At moments I am uneasy, dividing my few remaining years of teaching be-

tween Shakespeare and the art of reading poems. Yet what else ought I to teach?
I am not qualified to instruct in Pirke Aboth, let alone the more formidable
tractates of the Bavli. How can Jewish culture be extended by deep reading of
The Merchant of Venice or *Song of Myself*? It cannot, and I must acknowledge that
this is not my role.

My current students (all undergraduates, by my choice) are wonderfully
varied since Yale attracts them as an international university still renowned
for literary study. The presence of so many Asians and Asian Americans helps
me understand more of whatever true function I still have at eighty. Whatever
one's personal tradition, one teaches in the name of aesthetic and cognitive
standards and values that are no longer exclusively Western.

No single scholar-critic can assert a mastery of all traditions, Eastern and
Western. By centering upon Shakespeare in my teaching, I find an entry into
Asian response. If there is a single universal author, it must be Shakespeare,
who places all of humanity into his heterocosm. Is it even a heterocosm? One
might say that of Dante, Cervantes, Tolstoy, Dickens, even Whitman, but Shakespeare seems to have usurped reality. In the pure good of theory that is not
possible, yet only Shakespeare sustains the illusion that his women and men
walk forth among us.

Cynicism abounds. Reality is becoming virtual, bad books drive out good,
reading is a dying art. What matter? Those who go on reading deeply—a universal remnant, in all generations and in all lands—will preserve what they will
come to possess by memory. I intend no literary idealism by such reflection,
but only empirical observation. A populist—*not* a popularizer—I receive all but
daily a flood of messages calling on me to keep defending the faith that canonical literature is necessary if we are to learn to see, hear, feel, and think. I am
mildly amused when journalists assure us the canon wars are over—"despite
the best efforts of Harold Bloom," to quote one of them. That is not the burden
of a multitude of communications directed to me. Literary criticism cannot
reverse authentic declines in high culture, but it can bear witness. Growing
old, I intensify my personal quest to gain more vitality from the literary text.

All literary influence is labyrinthine. Belated authors wander the maze as if
an exit could be found, until the strong among them realize that the windings
of the labyrinth are all internal. No critic, however generously motivated, can
help a deep reader escape from the labyrinth of influence. I have learned that
my function is to help you get lost.

Shakespeare, the Founder

SHAKESPEARE'S PEOPLE

professional teacher these past fifty-five years, I have for a long time
now led two discussion groups, one on Shakespeare and the other on
poets from Chaucer to Hart Crane. My experience of the two is very
different. I attempt to unravel rhetoric in Shakespeare, as I do in Milton or
Keats or Crane, but then urgencies arise that militate against this. Falstaff transcends even the florabundance of his diction and images, and Hamlet sublimely
parodies our analytics. Teaching Shakespeare you teach consciousness, the
drive and its defenses, the disorders of the human, the abysses of personality,
the warping of ethos into pathos. That is to say, you teach the range of love, of
suffering, of the tragedy of the familial. You dimly hope to win some iota of
Shakespeare's own detachment or disinterestedness, but you come up against
the chagrin of recognizing that what you considered your own emotions were
originally Shakespeare's thoughts.

That life imitates art is an ancient realization, famously revitalized by Oscar
Wilde. If Shakespeare's protagonists indeed are "free artists of themselves,"
as Hegel suggests, we should be not surprised that they move us to desire such
freedom for ourselves, even though we cannot be Falstaff or Cleopatra. Actors
know this better than most of us can. Their purpose in playing Shakespeare is
to assert their own disciplined freedom against the challenge of roles too large
to be realized: Hamlet, Lear, Othello, Macbeth. And yet the roles themselves

threaten the plays: Hamlet and Lear cannot be cabined, cribbed, confined by Shakespeare's text. They break the vessels that he prepared for them.

Vagaries of fashion drift out of the academy even as they first flood in. The Shakespearean critics who to me matter most before our own time and after Johnson are Maurice Morgann, Samuel Taylor Coleridge, William Hazlitt, Algernon Charles Swinburne, and A. C. Bradley. Even in our bad era we have had Harold Goddard, William Empson, Kenneth Burke, Frank Kermode, and A. D. Nuttall, who maintained the realization that Shakespeare most mattered because his men and women are ever-living representations of complete human beings. What informs such a realization? It precedes all criticism of Shakespeare, and only developing it in something like Shakespeare's own spirit can hope, in this belated age, to transmute opinion into true criticism. By Shakespeare's own spirit I mean here his capacious detachment or remove, that Kierkegaardian "resonance of the opposite." The art of writing lines, replies, which express a passion with full tone and complete imaginative intensity, and in which you can none the less catch the resonance of its opposite—this is an art which no poet has practiced except the unique poet Shakespeare. Such resonance enables our sympathy with Iago, Edmund, and Macbeth, who by negation speak *for us* as much as to us. Hazlitt said, "We are Hamlet." Darker to say, "We are Iago." Dostoyevsky, unlike Tolstoy a thankful receiver of Shakespeare, would not have wished us to say, "We are Svidrigailov" or "We are Stavrogin," but Shakespeare is larger. No one could want to be the cad Bertram in *All's Well That Ends Well,* yet there is a touch of Parolles in nearly everyone I have known: "Merely the thing I am shall make me live."

The miracle of Shakespearean representation is its contaminating power: one hundred major characters and a thousand adjacent figures throng our streets and sidle into our lives. Dickens and Balzac, Austen and Proust more selectively have something of this force to contaminate a heterocosm. Joyce, had he chosen, might have excelled them all, but he isolated his energy upon language, allowing only Leopold Bloom—Poldy—a Shakespearean variety and scope in personality and character.

Joyce envied Shakespeare his audience at the Globe, which had the amplitude to allow an art that appealed to all social classes and degrees of literacy. Shakespeare, after his apprenticeship to Marlowe, educated that audience beyond its limits. Then, schooled by Shakespeare, audiences infuriated Ben Jonson by rejecting his stiffly classical tragedies *Cataline* and *Sejanus.* Reading them now, I wince, embarrassed for this superb poet and moralist, whose *Volpone* and *The Alchemist* remain wonderfully playable and readable. Shakespeare's Roman tragedies had spoiled Jonson's for audiences, to Jonson's understandable resentment.

Consciousness is the *materia poetica* that Shakespeare sculpts as Michelangelo sculpts marble. We *feel* the consciousness of Hamlet or Iago, and our own consciousness strangely expands. The experience of reading Shakespeare is one of a greater widening of our consciousness into what initially must seem a strangeness of woe or wonder. As we go out to meet a larger consciousness, we metamorphose into a provisional acceptance that sets aside moral judgment, while wonder transmutes into a more imaginative understanding.

Shakespeare's most capacious consciousnesses are those of Falstaff, Hamlet, Iago, and Cleopatra. That is a common judgment and accurate. Some more limited cognizances in the plays are nearly as enigmatic: Hal/Henry V, Shylock, Malvolio, Vincentio, Leontes, Prospero, Othello, Edmund, Macbeth. For me the strangest and most enigmatic is Edgar, who has defied the understanding of almost all critics and failed to provoke sympathy all but universally. But the failure is ours: we wonder at him and refuse to reimagine his strangeness for ourselves.

Partly this is a matter of Shakespearean perspectivism, which frequently gives us personages more adroit in self-understanding than we manage to be. Hamlet is notoriously interpreted by directors, actors, and scholars so shallowly as to seem transparent. If you cannot even be certain that your murderous Cain of an uncle is not actually your biological father, what can you know? If everything is questionable, is even the fiction of cause and effect plausible? Hamlet's worthiest disciples are Nietzsche and Kierkegaard, also free artists of themselves. Nietzsche emphasizes that anything we can express is already dead in our hearts. That is why Hamlet comes to feel such contempt for the act of speaking. Kierkegaard instructs us to listen for "the resonance of the opposite" each time Hamlet utters a conviction or an affect.

Shakespeare himself is neither Nietzschean nor Kierkegaardian, atheist nor Christian, nihilist nor humanist, and he is no more Falstaff than he is Hamlet. Everyone and no one, as Borges remarked. Nevertheless I persuade myself that I find him more uncannily in certain utterances than in most others. No one speaks for him or as him, but some speeches resonate with peculiar authority. Shylock's "gaping pig" tirade hurts me more than I am easy in acknowledging, though I do not know why. Is he more mad or malevolent? Or even if it be half and half, can we doubt that indeed he would happily have carved up Antonio?—a part I suppose was played by Shakespeare himself, with Burbage exuberantly rendering Shylock.

Zest, preternatural energy, linguistic spirit: these are the marks of the great villains, comic and tragic—of Shylock, Iago, Edmund, Macbeth—and yet that exuberance is exceeded by the uninterpretable giant forms of Falstaff, Hamlet, and Cleopatra. Falstaff's gusto is high positive, though with the undersong of inevitable rejection. Cleopatra's insouciance, powered by her sexual artistry, is nearly as exuberant as Falstaff's. Hamlet, negative theologian of the stage and usurper of Shakespeare's guidance, has become so familiar to all the cosmos that we encounter unexpected surprise whenever we confront again the heart of his mystery, his refusal of Shakespeare's power to represent him, a refusal that threatens to turn us—whoever we are—into so many Guildensterns:

> Why, look you now, how unworthy a thing you make of me! You would play upon me, you would seem to know my stops, you would pluck out the heart of my mystery, you would sound me from my lowest note to my compass; and there is much music, excellent voice, in this little organ, yet cannot you make it speak. 'Sblood, do you think I am easier to be play'd on than a pipe? Call me what instrument you will, though you fret me, you cannot play upon me.

We remember this so well we are likely to smile, as when a good acquaintance arrives to tell us what we already knew. Yet we are, in relation to Hamlet, an audience of time-servers. We don't know him. If he and Shakespeare agree on anything, it is on his irremediable strangeness. Why does he mix up recorders with lutes, as he acknowledges ("Call me what instrument you will")? *Mystery* here is more than hiddenness or musical skill: it is a synonym or name for Hamlet himself. D. H. Lawrence started a poem, "It is Isis the mystery / Must be in love with me." What we know foremost about Hamlet-the-mystery is that he does not love us, or, indeed, anyone in the play, except perhaps the deceased Yorick. Iago loved Othello until that mortal god passed over him. Hamlet has a deep affinity with the loveless Edmund the Bastard. Criticism cannot sound Edmund to his limit, nor can it sound his half-brother Edgar, who is consumed by his love, both for Gloucester and for Lear.

Hamlet's intellect is simply too rapid for our ken. Recorder and lute are fused together in him. He is in every sense a comprehensive instrument for performance, whether music or drama. Of all tragic protagonists he is the ulti-mate homo ludens, as are the tragicomic Falstaff and the genre-obliterating

Cleopatra. These three play the parts of themselves in Shakespeare's theater of the mind. To some limited extent many of us do the same, but come to social and familial grief very rapidly and then surrender, content to dwindle into what the world and our own ambience concede to be our selves.

Falstaff is too amiable and Cleopatra too narcissistic to probe the heart of our mysteries. But Hamlet is extraordinarily aggressive and indicts our ease and our decorum. Something like this is the center of his strangeness. He is neither a malcontent nor a trimmer, and he loathes Elsinore. No other Shakespearean protagonist so clearly abominates the play in which he is condemned to suffer and to act.

Why then does he secure the affection of so many through the ages? I once thought this was because he so plainly does not need or want our love or esteem, but that now seems wrong to me. He prevents Horatio from suicide not out of his exaggerated regard for that straight man but because he fears a wounded name after his own departure. Yet he surely deserves a bad reputation. He murders Polonius without compunction, heedless of whom he strikes, and he sends the pathetic Rosencrantz and Guildenstern off to gratuitous execution. You could argue that morally he exceeds the shuffling Claudius in monstrosity. That is quite aside from his most hideous crime: the sadistic driving of Ophelia to madness and suicide. These are not aberrations of his antic disposition; they are Hamlet the Dane.

Nietzsche refuted Coleridge's notion that Hamlet thought too much by observing that the prince thought much too well and so thought himself through to the truth that itself is fatal. If this is to any degree mistaken, it might be that Nietzsche actually underestimates how much beyond nihilism Hamlet's voyage into the undiscovered country takes him. Dostoyevsky's nihilists—Svidrigailov, Smerdyakov, Stavrogin—are not in Hamlet's fictive class. Who else is? I would start with Iago, Edmund, and Leontes and would not know where to go outside of Shakespeare to search for more.

Hamlet centers the literary cosmos, Eastern as well as Western. His only rivals are comic—Don Quixote—or on the border of divinity: the Gospel of Mark's amazingly enigmatic Jesus, who is unsure who he is and keeps asking his thickheaded disciples, But who or what do people say I am? Don Quixote in contrast says he knows exactly who and what he is and who he may be if he chooses. Hamlet seems to me even stranger than Mark's Jesus and Cervantes's hero. He does not want to know who he is. How could he bear to be Claudius's son? And he knows what he does not want to be: the avenger in a tragedy of blood.

Hamlet the prince and player is one kind of mystery or strangeness. His play notoriously is another, one that breaks with theatrical convention and literary tradition. Joseph Loewenstein sagely argued that *Hamlet* is an agonistic play, overgoing Thomas Kyd and Christopher Marlowe (and Robert Greene, who had defamed Shakespeare) by returning to Vergil. How much of Euripides Shakespeare could have read is uncertain, and perhaps I confound Euripides with Montaigne, palpably a resort for *Hamlet* and for Hamlet, play and prince. The Euripidean unease with the gods, to grow stronger in *King Lear*, seems yet another strand in the Shakespearean capaciousness here. Nothing can go right in Elsinore because the nature of the cosmos is askew.

Angus Fletcher, commenting upon the later Wittgenstein's rather ambivalent vision of Shakespeare, notes that Wittgenstein is wholly metaphoric in characterizing him. I am fascinated that Fletcher is less concerned than I am about Wittgenstein's Tolstoyan reservations in regard to Shakespeare. Wittgenstein found Shakespeare too English, which is like asserting that Tolstoy was too Russian. But Fletcher is concerned with a rich formulation he terms "iconographies of thought" and is unbothered by the deprecation of "thinking in literature" by Hume, J. L. Austin, and Wittgenstein. "Deprecation" is not at all the precise word for Wittgenstein's stance toward Shakespeare, but what he extends with rhetorical open palm he qualifies with clenched fist. Wittgenstein's Shakespeare is a "creator of language" rather than a poet, a description I cannot understand. Yet metaphor is Shakespeare's instrument both for language making and for thinking. Unlike Aristotle, Wittgenstein evades the work of figuration, which may be why he undervalued Freud as a mere—if powerful—mythologist. Wittgenstein's "new natural linguistic forms" are, as Fletcher observes, the very outlines of thought. Consider Hamlet's bewildering cascade of metaphors for thinking or Shakespeare's own figures of thought in the Sonnets. Fletcher shows that Shakespeare's thinking embraces a larger scope of mental activities than the philosophical. These include "perceptions, cognitions of all sorts, judgments, ruminations, analysis, synthesis, and heightened figurations of inner states."

Reading Tolstoy, Wittgenstein was captured, like the rest of us, by what seems to be the earth itself crying out. Tolstoy is a total artist of narrative, in which the art itself is nature. Shakespeare differs because (except in the Sonnets) he thinks through his characters, and the strongest of them think by and with metaphor. We as yet do not know enough about our own thinking through, by, and with metaphor. Yet I venture the Nietzschean reflection that all metaphor is a mistaking in the name of life. Hart Crane, the most intensely metaphorical of all poets, is neglected as a thinker because his "logic of metaphor" is so difficult. "Adagios of islands" is glossed by Crane as the slow rocking movement of a small boat traversing islets, yet its meaning is covertly that of homoerotic sexual intercourse. Stevens in 1945 wrote a subtle poem with the excruciating title "Thinking of a Relation Between the Images of Metaphors." The wood doves, sacred to Venus, are singing, but the bass lie deep, fearful of the waterish spears of Indians who hunted their ancestors. A fisherman, all ear and eye, presumably represents the poet, who offers the dove singularity of survival by the master of metaphor:

> The fisherman might be the single man
> In whose breast, the dove, alighting, would grow still.

Since the wood dove, like Whitman's mockingbird and hermit thrush, aches for fulfillment, the metaphoric transposition of dove into fisherman is a token of thought usurping passion, a Shakespearean victory. Stevens is aware that we cannot work out any precise relationship between thinking and poetry, but in Shakespeare more than in anyone else they fuse.

Freud implied that only great souls (his own included) could liberate thinking from its sexual past, from the infant's curiosity as to origins. Remembering was the mode of freedom. Shakespeare, the sublime of literature, had no illusions that thought could be desexualized. The poetry of Donne, Jonson, Sidney, Spenser, and above all Marlowe and Marvell refute Freud's idealization as well. Milton, Shakespeare's unwilling ephebe, gives us the tragic thinker Satan as the archetype of this dilemma. Freud wanted to prefer Milton to Shakespeare, but was too intelligent a reader to manage the displacement.

Fletcher wonderfully contrasts Satan's way of thinking to Don Quixote's. Satan, magnificent solipsist, can hold a dialogue only with himself. The Knight and Sancho *can* listen to one another, and influence one another by conversation. In Shakespeare, I do not find that anyone ever truly listens to anyone else: whom can Hamlet hear except the Ghost? The dying Antony cannot persuade Cleopatra to comprehend him because she is acting the great part of Cleopatra. Prospero will not listen, nor will Lear or Macbeth. Tragedy in Shakespeare has many roots and many consequences, one of which is that it has persuaded us not to listen to one another.

Yet ultimately it is misleading to speak of Shakespeare the thinker. Milton the thinker is possible, as is Hamlet the thinker, but Shakespeare the speculator or the wonderer better suits the poet-dramatist who makes us into wonder-wounded hearers. Shakespeare the inventor would be admirable, but few understand any more what Dr. Johnson meant by "the essence of poetry is invention."

Philosophy commences in wonder but journeys into the probable. Shakespeare never abandons the possible, and we abide there with him.

Genre has little relevance for apprehending Shakespeare. In its larger contours his work moved from comedy to tragedy and on to a final phase some scholars miscall romance. *The Winter's Tale* and *The Tempest* are of no genre yet usefully can be named tragicomedy. His two central achievements in my judgment are the Falstaffiad (*Henry IV, Parts 1 and 2* and Mistress Quickly's elegy for Sir John in *Henry V*) and *Hamlet*. To call the Falstaff plays histories does not illuminate; perhaps tragicomedies is a better identification. *Hamlet,* a poem unlimited, after four centuries remains the most experimental drama ever written. The dark comedies and tragedies of blood that followed were made possible by the composition of *Hamlet.*

The succession of the grandest Shakespearean characters moves from Falstaff and Rosalind through Hamlet on to Iago, Lear, Macbeth, Cleopatra, and Prospero. The immense wealth of Shakespeare's invention also comprises the Bastard Faulconbridge, Juliet, Bottom, Shylock, Hal/Henry V, Brutus, Malvolio, Othello, Edmund, Edgar, Antony, Leontes, Caliban, and so many more. But the central triad remains Falstaff, Hamlet, and Cleopatra, the quick of an invented world.

At the close of Plato's *Symposium,* Socrates explains to Aristophanes and Agathon (a young tragic dramatist) that authors should be able to write both comedy and tragedy. The challenge ultimately was accepted by Ben Jonson, who failed at tragedy, and by Shakespeare, still unique among the world's playwrights for his achievements in both. Molière composed comedies and Racine tragedies, as did Schiller and Goethe. Kleist is of no genre, but he is dark, and so are Chekhov, Ibsen, Pirandello, Beckett—all masters of tragicomedy.

There are many unanswerable paradoxes presented by Shakespeare but one such is, How could the same dramatist have written *As You Like It* and *Othello, A Midsummer Night's Dream* and *King Lear, Twelfth Night* and *Macbeth*? Yet even that is less enigmatic than, How could *anyone* have composed *Hamlet*? Of all literary works I have read it remains the most challenging. Why does its protagonist take up all imaginative space? Everything else in Western literature either prepares for it or dwells in its enduring shadow.

There is no useful critical distinction between prince and play. How many readers and audiences these four centuries have had the odd conviction that Hamlet is their secret sharer, a "real person" somehow dropped onto a stage where actors surround him? Out-Pirandelloing the Sicilian master, Hamlet seems to protest being in any play at all, let alone what he scorns as the wrong play for someone of his genius. Indeed, a revenge tragedy is an absurd vehicle for a consciousness unlimited. Any malcontent could hack Claudius down in act 1, or, if momentarily balked, could keep at it like a monomaniac until the slaughter was accomplished. Hamlet alone senses that his quest is metaphysical, perhaps an agon with God or the gods in order to win the name Hamlet away from his putative father. Who is the usurper: the warrior King Hamlet, the adulterous King Claudius, or the Black Prince?

In *The Question of Hamlet* (1959), Harry Levin accurately observed that everything in *Hamlet* was questionable, including the play's questionings. "What do I know?" might be the play's motto. Clearly the prince has read Montaigne as deeply as we go on reading Freud, who teaches us to question our own moral psychology.

Hamlet's capacious consciousness cannot be overemphasized. No other character in all Western literature can rival the prince in quickness of mind. Where else is intelligence so persuasively dramatized? One thinks of Molière's Alceste, but even he is too limited in range of intellect. There is no circumference to Hamlet's mind: his circles of thought spiral outward and downward. To ask why Shakespeare endowed Hamlet with what I assume is the full scope of the poet's own cognitive strength seems to me a risk, for how can we surmise an answer? The poetic mind at its most incandescent changes our concept of motives, which was one of Kenneth Burke's teachings. Shakespearean motivation in his greatest villains—Iago, Macbeth, Edmund—is so fused as to appear motiveless. Iago feels betrayed by the commander for whom, as flag officer, he was prepared to die. Macbeth, sexually baffled in his enormous desire for his wife, evidently hopes to reestablish his manhood in her estimate. Edmund truly is motiveless: who can believe his assertion that he needs to stand up for bastardhood? What is desire to Edmund? He cares neither for Goneril nor Regan, Gloucester nor Edgar, Lear nor Cordelia. Does he care for his own life? He throws it away against a nameless avenger who turns out to be his transfigured half-brother. Monstrously intelligent, Edmund suspects who his adversary is and what the result is likely to be, but for the bastard usurper sprezzatura is as much a necessity as it was for Hotspur, or for the poetry of Yeats.

It was Yeats himself who, in a rather brutal letter to Sean O'Casey explaining the Abbey Theater's refusal of *The Silver Tassie* in 1920, recognized this relationship:

> Dramatic action is the fire that must burn up everything but itself;
> there should be no room in a play for anything that does not belong
> to it; the whole history of the world must be reduced to wallpaper
> in front of which the characters must pose and speak.
>
> Among the things that dramatic action must burn up are the
> author's opinions; while he is writing he has no business to know
> anything that is not a portion of that action. Do you suppose for
> one moment that Shakespeare educated Hamlet and King Lear by tell-
> ing them what he thought and believed? As I see it, Hamlet and Lear
> educated Shakespeare, and I have no doubt that in the process of that
> education he found out that he was an altogether different man to
> what he thought himself, and had altogether different beliefs. A dra-
> matist can help his characters to educate him by thinking and studying
> everything that gives them the language they are groping for through
> his hands and eyes, but the control must be theirs, and that is why the
> ancient philosophers thought a poet or dramatist Daimon-possessed.

Setting aside the blatant unfairness of bringing up *Hamlet* and *King Lear* to demolish O'Casey's fair-to-middling drama, this seems to me a classical statement of the true relation between Shakespeare and his central creations. Yeats, one of the strongest lyric poets in the language, courted the daimon, yet one hardly could say that even the best of his stage dramas burns up his opinions. Is Shakespeare unique in his uncanny detachment? There are also Molière, Chekhov, and Pirandello, though not Racine or Ibsen, who each had his own eminence but was given to visions of the decorums of tragedy.

Shakespeare and Dante, Yeats emphasized in his *Autobiographies,* were poets who achieved a unity of being in their work that gave us "the recreation of the man through the art, the birth of a new species of man." If that is so, then Dante re-created only himself, the Pilgrim. Shakespeare as a person remained one of the old species: Falstaff, Rosalind, Hamlet, Iago, Macbeth, and Cleopatra were a new reinvention of the human.

Confusing Shakespeare with God is ultimately legitimate. Other writers—Eastern and Western—attain sublimity and can give us one to three memorable beings, their self-representations included. Shakespeare's singularity prevails: about a hundred major roles and a thousand minor ones who exist oddly separate from our apperceptions. In cognitive originality, sweep of consciousness, creation of language, Shakespeare surpasses all others, though necessarily only in degree, not kind. Yet so bewildering is the all but unique gift of producing human beings in full, depth beneath depth, that we cannot get our minds around it. We think we have done so, but then the wonder wounds us again. At some strange point the difference of degree transmutes to one of kind.

Strangeness, of a very particular sort, always has been a mark of the highest imaginative literature. Yet the world has so absorbed Shakespeare, particularly from the early nineteenth century through now, that we need to read him again as if no one ever had read him before. Since our theaters are in decline, he is best read in solitude, while you keep in mind that he writes to engross a live audience, each person aware of being surrounded by others, many of them strangers. We can believe that the defining moment of Shakespeare's life and work came when he first attended Marlowe's *Tamburlaine* and observed the enthrallment of the audience by the power of Marlovian rhetoric.

Audacity, eloquence, at times a noble pathos—all are part of Marlowe's gift and scope. Yet Tamburlaine, Faustus, the Guise, Barabas, even Edward II are marvelous cartoons rather than persons. Ben Jonson's Volpone would be a monstrous human except that Jonson's art wants him to be an emblem. Middleton, Webster, Ford, Beaumont and Fletcher emerge from the Shakespearean shadow in flare-ups of recognizable human possibilities, but only the *cry* of the human abides in them. Embedding Shakespeare in his era is not a kindness to his fellows and rivals. In peripheral ways it can be useful for introducing ourselves to him, but he lights up contexts far more than they illuminate him.

Harold Goddard preceded me at locating Shakespeare's breakthrough into full representation of the human with the Bastard Faulconbridge in *King John.* As the natural son of Richard Lionheart, Faulconbridge is not Shakespeare's invention but taken over from an earlier play, *The Troublesome Raigne of King John.* Transfiguring the derivation, Shakespeare's Bastard speaks what might indeed be his dramatist's own credo at setting out upon a mature career:

> And not alone in habit and device,
> Exterior form, outward accoutrement,
> But from the inward motion to deliver
> Sweet, sweet, sweet poison for the age's tooth,

> Which though I will not practice to deceive,
>
> Yet to avoid deceit, I mean to learn.

[1.1.210–15]

This could serve as Prince Hamlet's motto, but then the Bastard also is of royal blood. "The inward motion" and that thrice repeated "sweet," oxymoronically modify a "poison" which is the truth: like Faulconbridge, the aspiration is too large for *King John.* Something in Shakespeare, perhaps as early as 1590, strains toward a larger art than the London stage as yet had seen.

Largeness is endemic in Shakespeare, even in the Sonnets, where a pervasive irony continues to evade us. The Fair Young Nobleman, quite possibly a composite of the earls of Southampton and Pembroke, is very bad news, perpetually praised by Shakespeare as the proper object of total love even though plainly he is a spoiled narcissistic brat, a sadomasochist lost in a Platonic dream of himself. Mere irony toward him is forsworn: it would not suffice. Empson is virtually unique in expressing cognizance of this. Shakespeare does not signal to us what is going on in the sequence (if it is a sequence) because all the Sonnets are hugely tropological. Doubtless there are stories at the base of it. Evidently Shakespeare, like most true poets of the time, had to rely on aristocratic patronage until the share he purchased in his stage company provided him with a robust income. Something of the atmosphere of a highly cultivated, rather decadent aristocratic set lingers throughout the Sonnets. Highly valued but never wholly accepted by Southampton and later Pembroke, Shakespeare, we can surmise, fused together the two young exquisites, as well as the Rival Poets and possibly also two or even three Dark Ladies.

I repeat myself because my subject is the breaking of genre, and Shakespeare always is too large for genre. If genre breaks, then so does the influence process, which cannot breathe where genres splinter. Creative misreading within a genre is coherent: across genres our consciousness of influence falters. Why? Critics have charted Shakespeare's vast effect upon the nineteenth-century novel: Russian, German, French, Scottish, Italian, English, American. Dostoyevsky, Goethe, Stendhal, Scott, Alessandro Manzoni, Dickens, Melville were all powerful creators, and yet Shakespearean borrowings tend to jostle in their texts, and only rarely cease to be obtrusive. The touch of Falstaff in old Karamazov troubles me, as Wilhelm Meister playing Hamlet is also a distraction. *The Charterhouse of Parma* might be even better without its aura of *Romeo and Juliet,* and allusions to Shakespeare work to slow the pace of *Redgauntlet* and

The Heart of Midlothian. Manzoni's lovers are more than vivid enough without Shakespearean enhancement, while Pip and David Copperfield are somewhat at variance with overtones of Prince Hamlet. Most strikingly, *Pierre* sinks beneath Hamletian weightings, and even Captain Ahab cannot challenge Macbeth, whom he echoes too readily.

The burden is that Shakespeare, more even than Dante, is too immense to be accommodated by those who came later unless he is modulated into a lyrical ancestor, Keats's accomplishment in his great odes or Whitman's in his surprising allusion to King Lear's godson Edgar in "Crossing Brooklyn Ferry." Within drama, Shakespeare must be handled obliquely, as he was by Ibsen, Chekhov, Pirandello, and Beckett, or else you end up with Arthur Miller's involuntary parodies of tragedy.

Some scholars have surmised that Shakespeare abandoned acting as he labored on *Measure for Measure* and *Othello,* which seems correct to me. Perhaps he doubled as the ghost and Player-King in *Hamlet* and took the role of the French king in *All's Well That Ends Well* but recoiled from playing Vincentio in his troubled farewell to comedy, the wonderfully rancid *Measure for Measure.* Molière acted right down to his end in and as *The Imaginary Invalid,* but Shakespeare always had been a role player or character actor, perpetually secondary to Richard Burbage and to the company's clown, first Will Kemp and then Robert Armin. A new kind of perspectivism enters *Measure for Measure* and *Othello,* as Shakespeare learns to trust his audience more.

In fourteen consecutive months, from 1605 to 1606, Shakespeare composed *King Lear, Macbeth,* and *Antony and Cleopatra.* He was forty-one to forty-two and clearly upon his heights as a dramatist. *King Lear* and *Macbeth,* like *Othello,* are tragedies of blood, but what genre is *Antony and Cleopatra*? Properly directed and acted it is the funniest of all Shakespearean plays, though as a double tragedy it eclipses *Romeo and Juliet.* Tragicomedy and history play do not fit the overwhelming conclusions of act 4, the death of Antony, and of act 5, Cleopatra's sublime self-immolation, in contrast to Antony's bungled suicide. And yet Antony's painful death is qualified for us by Cleopatra's superb role-playing: we attend to her far more than to him. Cleopatra's death is worthy of her self-dramatizing myth, but qualified by the extraordinary dialogue between her and the asp-selling clown: "Will it eat me?" Like *Hamlet, Antony and Cleopatra* is a poem unlimited, beyond genre. A. C. Bradley, who resisted its tragic dimension, nevertheless exalted Cleopatra as the inexhaustible equal of Falstaff, Hamlet, Iago.

We have not yet caught up to these characters, nor to their plays.

THE RIVAL POET

"King Lear"

C hristopher Marlowe in his *Tamburlaine*, a brazen attack upon *any* societal morality, associates poetry, love, and warfare as closely related expressions of power. Marlowe, by temperament and conviction, was not a Christian. His dialectics of power and of beauty are as pagan as Tamburlaine's. Except for his worship of power, Marlowe had no ideology.

Shakespeare's plays and poems are beyond institutional religion as they are beyond political ideology. Wary of the fate of Marlowe—murdered by the Elizabethan CIA, which he had served—Shakespeare allowed himself no explicit critique of anything contemporary. And yet his daimon impelled a more profound break with Renaissance humanist tradition than Marlowe needed or wanted. We are in no position to perceive the scope of Shakespeare's originality because we are inside Shakespeare's rhetoric whether we have read him or not, and his tropes are largely his own creation.

Shakespeare clearly is not an exalter of power: even Henry V is presented equivocally, and it is not sentimentalism to affirm that Falstaff, both in his glory and when he is rejected, meant more to Shakespeare and his audience than did England's hero-king. Falstaff, in one perspective, is a mark of Shakespeare's emancipation from Marlowe, though traces will remain from *Henry V* on. I often ask myself, What would Marlowe have made of Sir John? The worlds of Tamburlaine, the Guise, Edward II, Barabas, and Dr. Faustus would be reduced to cartoon frames if the living being Falstaff were to burst into them.

Yet without Marlowe, Shakespeare would not have learned how to acquire immense power over an audience. Tamburlaine is Marlowe the poet-dramatist. Shakespeare, miraculously able to conceal the inner dynamics of his art, complexly parodies Marlowe in *Titus Andronicus* but does not free himself from his dangerous precursor in *Richard III*. In some ways Marlowe was never wholly exorcized; how could he be? I envision the young Shakespeare attending a performance of *Tamburlaine* and watching the audience with fascination. The possibility of the sublime of power—*King Lear, Macbeth, Antony and Cleopatra*—was born at the moment of Marlowe's impact upon Shakespeare.

How do you overcome a great original like Marlowe, with whom you served your apprenticeship? Marlowe and Shakespeare knew each other; they could not have avoided it. Shakespeare, evidently a cautious person dedicated to self-conservation, must have been careful to steer clear of Marlowe, a quick man with a dagger who was slain indeed by his own dagger (not a suicide but a state-arranged murder). Though there is Marlovian rhetoric as late as the post-Falstaffian *Henry V,* employed ironically, I would emphasize again Shakespeare's greatest debt to Marlowe: the example of gaining astonishing power over a large audience through one's rhetoric. Shakespeare's enormous vocabulary—more than twenty-one thousand words, some eighteen hundred of them fresh coinage—dwarfs Marlowe's, and the mature rhetoric (from about 1595 on) breaks not only with Marlowe but with all of Renaissance humanism. Yet always present in Shakespeare's consciousness there would have been an awareness of watching both *Tamburlaine* and its enthralled audience.

This kind of influence relationship may be unique. The stance of Euripides toward Aeschylus or of Dante in regard to Guido Cavalcanti is very different from Shakespeare's beholding a new theater in *Tamburlaine.* I do not undervalue Marlowe by observing that the grandest Shakespearean characters have an inwardness beyond Marlowe's genius. But to have invented a dramatic control *over the audience* in which Tamburlaine's vauntings enlist them as potential allies or victims is a surpassingly strange breakthrough. Shakespeare's infinite art far surpasses this, but required it as starting point.

Marlowe exults in the "pathetical persuasion" with which Tamburlaine converts the forces sent against him into his own cohorts and clearly implies that this rhetorical power mirrors the Marlovian capture of the audience. Iago is one of Shakespeare's ultimate triumphs over his apprenticeship to Marlowe's uncanny art. We the audience are in thrall to Iago and could share his demonic joy as he goes on discovering his genius. We don't altogether, though Shakespeare, as always, gives us no moral guidance whatsoever. The Christian moralist in Dr. Johnson reacted very fiercely against this Shakespearean refusal to moralize, until at last the Great Cham of literary criticism collapsed into the absurdity of preferring the poetaster Nahum Tate's revision of *King Lear,* which ends with the marriage of Cordelia and Edgar.

Yet Shakespeare swerved from Marlowe, where moral maxims abound but invert easily, to found a new freedom of distance, unlike any other stance in imaginative literature. Ben Jonson was a severe classical moralist, even as Marlowe was totally equivocal in his only apparent judgments. Long before Samuel Johnson, Shakespeare knew that the good and evil of eternity were too ponderous for the wings of wit. One of Shakespeare's inventions (prophetic of Nietzsche) was a new kind of perspectivism, in which what we see and hear is what we are.

It is not possible to think coherently about Shakespeare's deepest purposes in his giant art. Our philosophy or theology or politics are set aside by him, without even a casual shrug. Ideology is nothing to him. His surrogates in tran-scendence, Hamlet, and in immanence, Falstaff, expose all idealizing as so much cant. Action is discredited by Hamlet; "honor," responsibility, service to the state are laughed to nothingness by Falstaff.

How is it that Shakespeare, who had no designs upon us, surpasses any other writer—even Dante, Cervantes, and Tolstoy—in revealing the full burden of our mortality? The least tendentious of dramatists, he nevertheless teaches us the reality of our lives and the necessity of confronting our common limitations as humans. I say "teaches" but the use of this word is misleading since Shake-speare, so far as we can tell, has no desire to instruct us.

You can reread, teach, and write about Shakespeare all your life and never get beyond finding him an enigma. Milton, who wants to be a monist, remains binary, and perhaps was conflicted down to the end: *Samson Agonistes* is hardly a Christian dramatic poem. It is Miltonic and therefore personal. *Macbeth,* like *King Lear,* seems to me what William Elton called a pagan play for a Christian audience. Shakespeare cannot be discussed by invoking categories like the mo-nistic or the divided self. The late A. D. Nuttall wrote a wonderful final book in his *Shakespeare the Thinker,* which celebrates the poet-dramatist's freedom from all ideology. But I tend to shy away from philosophy in regard to Shakespeare, unless you wish to consider Montaigne a philosopher. A skeptical awareness that our lives are perpetually in flux, that we are always undergoing change, separates Montaigne and Shakespeare from Plato. Montaigne, who knows everything that matters, professes to know nothing. Shakespeare, preternaturally able to pick up on any hint, clue, or indirection, does not profess at all.

I venture that Shakespeare's marvelous remove stems in some large part from his influence relationship to Marlowe, who exalts the agonistic in art, love, war. Except in the Rival Poet sonnets, Shakespeare seldom expresses this agon, setting aside Prince Hal/Henry V. Shakespeare's contest with literary anteriority operates between the lines. His major influences after Marlowe are the Geneva Bible, Ovid, and Chaucer. They yield him materia poetica, which he cheerfully pillages wherever he can find it. After *Richard III* and a few moments in *Henry V,* he finds little in Marlowe to appropriate. The consciousness of what he never stopped owing to Marlowe is another matter, on which we can only speculate. Chaucer plagiarizes Boccaccio, whom he never mentions while citing fictive authorities. Yet the example of Boccaccio was even more important: storytelling about stories, Chaucer's resource, is quarried from the Italian precursor.

Shakespeare conceivably could have become himself without Marlowe, but his astounding power to bring us woe or wonder as we attend a performance or enact a scene in the theater of mind might have been curtailed, or at least postponed. Shakespeare took his *idea* of an audience from Marlowe and then refined it.

The traces of Renaissance humanism in Marlowe's plays and poems can be oddly discordant, though they abide, but the usurpation of power is a debased Machiavellianism that would have startled Erasmus. We do not know how Athenian audiences were affected by the three great tragic dramatists. Norman Austin points out that, as for Plato, their agon was with Homer. When I reflect on Marlowe's enterprise, I find it to be without precedent, even though Shakespeare's capaciousness has obscured Marlowe's audacity. A grand nihilist, Marlowe saw all ideology as absurd. Distrusting state ideologues who had murdered Marlowe and broken Thomas Kyd by torture, Shakespeare grew into his astonishing remove—but that word is arbitrary. No one has been able to describe with exactitude where Shakespeare stands with regard to his own creation. Our best hope is to trace the crossings between the early and later plays. And here I believe that Shakespeare's ever-evolving relationship to Marlowe is vital. In early plays, such as *Titus Andronicus,* Marlowe is a looming presence who threatens to overwhelm Shakespeare; in later plays like *Lear* and *The Tempest,* Marlowe is a possession, subsumed by Shakespeare's effort to overcome his own giant art.

* * *

Shakespeare employs the word *influence* in two senses: an astral influx, and inspiration. But whose breath is it that animates early Shakespeare, from the *Henry* plays on through *King John*? I surmise that Shakespeare would have answered, "Marlowe's." Soon enough, influence ceased to be inspiration in the mature Shakespeare, but there is a large irony, probably self-directed, in his conversion of the occult inflow into the process of absorbing the precursor. The Latin for "inspiration," the divine *afflatus*, reflects the tradition of invoking a muse, most familiar to us from Homer on.

In the Sonnets, Shakespeare equivocally is inspired by the rather dreadful Fair Young Nobleman, as destructive a muse as is the Dark Lady. Of the tragic muse, or the comic, the plays tell us nothing explicit. When *Henry IV, Part 1* opens, Falstaff has long ceased to be an influence upon Prince Hal. Whatever displaced filial affection for Falstaff remains to Hal is dwarfed by negative ambivalence, which plays with the idea of hanging the reprobate knight, as a kind of revenge for having once been influenced.

Empson and Barber each suggested that the Falstaff-Hal relationship mirrors the Shakespeare-Southampton tie in the Sonnets. Does that imply a prior influence of Shakespeare upon the nobleman, with subsequent resentment? Hal's murderousness is akin to a repressed element in latecomer writers when they confront their only begetters. In Hal's obsessive need to prove Falstaff a coward, there is again an analogue to misprision of the forerunner.

Ruefully fond of legal terms, Shakespeare, whose Jack Cade had cried out to his followers that the first thing was to kill all the lawyers, fascinates me by his use of *misprision* in conjunction with *swerving* and *mistaking* in the superb Sonnet 87:

> Farewell, thou art too dear for my possessing,
> And like enough thou know'st thy estimate;
> The charter of thy worth gives thee releasing;
> My bonds in thee are all determinate.
> For how do I hold thee but by thy granting,
> And for that riches where is my deserving?
> The cause of this fair gift in me is wanting,
> And so my patent back again is swerving.
> Thyself thou gav'st, thy own worth then not knowing,
> Or me, to whom thou gav'st it, else mistaking,

> So thy great gift, upon misprision growing,
> Comes home again, on better judgment making.
> > Thus have I had thee as a dream doth flatter:
> > In sleep a king, but waking no such matter.

I appropriate from the preface to the second edition of *The Anxiety of Influence* part of my commentary on Sonnet 87:

> "Swerving" and "misprision" both depend upon "mistaking" as
> an ironical over-esteeming or over-estimation, here in Sonnet 87.
> Whether Shakespeare ruefully is lamenting, with a certain urbane
> reserve, the loss of the Earl of Southampton as lover, or as patron,
> or as friend, is not (fortunately) a matter upon which certitude is
> possible. Palpably and profoundly an erotic poem, Sonnet 87 (not by
> design) also can be read as an allegory of any writer's (or person's)
> relation to tradition, particularly as embodied in a figure taken as one's
> own forerunner. The speaker of Sonnet 87 is aware that he had been
> made an offer that he could not refuse, which is a dark insight into
> the nature of authentic tradition. "Misprision" for Shakespeare, as
> opposed to "mistaking," implied not only a misunderstanding or mis-
> reading but tended also to be a punning word-play suggesting unjust
> imprisonment. Perhaps "misprision" in Shakespeare also means a
> scornful underestimation: either way, he took the legal term and gave
> it an aura of deliberate or willful misinterpretation. "Swerving," in
> Sonnet 87, is only secondarily a returning; primarily it indicates an
> unhappy freedom.

I would revise this now to wonder if the allegory or irony of Shakespeare's relation to a precursor is not a deliberate matter here. The Rival Poet who flickers on and off in the Sonnets increasingly seems to me Marlowe and not George Chapman, who was hardly a fit agonist for Shakespeare. Sonnet 87 is homoerotic, and a shadow of past poetic anxiety may linger in it also. Swerving from Marlowe, Shakespeare found the freedom of his own authentic dramatic genius for internalizing his protagonists, including the unhappy freedom of tragedy: Hamlet, Othello, Lear, Macbeth. Marlowe, more a great Ovidian poet than a playwright, had no interest in selves beyond his own. Tamburlaine, the Guise, Barabas, Edward II, and Faustus are all Marlowe, not his alter egos. Like Ben Jonson, his antithetical disciple, Marlowe is content with cartoons and caricatures, emptinesses into whom he can instill his amazingly effective hyperboles. "The proud full sail of his great verse," Shakespeare calls Marlowe's incantatory medium in a sonnet on the Rival Poet.

Assimilating Marlowe to one's own destructive muse—Southampton or another—could have been performed even by a poet who did not have Shakespeare's capacious soul. To *integrate* Marlowe with an equivocal male muse is to touch the negative sublime and is worthier of Shakespeare's uniqueness. After Marlowe's murder in a Deptford tavern, he haunts Shakespeare, rather surprisingly in *As You Like It,* the most high-spirited of Shakespeare's plays.

The ghostly Marlowe, in my unsupported surmise, also inhabits the formidable Edmund, arch-villain of *King Lear.* William Elton helpfully remarked the proleptic confluence of Don Juan and the Machiavel in Edmund, an amalgam evidently visible in Marlowe's public persona and totally lacking in the colorless Shakespeare. Marlowe's actual psychological orientation, like his religious stance, we never will know. Francis Walsingham's CIA not only terminated him with maximum prejudice, it tortured his friend Thomas Kyd so as to obtain a confession establishing Marlowe as an atheist and a sodomite. Edmund worships the goddess Nature and seduces both Goneril and Regan with insouciance.

One of the major unexplored topoi in Shakespeare is the struggle between the enemy half-brothers Edmund and Edgar. Shakespeare presents us with two enigmas: why does Edmund seek power, and what are we to think of the recalcitrant Edgar? A prominent modern critic calls Edgar "a weak and murderous character," which is altogether untrue. A more eminent exegete, the late A. D. Nuttall, located a sadistic element in Edgar (which I dispute) but interestingly viewed it as an expiatory gesture by Shakespeare in regard to the torments visited upon the audience of *King Lear.*

I think that neither Edgar nor Edmund can be apprehended in isolation from the other. Even in mutual relationship, it is uncertain whether either half-brother can be fully comprehended. Edmund burns away his self-understanding with titanic ironies, while Edgar defies any reasonable limits by punishing himself for his gullibility toward Edmund. Intellectually Edmund is the superior and possesses a dangerous capacity for self-interest that is free of all affect, including love, morality, and compassion. In contrast, Edgar learns reality slowly, yet so surely that he becomes the inevitable avenger of his father and the certain destroyer of Edmund, who simply has no chance against him in their final duel to the death.

Edgar is the legitimate son of Gloucester and is Lear's godson. Shakespeare jumps over several intervening kings so as to present Edgar, at the play's close, as the reluctant new king of Britain, following Lear. Tradition, known to many in Shakespeare's audience, told of Edgar's troubled reign fighting the wolves that had overrun the kingdom. Shakespeare subtly prefigures the darkness of Edgar's fate throughout the play. There is a continuous flow of radical change as Edgar develops, while Edmund continually unfolds until he receives his death wound and only then starts to change, a shattering moment too late to save Cordelia, whose murder he had commanded.

Perhaps Nuttall is partly correct in venturing that Shakespeare projects onto Edgar the dramatist's own unease at his audience's suffering, so that the blinded and suicidal Gloucester becomes our surrogate. I would go beyond Nuttall and suggest that Edgar, throughout the play, is a darkening self-portrait of crucial elements in Shakespeare's poetic mind. Edmund, who is overtly theatrical, delights in his Marlovian rhetorical power over everyone to whom he speaks. Is that why Edmund and Lear never address each other, even though they are onstage together at the inception and conclusion of the tragedy?

Shakespeare, as I observe throughout, is the major master of ellipsis in the history of theater. We have to interpret what he leaves out, a challenge from *The Comedy of Errors* through *The Tempest*. In *The Tragedy of King Lear,* much is given to our own perspectivizing, which is most challenged by the antithetical person-alities of Edgar and Edmund. Meditating upon their catastrophic relationship, I am tempted to the surmise that poems in regard to one another resemble that relationship, and so do poets. Shakespeare, subtlest of dramatists, has made both half-brothers difficult to apprehend, though once we come to know them deeply they *can* be comprehended, unlike Lear, who is beyond us. Edmund is seductive and Edgar seems antipathetic, but that is our weakness as readers. (I will not say "as audience," because every *King Lear* I have tried to attend has been lamentable. The great king is too sublime for stage representation, and Edgar's is too complex a role to be assimilated in any theater except the theater of mind. I can think of no part in all of Shakespeare that I have seen so ineptly preformed as Edgar's.)

Edmund's quest for power is affectless, and therefore initially resistant to analogies. It can be observed that Edmund *needs* no one, himself included. He seeks, however, rhetorical control over everyone, in what may be a Shakespear-ean tribute to Marlowe's singular drive. I rarely get the sense that Shakespeare relies solely on a sway of rhetoric to hold his audience. His irony is too vast for that, and is best exemplified by the monarch of wit, Falstaff, who mocks everything and everyone, and does not deign to spare himself. March Sir John into *King Lear*—outrageous notion—and he would infuriate the cold Edmund by unmasking him immediately. A. C. Bradley asked us to visualize Hamlet confronting Iago and driving the Venetian Machiavel to suicide by immediately parodying him. Falstaff and Hamlet share the genius of demystification in Shakespeare; sometimes in my unruly fashion I follow my much-missed friend, the late Anthony Burgess, in the mental enterprise of wondering how Hamlet and Falstaff would have fared in the same play. Neither of them given to silences, or addicted to listening, possibly they might simply talk past one another, yet the two most capacious consciousnesses in all imaginative literature might have surpassed expectation.

The Marlovian Edmund exercises an ambivalent power over the audience; the Shakespearean Edgar does not. One benefit of mastering the uses of misprision in literature is to learn how to interpret Edgar, who until now has been a failing test for criticism. It surprises my students when I point out to them that Edgar speaks far more lines in the play than anyone except Lear. The centrality of Edgar for Shakespeare's contemporary audience can be judged from the title page of the First Quarto: "M. William Shak-speare: His True Chronicle Historie of the life and death of King Lear and his three Daughters. With the unfortunate life of Edgar, sonne and heire to the Earle of Gloster, and his sullen and assumed humor of Tom of Bedlam." Shakespeare uses *sullen* to mean a kind of madness of melancholia, but also mournfulness. Uncannily, it is Edmund who first mentions Tom of Bedlam (1.2.134–36), just as Edgar makes his first entrance: "Pat! He comes like the catastrophe of the old comedy. My cue is villainous melancholy, with a sigh like Tom o' Bedlam."

Since Edgar does not hear this, there is a suggestion of a kind of occult connection between the half-brothers. Edmund, as dramaturgical as Iago, confronts a far easier gull than the formidable Othello. Edgar is credulous, gentle, innocent, and without guile, and swiftly becomes Edmund's fool or victim. Shakespeare does not give us Edgar's motives for descending past the bottom of the social scale and assuming the disguise of a roaring Mad Tom: "Poor Tom! / That's something yet. Edgar I nothing am." This total descent is hardly a weak or murderous character, though a masochistic strain of self-punishment is clear enough. When poor Tom and the mad King Lear encounter one another (act 3, scene 4) we marvel at the histrionic skill of Edgar, who could have been playing a Bedlamite all his days. Few passages even in Shakespeare are as evocative as Edgar's response to the king's "Art thou come to this?"

Who gives any thing to poor Tom? whom the foul fiend hath led through fire and through flame, through ford and whirlpool, o'er bog and quagmire; that hath laid knives under his pillow, and halters in his pew, set ratsbane by his porridge, made him proud of heart, to ride on a bay trotting-horse over four-inch'd bridges, to course his own shadow for a traitor. Bless thy five wits! Tom's a-cold—O do de, do de, do de. Bless thee from whirlwinds, star-blasting, and taking! Do poor Tom some charity, whom the foul fiend vexes. There could I have him now—and there—and there again—and there.

Ravening self-abnegation is Edgar's downward path to a limited kind of wisdom. He seeks a torturous path upward that will lead him to save his father, though nothing can ever fully explain why his father's despair is "trifled" with by him (as he admits). There is also the drive to vindicate familial honor by cutting down Edmund, which in the climactic duel Edgar performs with frightening ease. Playing Tom o' Bedlam is an education in internal violence, and to some degree Edgar approaches madness by simulating it, in Hamlet's wake. When the insane king addresses his disguised godson as his "philosopher," Shakespeare's unending irony compellingly indicates Poor Tom's mentorship as Lear descends into the abyss. The Fool's fury and Edgar's dissociative refrains fuse to further madden the figure of ultimate authority who both of them catastrophically love.

My late friend William Elton, in his splendid *King Lear and the Gods,* is my precursor in tracing Edgar's development. Elton was concerned with Edgar's relations to the play's pagan deities, but I want a change in emphasis, to chart Edgar's difficult development until at last, in the First Folio text, he takes Albany's place as the unhappy new monarch of Britain. To term Edgar's psychic journey "difficult" understates his transformations. He ends act 3, scene 4, with an extraordinary snatch of verse that we have no evidence not to attribute to Shakespeare himself:

> Child Rowland to the dark tower came,
> His word was still, "Fie, foh, and fum,
> I smell the blood of a British man."

Two scenes later that will be the blood of his father, Gloucester, streaming from the eyes gouged out by Cornwell. There is generally a prolepsis of the atrocities performed in *King Lear,* and they tend to be uttered by one of Gloucester's sons. The motto of the high tragedy could be Edgar's gnomic summary of Lear, Gloucester, and their offspring: "He childed as I fathered!" Goneril, Regan, and even Edmund are peripheral to that gnome. Lear and Cordelia and Edgar and Gloucester are central. The two loving children were stubborn in their recalcitrance, while both loving fathers were blind, particularly before Gloucester literally was blinded and Lear went mad. Edgar prophesies his own radical "cure" from Gloucester's suicidal drive and looks back at Cordelia's silence, which precipitated the double tragedy. Sonship and daughterhood, like fathering, themselves are seen as tragic by Edgar, who speaks for the play. Whether he is a surrogate for Shakespeare is undecidable, but no one else in this drama fulfills such a role. Perhaps no one could in an apocalypse.

Edmund's forerunners are the Marlovian overreachers Aaron the Moor and Richard III. The creation of Iago—the peer of Falstaff, Hamlet, Cleopatra—marked the triumphant end of the Marlovian strain in Shakespeare. Marlowe returns in Edmund but subdued to Shakespearean nature. His cheerful pledge to Goneril: "Yours in the ranks of death" is true prophecy:

> I was contracted to them both; all three
> Now marry in an instant.

It takes a Marlovian overreacher to make a double date with Goneril and Regan, and Edmund delights us in this. Delight and Edgar are antithetical. Someone in the play must suffer vicariously for everyone else, and Shakespeare elects Edgar. In cutting down Edmund he finally puts paid to Marlowe. Nothing is got for nothing. Who is the interpreter and—if Shakespeare—what is the power he has sought to gain over his own text?

King Lear, set in a Britain a century or so after King Solomon (whether or not Shakespeare imagined that), seems to model its magnificent monarch after the Hebrew ruler and not after Job, as many scholars have thought. There are allusions to the book of Job but also to Ecclesiastes and the Wisdom of Solomon. For a pagan drama, *King Lear* is rich in biblical echoes, those of the New Testament perhaps being subtler. These allusions do not constitute a pattern of meaning as they would in Blake or D. H. Lawrence or Faulkner. Shakespeare evokes auras but evades doctrines.

James I, the wisest fool in Christendom, delighted by comparisons with Solomon, might be remembered as James the Wise if not for his absurdities. To this day he is the only intellectual among the British monarchs. Lear, like

Othello and Macbeth, is not particularly intelligent: his majestic qualities are elsewhere. No one else in all literature competes with Lear's enormous affections, turbulent emotions, and outbreaking sublimities. He is created on so grand a scale that even in Shakespeare he has no rival to challenge him. Hamlet the intellectual is closest in eminence but leaves the audience's realm throughout act 5, where we rely wholly upon Horatio to mediate the prince for us.

All attempts to read *King Lear* as a positive, hopeful Christian drama are weak and unconvincing, but so drastic is the play that desperate attempts to soften it are understandable if deplorable. It is the most harrowing of all literary works, ever. Shakespeare pulls us in, exhausts us, and releases us to nihilism. Lear is neither saved nor redeemed, Cordelia is murdered, and Edgar survives as a warrior-king who, by one English tradition, goes down battling the wolves that overran the kingdom.

Edgar, after Hamlet, is the central enigma in Shakespearean tragedy. It is impossible to arrive at any categorical conclusion in regard to him. He proclaims that ripeness is all while his own career evidences that ripeness is catastrophe. Throughout the labyrinth of *King Lear,* Shakespeare's sinuous windings of intelligence, which remain detached in *Hamlet* and *Othello,* seem to compel authorial attachments to the perplexed survivors Kent, Albany, and above all Edgar.

In the early *King John,* the Bastard Faulconbridge at certain moments becomes almost a surrogate for the young Shakespeare, who was still working through his dramatic apprenticeship to Marlowe. Hamlet rebels against apprenticeship to Shakespeare and—in my reading—carves his rebellion against the play to an extreme edge still unmatched in the history of drama. If you prefer, Shakespeare employs Hamlet to break every canon of stage representation. From act 2, scene 2, through act 3, scene 2, no audience could possibly absorb what unfolds before it. And yet Hamlet is played by Burbage as Shakespeare admonishing an actor (possibly played by Shakespeare himself, doubling as Player-King and Ghost). That theatrical in-joke certainly would have sent a packed house into an uproar. A momentary identification of Hamlet and his creator is soon voided, but James Joyce would not let us forget it.

No one should identify "Shakespeare" with the amazingly recalcitrant Edgar, who surpasses even Cordelia in benign obduracy. After all, Edgar is himself a king's godson and the next monarch of Britain. Who played Edgar in 1609 at the court of James I? Until now I had assumed that Robert Armin acted the Fool, since Burbage-as-Shakespeare-as-Hamlet is protesting Will Kemp's lack of discipline, and Kemp undoubtedly was still the Gravedigger in *Hamlet*. Shakespeare exiled Kemp after that, and the dancer-comedian was replaced by the ugly but sweet-voiced Armin as the company's head clown. I incline now to suggestions that precede me (I cannot recall where) that Edgar, the principal part in number of lines after Lear, was acted by Armin, the star after Burbage in the Globe galaxy. No one doubts that Burbage added Lear, Macbeth, and Antony to his turns as Hamlet and Othello. Whoever played Iago was given the part of Edmund, and presumably the same boy played Cordelia and the Fool, who are never onstage together.

Armin as Edgar is a vision that might help revise misapprehensions of the role, which seems to me the most Protean in Shakespeare. Casting Armin as Edgar would have been a brilliant experiment, and perhaps I incline to it because every Edgar I have seen has been an absurdity, a bad or miscast actor guided by a hopelessly lost director.

Reginald Foakes, an astute Shakespearean critic, remarks that "Edgar is most vividly present when on the run." When he stops running, Protean Edgar metamorphoses into an unstoppable avenger against whom the warlike Edmund has no chance and soon is cut down. In a play of countless tragic ironies this implacable adversary who destroys Edmund was created by Edmund himself when he victimized his gullible brother, thus beginning the long pilgrimage in which a Tom o' Bedlam beggar at last became a nameless knight and then a new king.

Idealizing Edgar will not bring him closer, yet finding cruelty in him is also an estrangement. He is immensely difficult to characterize. Unlike Edmund, who is charmingly funny and high-spirited as he fuses Machiavelli with Don Juan, Edgar has no sense of humor and no sprezzatura. To survive he practices disguises, affects a stoicism he never feels, recoils from affect (as best he can), and punishes himself by a voluntary descent into the lowest stratum of the kingdom, degradation as a vagrant madman begging food, shelter, and raiment.

Why then am I impelled to find in his uncanny role a surrogate for his creator, not Shakespeare the man but Shakespeare the dramatist of *King Lear*, which bursts the limits of art? Nothing that Edgar *says* links him to Shakespeare. Yet Edgar's actions and failures to act, his evasions and negative energies, seem to hint at authorial remorse for imposing agonies upon us, readers and auditors of a literary work as appalling as Titian's apocalyptic painting of Apollo flaying Marsyas, which I saw displayed on loan from the Kroměřížska Museum in the Czech Republic to the National Gallery in Washington, D.C., many years ago. I remember standing transfixed in front of the picture for more than an hour until my friend, the late painter Larry Day who had taken me to see it, suddenly murmured, "It is act 4 of *King Lear,* isn't it?"

Agonies are only one of Edgar's changes of garments, which must be why Walt Whitman subtly echoes Edgar in "Crossing Brooklyn Ferry," section 6. There are many perspectives moving like waves of darkness across our shocked spirits as we read *King Lear,* and Shakespeare privileges none of them. There are only three survivors. Albany, I think, abdicates, presumably because of his guilt at necessarily battling invaders who came to rescue Lear. Kent, loyal to the end, wants only to journey to the undiscovered country where his king has gone. In all of Shakespeare, no new monarch comes to his throne as despairingly as does Edgar. The final quatrain is assigned to him in the First Folio, and I take the thrice repeated "we" to be royal rather than an awkward plural for joint rule by Albany and Edgar. Many in the audience would have known that the historical King Edgar would also see too much but certainly would not reach Lear's eighty years:

> The weight of this sad time we must obey,
> Speak what we feel, not what we ought to say:
> The oldest hath borne most; we that are young
> Shall never see so much, nor live so long.

Detachment is the trait Edgar shares with Shakespeare. It or something similar may be regarded as Shakespeare's stance toward all his characters. When Edgar deceives Gloucester in the attempted suicide, he miserably hopes to cure his father's despair by "trifling" with it. Unlike his enemy half-brother, he has no talent for trifling with the lives of others. Something transverse is enacted here. The Marlovian Edmund possesses a large measure—as Iago did—of Shakespeare's genius for botching the lives of those he limned in his night-pieces. Edgar cannot do it except ineptly, but there is nothing Marlovian about Edgar, whom I would term one of the most Shakespearean of all the shadows inhabiting the tragedies.

SHAKESPEARE'S ELLIPSIS

"The Tempest"

After Chaucer and Marlowe, Shakespeare's major precursor was the English Bible: the Bishops' Bible up through 1595 and the Geneva Bible from 1596 on, the year that Shylock and Falstaff were created. In speaking of the Bible's influence on Shakespeare, I am referring not to faith or spirituality but to the arts of language: diction, grammar, syntax, rhetorical figures, and the logic of argument. Whether Shakespeare knew it or not, that meant that his deepest model for prose style was the Protestant martyr William Tyndale, whose stark eloquence constitutes about 40 percent of the Geneva Bible, becoming a higher ratio in the Pentateuch and the New Testament. Since Shakespeare's own father was a recusant Catholic, many scholars ascribe Catholic sympathies to the poet-playwright, a judgment that I find rather dubious. I do not know whether Shakespeare the man was Protestant or Catholic, skeptic or occultist, Hermetist or nihilist (though I suspect that last possibility), but the dramatist regularly drew upon the arch-Protestant Geneva Bible throughout the last seventeen years of his productivity. Milton also favored the Geneva Bible, though increasingly I wonder whether the final Milton was not a post-Protestant sect of one, anticipating William Blake and Emily Dickinson.

Among other precursors Ovid gave Shakespeare confirmation of his love of flux and change, the qualities Plato most abhorred. Marlowe at first all but overwhelmed Shakespeare, even in the deliberate parody that is *Titus Andronicus* and the Machiavel Richard III. But Shakespeare so powerfully accomplished a misprision of Marlowe, from at least *Richard II* on, that all the traces of Marlowe became tightly controlled illusions. Chaucer was as crucial to an element in Shakespeare's creation of fictive personalities as Tyndale was to aspects of Shakespeare's style. Elsewhere I have followed Talbot Donaldson's *The Swan at the Well: Shakespeare Reading Chaucer* in depicting the effect of the Wife of Bath upon Sir John Falstaff, and I hold to my earlier notion that Shakespeare took a hint from Chaucer in representing persons who change by self-overhearing. Yet even Chaucer, the strongest writer in the language except for Shakespeare, was not the definitive precursor Shakespeare became for himself from 1596 on, when he turned thirty-two and brought Shylock and Falstaff into being.

Can we speak of "Shakespeare Agonistes"? I think there was no such poet. You can speak of "Chaucer Agonistes," who credited nonexistent authorities and would not mention Boccaccio. "Milton Agonistes" should be a byword, but Shakespeare subsumed his influences: Ovid and Marlowe on the surface, William Tyndale and Chaucer far within.

Backgrounding Shakespeare, old style or new, wearies me. Shakespeare and his contemporary dramatist Philip Massinger look the same when the history of their own time is allowed to interpret them. Yet Massinger's writing concerns only a few specialized scholars. Shakespeare's changed everyone, Massinger included, and goes on changing you, me, even the Historicizers and Cynics. What Shakespeare leaves out is more important than what other Elizabethan-Jacobean dramatists put in. All the many elements in Shakespeare's strangeness could plausibly be reduced to his perpetually augmenting elliptical tendency, his development of the art of leaving things out. Appropriately confident of his magical powers over groundlings and the elite alike, he wrote increasingly for something agonistic in himself.

Aldous Huxley has a shrewd essay called "Tragedy and the Whole Truth," which argues that in Homer, when you lose your shipmates you sit down anyway to your meat and wine with gusto and then sleep your losses away. This is counter to Sophoclean tragedy, in which loss is irrevocable and endlessly dark. In Shakespearean tragedy, the Homeric and the Sophoclean fuse, with the English Bible never far away. Genre vanishes in Shakespeare because, contra Huxley, he wants to give himself and you both tragedy and the whole truth. Hamlet, however affected by what appears to be his supposed father's ghost, cannot stop jesting in the mode of his authentic mingled mother-father Yorick, and disrespectfully addresses the Ghost as "old mole."

To accommodate tragedy and the whole truth simultaneously, you must leave as much out as possible, while yet indicating the absences. No alert reader doubts either the tragedy or whole truth of the excruciating plays *Othello* and *King Lear*, both of which are fields of inference where we get lost without realizing our waywardness. When I tell an audience or a student-discussion group that the marriage of Othello and Desdemona was probably never consummated, only rarely do I not face dissent. This is akin to my reception when I insist that the enigmatic Edgar is the other tragic protagonist of *King Lear,* and that he is much its most admirable character, a hero of endurance though with many flaws, who makes mistakes of judgment out of an overwhelming love he cannot learn fully to sustain. Skeptical auditors understandably protest to me, If such interpretations are accurate, why does Shakespeare make it so difficult to arrive at them?

Begin at the other side of this protest: What is clarified in *Othello* if the Moor has never known his wife? What is yet more shattering about *King Lear* if its pragmatic center is Edgar and not the ruined godfather whom he loves and worships? The heroic Moor's vulnerability to Iago's demonic genius becomes far more understandable, particularly if Iago suspects Othello's ambivalent re-luctance to posses Desdemona. Edgar is Shakespeare's most profound embodi-ment of self-punishment, of the spirit splitting apart in the defensive process. If we meditate deeply upon Edgar, we realign Lear's tragedy, since only Edgar and Edmund give us perspectives other than Lear's own on the great king's downward and outward fall into his abyss. This most elaborate of Shakespeare's domestic tragedies depends for its final coherence on the interplay between Lear's incredibly intense feelings, Edmund's icy freedom from all affect, and Edgar's stubborn sufferings, including his acedia, Tom o' Bedlam's "sullen and assumed humor" as the First Quarto's title page phrases it.

Whenever I search for precedents rather than sources for Shakespeare, I arrive more often at Chaucer than at the English Bible, Ovid, or the Ovidian Marlowe. William Blake, commenting on the Wife of Bath, seems to have inter-preted her as the incarnation of what he dreaded: the Female Will. These days, I find it necessary to emphasize that Blake found the Female Will as much in men as in women. Chaucer the pilgrim delights in Alice, Wife of Bath, and so do we. Still, even if she disposed of her first three rather feeble husbands with her generously active loins, there is an ellipsis just before her fourth husband so conveniently goes to his funeral, freeing her for the love of her life, her young fifth mate, whom she generously laments. Evidently the inconvenient fourth husband was dealt with handily.

From Chaucer, Shakespeare learned how to conceal his irony by expanding it until sight alone cannot apprehend it. With Hamlet we cannot even hear it. No other literary personage so rarely says what he means or means what he says. This misled the clerical T. S. Eliot, who had unresolved ambivalences toward his own mother, into judging Hamlet to be J. Alfred Prufrock and Shakespeare's play to be "most certainly an artistic failure." With the possible exception of *King Lear, Hamlet* is most certainly the supreme artistic success in Western literature. Eliot, alas a great if tendentious poet, most certainly was one of the worst literary critics of the twentieth century. His refined contempt for Sigmund Freud, the Montaigne of his era, crippled the anti-Semitic oracle who held in sway the academies in my youth.

Richard Ellmann assured me that Joyce always championed the brilliant reading of *Hamlet* given by Stephen in the National Library scene of *Ulysses*. Implicit in that interpretation is the view that Shakespeare's fatherly love for his Hamlet repeats the pattern of Falstaff's love for Hal, a pattern William Empson and C. L. Barber found present in the Sonnets in Shakespeare's betrayed love for Southampton and Pembroke.

The greatest ellipsis in *Hamlet* is its long foregrounding, in which the prince's soul has died. We have to surmise why and how, since the magnitude of his sickness-unto-death has to have long preceded his father's death and mother's remarriage. Our crucial clue is the prince's relationship to Yorick, who bore the boy on his back a thousand times and exchanged so many kisses with an affection-starved child. The signature of the play *Hamlet* is the mature prince holding the skull of Yorick and asking it cruel, unanswerable questions.

There is an occult relation between Hamlet's long malaise and the play's unique and dazzling enigma, the gap cut in mimesis from act 2, scene 2, through act 3, scene 2. We behold and hear not an imitation of an action but rather representations of prior representations. The covenant between stage and audience is abrogated in favor of a dance of shadows, where only the manipulator Hamlet is real. Destroying its own genre, the play thus gives us an unfathered Hamlet. Shakespeare scrambles after him, but Hamlet keeps getting away, Hobgoblin run off with the garland of Apollo.

How can a stage play center both upon the meaning of an apocalyptic self-consciousness and on the transcendence of playacting that all but purges consciousness of self in act 5? That only leads to further questions in this labyrinth of ellipses: Why does Hamlet return to Elsinore after his aborted voyage to England? He has no plan and refuses to devise one. Why go into the obvious mousetrap of the duel with Laertes? If indeed we know absolutely nothing of anything we leave behind us, then one time for departure is as good as another, but surely Hamlet knows more than the rest of us about the meaning and nature of time. We have listened to seven of his soliloquies, yet we badly need an eighth one, which Shakespeare declines to provide.

Other ellipses abound in Shakespeare. Of Shakespeare's greatest figures—Falstaff, Hamlet, Iago, Cleopatra—only Hamlet has parents, dubious as one of them may be. In 1980, R. W. Desai suggested Claudius as Hamlet's likely father. But neither we nor the prince know how far back the sexual relationship between uncle and mother went. Hamlet, whose ironic mode of operation is not to say what he means or mean what he says, will not voice this perplexity, yet it must numb him. Cutting down a murderous uncle is one matter, killing the father quite another.

Hamlet claims his proper name, no longer his putative father's, by having cast the Ghost out into the North Sea, as it were. He returns as Hamlet the Dane, perhaps conceding that the satyr Claudius may well be his phallic father. We do not know, nor does he. Yorick, the imaginative father who loved and nurtured the little boy until he was seven, can be regarded as the grandest ellipsis in Hamlet's elliptical tragedy. No one need be gulled by Hamlet's disgust as he beholds Yorick's skull. Even on the other side of affection, Hamlet in the graveyard elegizes Yorick as his true mothering father, the author of his wit.

Of Falstaff, Shakespeare says only that the globelike wit served as a page to John of Gaunt, King Henry IV's father. Of Iago, we surmise only that as Othello's flag officer he started out worshiping his captain as the war god. Of the pre-Antony Serpent of the Nile, we are told that Pompey and Caesar enjoyed her, but only Caesar—before Antony—engendered a bastard son. Why give us such greatness and yet tell us so little?

Shakespeare's bastards commence with the wonderful Faulconbridge in *King John* and then darken with the thuggish Don John in *Much Ado About Nothing*. The spectacular genius of bastardy is Edmund, yet Brutus and Hamlet are ambiguous possibilities on the way. In the second part of *Henry VI*, Suffolk speaks proudly before being led away to execution: "Brutus' bastard hand / Stabb'd Julius Caesar" (4.1.136–37). Plutarch mentions the scandal (from Suetonius) that Brutus was Caesar's son, and Shakespeare hints at this without making it overt in *Julius Caesar*. Evidently Brutus and Caesar know their true relationship, and Hamlet and Claudius cannot evade it.

Elliptical Shakespeare is echoed by Joyce's Stephen in the National Library scene, where we are told that fatherhood is always a fiction. Joyce cunningly counterpoints this with his insistence on the Jewishness of Poldy Bloom. Joyce, Bloom himself, and all Dublin agree on this identification but count for little against the Talmud. Poldy's father is the Hungarian Jew Virag, but his mother and her mother were Catholic. This turns the Talmud on its head. Normative Judaism simply did not care who your father was: only the child of a Jewish mother is a Jew, period.

Picasso is reputed to have said he did not care who influenced him but he did not want to influence himself. Yet I follow Paul Valéry in believing that self-influence bespeaks a singular literary achievement, a sublime form of self-possession found only in the strongest of strong writers. The most vital-izing candidate for Valérian investigation has to be Shakespeare's misprision of Shakespeare. As an influence upon himself, Shakespeare sets the terms for Valéry's admonition that we must learn how to comprehend the influence of a mind on itself. Depending on how you count, Shakespeare wrote thirty-eight plays, of which twenty-five or so are altogether worthy of him. Tastes vary: as a devout Falstaffian I cannot endure *The Merry Wives of Windsor,* and *The Two Gentlemen of Verona* is little better, despite an adorable dog. *Titus Andronicus,* to me, is a Marlovian send-up, as though the young Shakespeare were saying, "If they want blood, let them have this!"

The Bastard Faulconbridge in *King John* begins the true Shakespeare. But his first triumph is what I go on calling the Falstaffiad: the two parts of *Henry IV* and Mistress Quickly's Cockney prose elegy for Sir John in *Henry V.* The instant success of Falstaff transformed Shakespeare's career: the apprenticeship to Marlowe ended and an absolute self-reliance commenced. Falstaff replaced Marlowe as Shakespeare's precursor.

This hardly denies the other forerunners: Ovid, Chaucer, Tyndale's New Tes-tament, Montaigne. Yet as Giambattista Vico recognized, we know only what we ourselves have made, and Shakespeare knew Falstaff. Cast aside what scholars go on canting about the immortal Falstaff, though they have Hal/Henry V on their side. Shakespeare's auditors and readers fell in love with Falstaff because he carried the secular blessing: "Give me life!" Hamlet, Iago, Lear and the Fool, Edgar and Edmund, Macbeth: these are not life's ambassadors to us. Cleopatra is and is not; Bernard Shaw shrewdly denounced her and Falstaff together even as he expressed pity that Shakespeare's mind was so much less capacious than that of the creator of *Caesar and Cleopatra.*

Falstaff engendered Hamlet, and the Black Prince made possible Iago and Macbeth. What the Gnostics called the *pleroma*, the fullness, always abides with Falstaff. Hamlet ironically swerves from the giant of comedy, a swerve answered by Shakespeare's antithetical completion of stage acting in *Measure for Measure* and *Othello*. Read together, *Measure for Measure* and *Othello* are a comprehensive synecdoche for Shakespeare's art as a dramatist, however you choose to interpret Duke Vincentio in that broad range that goes from benevolent intervener to Iagolike play-botcher.

In the revisionary scheme I propose, *King Lear* and *Macbeth* together are a radical *kenosis*, an undoing of the Falstaffian pleroma. A compensating sublime can be read in Shakespeare's daimonic response, *Antony and Cleopatra*, the farthest horizon of his career, from which he ascetically withdraws in *Coriolanus*. *The Winter's Tale* and *The Tempest* appear as a final glory, an ever-early candor, far-fetched yet homelike on arrival. Leontes, Hermione, Perdita, and Autolycus are one version of finale; Prospero, Ariel, and Caliban are quite another. Falstaff could have said much to Autolycus, but little or nothing to Ariel. *The Tempest* is a wilder shore than *The Winter's Tale* and is its poet's most surprising play, not to be transcended, his last and best comedy, and an extraordinary departure even for the most self-revisionary of all writers ever.

Trace a thread through the dark backward and abyss of time from *The Tempest* (1611) to the *Henry IV* plays (1596–98). Those fifteen years of creation eclipse any other individual achievement in Western literature, an audacious assertion since it includes the ancient Greeks, Romans, and Hebrews, Dante, Cervantes, Montaigne, Milton, Goethe, Blake, Tolstoy, Whitman, Proust, Joyce, and comparable splendors. Call that single thread a perpetual agon between Shakespeare and Shakespeare, later and earlier. Prospero, Leontes, Coriolanus, Antony, Macbeth, Lear, Othello, Hamlet, Falstaff: Does that ninefold have any sublimity in common? Go to the other sex. Miranda, Hermione, Perdita, Volumnia, Cleopatra, Lady Macbeth, Cordelia, Desdemona, Ophelia: Do they share anything? So varied are Shakespeare's men and women—and these two minefields exclude clowns and most villains—that we are liable to lose our sense of wonder that a single mind conceived them. The wonder matters because if they had not made a difference we would be something else from what we are.

Falstaff is the matrix from which Shakespeare's mature art of characterization emanated. Even the Bastard Faulconbridge, Juliet, Bottom, and Shylock do not reverberate with Falstaff's richness of being. He is brother to the Wife of Bath, and he is Cleopatra's histrionic rival. The reaction of Shakespeare's contemporary audience to the fat knight retains a critical accuracy we are in danger of losing, despite Dr. Johnson, A. C. Bradley, and Harold Goddard, all of whom saw Falstaff plain.

I do not know of any recent modes of criticism that can explain how meaning gets started in a dramatic character. Falstaff is how meaning gets started, as are Hamlet, Iago, Cleopatra. Prospero is how meaning ebbs out and away, for even Prospero is one of the fools of time. Falstaff is not. Dying, to Mistress Quickly's Cockney prose music, he is a child again, smiling upon his fingers' ends, and singing the Twenty-Third Psalm. He spends his life bidding time stand aside. It will not, and yet we will see no triumph of time over Sir John Falstaff. Betrayed love achieves victory; can that be total defeat?

Falstaff, through florabundance, excess, overflow, creates meaning. Such creation can take place only because Falstaff creates love, laughter, a rejoicing in mere being, the ecstasy of existence. There is a highly deliberate diminishment in Shakespeare's long movement from Falstaff to Prospero, who empties out meaning and ends triumphant but in despair, departing his island back for Milan, where every third thought shall be his grave. Ariel is released to his elements, fire and air, while Caliban is acknowledged, earth and water together, a failed adoption yet now a thing of darkness that indeed is Prospero's own.

Of Prospero the anti-Faustus we have heard too little; Ariel and Mephistopheles are so different that their functional parallel cannot be summoned to an audience's consciousness. But Prospero himself is difficult to absorb:

> Graves at my command
> Have wak'd their sleepers, op'd, and let 'em forth
> By my so potent art.

[5.1.48–50]

A Hermetist magus who resurrects the dead cannot be accommodated by Christian doctrine. Analogues between Shakespeare and Prospero are peculiarly wavering: they are and are not there. Shakespeare resurrects the mighty dead—Julius Caesar, Mark Antony, Henry V, Henry VIII—by his magical art of representation. His histories, like his comedies and his tragedies, are of no genre, and really are alternative histories that have triumphed over the facts. Evidently Richard III was a humane king and Henry VII a villain, yet Shakespeare altered that forever.

In Milan, princely administration (at which he had failed) will be Prospero's first thought, and reeducating Caliban the second. That leaves only death to close a joyless existence. Whether you interpret Prospero as the greatest of white magicians or as an overworked theatrical director—stage manager or as Shakespeare himself, is that a proper end for a final comedy? *The Tempest* is an awesomely original play, still poorly read and badly produced, but it is curiously fragile. Substitute Falstaff for Trinculo, and the final play Shakespeare indisputably written solely by himself would explode.

Is there no way to cast our hook so as to rescue Prospero's drowned book? On our stages the current obsession with the gloriously pitiful Caliban should yield to an increased joy in Ariel, who intoxicated Shelley and Hart Crane. It is Prospero's and Ariel's play, not Caliban's, though the island *is* his. Robert Browning gave us an extraordinary dramatic monologue, "Caliban upon Setebos," which I greatly prefer to W. H. Auden's *The Sea and the Mirror,* even though Caliban (presumably after his Milan reeducation) speaks there in the tonalities of the later Henry James, who shared Shelley's and Browning's passion for *The Tempest.*

I recall walking out of a performance of George C. Wolfe's travesty of *The Tempest,* which presented Caliban as a heroic West Indian freedom fighter and added Ariel, an equally fierce Prospero hater, as a West Indian female rebel. In my remaining lifetime, *The Tempest,* as Shakespeare composed it, is not likely to be performed again. Perhaps that doesn't matter: reading and studying the actual play will continue, and sociopolitical fashions will ebb away. The sorrow is that near the close of his work Shakespeare wrote what might be the funniest of his comedies, though its laughter is not akin to Falstaff's aggressive vitalism or to Cleopatra's vitally darker wit. *The Tempest*'s comic strength lies in so sophisticated an irony that we are slow to comprehend it:

Gonzalo: How lush and lusty the grass looks! How green!
Antonio: The ground indeed is tawny.
Sebastian: With an eye of green in't.
Antonio: He misses not much.
Sebastian: No; he doth but mistake the truth totally.

[2.1.52–56]

You see what you are. The good Gonzalo beholds an earthly paradise, while Antonio and Sebastian, accomplished and prospective usurpers, respectively, regard things as they are, and to a usurping potential advantage. If *The Tempest* still holds up the mirror to nature, then it is only to human nature. Caliban presumably is only half human and Ariel not human at all, but Antonio, Sebastian, Trinculo, and Stephano are all too human.

The only human in the play who is more than a sketch is the magus Prospero, as enigmatic a personality as Shakespeare ever created. He is one of those teachers who is always convinced his auditors are not quite attentive. "Mark me" and "Dost thou hear?" keep breaking from him. Perhaps, nearing the end of Shakespeare's enterprise, Prospero realizes incessantly a truth of all the plays: no one really listens to what anyone else is saying. Here life has imitated Shakespeare: the more we read him, the less we listen to one another. With Cleopatra, we keep saying, "No, let me speak!"

Never far from anger, grumpy Prospero is capable of addressing Ariel as if he were Caliban: "Thou liest, malignant thing!" And yet we are with and for Prospero since *The Tempest* yields us no choice. Even granting that he has been betrayed, his coldness is irksome. We forgive him because of his grand recovery in acts 4 and 5, particularly since his temporal anxiety is revelatory of our own. He keeps wanting to know the time yet almost forgets the conspiracy of Caliban, Stephano, and Trinculo against his life: "The minute of their plot / Is almost come." His immense power over illusory space gives him no freedom from time.

Why does Shakespeare, in Prospero's abjuration speech, extend the mage's "rough magic" to the shocking impiety of having resurrected the dead?

> Graves at my command
> Have wak'd their sleepers, op'd, and let 'em forth
> By my so potent art.

The tone has no trace of guilt, but why has Prospero indulged himself in this extravagant activity? The Renaissance mage—say, Giordano Bruno or Dr. John Dee—might seek to perfect nature (as in alchemy) but would not desire to resurrect the dead. Prospero dwarfs Dr. Dee, the royal astrologer sometimes considered to have been his model. The least that must be affirmed of Prospero is the awesomeness of his power. Marlowe's Faustus performs paltry tricks; Prospero is the authentic "favored one" and has mastered reality, except for the chastening riddle of time.

Shakespeare's art of ellipsis is so flagrantly triumphant in *The Tempest* that we tend not to see how it governs the play. After the illusory opening storm, *nothing happens.* If *Othello* is overplotted, then *The Tempest* is a plotless experiment. Even the evident act of abdicating white magic is equivocal. Prospero's authority is not diminished at the close, and I do not believe his Ovidian renunciation. He is not Medea, and his breaking of staff and drowning of book are promises for a future beyond *The Tempest*'s scope.

Perform Prospero's drama as postcolonial allegory or anti-imperialist satire, and it certainly is no comedy. Yet it should be Shakespeare's final comedy, of a new kind we have not yet learned to apprehend. We never can be certain what is or is not happening in the play, but that seems the essence of Shakespearean New Comedy. Any knowledge the work might give us would be purchased at the cost of his power over us. Power becomes comic only if it is mocked. I would suggest that Prospero, more favored than Faustus, nevertheless is a tragicomic protagonist, but so are Caliban and all the humans in the play, except the young lovers Miranda and Ferdinand. Ariel also is exempt from comedy.

I call *The Tempest* a tragicomedy since that, rather than romance, approximates its uncanny genre, yet tragicomedy suits *The Winter's Tale* better than *The Tempest.* No one dies or is wounded in body or soul in *The Tempest,* but we simply don't have a genre that will fit Shakespeare's final full-scale originality. I suspect that if questioned he would have replied "comedy" but would merely have meant all's well that ends, however we modify the final "well."

How can we accommodate a concept of comedy to Prospero? For Shakespeare's initial audience and for centuries afterward, Caliban was nothing but comic. Doubtless he was not played by Shakespeare's chief clown Robert Armin, whose admired singing voice make him the likely Ariel. Stage tradition before our Age of Political Correctness was likely to give the audience a half-fish or half-amphibian as Caliban. That seems to me no worse than the heroic rebel Caliban in most of our current stagings.

Authenticity in culture involves an augmenting of the foundations, according to Hannah Arendt in *Between Past and Future* (1961). By general consent, Shakespeare augments the foundations of drama in *The Tempest.* He does this by demonstrating the dramatist's freedom from history. All attempts to New Historicize *The Tempest* have proved feeble and are already sadly archaic. The freshness of this elliptical play evades every sociopolitical net. How do you catch a wind?

Marlowe, Shakespeare's dangerous forerunner, ended his truncated career with Doctor Faustus. Prospero parodies and trumps Faustus, even in his name. The first Faustus, by Christian tradition, was Simon Magus of Samaria, who went to Rome, where he took the cognomen of Faustus (the "favored one") and then supposedly perished in a levitation contest with Saint Peter. Shakespeare, I surmise, wrote *The Tempest* in belated competition with Marlowe's last play, eighteen years after Marlowe's murder.

Shakespeare parodies Marlowe's *Faustus* in *Richard II* and alludes several times to Marlowe's work and death in *As You Like It,* least Marlovian of comedies. In *The Tempest,* he perhaps attempts a highly personal exorcism of a theatrical ghost who had gone on haunting him, albeit in a new way, mediated by his agon with his own earlier work. Shakespeare undoubtedly knew Marlowe personally, though he kept a distance from the theatrical rhetoric that had fostered him in *Titus Andronicus* and the *Henry VI* plays, culminating in the highly Marlovian *Richard III.* Yet something in him, I would guess, always was grateful to Marlowe's genius even as his scarcely older precursor increasingly became the way not to go, in art as well as in life. Forbidden knowledge, a Marlovian commonplace, is not a continuity between *Dr. Faustus* and *The Tempest,* since Prospero blamelessly goes far beyond Faustus in the Hermetic quest. But this is a Hermetism purged of the search for God, purified indeed of any transcendental yearnings. Prospero's art is a science that governs nature through sprites or angels, Ariel and his peers. That is not quite an allegory of Shakespeare's art in this play if only because *The Tempest* labors intensely to cleanse us of any anticipatory images we might bring to its interpretation. We are all made into Miranda, who is to "sit still, and hear the last of our sea-sorrow." We *are* persuaded to sit still in expectation of hearing some revelation from the magical Prospero, but we do not receive even an iota. In dramatic terms, he has none to impart. Had Shakespeare invented something, it would have emerged as parody, and *The Tempest* would have piled up with absurdities, like *Cymbeline.*

What is not at all absurd in *The Tempest* is Prospero's will to power, over the elements and everyone in the play, himself included. So overwhelmingly strong a will comes at the high cost of human sympathy, and I have never encountered a playgoer or reader who likes Prospero. It is not only his nervous severity that troubles us. More unsettling is the effect of his magical art. If the opening tempest was merely an illusion, then how can we trust any event or appearance in this play, since he has contrived them all? The island is enchanted: are there any limits to this enchantment?

The love between Miranda and Fernando is not illusive, though also plotted by Prospero. He provides the context yet not the natural magic of their mutual falling in love. Prospero's mastery of place cannot control time or the timelessness that the lovers create. Wry comedy ensues as time's sway nearly destroys Prospero, who is about to miss his cue:

> I had forgot that foul conspiracy
> Of the beast Caliban and his confederates
> Against my life. The minute of their plot
> Is almost come.

[4.1.139–42]

The limitation of Prospero's art is time. No other play by Shakespeare, not even the sunrise-to-sunset *Comedy of Errors,* so enacts itself that lapsed time and performance time almost are one. We expect a lyric or a meditation to be a brief fiction of duration; that is not our experience of Shakespearean drama. *The Tempest* is a tense experimental play; it might as well be entitled *Time.* Prospero knows our reprieve is not so indefinite as we might wish; we are all condemned men and women. He had three labors, only two of them expected: the safe restoration of his daughter through a dynastic marriage; the restitution of his duchy of Milan, for whose governance he has neither aptitude nor enthusiasm; the surprising resumption of his failed adoption of Caliban, the thing of darkness he again acknowledges as his own. Prospero, in all three endeavors, acknowledges implicitly the triumph of time.

From Coleridge to the present—when it is out of fashion—there is some intimation of identity between Prospero and Shakespeare, an uncritical apprehension that secures some warrant when we consider how absurd it might be to compound Leontes with his creator. *The Winter's Tale* I find aesthetically superior to *The Tempest,* yet it troubles my imagination less. The drama of Prospero, Ariel, Caliban unsettles the spirit; it has no Autolycus or Perdita to delight us. Henry James seems to have given *The Tempest* primacy over the rest of Shakespeare; that may be why W. H. Auden startles in *The Sea and the Mirror* by having his Caliban speak indubitably in the manner of the later James. *The Tempest* provokes you to make something of your own from it. Shelley and Hart Crane found themselves in Ariel, while Robert Browning quarried from *The Tempest* his still under-esteemed dramatic monologue "Caliban upon Setebos," a far subtler development of Shakespeare's grotesquely pathetic yet sublime creature than our current bad conscience permits us.

I cannot think of another play by Shakespeare that truly resembles *The Tempest.* Even *The Winter's Tale* has affinities, to *Pericles* and to *Cymbeline,* but

The Tempest stands apart from the other three late tragicomedies and from the even more brilliantly cold Shakespearean portion of *The Two Noble Kinsmen*. Beckett seems straightforward compared to *The Tempest*, which remains the most elliptical play I know. Even as *Hamlet* still seems the most experimental of plays, because of the wild sequence from act 2, scene 2, through act 3, scene 2, so *The Tempest* manages to achieve coherence while leaving out most of what we might expect to be given us. Where are we anyway? Shakespeare had delightedly outraged Ben Jonson by giving Bohemia a seacoast in *The Winter's Tale*. He goes one better in *The Tempest* by locating Bermuda in the Mediterranean somewhere between Italy and Tunis. Weather on the Enchanted Island is glorious except when Prospero is moved to create the illusion of a storm. The landscape, seascape, skyscape also are illusory, since Ariel and his fellow sprites perpetually are out and about ordering sensations and perceptions. And music seems always in the air, Ariel and his company being singing sprites. Yet as poor Caliban keeps lamenting, this is no island paradise, since the sprites pinch and goad him endlessly for discipline and correction.

Shakespeare at once throws away all the rules of stage representation while also imposing a strict time frame and unity of apparent space. Indeed, he writes as though no one, including William Shakespeare, ever has written a play before *The Tempest*. Without precursors, it fathers itself. The opening, the title's tempest out at sea, is memorable for its boatswain, plainspoken and realistic, who shouts, "Use your authority!" to the amiable and good Gonzalo, certainly the sweetest character in the entire play. But no authority (except Prospero's) could quell the storm. You cannot know from the first scene that there is no storm anyway. Since Shakespeare chose the title, we are puzzled at his naming a play for a nonevent.

Shakespeare had been working at perspectivism from his career's start but had achieved an absolute mastery of it only with *Antony and Cleopatra*. Simply, if you want to view Cleopatra as an imperial whore and Antony as her declining victim, you can do so, and that will show you and others just who you are. If you see her as a sublimity and Antony as her life's great love, that will show something else. Shakespeare hands the choice to you and avoids judgment. With *The Tempest* all perspectives are possible at once, and so you need not choose. Prospero's magical will prevails.

Shakespeare directly juxtaposes the mutual cursing of Caliban and Prospero, pupil and teacher, with the exquisite interplay of Ferdinand's lament and Ariel's song. As an aesthetic effect this is extraordinary even for Shakespeare:

Ferdinand:	Where should this music be? I' th' air, or th' earth?
	It sounds no more, and sure it waits upon
	Some god o' th' island. Sitting on a bank,
	Weeping again the King my father's wreck,
	This music crept by me upon the waters,
	Allaying both their fury and my passion
	With its sweet air. Thence I have followed it
	(Or it hath drawn me, rather) but 'tis gone.
	No, it begins again.

Ariel [*Sings.*]:	Full fathom five they father lies,
	Of his bones are coral made;
	Those are pearls that were his eyes,
	Nothing of him that doth fade
	But doth suffer a sea-change
	Into something rich and strange.
	Sea nymphs hourly ring his knell.

Burthen [*within*]:	Ding dong.

Ariel:	Hark, now I hear them—ding dong bell.

Ferdinand:	The ditty does remember my drowned father;
	This is no mortal business nor no sound
	That the earth owes. I hear it now above me.

[1.2.388–408]

Eliot's *The Waste Land* and lyrics by Shelley and Hart Crane meet and mingle in this matrix of so much later poetry in the language. To this music Miranda and Ferdinand meet, instantly fall in love, and thus accomplish the authentic triumph of Prospero's art. For this one moment we are deceived into thinking that Prospero allows a natural epiphany its full glory, yet he wills otherwise.

Since it is Prospero's play and not Ariel's or Caliban's, Shakespeare risks alienating us altogether by the magician's hardness. Poor Miranda speaks wistfully for all of us when she says to the spellbound Ferdinand, "My father's of a better nature, sir, / Than he appears by speech." Yes and no, for Prospero has a kind of inwardness we have not met before, in Shakespeare or any other writer. The labyrinthine journey to the inmost self, inaugurated by Shakespeare from Hamlet through Macbeth, ended with Cleopatra and her Antony. That matrix of darkness is present in *Measure for Measure*'s Vincentio and Angelo, but is revealed to us only in bursts. When deep inwardness returns in Leontes it is a horror, the spider in the cup.

Prospero's difference presumably is the fruit of his magical art. With each occult victory he had become more inaccessible to himself and so to us. If there is a high cost to forbidden knowledge, it yet works out very differently for the magi of Marlowe and of Shakespeare. Faustus is hauled off to hell; Marlowe dies in agony in a Deptford tavern. Prospero departs with Caliban for Milan, where every third thought will be the grave awaiting even the greatest of magi. Shakespeare departs soon after for Stratford to live without players and audience. We do not know why. Unlike Dante and Whitman and Joyce, the poet of *The Tempest* intended no Third Testament, no new Bible.

As a secularist with Gnostic proclivities, and above all as a literary aesthete, I preach Bardolatry as the most benign of all religions. The painter J. M. W. Turner and his critical apostle John Ruskin saw the sun as God. For me, Shakespeare is God. Tropologically, call that the sun if you want to. The First Folio for me is also the First Testament. How wise its editors (who had Ben Jonson's advice) were to open it with *The Tempest,* recognizing that this uncanny comedy declined to be an apocalypse.

POSSESSION IN MANY MODES

The Sonnets

The formalist critic L. C. Knights mocked the character-based criticism of A. C. Bradley by saucily asking, "How many children had Lady Macbeth?" Knights's question was intended to suggest the absurdity of treating fictional characters as both living creatures and valid objects of study. But I think it an excellent question and tend to surmise: just one, murdered with her first husband.

More compelling still is the question of why this erotically charged woman chose to marry Macbeth. The Macbeths began as the best marriage in all Shakespeare. And if that is a jest, it is Shakespeare's. A love match, founded on desire and ambition, this was murderous from the start, well before King Duncan was slain. Read the text closely—as I have done in *Shakespeare: The Invention of the Human* (1996)—and it suggests that Macbeth is impeded by overwhelming desire for his wife and is so anxious and hasty that sexually he keeps missing his cue. He is far more effectual on the battlefield than alone with his wife.

I remember many years ago in London watching Michael Redgrave as a properly frightening Macbeth and Ann Todd as a vibrant Lady Macbeth. When she cried out, "Unsex me here!" she doubled over, clutching what King Lear and Sonnet 129 refer to as "hell." Like doubtless many other males in the audience, I was moved indeed.

I find it odd that we know her only as "Lady Macbeth"; why does Shakespeare not give this vital woman her own name? It is her creator's design to remove her from much of the play that dooms her to madness and suicide. Like Dr. Johnson I am troubled by "She should have died hereafter." There will be no time for such a word in the world Macbeth has botched to a false creation. That the death of his wife hardly prevails in Macbeth's consciousness is weird when the tragedy is of the imagination itself.

The scene of Banquo's ghost raises again what may be this scary tragedy's prime question: Was it for a desolate occasion like this that the Macbeths murdered to usurp the throne? The thanes stay not upon the order of their going but go at their angry queen's command, glad to escape with their lives. Childless, Macbeth murders Macduff's children after Fleance gets away to found the Stuart line of Scottish (and English) kings. A great voice, not his own, keeps breaking into Macbeth's soliloquies, in contrast to Hamlet, whose many voices emanate from a coherent center. Possession in several modes renders *Macbeth* the uncanniest of Shakespearean dramas. Nietzsche recognized *Macbeth*'s freedom from all moralities: he did not term this nihilistic, yet it is a Gnostic drama, still in the *kenoma*, the cosmological emptiness carried over from *King Lear*. In both tragedies, Creation and Fall are the same event. The audience suffers *being thrown* into an emptiness. Yet Shakespeare's gnosis is his own. Edmund and Macbeth are both Demiurges, but they could not be more different. Edmund is beyond affect until he receives his death wound from Edgar. Macbeth, except for Lear, experiences the most turbulent emotions in Shakespeare.

What Hamlet did to Shakespeare himself is perpetually in dispute. Who won the victory in the agon between creature and creator? My brief book on that struggle, *Hamlet: Poem Unlimited*, received a mixed reaction, which did not surprise me since the matter is a vexed one. Falstaff refused to be held captive by the two parts of *Henry IV* yet did not destroy the coherence of that great double play—is it Shakespeare's greatest achievement? But Hamlet broke the vessels even as Yahweh did in the Creation. God ruined many worlds before this one. Shakespeare, God of literature, ruined *Hamlet*, or else Hamlet ruined his play. But what is "ruin" in the realm of the aesthetic?

Owen Barfield, in his wonderful *Poetic Diction: A Study of Meaning*, reminds us that the root meaning of the verb *to ruin* is "rushing to a collapse." In Shakespeare *ruin*, whether as verb or substantive, has an aura: the splendor of Lear in his madness or of Antony in his fall. We experience a pleasure in and of ruin surpassing that of the world traveler. T. S. Eliot would have been sounder had he called the endless puzzle of Shakespeare's struggle with his own angel,

Hamlet, a sublime ruin instead of an aesthetic failure. Neither prince nor dramatist wins that contest. It is very like Jacob's wrestling with the Angel of Death, which results in the Hebrew Patriarch's blessing of the new name, Israel, but at the expense of a permanent laming, an ironic vision of the fate of the Jewish people. Who recovers a new name: Hamlet, Will Shakespeare, or both?

Grappling with Laertes at Ophelia's grave, the prince cries out, "It is I, Hamlet the Dane." That is the old name, but newly reft from the ghostly father. Shakespeare already had won back his name from time's revenges through the making of Falstaff. *Hamlet* confirmed the victory.

"Am I still Shakespeare?" That is the question implied by the crisis-points in the development of Shakespeare's ever-living art. Shylock and Falstaff sprang up close together, followed by Hamlet and Malvolio four to five years later. Duke Vincentio and Iago, Edgar and Lear, Macbeth and Cleopatra followed in a rush. Leontes and Prospero come four or five years on from then. This chronology is rough, and useless except for the progression in crises. My choice of these dozen figures is arbitrary except that *for me* they are like numerals on a clock or watch. The complete fire is death, yet that came five years after Prospero. Shakespeare's few peers through the age wrote until they died, but Shakespeare abandoned his art. Why? We never will know, yet he seems to have created nothing for at least the last three years of his life. Why did the greatest figure in imaginative achievement shrug and resign himself well before his fiftieth birthday?

I recall discussing this many times with my friend the novelist Anthony Burgess, who held hard to his belief that the poet-dramatist had suffered from syphilis, a conjecture Burgess based upon Sonnets 153 and 154, the "Epilogue" of Pandarus in *Troilus and Cressida*, and Timon's tirades addressing the whores in *Timon of Athens.* This putative illness is vividly conveyed in Burgess's splendid novel concerning Shakespeare, *Nothing Like the Sun*, but has no other warrant. I observed to Burgess that the plays and poems could be employed for hosts of contrary conjectures, and he amiably agreed. Other Bardolators have suggested that Shakespeare had hoarded more than enough money for his Stratford retirement and simply wearied of writing for the theater. I think we do him wrong, he being so majestical, to offer so weak a surmise. Instead I desire to speculate upon this subsiding into the rest of silence.

Detachment in nearly all among us coarsens and becomes indifference; not in Shakespeare. We need a more precise word than *detachment* for Shakespeare's stance in plays and sonnets, but I am never quite sure what it might be. *Indifference* is wrong. Shakespeare cares more for Falstaff than most scholars do, yet he allows his richest singularity to die broken by betrayed love. *Remove* comes closer, since Shakespeare is the major dealer in ellipsis among all the great writers.

We cannot know whether the Sonnets are removed from the authentic self or only from its representation, since their speaker wants us to take him as a poet-actor and not an inwardness. He declines *to overhear himself*; he is a negative whether absent or present, which allows him the audacious blasphemy of Sonnet 121, appropriating Yahweh's words to Moses (Exodus 3:14): "I am that I am":

> 'Tis better to be vile than vile esteemed,
> When not to be receives reproach of being,
> And the just pleasure lost, which is so deemed
> Not by our feeling but by others' seeing.
> For why should others' false adulterate eyes
> Give salutation to my sportive blood?
> Or on my frailties why are frailer spies,
> Which in their wills count bad what I think good?
> No, I am that I am, and they that level
> At my abuses reckon up their own;
> I may be straight though they themselves be bevel;
> By their rank thoughts my deeds must not be shown,
>> Unless this general evil they maintain:
>> All men are bad and in their badness reign.

I do not understand why Stephen Booth—an admirable exegete—believes the allusion to Yahweh's self-naming causes the poem's speaker to "sound smug, presumptuous, and stupid." If Shakespeare in some way does not accept a degree of self-representation in Sonnet 121, then how can the poem cohere? The allusion may well be ironic in that Shakespeare profoundly understands a god who names himself: "I will be [where and when] I will be," or even "When I will not to be here, then I will not be." Will is at the center, not the "others" whose "wills count bad what I think good."

Is Shakespeare in the Sonnets also the creator of Falstaff, Hamlet, Iago, and Cleopatra? In *Motives of Eloquence* (1976), Richard Lanham, Renaissance rhetorician for our time, emphasized the narrator's detachment in "Venus and

Adonis": "What do we think of him? He possesses a rich poetic power but no judgment to go with it. To him Shakespeare has lent his pen but not his mind." The narrator of the Sonnets may not be Shakespeare in full compass, but he shares the poet-dramatist's mind. Lanham also remarked that there are at least as many different "I"s as there are Sonnets. Some of these "I"s are able to turn "injury into poetry" (C. L. Barber's formulation), while others fall short, or perhaps do not quite want such a "transmemberment of song" (Hart Crane). When Shakespeare holds back in the Sonnets, he chooses lyric over drama. And yet the poet of *A Midsummer Night's Dream,* of the fifth act at Belmont of *The Merchant of Venice,* of *Romeo and Juliet* and *Richard II* is the ultimate lyrical dramatist. That fusion comes apart in the Sonnets.

One of my students observed in class discussion some years ago that many of the Sonnets depend upon Shakespeare narrating his own sufferings and humiliations as though they were someone else's. Yes and no, I recall replying, since they are never presented as though indeed they were painful and debasing. Unless Shakespeare prophesied Nietzsche's apothegm "That which does not destroy me strengthens me," we are given a reticence preternaturally reliant upon the exclusion of pathos. And yet the rhetoric of the Sonnets is not Ovidian-Marlovian.

The most illuminating essay on this that I have read is Thomas M. Greene's "Pitiful Thrivers: Failed Husbandry in the Sonnets" (1985). Here is Greene's poignant conclusion:

> The Sonnets can be read to the end as attempts to cope with progres-
> sively powerful and painful forms of cost and expense. The bourgeois
> desire to balance cosmic and human budgets seems to be thwarted by a
> radical flaw in the universe, in emotion, in value, and in language. This
> flaw is already acted out at the beginning by the onanistic friend who
> "feed'st thy lights flame with selfe substantiall fewell" (1). In Sonnet
> 73, the metaphoric fire lies in its ashes as on a deathbed, "consum'd
> with that which it was nurrisht by." This becomes, in the terrible Son-
> net 129, "a blisse in proofe and proud and very wo," a line always, un-
> necessarily, emended. The vulnerability of the Sonnets lies in their
> ceaselessly resistant reflection of this flaw, their stubborn reliance on
> economies incapable of correcting it, their use of language so wealthy,
> so charged with "difference," as to be erosive. The vulnerability of the
> Sonnets might be said to resemble that nameless flaw that afflicts their

speaker, but in their case the flaw is not ultimately disastrous. They are not consumed by the extravagant husbandry that produced them. Their effort to resist, to compensate, to register in spite of slippage, balances their loss with store. They leave us with the awesome cost, and reward, of their conative contention. The vulnerability is inseparable from the striving that leads us to them: the "poet's" expense and Shakespeare's expense.

Emerson's Gnostic observation—"There is a crack in everything that God has made"—is akin to Greene's "radical flaw in the universe, in emotion, in value, and in language." But that is Hamlet's cosmos, and Lear's, and Macbeth's. The more than overwhelming force of the major tragedies is circumvented in the Sonnets, except perhaps for the death march of 129, and the "Desire is death" litany of 147, to me the most terrifying erotic poem I know. Once again, what compelled (if that is the right word) Shakespeare to hold back?

Only the force of Shakespeare's own mind could defend it from itself. Shakespeare, almost all deep readers agree, excelled in intellectual power, wisdom, and linguistic vitality, but the three together are surpassed by his rarest gift: the creation of personalities. *People* is the word I prefer, though that restarts wearisome arguments. Even Cervantes and Tolstoy are not that prodigal at repopulating a heterocosm.

Of the two intensely erotic relationships in the Sonnets, each may be at least a doubling (Southampton *and* Pembroke, Mary Fitton *and* Emilia Bassano Lanier *and* Lucy Negro). Even the Rival Poet may be a tripling (Chapman, Jonson, Marlowe), which would be less provocative than the strong possibility that both the Fair Young Nobleman and the Dark Lady are composites. Many if not most of us realize in retrospect that a lifetime's attachments tend to arrange themselves into recurrent patterns. Fusion re-imagines erotic singularities, however intense and long lingering, and makes them seem only fictions of duration, uneasily akin to poems and literary narratives.

Greene's emphasis upon fluctuations in value is cruelly sustained by the language of trade and economy in the Sonnets. Is that language consistently ironic? I think not, though an ironist so towering as Shakespeare works beyond our ken. Sonnet 87—"Farewell, thou art too dear for my possessing"—upon which I have attempted to found a poetics of influence, piles up an extraordinary heap of commercial diction endlessly paradoxical in its referential power: "dear," "possessing," "estimate," "charter," "worth," "releasing," "bonds," "determi-

nate," "granting," "riches," "deserving," "gift," "wanting," "patent," "swerving,"
"gav'ot," "mistaking," "misprision," "growing." Those twenty words are packed
into the first eleven lines of the poem; is this the feared end of an erotic or of
a financial partnership? There is a tradition that Shakespeare purchased his
share in the Lord Chamberlain's company of actors with a thousand pounds
borrowed from his patron, the earl of Southampton.

The creator of Hamlet trades in the commodity of what Emerson was to call
"the great and creative self." The dramatist of Falstaff and Hamlet, Iago and
Cleopatra transcends any pragmatics of self-reliance. And yet the poet of the
Sonnets engages himself in so Proustian a quest for small and large evidences
of betrayal and devaluation that we might recall the more comic sorrows of
Swann and Marcel, except that Shakespeare does go through all this for a man
and a woman who surprisingly did suit him and evidently were authentically
his style and mode.

Shakespeare's erotic vision in the comic sphere concludes in *Measure for
Measure,* while in tragedy it culminated in *Timon of Athens.* The late tragicomedies (they are *not* romances) flame out in the jealous madness of Leontes
and the stance beyond detachment of Prospero. In the Sonnets, Shakespeare
reveals nothing of his own personality while rendering both the Fair Young
Nobleman and the Dark Lady sexual minefields. As readers we might murmur
that they deserve one another, a judgment that is alien to Shakespeare. And
yet the surprising misogyny provoked by his Dark Lady (a stance nowhere evident in the plays) is not justified by him, and his endless celebrations of the
Fair Young Nobleman do not bring forward a single good quality in that lethal
spoiled aristocrat. Southampton/Pembroke is merely beautiful while Mary/
Emilia/Lucy is a furnace, prophetic of Lady Emma Hamilton's Electric Bed,
which became Admiral Horatio Nelson's Promised Land aboard the *Victory.*

Even in the Sonnets we are allowed our own perspectives but always at the
risk of exposing ourselves while the poet remains sequestered. No one except the narrator of the Sonnets is capable of any affection for the Fair Young
Nobleman, but I hardly know a male reader who does not share my lust for the
Dark Lady. No other love poem in the English language has an affect as grim
as Sonnet 147:

> My love is as a fever, longing still
> For that which longer nurseth the disease,
> Feeding on that which doth preserve the ill,

Th' uncertain sickly appetite to please.
My reason, the physician to my love,
Angry that his prescriptions are not kept,
Hath left me, and I desperate now approve
Desire is death, which physic did except.
Past cure I am, now reason is past care,
And frantic mad with evermore unrest;
My thoughts and my discourse as madmen's are,
At random from the truth vainly expressed:
    For I have sworn thee fair, and thought thee bright,
    Who are as black as hell, as dark as night.

Falling in love with an illness of the self, near enough to a sickness-unto-death, is to drive beyond the pleasure principle. I cannot recall any mention of the features of the beloved young man, but am all too aware that the mistress' eyes are raven black, doubtless like those two pitch-balls stuck in Rosaline's face in *Love's Labour's Lost*. Whatever Shakespeare's relation to Southampton or to Pembroke (or to both) it was temperance itself when compared to the furnace of the Dark Lady (or Ladies). "Desire is death": so grand a finale of seem achieves perfection neither of the work nor of the life. For a moment only, the poet-narrator joins himself to Iago and to Edmund.

Do the "pitiful thrivers" of Sonnet 125 exist in the same cosmos that commences two sonnets later? The language of expense, bonds, usury prevails, yet the trade more clearly is erotic, not commercial. Of the Dark Lady, Greene ventures that she "perhaps is the one thriver in the work who is not pitiful."

No one would defend the "loyalties" of the Sonnets, but since they have no world-without-end bargains is there warrant for terming their bargains "tawdry"? No valid promises were made, no pledges enacted, among this triangle. No one emerges in a posture other than prone. Except for the Stony Rimes of Dante, no other "love poems" are so finally forbidding.

Shakespeare does not compose the Sonnets *as* Shakespeare, creator of Falstaff, Hamlet, Rosalind, Feste. Wit is too besieged in the Sonnets by a strict restraint of ethos and pathos; logos reigns almost unchallenged. That "almost" reflects Rosalie Colie's sensitive reading in her *Shakespeare's Living Art* (1974), which emphasizes style as doing the work of ethos in the Sonnets. The Sonnets are neither comedy nor tragedy. They are early romance, internalized for their speaker-narrator if not perhaps for their poet. Do they tell a story? Everything that happens has occurred before and will come again. The Falstaffiad/Henriad tells a story, one that in a profound sense is over when we first encounter Falstaff and Hal. No one triangulated their dark story: Henry IV and Hotspur are not Dark Lady and Rival Poet. Did Shakespeare have a nightmare sense of repetition when (if) he experienced with Pembroke what he had suffered with Southampton? How good it is that we cannot and will never know.

There is no Falstaff in the Sonnets; the Falstaff-in-Shakespeare is there in dilemma or predicament, not in wit and vitalistic outcry. Empson had to find Falstaff in Shakespeare the sonneteer because his Falstaff (like the great poet-critic himself) was bisexual. Hal/Henry V is of that double persuasion; Falstaff never is a double man, in Eros or in fending off time, death, and the state. It is not that Falstaff (like Hamlet or even Cleopatra) is too good for his play(s) but that they are not good enough for him. Nothing, even by Shakespeare, overmatches the double play of *Henry IV,* but even that Homeric and Aristophanic wealth cannot contain Sir John, who as life itself breaks every vessel that would contain his force.

Does Shakespeare the poet break the vessels in the Sonnets? Start at the beginning and read your way through. From 19 on ("Devouring time, blunt thou the lion's paws") you will stop many times: 20, 29, 30, 40, 53, 55, 66, 73, 86, 87, 94, 107, 110, 116, 121, 125, 129, 130, 135, 138, 144, 146, and 147 among them. That is two dozen poems I have chosen personally; others may choose differently. Whichever you choose, they touch very near the limits of art.

Shakespeare—to know whom is to have acquired knowledge—might have had no quarrel with Francis Bacon's essay "Of Love," which he must have read: *That it is impossible to love and to be wise.* In Samuel Johnson that became the reflection, Love is the wisdom of fools and the folly of the wise. That seems to me a fit motto for Shakespeare's Sonnets.

"HAMLET" AND THE ART OF KNOWING

Time hath, my lord, a wallet at his back
Wherein he puts alms for oblivion.
—*Ulysses to Achilles,* Troilus and Cressida

The place of the tragedy *Hamlet* in Shakespeare's canon is suggestively parallel to that of Mark's Gospel in the English Bible. Remarkably, Mark's Jesus finds his way back to the J or Yahwist portion of the text of Genesis, Exodus, Numbers. He is for Yahweh alone and not for the God of the Priestly Writer or the Deuteronomist. His Yahweh is personal, passionate, and thus very far from a theological god. It is doubtless strange of me to say this but something of the Marcan Jesus, abrupt and startling, abides in the aura of Prince Hamlet.

There is frequent controversy as to whether *Hamlet* is more a Protestant or a Catholic play. Neither, I would suggest, though Protestantism would be closer if only because Hamlet's stance toward divinity is unmediated. He is not a Faustian figure and would not cry out with Marlowe's damned scholar, "See, see where Christ's blood streams in the firmament!" His consciousness turns ever more inward, away from credences and into the labyrinth of questionings, where the Montaigne of John Florio's edition went before him.

Montaigne asked, "What do I know?" Hamlet, as befits a king's son, could not phrase it that way. Instead he challenges individuals in his audience: "What

do you know?"—aware that we know less then he does. That makes more pregnant his final direct address to us:

> You that look pale, and tremble at this chance,
> That are but mutes or audience to this act
> Had I but time—as this fell sergeant, Death,
> Is strict in his arrest—O, I could tell you—
> But let it be.

[5.2.334–38]

Are we mutes onstage or audience in front of it? Of the speaking parts in the
play, Horatio, the head-bashing bully-boy Fortinbras, and the fop Osric remain alive. Only Horatio represents us, but Hamlet also is prepared to let us
represent ourselves. To what purpose? What could he have told us?

Once I thought that would have been personal, a discovery of what he himself
had represented. Now I grow uncertain. The longer I read, teach, and meditate
upon *Hamlet,* the stranger the play becomes to me. I resort to my variation upon
what Kenneth Burke taught me: What was Shakespeare trying to do for himself,
as person and as poet-dramatist, by composing *Hamlet*?

James Joyce answered the personal question by invoking the deaths of
Shakespeare's father and son Hamnet. Anthony Burgess, Joyce's disciple,
charmed me on one of our Fundador-soaked evenings together by a Joycean
insight: Anne Hathaway had surpassed herself by adultery with both of Shakespeare's brothers. Being less baroque in this, I prefer to ask, What did Shakespeare intend to do for himself as dramatist by this magnificent breakthrough,
still the most experimental play ever composed?

Falstaff already had captured London; Hamlet confirmed the conquest. The
two brought Shakespeare to glory, but his restless agon with all of literature
took him onward to the Gnostic sublimity of *King Lear* and *Macbeth.* Creation
and Fall become one event in the later Shakespeare. Are they a simultaneous
catastrophe in *Hamlet* as well?

Whatever Demiurge created Prince Hamlet, it does seem to have been what
Melville termed an "anarch hand" tearing the "human integral" asunder. One
sees why actresses venture to play Hamlet: in some ways he is the Hermetic
androgyne before the Creation-Fall. It may or may not be accurate to define
certain characteristics of consciousness as being either male or female. What
is exact is to see and say that Hamlet contains virtually all women and all men.

Stand back from that assertion and it can seem insane. Assume that Peter Alexander, and Harold Bloom in his wake, could be right in ascribing the missing Ur-*Hamlet* of 1588 or so to Shakespeare himself and not to Marlowe's crony Thomas Kyd. In 1604 a writer observed that tragedy "should please all, like Prince Hamlet," which follows Gabriel Harvey's saying in 1600 that "the wiser sort" are pleased by the tragedy of Hamlet. I will not ask who among us four centuries later are of the wiser sort. G. K. Chesterton, writing in 1901, still speaks to my sense both of Falstaff and of Hamlet: "Falstaff was neither brave nor honest, nor chaste, nor temperate, nor clean, but he had the eighth cardinal virtue for which no name has ever been found. Hamlet was not fitted for this world; but Shakespeare does not dare to say whether he was too good or too bad for it" ("The True Hamlet"). Surely Falstaff was too good for this world, while Hamlet was both too good and too bad to be fitted for our world, which remains Elsinore writ large.

The actual fortress-castle at Elsinore could hardly be larger. I was taken to see it in 2005, when I was in Denmark to receive the Hans Christian Andersen Bicentennial Award. The visual experience stunned me and belatedly changed my mind about some aspects of the play. Where and how Shakespeare lived during some of the middle to later years of the 1580s is lost to us. Could he have gone abroad with a company of English actors, who perhaps even played the Ur-*Hamlet*? That is merely wild speculation on my part, yet the scale and rugged brutalism of the Elsinore fortress troubled me with the intuition that he had been there. The great hall in which the duel is staged is gigantic, and the commanding position of the fortress over the water gives a vivid conviction of how powerful the Danish monarchy still was in Shakespeare's day. Above all the scale of Elsinore, a sublime ruggedness of context indoors and outdoors, lingers in memory as the stage for Hamlet's curtailed life and early death.

How early that death is remains undecidable. Shakespeare, elliptical and crazily random in this lawless drama, gives us an undergraduate Hamlet at the start, presumably twenty or less, and a thirty-year-old in the graveyard scene. The lapsed time of the play can only be a week or at most two. This does not matter compared to greater ellipses. How far back does the sexual relationship between Gertrude and Claudius go? Was there any complicity, however passive, on Gertrude's part in the fratricide? How intense, on Hamlet's side, was the romance—if any—with Ophelia? More important than all these: How is Prince Hamlet so conversant not only with Shakespeare's own company of players but with the context that makes relevant London theatrical gossip? It is a legitimate inference that he may have spent more time at the Globe than in pursuing his studies at the Lutheran University of Wittenberg.

Hamlet in the play is rather more than a theatrical amateur play-botcher. His admonitions to the players—clearly directed to the clown Will Kemp, in particular, who must have played the Gravedigger—seem more incontrovertibly the utterance of Shakespeare himself than anything else in the thirty-eight or so dramas we confidently can ascribe to the world's central poet-playwright.

When the Christian Bible is treated as a single work, say in the King James Version, I become unhappy. There are copious reasons for my discontent, quite aside from the captivity of the Jewish Bible, being dragged along by Christian triumphalism. Yet I have expounded my stance upon this in print, all too often for some. William Shakespeare of Stratford really did write almost everything attributed to him; partisans of Marlowe, Oxford, Bacon, or Middleton can be waved aside. I grant that the texts are multiform and frequently unreliable, so that we cannot quite know what is or what is not in *Hamlet* or *King Lear.* And I will not appeal to our mutual experience of attending performances of Shakespeare, since not infrequently I walk out at the first intermission, reflecting that at eighty I do not need to endure any more high-concept directors, who should be shot at dawn.

I am a common reader who goes through Shakespeare again, from start to finish, each year, in and out of the classroom. He did not intend his quarter-century of playwriting as a unitary effort, but his friends gathered almost all of the plays together in 1623, seven years after his death, in what we now term the First Folio. Ben Jonson advised the actor-editors, doubtless reflecting on his own just audacity in having brought forth his *Works* in a folio of 1616 (which, however, did not contain his plays). Yet Jonson not only encouraged Shakespeare's friends; he prefaced the First Folio with a great poem to Shakespeare's memory and plays, many of which he must have read for a first time. The poem, eighty lines in superb couplets, implicitly treats the plays as a life work, and so a single one. Jonson urges us to "Look how the father's face / Lives in his issue," which makes the individual plays Shakespeare's daughters and sons. I would like to think that *Titus Andronicus* and *The Merry Wives of Windsor* do not much resemble their father, though even they have their admirers. *Titus Andronicus* I take as a spoof, a send-up of Marlowe, Thomas Kyd, and George Peele, while *Merry Wives* travesties the greatness of Falstaff in the *Henry IV* plays.

Shakespeare's immediate precursor was Marlowe, only a few months older

but the beneficiary of a running start as an undergraduate. Marlowe was murdered in 1593, when he and Shakespeare were twenty nine. Had Shakespeare
died with Marlowe, he would have left us the three parts of *Henry VI* and *Richard
III,* but not much more, if scholars are accurate in their datings. Popular as
Richard III remains, it does not measure up to the *Tamburlaine* plays, *The Jew of
Malta,* and *Faustus.* Had Marlowe lived, he would have continued to unfold, but
he was unlikely to change. No writer ever has transformed himself as Shakespeare did from 1594 to 1613. In just short of two decades, at least twenty-seven
permanent dramas came forth, accompanied by what are among the finest
short poems in the language.

As with the indubitable villains Macbeth, Iago, and Edmund, Hamlet's atmosphere is conjecture: his imagination is proleptic, his mode is prophecy.
Macbeth is preternatural; he has second sight and he hallucinates. Iago antici-
pates Milton's Satan, in whom Angus Fletcher finds the masterpiece of tragic
isolation and negativity. What troubles Satan is his mixed heritage: Hamlet,
Macbeth, Iago. He has little in him of Edmund's zestful blend of Don Juan and
an English Machiavel, though he lusts after both Eve and Adam. His cosmological despair is Hamlet's; his temporal anxieties are Macbeth's; his sense of
injured merit is Iago's. In *Colors of the Mind,* Fletcher generously illuminates the
iconography of fallen thought in Satan, doomed to the rigors of endless self-
justification, the solipsist's dilemma. When I was younger, my passion was for
Satan; now I am warier, since solipsism cannot die its own death. With grim
eloquence, Fletcher distinguishes Satan from his prime precursor, Hamlet:
"Milton has created the largest and most heroic image of the hero as suffering
thinker, or, to personify, of thinking as suffering. For unlike Hamlet, who dies
in a wild melodrama of dueling, the defeated antagonist of Jesus can only watch
his opponent go quietly home to his Mother's house."

Has Fletcher not stacked the deck? Or had Milton done that for him? But
few believe that the hero of Western consciousness goes down appropriately in
Claudius's poisoned duel. Hamlet, as much an enigmatic Redeemer as Mark's
Jesus, is given nothing better to do than to chop down Claudius, not a mighty
opposite but a frantic Machiavel to whom no one would assign a passing grade.
Milton, far more deeply affected by Shakespeare than he knew, makes his own
sacrifice in chronicling Satan. Where is Lucifer, the unfallen Satan? When we
first see Hamlet, he is already ruined. The Ghost can do no more to him than
the Prince has done to himself. He is the wrong man in the wrong place at the
wrong time, and he knows it. Satan begins in the right place, but why will Milton

not represent it? I fear this is Milton's tribute to Hamlet, Macbeth, Iago, and the inescapable forerunner, Shakespeare.

Try to envision a first two books of *Paradise Lost* with a gloriously unfallen Lucifer; we would be stopped upon his wings by sound. Our Adversary seems trouble enough without added sublimity. Ophelia praises a Hamlet we never see; Satan studies the nostalgias but already is crippled by temporal anxieties. I cannot locate C. S. Lewis's temper-tantrum Satan. Something has gone wrong with the hero-villain, but no one as yet is able to tell us what.

Milton, undaunted, could have given us an unfallen Lucifer had he chosen to do so; some traces survive. Shakespeare, even in the graveyard, shows us splinters of an angelic Hamlet but will never allow us to see the undiminished Prince. And yet Satan and Hamlet both think their ways into the desolation of reality. Man's life is thought, and all of us are fallen angels: Satan, Hamlet, Shakespeare, the reader.

Wisdom is Hebrew as well as Greek, but literary criticism was wholly Greek in its origins, and tendentiously ideological when Plato malformed it. Shakespeare plays with transcendence for mostly comic effects, but has no use for Plato's transcendental Forms, scarcely of interest to a consciousness that loves change. Metamorphosis for Shakespeare is another mode of thinking in his theater of mind, where Hamlet abides as monarch of wit. Whatever his illnesses (and these all seem north-by-northwest) Hamlet leads any competitors (Oedipus included) in *recognition,* perhaps the central act of thinking in imaginative literature. Fletcher cites Heidegger's wordplay on the link in etymology between *thinking* and *thanking,* so that memory is made into both cognition and praise, as it is in the Psalms. Recognition, in that context, need not be resolution but generally is only partial, since full recognition concludes thinking in literature.

In a later study, *Time, Space, and Motion in the Age of Shakespeare* (2007), Fletcher identifies our sense of remaining time with Shakespeare's large view of "nature." That sense itself is a Shakespearean enlargement of Aristotle's "recognition," defined by the philosopher as "a change from ignorance to knowledge," knowledge that is hard to accept. There are great figures who refuse tragedy, Falstaff and Don Quixote in particular. Both of them are too intelligent not to know that what they refuse is the catastrophe of recognition. Shakespeare abounds in those who refuse recognition: Bottom, Shylock, Malvolio are among them. Falstaff, a thinker incessant and powerful enough to have challenged even Hamlet, Rosalind, and Cleopatra, is wary even of partial recognition.

Fletcher shows us this refusal flowering into the soliloquy, where no one can approach Shakespeare's giant art. Hamlet's soliloquies, now shunned by many directors and actors, are the masterpieces of Shakespeare the thinker.

Exportable to the entire world except for France—despite Stendhal, Victor Hugo, and Balzac—the Shakespearean soliloquy expires upon the French stage. Voltaire thought Shakespeare "barbaric," and French drama, until Alfred Jarry and the Absurdists, avoided dramatic monologue. It is the heroic praxis of Racine always to provide an interlocutor or at least auditor upon the stage. I have seen no study of Shakespeare's soliloquies altogether worthy of them, but they are a high art within his art, and constitute the royal road to his enhancement of our own sense of personality. We *hear* Falstaff, Hamlet, Iago, but they *overhear* themselves, and change through that self-overhearing. Will as deepest desire is surprised by this overhearing, and Shakespeare, who played endlessly upon his first name, might be said to develop will-overhearing while gradually abandoning self-overhearing.

I revise here my earlier notion that Shakespeare's reinvention of the human centers upon change through overhearing. Except for one unsympathetic but clever critic, who remarked that what was being overheard was Shakespeare himself, my rumination met either silence or poor wit (Shakespeare did *not* invent the lightbulb; Edison did). My intellectual debt in this area was to John Stuart Mill, who wrote that poetry is not heard but overheard. But by what psychic agency or component of glory?

Shakespeare's secret, his guide through the labyrinth of influence exercised upon him by his own mind and works, was a discovery I should have termed the selfsame or the will overhearing itself. In Shakespeare, the knit of identity is not psyche or the soul but the daimon, pneuma, spark of will, what Nietzsche and Yeats called the antithetical self as opposed to a primary self. I do not believe that Shakespeare was a Hermetist (Frances Yates) or at times an Ophitic Gnostic (A. D. Nuttall), but this greatest of all poets possessed his own way of knowing, which never can be fully deciphered by us except through endless deep rereadings. Possess Hamlet by memory and he ceases to seem merely clever or as crazy as the rest of us. G. Wilson Knight said that Hamlet's was "the embassy of death" from that undiscovered country. D. H. Lawrence reacted to Hamlet's soliloquies pretty much as to Whitman's poems. Hamlet/ Shakespeare and Walt/Whitman at once were "obscene knowers" (Lawrence's term) and also minds that broke the new road.

MILTON'S HAMLET

William Empson pronounced *Paradise Lost* to be "horrible and wonderful," akin to Aztec or Benin sculpture or to the novels of Kafka, and further claimed that its God was wonderful because he was so horrible. I swerve away here from Empson's account in *Milton's God* (1961). As I go on reading the dramatic epic, it has at least two gods, one an irascible heavenly tyrant and the other a Spirit that prefers the pure and upright heart of John Milton to all temples of worship.

What Spirit is that? In his edition, Alistair Fowler, who finds in Milton's God a universal father figure, identifies the Spirit with the Pauline Holy Ghost, which would not have pleased John Milton, a sect of one (rather like Blake, Shelley, Emerson, Whitman, Dickinson, and other descendants of the Miltonic Inner Light). I would prefer to name the Spirit as the bells that break down Milton's lonely tower and swing he knows not where. Internalizing the muse as his own image of voice, Milton worships his own inspiration. How could it be otherwise? Those haunted by Shakespeare, Milton's only audience then and now, are readers who can enter the Globe's theater of mind. Shakespeare had his auditors, envied by Milton and Joyce.

In old age, time becomes urgent, and this makes me unwilling to tolerate learned ignorance. I dismiss as irrelevant anyone trying to argue that Shakespeare wrote as an ardent Christian, whether Protestant or recusant Catholic. But was Milton a Christian? Milton believed in Milton quite overtly, and he believed also in Shakespeare, rather more than in the English Bible. The Bible and Homer, Vergil and Dante, Tasso and Spenser are fecund resources for Milton. Shakespeare is different: he comes unbidden.

Shelley once said that the Devil owes everything to Milton, but Milton's Satan owed the soliloquy to Hamlet. In a sense everything that both Hamlet and Satan say is soliloquy: their mutual spirits wither gloriously in the air of solitude. Each addresses (when it most matters) only himself, for who else seems real? We do not believe in Hamlet's love for anyone (except Yorick, in the prince's childhood) or in Satan's, except that Satan at least would want to love himself while Hamlet doesn't even want that.

Macbeth gave Satan his proleptic anguish, Iago his sense of injured merit, and Edmund a desire to stand up for bastards. Yet Hamlet gave Satan, Satan: the prison-house of the self. *Samson Agonistes,* a stunning display of Milton's rhetorical genius, breaks from Shakespeare's influence at the high cost of expelling inwardness. Only a few Shakespearean echoes sneak into *Samson Agonistes,* and they jar. When Manoa applies "miserable change" to Samson, the phrase serves only to indicate the abyss between the Herculean hero Antony and the Hebrew champion. Nothing so clearly illustrates the Shakespearean personality of Satan as the lunatic speculation, How could you fit him into *Samson Agonistes?*

Setting aside T. S. Eliot's dismissal of him as another curly-haired Lord Byron, Milton's Satan is unquestionably one of the sublime hero-villains, fit to associate with the visionary company of his Shakespearean precursors Hamlet and Iago, Edmund and Macbeth, and with such descendants as Captain Ahab, Shrike of *Miss Lonelyhearts,* and Judge Holden of Cormac McCarthy's *Blood Meridian.* In transatlantic phone conversations with the late A. D. Nuttall, a friend I never met, he liked to remind me that Milton rigorously excluded any mention of Prometheus from *Paradise Lost.* And yet Blake's Prometheus, Orc, and Shelley's Prometheus Rising, attend me whenever I brood on Milton's grandest creation, the High Romantic Shelleyan Satan of *Paradise Lost.* Not Byron or Blake but Shelley: Satan also goes on until he is stopped, and he never is stopped. Idolator of the sacred Milton as of the supernal Shakespeare, I nevertheless dismiss the palpable bad taste of a hissing Satan on the Dead Sea shore. There is no such Satan, and Milton knew it.

What do we love most about our wicked kinsman Satan? Sometimes I envision him on the Yiddish stage of my youth, played all-out by Maurice Schwartz as I saw him playing Shylock and Lear. A Yiddisher Satan would have had the necessary swagger, inherited by Schwartz from Jacob Adler and Boris Thomashefsky, both alas before my time as a child born in 1930. But that would have been swagger with pathos, akin to Schwartz as Shylock, dropping the scalpel with a shudder as he approached Antonio the trembling *shagitz* and crying out with a tremor that shook the Second Avenue Theater: *Ik bin doch a Yid!* Not that I see Uncle Satan murmuring, "Well after all, I *am* Jewish," but rather that he declines the role of vulgarian proposed for him by T. S. Eliot and C. S. Lewis. Satan did not attend Harvard or Yale, Oxford or Cambridge. Doubtless he assiduously studied Talmud until expelled by furious rabbis, compelled to recognize another *Acher,* the Stranger they rejected in Elisha Ben Abuya, with whom I have identified for more than sixty years.

Neil Forsyth's *The Satanic Epic* (2003) is my particular favorite among recent studies of *Paradise Lost.* Forsyth intimates that Milton's God may be just as much a hero-villain as Satan is, but Forsyth declines to see Milton's refusal to portray Lucifer (the unfallen Satan) as a flaw or a descent from the Shakespearean fullness. That Miltonic falling away from Shakespeare's pleroma is my subject here.

Imagine Milton's uncompleted tragedy *Adam Unparadised* as composed by Shakespeare. Its prime personages would have been Lucifer, Adam, Eve, and God: three hero-villains and a witty heroine. Christ, a worse disaster even than God in *Paradise Lost,* would not have appeared. Lucifer might have resembled Prince Hamlet, while Adam could combine aspects of the uxorious Othello and the slow learner Edgar of *King Lear.* God of course would be Lear, and Eve a synthesis of Rosalind and other comedic splendors in Shakespeare.

Shakespeare's grandest originality always was the imagining of change; he would have been delighted to represent Lucifer overhearing himself and then undergoing change to the music of perpetual surprise. Ovidian to his core, the dramatist loved change; the quasi-Platonist Milton employed Circe, mistress of bestial transformations, as the symbol of all metamorphosis. Lusting after Eve as intensely as do Adam and Satan, the epic poet nevertheless associates her with the Homeric Circe. Shakespeare makes us admire Rosalind as a goddess of erotic transformations, an all-but-universal matchmaker. And though she warns Orlando that as a woman she is changeable, her love actually is constant, as is Eve's for Adam.

Lucifer is the unfallen Satan, never quite shown to us by Milton. The origins of Lucifer (the light-bearer, in Saint Jerome's Latin) are in the ancient bright Star of Morning: Athtar, Phaethon, Helel (this last in Isaiah 14, *Helel ben Shahar,* shining Son of Dawn), applied to the defeated king of Babylon. Assimilated to the downfall of the Covering Cherub, the prince of Tyre in Ezekiel, the Morning Star became the vision of prelapsarian Satan. But where is he in Milton?

At the close of book 3 the heroic Satan, voyaging to the New World of Eden (Hebrew for "delight") pauses atop Mount Niphates, on the border between Syria and Armenia. Starting book 4 he utters an extraordinary soliloquy (lines 32–113), which was written years before *Paradise Lost* and meant to open *Adam Unparadised.* Here the speaker addresses first the sun and then himself alone. The overt model is the beginning of *Prometheus Bound* by Aeschylus, but hidden in these sonorous tonalities is the voice of the Prince of Denmark:

> O thou that with surpassing glory crowned,
> Lookst from thy sole dominion like the God
> Of this new world; at whose sight all the stars
> Hide their diminished heads; to thee I call,
> But with no friendly voice, and add thy name
> O sun, to tell thee how I hate thy beams
> That bring to my remembrance from what state
> I fell, how glorious once above thy sphere;
> Till pride and worse ambition threw me down
> Warring in heaven against heaven's matchless king:
> Ah wherefore! he deserved no such return
> From me, whom he created what I was
> In that bright eminence, and with his good
> Upbraided none; nor was his service hard.
> What could be less than to afford him praise,
> The easiest recompense, and pay him thanks,
> How due! Yet all his good proved ill in me,
> And wrought but malice; lifted up so high
> I sdeigned subjection, and thought one step higher
> Would set me highest, and in a moment quit
> The debt immense of endless gratitude,
> So burdensome, still paying, still to owe;
> Forgetful what from him I still received,
> And understood not that a grateful mind
> By owing owes not, but still pays, at once
> Indebted and discharged; what burden then?
> O had his powerful destiny ordained

Me some inferior angel, I had stood
Then happy; no unbounded hope had raised
Ambition. Yet why not? Some other power
As great might have aspired, and me though mean
Drawn to his part; but other powers as great
Fell not, but stand unshaken, from within
Or from without, to all temptations armed.
Hadst thou the same free will and power to stand?
Thou hadst: whom hast thou then or what to accuse,
But heaven's free love dealt equally to all?
Be then his love accursed, since love or hate,
To me alike, it deals eternal woe.
Nay cursed be thou; since against his thy will
Chose freely what it now so justly rues.
Me miserable! Which way shall I fly
Infinite wrath, and infinite despair?
Which way I fly is Hell; myself am Hell;
And in the lowest deep a lower deep
Still threatening to devour me opens wide,
To which the hell I suffer seems a heaven.
O then at last relent: is there no place
Left for repentance, none for pardon left?
None left but by submission; and that word
Disdain forbids me, and my dread of shame
Among the spirits beneath, whom I seduced
With other promises and other vaunts
Than to submit, boasting I could subdue
The Omnipotent. Ay me, they little know
How dearly I abide that boast so vain,
Under what torments inwardly I groan;
While they adore me on the throne of hell,
With diadem and scepter high advanced
The lower still I fall, only supreme
In misery; such joy ambition finds.
But say I could repent and could obtain
By act of grace my former state; how soon
Would height recall high thoughts, how soon unsay

What feigned submission swore: ease would recant
Vows made in pain, as violent and void.
For never can true reconcilement grow
Where wounds of deadly hate have pierced so deep:
Which would but lead me to a worse relapse
And heavier fall: so should I purchase dear
Short intermission bought with double smart.
This knows my punisher; therefore as far
From granting he, as I from begging peace:
All hope excluded thus, behold instead
Of us outcast, exiled, his new delight,
Mankind created, and for him this world.
So farewell hope, and with hope farewell fear,
Farewell remorse: all good to me is lost;
Evil be thou my good; by thee at least
Divided empire with heaven's king I hold
By thee, and more than half perhaps will raign;
As man ere long, and this new world shall know.

Depths beneath depths: this is Hamlet's infinite self-consciousness. It does not matter that Satan is an obsessed theist and Hamlet is not. Two angelic intellects inhabit a common abyss: the post-Enlightenment ever-augmenting inner self, of which Hamlet is a precursor, intervening between Luther and Calvin, and later Descartes and Spinoza. Milton's mind is so powerful that it almost holds off Hobbes and produces the last heroic poem, definable as the ascendancy of rhetoric over dialectic.

Satan's rhetoric atop Niphates emphasizes the infinitude of obligation: "The debt immense of endless gratitude, / So burdensome, still paying, still to owe." He goes on to blame himself but not persuasively, given Raphael's account in book 5 of how the rebellion began. Empson sensibly blamed God for starting all the trouble anyway:

Hear all ye angels, progeny of light,
Thrones, dominations, princedoms, virtues, powers,
Hear my decree, which unrevoked shall stand.
This day I have begot whom I declare
My only Son, and on this holy hill
Him have anointed, whom ye now behold

At my right hand; your head I him appoint;
And by myself have sworn to him shall bow
All knees in heaven, and shall confess him Lord:
Under his great viceregent reign abide
United as one individual soul
For ever happy: him who disobeys
Me disobeys, breaks union, and that day
Cast out from God and blessed vision, falls
Into utter darkness, deep engulfed, his place
Ordained without redemption, without end.

[5.600–615]

This is so outrageous that a Gnostic critic, like myself, could not be more delighted. It is like being surfeited with openings for rebuttal, and I do *not* believe Milton meant it as more than a trap for the unwary and literal-minded. He knew his poem had to get past the censor (as it did, quite readily), and he went far beyond Leo Strauss's subtle techniques for "writing between the lines." *Paradise Lost* is almost always weakly misread because scholars never become aware that Milton also partakes in Chaucer's and Shakespeare's irony that is "too large to be seen" (as G. K. Chesterton termed it). Miltonic ironies may even be the largest of the three: neither Chaucer nor Shakespeare was the champion of the losing side in civil wars featuring religious differences, usurpation, regicide, and enormous treasons. Chaucer served both Richard II and his usurper, Henry IV, evidently without discomfort, and Shakespeare avoided trouble under both Elizabeth I and James I. But Milton served Cromwell and then composed most of his masterpiece after Charles II returned to power. If Satan is subversive, then so is his creator, the poet-prophet of Cromwell's revolution. But Satan and Milton share far more than a talent for subversion.

Is *Paradise Lost* insincere? What else could or should the best long poem in the language be? Chaucer and Shakespeare invest their creative exuberance in uncovering the human. Milton is not that preternaturally gifted, though he surpasses all other poets in the language except those two miracles. Chaucer, despite his late recantation, was not particularly pious as a poet: the Prioress and her ghastly tale do not outweigh those splendid rogues the Summoner and the Friar, and their sublime companion, the obsessed Pardoner. Who knows, who cares, what Shakespeare the poet-dramatist *believed*? The abyss, to me, is the only safe answer. Why do scholars out-obsess the Pardoner in trying to establish what Milton the epic poet believed? Satan is Milton's Hamlet, another hero of consciousness. Like Hamlet, Satan at his strongest believes in nothing. When weak, he is a Christian and lapses into book 9's bad poet. In my final phone conversation with Nuttall, we agreed that Milton at the close believed in absolutely nothing, except perhaps his own Inner Light. His affinities were with Henry Vane the Younger, Thomas Ellwood and the Quakers, and, as Christopher Hill insisted, the delightfully named Muggletonians. The God of *Paradise Lost* is a nightmare of bad poetry and evil religion, vindicating everything Shelley and Blake said about him. Milton, profoundly devious, wanted to believe in his own uprightness and purity. His vocation was his belief: Homeric poetry.

Satan's five soliloquies follow in the wake of Hamlet's seven self-communings. Read in juxtaposition, these monologues establish Hamlet as Satan's prime forerunner. But there is no true agon; Hamlet's consciousness is far wider than Satan's. Depth need not be compared: prince and angel alike inhabit an abyss. Hamlet is unique because he overflows with meaning. Context cannot confine him. Satan continues meanings but cannot engender them: Hamlet is a supreme interpreter, Satan a case for interpretation.

For all his supposed solipsism, Hamlet is genuinely interested in everyone he encounters, even the fop Osric. It is not clear whether Satan can perceive other selves. And yet the alert reader's sympathies are with Satan, particularly when he regards God as a usurper, Christ as an upstart, and Abdiel as a time-server. Whose poem is it, anyway? Satan's, Eve's, Adam's, in that order, unless you want to argue it is the reader's. Yet I certainly do not regard the poem as mine, nor Milton's. As narrator, Milton bravely tries to usurp Satan, which leads to the poem's largest flaw: editorializing. Satan earns his bad eminence; Milton is unsporting when he should show more gratitude to his star pupil.

One of the best Miltonic studies, J. M. Evan's *"Paradise Lost" and the Genesis Tradition* (1968), showed how urgently the poet had to hold off the irreconcilable authors of Genesis, the tenth-century B.C.E. Yahwist and the fifth-century B.C.E. Priestly Writer. The Yahwist's God is a person and a fierce personality; the Priestly Author's deity is an unblooded abstraction. Milton's God, like the Yahwist's, is human-all-too-human. The recent biography *John Milton: Life, Work, and Thought*, by Gordon Campbell and Thomas N. Corns, begins by characterizing its subject as "flawed, self-contradictory, self-serving, arrogant, passionate, ruthless, ambitious, and cunning." All true and even truer of Yahweh and of Milton's God: the poet and the archaic Hebrew Divinity were made for each other.

Milton, as I read him, inaugurated the literary tradition of Protestantism without Christianity, to be followed by Blake, Shelley, Emerson, Whitman, Dickinson, the Brontës, Browning, Hardy, and Lawrence, among others. *Paradise Lost* is the English Protestant epic, but it is *not* a Christian poem. The Son hardly seems the Jesus of the gospel of Mark, while Milton has the same distaste for the Crucifixion that I share myself. Mounting the chariot of Paternal Deity, Milton's Son leads an armored attack upon Satan and the rebel host which throws the fallen angels out of heaven and into the abyss. The chariot's flames ignite Satan's legions and pragmatically create hell when the defeated go crashing down. Milton, far more ironical a poet than he is generally judged to be, has shown us the Son creating hell.

If the epic's God and his Son are so equivocal, so must be its Satan. Only Adam and Eve share the poem's glory with Satan, and they are free of his death drive beyond the pleasure principle. The Satanic epic and the Adamic epic diverge, more because of Eve than of Adam. He has limitations, some perhaps unintended by Milton. Eve has none that matter, which cannot be what the man Milton meant to convey. But the poet Milton surpasses himself in *Paradise Lost* and transcends the political man.

I recall first reading the poem when I was thirteen, thrilling to Satan and falling in love with Eve. In those years I fell regularly in love with fictive heroines and encountered Eve after a year of infatuation with Thomas Hardy's heroines, particularly Eustacia Vye in *The Return of the Native* and Marty South in *The Woodlanders.* I all but wept when Marty South cut off her long, beautiful hair, while I joined Milton and Satan in their lust for Eve's wanton tresses. Milton's fierce heterosexuality can be located about midway between Browning's strenuous longings for womankind and Shakespeare's erotic suffering in the Dark Lady sonnets.

Compared to Milton's and to Satan's, Adam's normative and loving desire for Eve is refreshing. Despite Milton's archaic patriarchal stance (he would have practiced polygamy had it been permitted), his shaping power broke loose from him and gave us an Eve naturally superior to her Adam. Shakespearean irony constantly presents his theater with heroines far more vital than their men: Juliet, Rosalind, Lady Macbeth, Cleopatra, Imogen, and so many more. Miltonic irony differs from Chaucerian defense and Shakespearean invention by its wildness; it is not at all clear that Milton could control it even when he wanted to. Does he will to master it? I think not, which is one of the reasons *Paradise Lost* is so endlessly surprising. This model monist, in metaphysics and in theology, is also psychologically forever falling into dualism. Head and heart are monistic, but also opposed to one another, and their strife allows a siege of contraries onto the cosmological stage of the major epic in the English language.

I first learned to read Milton deeply from a brief book, *An Anatomy of Milton's Verse*, by W. B. C. Watkins (1955). I purchased it upon its publication, and have been rereading this introduction to Milton ever since. Watkins, now rarely consulted, was an immensely gifted scholarly critic who wrote on Shakespeare, Spenser, Dr. Johnson, Swift, and Laurence Sterne in addition to Milton. I recall first being arrested by an extraordinary paragraph in *An Anatomy of Milton's Verse* that stresses how Milton's monism works:

> We cannot overstress a fundamental truth about Milton which we find endlessly proliferated in his work. At his most creative, he accepts the whole range from the physical, specifically the senses, to the ultimate Divine as *absolutely unbroken*. This glad acceptance means that he is free to speak of any order of being (extending to inanimate matter) in identical sensuous terms as the great common denominator. For our purposes there is no need to query this or to attempt logical reconciliation with his intellectual beliefs, since we are concerned entirely with his practice and with his remarkable, though not completely successful attempt to make all that he has to say at once perceptible through the senses and intelligible to the mind. Few poets (Lucretius, Dante, Spenser, occasionally Wordsworth) have come so close to making what are ordinarily abstract concepts thus tangible.

Watkins perceptively indicated Milton's anticipation of *Finnegans Wake*. What he catches is Milton's surprising Lucretianism, shared, as we shall see, by Shelley, Whitman, and Stevens as well as Joyce. The insights of Watkins were expanded by William Kerrigan's Freudian study *The Sacred Complex* (1983), where "Miltonic Christianity is the Oedipus complex." Fair enough, though I would join Nuttall in judging that *Paradise Lost* transcends the Oedipal agon and transmutes Miltonic religion into what I would call High Romanticism. Milton's God within is neither Yahweh nor Jesus, though it could be called Hermetist. On that reading, there is more of God in Eve and Adam than in Satan, Messiah, or the Paternal Deity of *Paradise Lost*.

Nuttall wittily observed that "Milton is too intelligent for his own monism." Unfortunately, Nuttall was a touch too impressed by Milton's "ethical will," which *The Alternative Trinity* (1988) audaciously concluded had led the epic poet into espousing the Gnostic heresy: "Even monist, Arian Milton was surprised by the element of Gnosticism in his own mind into a kind of revolution within the Godhead." I wonder: If Milton is too intelligent for his own monism, is he not also too passionate and sensuous for his own "dualism"? In *The Matter of Revelation* (1996), John Rogers argued learnedly for a "vitalist" Milton and so found yet another path out of *Paradise Lost*'s theological maze: "There is a sense in which Milton's stated goal to 'assert Eternal Providence' may acquire its ultimate meaning from the Latin root, *asserere,* to declare a slave free. *Paradise Lost* can engender its theology of free will, its politics of self-rule, and its ethos of individualism only by liberating providence from the tyrannical bonds of an authoritarian logic."

The creator God of book 7 is a vitalist in the seventeenth-century monistic sense: he endues every substance with animate energy, self-propelling and self-fulfilling. But John Milton composed book 7, gorgeously expanding the biblical account of beginnings. God Milton is not only present at the Creation and represents it for us; he transmembers both the Yahwist and Priestly texts of the cosmological event. Whether the surging power of book 7 truly balances Satan's eloquent energies I now tend to doubt, and prefer to find Satan's poetic rival only in Eve and in Milton's four invocations. Can they be termed John Milton's own soliloquies?

How might Shakespeare have managed the transition from Lucifer to Satan? Iago and Edmund are already fallen when first we encounter them, and Macbeth is so open to the night world that he scarcely needs to fall. Hamlet, however, begins and ends as a Lucifer, the Morning and Evening Star of all those who think much too well. Despite certain verbal gestures he can encounter nothing transcendental except his own spirit. One as yet untried way of reading his drama would be to consider it a quest to discover values outside his knowledge of self that might hold him to life. Though he believes (or says he believes) he has found an immediate justice in Horatio, I suspect this finding. Is it not a Shakespearean device to convert us, audience and readership, into so many idolatrous Horatios? Something is always missing in Horatio, but *that* ellipsis is our own. Shakespeare, with benign irony, reminds us that something is always missing in ourselves.

Hamlet is so bewilderingly overrich that it takes us a while to see how elliptical he is in himself. Horatio's adoring vacuity too easily can become our own, but it is very difficult to become Hamlet's skilled auditor, and turning into an anti-Horatio will not help either. Satan has no Horatio, and he needs one. His partner Beëzelbub surpasses Horatio in colorlessness and is merely Satan's yes-man. Horatio tactfully tends to modify Hamlet's observations while mostly agreeing with them, but Beëzelbub is only an instrument. There is then no one to mediate Satan for us except Milton the narrator, who frequently mars the heroism of Satan by the sort of pious editorializing that would better have been left to C. S. Lewis and T. S. Eliot.

An unmediated Satan raises other problems in representation, all of them working against Milton's creation of a Lucifer of undiminished splendor. The strict avoidance of any references to Prometheus in an epic so archaic and classical as *Paradise Lost* indicates Miltonic anxiety, for Lucifer and Prometheus form a triad with Hamlet, as Victor Hugo majestically implied. Let us take a step even beyond Hugo's sublimity: the triad is an identity. Lucifer, Prometheus, and Hamlet all are light-bringers: all steal fire from heaven. Hamlet knows everything because he has ransacked everything. Like Shakespeare, his dark brother, Hamlet is a magpie. Montaigne usurped the image of Socrates, playing Xenophon against Plato. Hamlet makes of Montaigne *his* Socrates, while Shakespeare separately dreamed Falstaff as the Socrates of Eastcheap.

Prometheus and Hamlet are inventors (in the broadest sense of the word) and share the arts of deception: cunning, slyness, lying like truth. But that is to see them from a sky god's perspective, and not from their own. Lucifer, I take it, was too grand for such subtle evasiveness until he fell into the state of Satan. It can be difficult to distinguish Lucifer in his full glory from Christ in Revelation 22:16, and the two figures are associated again in the Easter eve exaltation of the paschal candle.

Nuttall's surmise was that Prometheus is never mentioned in *Paradise Lost* because he was too relevant and might have tempted readers to a subversive or Gnostic reading of the epic. Since Nuttall shows us Milton tempting himself to just such a reading, I am skeptical. Prometheus is the figure of rebellion against the father and assimilates all too early to Satan. But as an image of new thought he suggests a closer connection to Hamlet than to Satan. Whose son is Hamlet? We do not know, nor does Hamlet, for, once again, when did the love affair of Claudius and Gertrude begin?

Tracing the psychogenesis of *Paradise Lost*, Kerrigan reveals Milton's dividing up of his revered father: obedience except *as a poet*. Like Satan, the poet-in-Milton knows no time when he was not as now. This allowed a transcendence of any anxiety of influence in regard to the senior Milton, a talented composer and successful scrivener, and also in the poet's stance toward the Bible, the classical epics, and their progeny in Dante, Tasso, and Spenser. Why did such freedom not spring into being in respect to William Shakespeare? The Promethean fire, for *Paradise Lost*'s Satan, had to be stolen from Hamlet the Dane. Milton's permanent anxiety of influence always remained his obligation to Shakespeare. Lucifer's soliloquies are not Satan's fivefold. They are Hamlet's seven voyages into the ever-deepening abyss of self-consciousness.

In his youth, Milton audaciously contemplated writing his own *Macbeth* and inevitably never got past the title. In *Paradise Lost* he wrote his *Hamlet* but without the Prince of Denmark as protagonist: Satan is the badly fallen Hamlet. Lucifer does not appear in Milton's epic because too palpably he would have been Hamlet. Is that assertion arbitrary? I enlist Neil Forsyth as a supporting witness: "The sympathy we are invited to feel for each has a similar occasion—their magnificent and tormented soliloquies; and in each case they are eventual victims of parallel revenge plots against themselves, but worked out in secret and so without their knowledge. In Hamlet's case, the patent villainy of Claudius's counterplot intensifies our fearful sympathy with the hero, while Shelley, Empson, and other accomplished readers have testified that they have similar reactions to Milton's Satan and his villainous God."

That is certainly a fair start; juxtaposed readings of Hamlet's and Satan's soliloquies are relevant here, but I am content to rely upon my readers for that. I turn instead to Milton's own soliloquies in the epic's invocations, where the triad of Hamlet, Satan, and Prometheus hover close by. Wonderful as are Satan's five interior monologues, they do not challenge the four invocations, which are of Hamletian ambivalence and memorably eloquent. Hamlet and Milton, like Satan, are histrionic: violently aware of being onstage in the theater of the reader's mind. All of them want the play, even at the expense of epic.

Hamlet, and Milton and Satan after him, desires to manifest the power of his mind over "a universe of death" (*Paradise Lost*, 2.622). The method of Hamlet depends upon incessant self-questionings, more the mode of Satan than of Milton himself. Yet all three are ambitious poets, and all attained the sublime. In Milton and Satan the bells break down their tower, and swing we know not where. Hamlet is different: the lonely tower of his infinite consciousness breaks down his poetic gift, and he chooses silence.

I brush aside all academic critics—dryasdusts and moldyfigs—who tell me that Shakespeare and Milton are dramatic poets while Hamlet and Satan are mere personae. Nonsense. Hamlet and Satan are poets setting out for themselves in violent dissociations from their rivals, Shakespeare and Milton. For Hamlet and Shakespeare as agonists, I refer my readers to my *Hamlet: Poem Unlimited.* Here I am concerned with Milton's agon in regard to Shakespeare, and Satan's agon with Milton. The struggle with Shakespeare is concealed; Satan's discomfort with Milton is the nucleus of *Paradise Lost.*

Hamlet rebels against being placed in a revenge tragedy, hardly a subgenre worthy of his amazing sense of self. He merits a cosmological drama akin to *King Lear* or *Macbeth,* but perhaps Shakespeare was not quite prepared to write one in 1600. Satan is placed in a cosmological tragedy, which may be rather more than Milton thought the fallen Lucifer deserved. What could a confrontation between Hamlet and the enthroned Father of *Paradise Lost* have resembled? Claudius and the epic's ostensible God have some qualities in common, and the wretched usurper hardly is Hamlet's mighty opposite. He tends not to comprehend what his uncanny nephew is saying. Clearly he is out of his league, as Milton's God also would have been if Hamlet were the Old Enemy.

Except for a handful of diehards, the ostensible God of *Paradise Lost* now lacks defenders. A nasty old schoolmaster of souls, he is afflicted by ill temper and takes a sadomasochistic pleasure in making threats. He certainly is not the Yahweh of the J Writer, and why Milton conceived him I cannot imagine. You can take up a post-Empsonian posture and argue perversely that he is so bad that he is rather good, but for that a good soaking in wine seems necessary.

Milton's God is "the Father," which distresses many among us for a galaxy of different, indeed clashing, reasons. One labyrinth in which the Father, Minotaur-like, can be slain, is the Gnostic model adopted by learned skeptics from Denis Saurat to A. D. Nuttall. I am reasonably certain that you can associate Sir Henry Vane's and the Muggletonians' Inner Light with Milton's temple-of-one, but Kabbalah and Ophite Gnosticism remain remote from the shadowy abyss of *Paradise Lost.* Robert Fludd and Renaissance Hermetism seem not as alien, but would be hazy analogues at best. Milton may *seem* more normative than William Blake, but is he? His heresies, taken together, are impressive, but secondary. His rugged temperament matters most. Religion, politics, and morals all ensue from his pride, matched only by Dante's among the poets.

Satan's pride is all but equal to his creator's (Milton, not God). It is not customary to speak of Prince Hamlet's pride, but it is present even when he denounces himself. Asserted, it overwhelms: "It is I, / Hamlet the Dane." Satanic pride is hierarchical; Hamlet's pride is vocational: *a dramatist's pride.* Evidently

Shakespeare evaded *that* sense of glory. The Sonnets are much occupied with poetic pride, which appears to be why the Rival Poet is strikingly invoked. Even as a lyric poet Shakespeare is a rueful player, and there he *is* close to Hamlet, except that Hamlet seems to forsake ambivalence only when he is playing.

Satan is about as playful as Milton, notoriously the strongest author totally lacking a comic spirit. If my suggestion that the unfallen Lucifer would have to resemble Hamlet has any merit, then one sees again why Milton could not portray Lucifer for us. Prelapsarian Lucifer would have been ironically histrionic, like Hamlet. Father and Son would not have been amused as an audience for Luciferic skits, designed by Lucifer with perhaps a scherzo of theological satire. But I go too far in this.

Hamlet is his own best audience, which is true of Falstaff as well, though it sobers me that Iago and Edmund also play to their own appreciative pleasure. Satan's ironies are poor stuff, really too obvious to be worth noticing. Milton's own ironies are poor stuff in themselves, unworthy of the greatest poet in the language after Chaucer and Shakespeare. Jonathan Swift, the total yet dangerously subtle ironist, would be an impossible standard for Milton, but Chaucer and Shakespeare had much to teach Milton that he did not care to learn. A Hamlet-like Lucifer would violate the visionary intensity of *Paradise Lost,* and doubtless more would be lost than gained had Milton taken up the Shakespearean challenge.

JOYCE...DANTE...SHAKESPEARE... MILTON

I f Joyce and Proust are the sublime of twentieth-century Western literature, there perhaps are other major poets, novelists, storywriters, and dramatists who approach that eminence, but not even Kafka, Yeats, or anyone else you care to nominate is likely to prove as central as the creators of *Ulysses, Finnegans Wake,* and *In Search of Lost Time.* Evidently the two met once only, at a Parisian dinner table. Joyce had read a little Proust but found it ordinary, while Proust had never heard of Joyce. The Irish genius lamented his eyesight and headaches, while the seer of Sodom and Gomorrah complained of his digestion. Even their infirmities were unshared, though later Joyce silently attended Proust's funeral.

Shakespeare hovered in both of them, much more extensively in Joyce. Flaubert too was a common ancestor, though less crucial to Joyce than was Dante. Proust is the ironic humorist of sexual jealousy, even as Shakespeare was its tragic ironist. Joyce's Poldy in *Ulysses* evades being destroyed by erotic jealousy: the good man's curiosity is too humane for that hellish abyss.

Among the major writers in English, Joyce's agon with Shakespeare is matched only by Milton's. It is possible that blind Milton and the near-blind Joyce, who worked at least sixteen years on the *Wake,* relied upon auditory memories of reciting Shakespeare out loud to themselves, since both *Paradise Lost* and the *Wake* sometimes seem to be echo chambers alive with Shakespearean revelations. The large difference is that the Joycean resoundings are explicit, while the Miltonic echoes frequently appear to be inadvertent.

Was John Milton, then, a more wonder-wounded *hearer* than was James Joyce of Shakespeare, or is it that Joyce chose the mask of manipulator to disguise his own wound with richness?

I began reading *Finnegans Wake* as a Cornell undergraduate in October 1947, and I find that date written next to my signature in the first copy I owned, and in my worn-through *Skeleton Key to "Finnegans Wake,"* by Joseph Campbell and Henry Morton Robinson (1944). Fortunately, my early efforts were reinforced by participating in Thornton Wilder's informal discussion groups during my Yale graduate school years. Sometime later, as a young faculty member, I myself wearily emulated Wilder by leading another informal seminar, by then employing a 1958 Viking Press edition, which is before me as I write, heavily annotated by rather Blakean marginalia. In subsequent years, I discussed the *Wake* first with Matthew Hodgart, and then with Anthony Burgess. Hodgart emphasized Shakespeare's presence, while Burgess was more interested in Lewis Carroll as presiding genius of Joyce's dream epic. All critical reading of difficult texts is mediated by others, to one degree or another, but I mention these mediations because Wilder, Hodgart, and Burgess helped me to rather complementary understandings of the book.

I was concerned then as now with a cluster of linked questions. Is it one of the costs of Joyce's vast experiment that the *Wake*—unlike, say, the Bible, Plato, Dante, Shakespeare, Cervantes, Milton—does not yield a fecundity of rival interpretations? Is the surface or textual complexity of this dream-book somewhat at variance with an underlying simplicity? *Strangeness,* the most canonical of literary qualities, exists in *Hamlet* at every level. Does the life story of H. C. Earwicker, Joyce's Everyman, ultimately lack this canonical quality? It is not possible to invoke a Johnsonian-Woolfian Common Reader as the true judge of the *Wake* because it has not had many common readers. Burgess, seeking them, edited *A Shorter "Finnegans Wake"* (1968), where he insisted on the "easy symbolism" of the book, an accurate insistence, perhaps too much so.

At eighty, I tend to wake up twice for the day, first anywhere between two and four, and a second time after, a few hours later, I have fallen asleep for an hour or two. I have stopped dreaming of the past, a foreign country no more to be visited, and have bad dreams instead of what vaguely seems the present. Freud now to me is least persuasive as a dream interpreter. Joyce, I think, means to convince us that we dream one universal cavalcade, but the Joycean mythology, oddly like Freud's, is Shakespearean. We are such stuff as dreams are made on, and our brief span ends in eternal sleep. Shakespeare neither affirms nor denies resurrection: affirmation and denial alike are alien to him. Joyce's dreamer Earwicker plays with a resurrection myth, but Earwicker is not James Joyce, whereas a fused Stephen-Bloom in *Ulysses* had been a portrait of the artist as a mature man. Still, Joyce—like Giordano Bruno the Nolan—was a Hermetist, and possibly less ironic in his esotericism than Yeats, who himself sometimes pretended to be more skeptical than actually he was. Hodgart took the *Wake*'s eclectic occultism quite seriously, and as his student (he was my tutor at Pembroke College, Cambridge) so do I. Several critics, the brilliant A. D. Nuttall in particular, locate a kind of Gnosticism in Shakespeare, as well as in Marlowe, Milton, and Blake. A confirmed Gnostic myself, I scarcely can trust my own perceptions on this, but follow cheerfully in the wake of others, and in that of the *Wake* itself.

In his memoir *James Joyce and the Making of "Ulysses"* (1934), the British painter Frank Budgen reports Joyce as saying, "In my case the thought is always simple." Shakespeare's thought is endlessly complex: lord of language and creator of hosts of personages, he also amazes by sheer cognitive originality. Joyce considered himself Shakespeare's true rival, and his power over language *is* Shakespearean. In *Ulysses* he creates Leopold Bloom, a complete human being, fit to discourse with Sancho Panza and Sir John Falstaff. The personages of the *Wake,* Earwicker and his family, are not persons but giant forms, like William Blake's Albion and his wife, sons, and daughters. Blake's *The Four Zoas, Milton,* and *Jerusalem* are marked by cognitive power and frequent magnificence of language. Joyce was enormously intelligent but chose to manifest this gift as ingenuity and cleverness. That is not intended by me as deprecation. As a follower of Vico and Bruno, Joyce believed in a kind of ancient wisdom. Samuel Beckett, who expounded the *Wake* best and earliest, ruefully relied more upon Descartes and Arthur Schopenhauer than on Vico and Bruno. Philosophy concerned Joyce only insofar as it could add to his word-hoard.

Conceptual originality certainly was implicit in Joyce, but he preferred to invest his creative desire elsewhere. Like Proust, Joyce was infinitely curious, and both were primarily comic in their genius. *Finnegans Wake,* even more than *Ulysses,* is humorous, not tragicomic. Readers who persevere with the *Wake* will laugh with it, as they do with Shakespeare, Dickens, and Proust. But there remains Joyce's deliberate choice of intellectual simplicity. Does the *Wake* generate enough mythological splendor to compensate for its evasion of what can be called literary *thinking?*

The experiential answer emphatically is positive. Hodgart would tell me to remember Wagner's texts, which I dislike but which yet disturb me by mythical force. Joyce absorbs virtually all mythologies, from the Egyptian Book of the Dead through the Bible to the Hellenes, but the fundamental undersong of *The Wake* is northern mythology, including the Ibsenite and the Wagnerian.

Deep readers of Joyce rarely are surprised by his extraordinary fusion of naturalism and symbolism, which allies him to Thomas Carlyle and also to Walt Whitman, among others. The affinity with Carlyle is greater: when I reread *Sartor Resartus,* I feel that it is overly influenced by the *Wake,* though Carlyle's now unread masterpiece actually compounds itself out of Goethe, Novalis, Jean Paul, and related Germanic sources. Even as Joyce had abandoned Irish Catholicism, so Carlyle had given up Scottish Calvinism. Professor Diogenes Teufelsdröck is not nearly so universal as Tim Finnegan, but *Sartor Resartus,* like the *Wake,* takes its title from a song, old Scottish countryside rather than Irish American ballad. The Scottish tailor, patched (and so edited), is akin to the Irish American construction worker who suffers a drunken fall from a ladder. I like to think of Carlyle attempting to read the *Wake.* It would have outraged him, but he might have found something of his own extravagance in it.

Extravagance etymologically means "wandering beyond limits," and the *Wake* goes much farther in transgressing every boundary than does *Sartor Resartus.* Carlyle wrote a mock-spiritual autobiography, but one of the great Joycean paradoxes is Stephen's version of the artist as Aristotle's Unmoved Mover, which is refuted by the overwhelmingly familial allegories of both *Ulysses* and the *Wake.* Perhaps Joyce fights against it; he is more Poldy than Stephen, more Earwicker than Shem the Penman, though the *Wake*'s family romances are so much more fabulistic than those of *Ulysses.* Edna O'Brien, in her brief biography of Joyce (1999), catches the Irishness of domestic conflict and desire more vividly than anyone else has to date.

Part of Joyce's universality, like Shakespeare's, is his skill at rendering what Freud called "family romances." The *Wake* frequently is rescued from its mythologizings by the intensity of Earwicker's barely repressed desire for Isabel, his daughter. Freud's interpretation of *King Lear* was Joycean before Joyce, but has little to do with Shakespeare's play and instead reflects Freud's own partly evaded love for his daughter, Anna.

The agon between Joyce and Shakespeare scarcely can be overemphasized: the Irishman's prose epics sail in Shakespeare's wake, which would be an apt alternate title for *Finnegans Wake.* Joyce seems to have known Shakespeare as well as he knew Dante. The extraordinary language making of Earwicker's saga is both Shakespearean and a defense against Shakespeare, rather like Beckett's turn to composition in French lest he continue writing books as Joycean as the delightful *Murphy* and the unsatisfactory *A Dream of Fair to Middling Women.* Translating his own French back into English, Beckett emerged Joycean neither in mode nor in style and became a strong fourth with Joyce, Proust, and Kafka as the masters of prose fiction in the twentieth century, transcending Thomas Mann, Joseph Conrad, D. H. Lawrence, Virginia Woolf, and William Faulkner.

Only surmise is possible as to what Joyce might have written had he not died in his late fifties. Of Shakespeare, dead at fifty-two, no one need lament: the greatest of all writers had given up creating stage plays for some three years. Cervantes, Tolstoy, and Henry James went on working until the end, but Shakespeare simply retired. For whatever reason, he had lost interest after his share in *The Two Noble Kinsmen,* written with John Fletcher. But Joyce doubtless would have kept writing, evidently an epic on the sea. Where might Shakespeare have been in that project? Had he truly been exorcised in the *Wake*? Can you contemplate a sea epic without grappling with Shakespeare, as Melville did in *Moby-Dick*? There are only two or three references to Melville in the *Wake;* presumably he might have interested Joyce more in that ultimate epic.

Ulysses, as critics came to see, gave us Joyce's portrait of citizen Shakespeare in Poldy, regarded by Dublin and himself as a Jew though he had an Irish Catholic mother and grandmother and had undergone three separate baptisms. But then Stephen (less convincingly) wants to see himself as Shakespeare, though he argues to prove that Shakespeare was a Jew. Sometimes I wonder why Stephen does not anticipate Kenneth Gross's *Shylock Is Shakespeare* (2006). Falstaff, Hamlet, Iago, Cleopatra, Malvolio, and many more also were Shakespeare, but none of these was a usurer, and Shakespeare was, quick to go to law to recover principal and exorbitant interest. Poldy Bloom is not a moneylender, and Stephen is something of a sponge, yet fused they are Joyce's Shakespeare. *Ulysses* is more a quest for Shakespeare than a voyage to the faithless Molly, while the *Wake* is the quest fulfilled, since Joyce regarded his final book as a fully achieved rival to Shakespeare, a magnificent echo chamber of his precursor, who himself was a cosmological echoer.

It would be absurdly inadequate to speak of "Shakespeare's influence" upon *Finnegans Wake. Hamlet* is everywhere in the *Wake,* with *Macbeth, Julius Caesar,* and *A Midsummer Night's Dream* nearly as prevalent. If Shylock is Shakespeare, then Falstaff is Bloom (not Poldy, but Harold) and the *Wake's* Falstaff is not merely a table of green fields but "a verytableland of bleakbard fields!" I am happier with that than with "fraudstuff" and its half-dozen variants in the *Wake*. As a commentary upon virtually all of literature, the *Wake* most constantly serves as Joyce's midrash upon Shakespeare. In the wake of Matthew Hodgart and Adaline Glasheen, there is a workmanlike study, *Shakespeare and Joyce* by Vincent John Cheng (1984), that provides a catalogue of Shakespearean al-lusions in the *Wake,* and subsequent studies have elaborated what may be an infinite matter. Challenged by Shakespeare as by no other, not even Dante, Joyce hunts his rival down as Captain Ahab pursues the White Whale. No more than Moby-Dick is Shakespeare definitively harpooned by Joyce, but neither Milton nor Melville comes so close to triumph over the Leviathan of literature.

Can so vast an allusive web as the *Wake* still be termed a product of influence? Yes, but only because after Shakespeare all indeed becomes after Shakespeare. The elder Alexandre Dumas observed that, after God, Shakespeare created the most, an apothegm quoted in the National Library scene of *Ulysses.* Whether or not one believes in Yahweh, Jesus, or Allah hardly affects the realization that, in some respects, Shakespeare invented us as we since have been. When I affirmed just that in my book *Shakespeare: The Invention of the Human,* I was widely trounced for the notion by secularists and the faithful alike. But I hold by it still, extending the fine observation of Nuttall, noted earlier, that without Shakespeare we never could have seen so much that already was there.

Joyce, though as great a creator of language as Shakespeare was, could not invent women and men on the Shakespearean scale. Repeopling Dublin was a vast project, but Shakespeare peopled a heterocosm, an alternative world sometimes more natural than nature. The *Wake* centers on Dublin, yet has its center everywhere, including nearly all sacred texts. In lifelong flight from a Jesuit education, Joyce had as secular a sensibility as Proust's or Beckett's, Mann's or Valéry's, Eugenio Montale's or Wallace Stevens's. All seven can be set against great writers like Kafka, Crane, Rainer Maria Rilke, Yeats—figures who sense the reality of a transcendence in which they themselves could not share.

The *Wake* is a scripture of no credence, as perhaps Shakespeare is now a worldwide scripture. Miguel de Unamuno considered *Don Quixote* to be the authentic Spanish scripture and referred to Cervantes's sad-faced Knight as "our Lord." Shakespeare and the *Wake* are scripture in that mode alone. At its heights, imaginative literature possesses the aura of a gnosis, however far away from Gnosticism. So I call the *Wake* a gnosis, even if I have less than a full knowledge of it. The *Wake*'s most devoted exegetes possess the book in every linguistic detail. I have learned to read through it, but only by continuously resorting to their aid, which is not the way I read Shakespeare and the Bible, Dante and Milton, Blake and Whitman—or *Ulysses* for that matter. Were I to live long enough, I might learn the *Wake* more thoroughly, and perhaps I yet will. For now, I know it just well enough to respect its kind of knowledge, even if I continue to be puzzled by its possibly only apparent simplicity at the level of plot and character.

Are the sacred books of the world invoked by Joyce as a defense against the *Wake*'s turning into a pure agon with Shakespeare? That is merely speculation, particularly since Lewis Carroll and Jonathan Swift are as canonical to Joyce as are the Bible, the Egyptian Book of the Dead, and the Qur'an; indeed, Carroll's *Sylvie and Bruno* and Swift's *A Tale of a Tub* probably provoked more reverence in Joyce than did the New Testament. As Shem the Penman, Joyce is as much his own Christ as Walt was Whitman's, while the resurrection of Finnegan/ Earwicker is closer to the Book of the Dead than to the Gospels. Whether Joyce would like it (or not) the form of resurrection in the *Wake* is Shakespearean, if only because Shakespeare is the *Wake* itself.

Macbeth had a particular fascination both for Milton and for Joyce. Why? Of all Shakespearean protagonists, Macbeth stands out for simultaneously evoking in us both moral revulsion and imaginative identification. I can see why that intrigued Milton, but Joyce never desired his readers to experience either relationship to any of his characters. I recall discussing with Matthew Hodgart the question of why *Macbeth* interested Joyce much more in the *Wake* than in *Ulysses*. Hodgart persuasively suggested to me that he judged Joyce to be a kind of heretic, Manichaean or Gnostic, in rebellion against Catholic dogma, and there are certainly Gnostic dualistic elements in *Macbeth*. Years later, Anthony Burgess, himself a lapsed Catholic of strong Manichaean leanings, made the same observation in response to my questioning. Both were deeper students of the *Wake* than I was then, or am now. Hodgart's point was that the *Wake* had a spiritual stance, a heterodox one, while Burgess charmingly urged me to re- alize that Gnosticism and hilarity were by no means antithetical phenomena. William Blake's Rabelaisian salutes to "Old Nobodaddy aloft" are among the instances that could be cited, and so are the parodistic outrages of Nathanael West's *Miss Lonelyhearts* and *A Cool Million*.

Joyce, like his disciple Samuel Beckett, had dark wit and enormous intel- lect, and I begin to doubt the surface simplicity of the story and persons who emerge from the linguistic labyrinth of the *Wake*. Like Leopold Bloom, whose half-Jewishness makes him a stranger to his fellow Dubliners, the protagonist of the *Wake* is an outsider, a Protestant Scandinavian married to a partly Slavic woman. Porter (evidently his waking name) dreams all of the book, which could be described as an incestuous visionary epic, since the hero's guilty lust is for his daughter, Isabel. Shelley and Byron shared a preoccupation with incest, which Byron accomplished with his half-sister, and the young Shelley may have desired (vainly) with *his* sisters. Incest, Shelley asserted, was the most poetical of circumstances. *Finnegans Wake* agrees, and makes of Shelley's *Prometheus Unbound* "Promiscuous Onebound."

Are all dreams incestuous? That query may be absurd, and yet the *Wake* is the dream-of-dreams in all literature. Nothing else is on so huge a scale as Joyce's Book of the Night. Or can we regard all of Shakespeare as one vast dream, as Joyce seems to do in the *Wake*?

Dante's *Paradiso,* like the rest of the *Commedia,* is a dreamlike fiction presented as truth. Joyce loved Dante with little of the ambivalence provoked in him by Shakespeare. Yet despite its multi-tongued diction, the *Wake*'s syntax remains Shakespearean. Dante was safely distant in language: Joyce's Italian was superb, but most of the readers of *Ulysses* and even of the *Wake* are at home in English, and to one degree or another are Shakespeare-haunted. Joyce was happier rereading Dante than Shakespeare. How much of Dante gets into the *Wake*?

No scholarly study yet published on Joyce and Shakespeare approaches the sensibility of *Joyce and Dante,* by Mary T. Reynolds (1981), whom I remember as a friend introduced to me at Yale by the grand Irish wit Mary Ellmann in the 1970s. Tea with the two Marys always was a delightful fusion of laughter and learning. Mary Reynolds taught me that Stephen and Poldy in *Ulysses* are dual figures not only of Shakespeare but of Dante. Vico, Joyce's guide in the *Wake,* remarked that Dante would have been the perfect poet except for his unfortunate immersion in theology. That remains an Italian but not an Anglo-American view, except in the anti-theological Joyce, who regarded the "hangman God" of Christianity with profound distaste. I myself read Dante as a thinker who implicitly prefers himself to Augustine, but Anglo-American scholarship smothers the *Commedia* beneath Augustine and Aquinas. Vico's essential principle is that we know only what we ourselves have made. W. B. Yeats said that only the great poets know reality because they themselves have created it. Joyce moves beyond Vico and Yeats into a place where William Blake had preceded the *Wake* in *his* book of the night, *The Four Zoas,* abandoned by Blake in manuscript. Joyce's Dante is Joyce's, as his Shakespeare was his own also. Proust does not attempt to take up all the space for himself, though that nearly was his achievement. Joyce, subsuming everything and everyone, intended to occupy all literary space. In *Finnegans Wake,* there are no limits to Joyce's scope. Like Milton, Joyce had to usurp Dante and Shakespeare in order to become absolute Joyce.

Except for Shakespeare, the *Commedia* resists usurpation more tenaciously than any other Western literary achievement, including Plato and the Bible. Only a master at inventing language could challenge Dante and Shakespeare, the geniuses of linguistic invention who provoked Joyce's answer, the *Wake.* Dante's astonishing linguistic mastery manifested itself both in his invention of terza rima and in his virtually single-handed imposition of Florentine Tuscan as the Italian literary language. Joyce was highly conscious of the extent to which Shakespeare had remolded Chaucer and William Tyndale into the English literary language: Yeats and Beckett were not Celts, and they never regarded Shakespearean English as alien to them. Joyce, the greatest master of English since Milton, nevertheless regarded it as an acquired language, even though he had spoken nothing else as a child. Perhaps he felt less remote from Dante's Tuscan than from Shakespeare's English.

Joyce, we know, guided the twenty-two-year-old Samuel Beckett in the essay "Dante . . . Bruno . . . Vico . . . Joyce," still a crucial introduction to the *Wake.* Linguistic survival, transmitted by etymology, is a Viconian lesson on Joyce's own view. Eleanor Cook, in her *Enigmas and Riddles in Literature* (2006), gives as one of the finest instances of linguistic transmission in the *Wake* Joyce's appropriation of Dante's entrance into Eden, *Purgatorio* 27. Walking side by side with the singing Matilde, we are given the perfection of vales of the Earthly Paradise. But for Dante, this is only a prelude to the enigma of Beatrice's arrival. Joyce stops short of the revelation of the sacred riddle, and hails the Earthly Paradise as being more than enough.

Spiritually, Joyce was careful about absorbing Dante. With Shakespeare, caution was not required, since Joyce harbored no Miltonic reservations toward him. Churchwardenly commentators, C. S. Lewis foremost among them, have inundated us with Milton's supposed piety. I follow Empson, Nuttall, and Neil Forsyth in observing that as a theodicy, *Paradise Lost* would be a disaster, rather than the heretical dramatic magnificence it manifestly is. It partly justifies Milton's better way to us, his readers, but scarcely justifies the ways of Milton's God, which I do not think Milton attempts, though he insists otherwise. Forsyth indicates the hidden genre of *Paradise Lost* as Shakespearean revenge tragedy, transmogrified into the most unlimited of all poems, *Hamlet*. I myself am personally fonder of Satan than I am of Hamlet, but the Prince of Denmark eclipses even the Prince of Darkness as the Western hero of consciousness and cognition. Did Milton admit Hamlet into his supposed epic, as Joyce did in Ulysses and the *Wake,* or did Hamlet force the gate?

On allusion and its discontents, the magister ludi is John Hollander, in his *The Figure of Echo* (1981). Hollander avoids distinguishing between intended and what I might call unruly allusions, and divides allusion in Milton and after into five types of echo: acoustical, allegorical, schematic, metaphorical, and metaleptic, illuminating this last mode with a marvelous excursus upon Angus Fletcher's trope of transumption, which I tend to call the Galileo syndrome. Milton, attempting to overgo Homer's shield of Achilles (*Iliad,* 19.373) and Spenser's shield of Radigund (*The Faerie Queene,* 5.5.3), compares Satan's "ponderous shield" to the moon as seen through Galileo's telescope:

> . . . his ponderous shield
> Ethereal temper, massy large and round
> Behind him cast; the broad circumference
> Hung on his shoulders like the moon, whose orb
> Through optic glass the Tuscan artist views
> At evening from the top of the Fesole,
> Or in Valdarno, to descry new lands,
> Rivers or Mountains in her spotty globe.

[Paradise Lost, 1.284–91]

Perhaps this ambivalent vision manifests Milton's nostalgia for an actual visit to Galileo, when the scientist was under house arrest by the Inquisition in Fiesole, in the valley of the Arno, and the English poet was allowed by "the Tuscan artist" to gaze at the moon through a telescope. Though some critics find this a dark reference, it impresses me primarily as praise for the compromised Galileo, who sensibly wished to avoid the fate of Giordano Bruno, "terribly burned" alive in Rome a generation before by the Inquisition. Whether Milton truly met Galileo (as asserted in Milton's most famous prose tract, *Areopagitica,* a defense of printing freedom) has been disputed, but that scarcely matters. Dr.

Samuel Johnson commended Milton for this passage, noting that "he crowds the imagination," an observation expanded by my "only begetter" in criticism, Angus Fletcher, in his *Allegory*, when he remarks that Johnson's Milton had a "transumptive" style of allusion. In Hollander's *The Figure of Echo*, transumption is named metaleptic echo and becomes the primary figure of interpretive allusion in all post-Shakespearean–Miltonic poetry. Philip Roth in his recent major phase transumes Falstaff in *Sabbath's Theater*, Shylock in *Operation Shylock*, and Lear's Cordelia in *Everyman*. In what I call in this book the death of Europe in our Evening Land, transumptive allusion expands to titanic dimensions.

Hollander defines transumptive allusion with useful tenacity, but Hollander, an immensely erudite scholar-poet-critic, can be simplified for common readers (like myself) by returning to Galileo in Milton. John Guillory, in his *Poetic Authority* (1983), indicates that Galileo is the only living contemporary mentioned by name in *Paradise Lost*. I can detect subtle allusions to Cromwell, Charles I, and the earl of Clarendon, among others, in the epic, yet Galileo, first as "the Tuscan artist" and next as "Astronomer" (3.589), appears as himself the third time around (5.261–63):

> As when by night the glass
> Of Galileo, less assured, observes
> Imagined lands and regions in the moon.

All three mentions stress both Galileo's art or science and its limitations when compared to the angelic view, whether fallen or unfallen. Galileo, like one aspect of the poet Milton, is necessarily belated, but the time-reversing rhetoric grants the visionary aspect of Milton a triumph unavailable to Galileo. Historically, Galileo recanted, though he knew he was right. Milton, blind and disgraced by the Restoration, which burned his books and for a time imprisoned him, recanted nothing. Doubtless his heroism was temperamental, but did he not recognize that it had affinities with the heroism of his own Satan in his great poem?

No two authentic readers ever will agree completely on the relation between Milton and his creature, Satan. For me (admittedly a Jewish Gnostic heretic), Satan is Milton's daimon, his alter ego, perhaps indeed the Miltonic genius. Blake, Shelley, Hazlitt, Empson, Nuttall, and Forsyth take up this stance, and I join myself to their visionary company. Shakespeare's influence upon Milton— on what level of awareness I cannot know—may be the largest overdetermination of Satan's ambivalent greatness. Let me venture that Satan is both Iago and

Othello, both Edmund and Lear, both Hamlet deranged and Hamlet sane, both Macbeth before the play begins and Macbeth in the tragedy of his bloody fall.

But what is missing is an actual representation of the Shakespearean moment of soliloquy in which Lucifer overhears himself and through that shock changes into Satan. Forsyth argues that in the grand soliloquy that comes soon after book 4 begins, lines 32–113 (quoted above in "Milton's Hamlet"), we hear both the nihilistic inwardness of the Hamlet-like unfallen Lucifer and the narcissistic self-devouring of fallen Satan, Iagolike in his sense of injured merit, and Macbethian in his imaginative despair. Since we know that Satan's soliloquy atop Mount Niphates was composed years earlier, to serve as the opening of *Adam Unparadised,* a drama rather than an epic, Forsyth has clear philological warrant for his judgment.

Yet what is lacking is the *moment of change,* a Shakespearean invention from which Milton shies. Anyone who watched Zero Mostel metamorphose into a rhinoceros in the film version of Ionesco's play will know what I mean. The transformation from human to rhinoceros, a triumph of Mostelian mime, is miniscule compared to the fall of Lucifer, Son of Morning, into Satan, deformed rebel. Shakespeare shows us the falls of Richard II, Othello, Macbeth, even Hamlet, who so brutally abuses Ophelia into madness. This was an agon that Milton would not enter. Why?

Leslie Brisman, in *Milton's Poetry of Choice and Its Romanic Heirs* (1973), follows Milton himself, who contended he had been freed from Shakespeare by willing "a better way" (the phrase itself, though, is Shakespeare's in *King Lear*). For Shakespeare, Chaucer was a resource, as Spenser was for Milton. But to writers as powerful as Milton and Joyce, Shakespeare is the most dangerous of sources. It is like Jacob wrestling the Angel of Death, and holding him to a stand-off, but at the cost of being forever lamed. How do you progress *beyond* Shakespeare? Milton thought he would manage that by self-limitation, by chastening his imagination. But Satan *wants* to be more like Hamlet, Macbeth, Iago, and their fellow protagonists. He also wants what he can never have: the undimmed glory of Lucifer. Joyce, who had a justified Irish dislike for the Cromwellian Milton but a Romantic admiration for Milton the rebel, rather complexly identified with the Miltonic Satan. Joyce also would not serve, whether as his early surrogate Stephen or as himself. And though Joyce reluctantly ranked Shakespeare over Dante—in response to the Desert Island question, Joyce grumpily replied that he wished he could take Dante but Shakespeare was *richer*—he accurately esteemed Dante above Milton, and tended to overstate

Dante's influence upon *Paradise Lost.* Dante trails behind Shakespeare in the *Wake,* and Milton well behind Dante, but it surprises me that Milton nevertheless lingers on. In Anna Livia Plurabelle's closing cadences, we are made to hear the exit from Eden that concludes *Paradise Lost.*

The language of the *Wake* is more Miltonic than Shakespearean, despite the packing of the text with so much of Shakespeare's output. Blind bards like the near-mythical Homer, Joyce, and Milton write for the ear, not for the eye, while Shakespeare addresses all five senses, as in Bottom's account of his bottomless dream. We associate Joyce with Lewis Carroll, as we should, but the *Wake* teaches us, more surprisingly, to group *Paradise Lost* with Carroll and even with Edward Lear's *Nonsense* books. One hears Miltonic, Tennysonian, and Joycean sonorities in "The Courtship of the Yonghy-Bonghy-Bo" and "The Dong with a Luminous Nose."

Joyce's defense against Shakespeare is total appropriation; Milton's is highly selective repression. The odd effect is that Shakespeare's influence is less distracting in the *Wake* than in *Paradise Lost.* That is an aesthetic advantage for the Irish wordmaster over the Cromwellian organ-voice of England, as I think the canny Joyce recognized. Sometimes it baffles me that Milton, most acutely self-conscious of poets since Pindar, is weirdly unknowing of his quasi-acoustical echoes of the "top bard." Here are Claudio, in *Measure for Measure,* fearfully exhorting his sister Isabella to save him from death by prostituting herself (though a novice nun) to Angelo, followed by Belial debating in hell and advocating the survival of consciousness for its own sake:

> Ay, but to die, and go we know not where;
> To lie in cold obstruction, and to rot;
> This sensible warm motion to become
> A kneaded clod; and the delighted spirit
> To bathe in fiery floods, or to reside
> In thrilling region of thick-ribbed ice;
> To be imprison'd in the viewless winds,
> And blown with restless violence round about
> The pendant world; or to be worse than worst
> Of those that lawless and incertain thoughts
> Imagine howling!—'tis too horrible!
> The weariest and most loathed worldly life
> That age, ache, [penury], and imprisonment

Can lay on nature is a paradise
To what we fear of death

[*Measure for Measure,* 3.1.117–31]

And that must end us, that must be our cure,
To be no more; sad cure; for who would lose,
Though full of pain, this intellectual being,
Those thoughts that wander through eternity,
To perish rather, swallowed up and lost
In the wide womb of uncreated night,
Devoid of sense and motion?

[*Paradise Lost,* 2.145–51]

Palpably Belial echoes Claudio, but to what cognitive and aesthetic purpose? I surmise none, and conclude that the allusion is wholly indeliberate. Milton can be a superb stationer of his allusions, but this is hardly the only instance of the "viewless winds" blowing from Shakespeare's cosmos into Milton's. James Joyce took care not to so internalize Shakespeare as to absorb his deep inwardness. John Milton read Shakespeare more intimately, and at a higher cost to himself. Shakespeare, "richer" than Dante, nevertheless could not possess Joyce as he did Milton. In 1630, the twenty-one-year-old Milton composed "On Shakespeare," a poem of seven couplets, celebrating "our wonder and astonishment" and darkly observing:

Then thou, our fancy of itself bereaving,
Dost make *us* marble with too much conceiving.

We forget our own imaginative power, confronted by Shakespeare's, and become *his* marble monument. Whether Joyce or Milton found the better way to confront Shakespeare is perhaps undecidable. The great Irish prose-poet and the greatest of English poets after Chaucer and Shakespeare are never more different than in their struggles with Shakespeare. Milton's agon is more mysterious than Joyce's, if only because we are compelled to see it through the lens of the Romantic poets, who were almost equally indebted to Shakespeare and to Milton. The Satan of *Paradise Lost* is not only a Jacobean hero-villain; he is an actor, and could have been played either by Shakespeare's star, Richard Burbage, or by Marlowe's equally eminent Edward Alleyn. Joyce wrote an Ibsenite play, *Exiles,* and himself was an amateur actor-singer of some skills. But even had *Adam Un-*

paradised been completed for the stage, or the unactable *Samson Agonistes* gone into actual performance, we would have been baffled had Milton performed in one or the other. It is, after all, a question of personality. Joyce could be shy, yet delighted in companions; Milton, politically and personally, was eclipsed by the Restoration. Shakespeare, a professional actor of the sort we now call a "character actor," frets in a sonnet at having worn motley, and evidently gave up acting while he prepared *Othello* and *Measure for Measure* for production.

Critics have described the *Wake* as a drama, but only for the theater of mind, while parts of *Ulysses* have been staged and filmed. But neither Joyce nor Milton invested his creative exuberance in drama. *Ulysses* is the apocalypse of the novel, whether of Flaubert or of Dickens, and the *Wake* is in the genre of *The Four Zoas*. *Paradise Lost* abandons drama for the epic of Homer, Vergil, and Dante, and for the visionary romances of Tasso and Spenser. Shakespeare essentially blocked stage greatness for all who came after him in English, down to this very day. Molière, Racine, Schiller, Chekhov, Pirandello would not have been able to function in English. Beckett escaped *Ulysses* and the *Wake* in his *Molloy* trilogy, and largely evades Shakespeare in *Waiting for Godot*. *Endgame* remains the great exception. There the protagonist Hamm is clearly Hamlet, and Clov is a Horatio who finally walks off the job. Beckett, who perhaps was the final great original in Western literary tradition—being the worthy heir of Joyce, Kafka, and Proust—was too authentic an agonist forever to avoid Shakespeare. *Endgame* wrestles *Hamlet,* just as Chekhov and Pirandello attempted that impossible match, in which they were bound to lose and knew it.

T. S. Eliot, worthy custodian of Anglo-Catholic conservative royalist European culture, bravely rejected *Hamlet* as an "aesthetic failure" while commending Djuna Barnes, Wyndham Lewis, and Pound, "the better maker," who told us, "All the jew part of the Bible is black evil." My favorite of all Eliot's dicta was that, being a Christian, he was prohibited by his faith from his not always polite anti-Semitism. Honest critics (we have a handful or two) like Louis Menand and Christopher Ricks have attempted to exorcize Eliot's loathing of Jews as a mere vagary. Is the creator of Bleistein and Rachel née Rabinowich coherent without his hatred and disdain? Like the current Pope Benedict, Eliot assured us that European culture would die if European Christianity died. It *is* dying to dead, and the world's religiosity (for more and better) abides elsewhere: Asia, Africa, the Americas, with new Christianities and militant Islam. Eliot, at his best an exquisite poet, as a prophet merits lumping in with C. S. Lewis, G. K. Chesterton, and W. H. Auden (though *he* decidedly was no anti-Semite).

* * *

Immanuel Kant rightly advised us that all aesthetic taste was subjective, but experience makes me doubt the formidable *Critique of Judgment*. Why, after all, do we venture to juxtapose Joyce with Dante and Shakespeare? If you lived most of your life in the twentieth century, then the writers of your time were Proust and Joyce, Kafka and Beckett, or if you loved great verse more than fictive prose, the poets of your era were Yeats and Valéry, Georg Trakl and Giuseppe Ungaretti, Osip Mandelstam and Eugenio Montale, Robert Frost and Wallace Stevens, Luis Cernuda and Hart Crane, Fernando Pessoa and Federico García Lorca, Octavio Paz and T. S. Eliot, and many more. Dramatists of universal value are fewer: perhaps Pirandello only, in the longest post-Ibsenite perspective. I myself place a particular value on those writers who composed greatly in prose *and* verse, Hardy and Lawrence, in particular. Joyce wrote an Ibsenite drama, *Exiles*, two volumes of lyrics, a superb book of stories, *Dubliners*, and a conventional enough coming-of-age novel, *The Portrait of the Artist as a Young Man*. Yet Joyce challenges the greatest—Dante, Shakespeare, Milton—only in his prose epics, *Ulysses* and *Finnegans Wake*. Proust competes with all prior novelists since Cervantes with *In Search of Lost Time*, while Kafka even more than Joyce himself became the Dante of his era though excelling primarily in fragments and apothegms. Beckett, a novelist, dramatist, and poet, like Kafka matters as an icon of creativity or, even better, a maker of icons. In their different ways, Jorge Luis Borges and Italo Calvino have something of the same functions.

Comparative estimates of aesthetic value initially can seem arbitrary, unless they are outlandish enough. If a student, friend, or acquaintance were to tell me that Pearl S. Buck was preferable to James Joyce and Marcel Proust, or that Stephen King was comparable to Franz Kafka and Samuel Beckett, I would not stay to argue. I could reflect that the Nobel Prize for Literature went to Buck and to neither Joyce nor Proust, and that King holds a lifetime achievement award from the organization that decides the National Book Awards.

Try to imagine someone reflecting upon an agon between Buck and Joyce, or discoursing on how Proust's influence affects King. Kant's aesthetic is too dignified for such surmises, and even the ruining chapels of Cultural Studies are queasy at dismissing aesthetic dignity. This is because of the pragmatics of mindfulness: Joyce could not replace Shakespeare, but *Ulysses,* next to *Hamlet* and its Shakespearean equals—*The Tempest, Henry IV, Part 1, Macbeth, King Lear,* and some others—has contaminated the cosmos of "information" and of oddly named "popular culture." This was clearer in my childhood, when the

Luce magazines (*Time, Life, Fortune*) were composed in Joycean cadences and diction, and it prevails, though diffused, in their ongoing rivals and successors.

Joyce, obsessed with Shakespeare as the word-rich Englishman, wanted to prefer Dante, and yet could not. What Joyce yielded to was the worldwide prevalence of Shakespeare. He envied the English wordman his audience at the Globe, but that is not the center of his creative emulation of the top bard. Joyce's egoism would have been absolute had Shakespeare not existed. Despite its Homeric structure, *Ulysses* is a dramatic poem for voices and edges near Shakespeare's art. We reread *Ulysses* for Poldy, who fuses Bottom and the gentler aspects of Falstaff.

Yet Joyce distrusted Poldy, just as Shakespeare became aware that Falstaff could not be cabined, cribbed, and confined. Falstaff and Hamlet get away from Shakespeare. I cherish the fantasy of Orson Welles, who wrote that on reaching England, Hamlet took up residence and bloomed into Falstaff. Stephen, Hamlet to Poldy's Falstaff, is inadequate (by design) to the task of reviving King Henry V. Joyce, who also desired to find a model in Ibsen, fell into the ennui of *Exiles.* Is it that Joyce, like Milton (and Henry James), had no gift for staged tragicomedy?

The binding agency that holds together Shakespeare, Milton, and Joyce, is their sense of how meaning gets started, which always is overflow. Falstaff, Hamlet, Adam, Satan, and Bloom all are troubling because they do not declare their own fictiveness. Effluence, not influence, is their true function in literary history. How many other authors transcend meaning-by-repetition? A few doubtless: Montaigne, Dickens, perhaps. "Montaigne" is a great creation, and Dickens flows eternal.

DR. JOHNSON AND CRITICAL INFLUENCE

At the age of nine Samuel Johnson first read *Hamlet,* sitting at home in the kitchen quite alone, and came to the entrance of the Ghost, which caused him to get up and go outside "that he might see people about him." Many years later, in his *Observations on Macbeth,* Johnson remembered that moment: "He that peruses Shakespeare looks around alarmed, and starts to find himself alone." There is the epitome of Johnson on Shakespeare: here is the writer and his critic who make us tremble like a guilty thing surprised when we first encounter the most vivid immediacy that imaginative literature can afford us.

Johnson as a literary critic means most to me in his apprehension of Shakespeare, even though I regard the late *Lives of the Poets* as his critical masterwork. Shakespeare confronts Johnson with an invaluable dilemma. In his own new way Johnson seems to me essentially a *biographical* critic. Johnsonian universals always are biographical, that is to say psychological, and that is the clue to his love and understanding of Shakespeare. For Johnson, Shakespeare is the absolute poet of human nature, and of our affections in particular. Now, just over three centuries after Johnson's birth (September 18, 1709), we have absurdly detailed information about Shakespeare's life but absolutely nothing that relates to his inwardness. Here I think we may know less than Johnson intimated, since Johnson's heart and mind were larger than ours, and Shakespeare's were surely the most capacious in the annals of the human.

Beneath his gruffness the bearlike Johnson shielded a tenderness toward human suffering almost beyond measure. My Johnsonian teacher, W. K. Wimsatt, was remarkably like our mutual hero in this, as in so many other ways.

Johnson on Shakespeare has moments I would term critical epiphanies. Here is Duke Vincentio in *Measure For Measure* (3.1.32–34) advising young Claudio to welcome execution:

> Duke: Thou hast nor youth, nor age:
>   But as it were an after-dinner's sleep,
>   Dreaming on both.

And here is Johnson's midrash:

> This is exquisitely imagined. When we are young we busy ourselves in
> forming schemes for succeeding time, and miss the gratifications that
> are before us; when we are old we amuse the languour of age with the
> recollection of youthful pleasures or performances; so that our life, of
> which no part is filled with the business of the present time, resembles
> our dreams after dinner, when the events of the morning are mingled
> with the designs of the evening.

The baroque cognitive music of Johnson's rolling periods suggests Sir Thomas Browne a century earlier and Walter Pater's subtle essay on *Measure for Measure* a century later. T. S. Eliot, caught by Duke Vincentio's dying fall, employed this passage as the epigraph to his *Gerontion,* of which I remember first the small lowercase crouching jew, emblem of Eliotic hatred for the free-thinking. Johnson, immune from rancor, commends Shakespeare for his perfect phrasing of our universal failure to live in the present moment.

Universal is a key word for Johnson's comprehension of Shakespeare's importance, since "universals" imbue the Johnsonian mode of criticism, empirical but deeply learned, a parallel discipline to David Hume's philosophy. Johnson and Hume, apart in religion, share common sense, an appeal to the common reader and the common possession of psychological universals. Yet Johnson loved Shakespeare, while Hume (like Wittgenstein) resented this writer who was the greatest of thinkers, subsuming everyone and everything, philosophers included. Hume, as powerful a historian as he was a philosopher, would not have been happy with Johnson's preference for biography over history, while Johnson might have assented to Emerson's "there is no history, only biography."

I recall discussing with Wimsatt Johnson's singular unfairness to Jonathan Swift, whose *A Tale of a Tub* had something of the same effect upon Johnson as it does on me, which helps me understand the strongest prose work, after Shakespeare and the English Bible, in the language. For sixty years now, since my nineteenth birthday, I religiously reread, every six months, *A Tale of a Tub* and its outrider, *A Digression Concerning Madness.* I have just finished reading it again, for what may be the 120th time, and I realize I now possess it by memory. Nothing else makes me so uncomfortable, and I imagine Wimsatt's ghost chuckling, "You should be!" Johnson's defense against the book's power upon him was to doubt Swift's authorship, a weirdness on the great critic's part that reminds me of Freud's defensive insistence that the earl of Oxford had written Shakespeare.

Perhaps the greatest among ironists—Swift and Johnson, Shakespeare and Freud—cannot survive in one another's aura. Ben Jonson was a satirist; Shakespeare, even in *Troilus and Cressida,* was something else. For all his Popean veneration, Johnson would not allow himself to be a satirist. Somewhere in this refusal is the dread of turning into Swift, of whom Johnson wrote in *The Lives of the Poets:* "He was not a man to be either loved or envied. He seems to have wasted life in discontent, by the rage of neglected pride and the languishment of unsatisfied desire." The acid of absolute satire is neither Johnsonian nor Shakespearean. Of everything on Shakespeare I have read, the most helpful is Johnson's preface to his edition of Shakespeare's plays. Nothing else devoted to Shakespeare brings to the sublime of all works of literature a total human being whose cognitive and affective endowments rival the plays he lovingly confronts.

Yet, again, as a critic of Shakespeare, Johnson has one acute limitation. Always a moralist above all, Johnson is too intelligent not to see that Shakespeare's purpose is very different:

> His first defect is that to which may be imputed most of the evil in books or in men. He sacrifices virtue to convenience, and is so much more careful to please than to instruct, that he seems to write without any moral purpose. From his writings indeed a system of social duty may be selected, for he that thinks reasonably must think morally; but his precepts and axioms drop casually from him; he makes no just distribution of good or evil, nor is always careful to shew in the virtuous a disapprobation of the of the wicked; he carries his persons indifferently through right or wrong, and at the close dismisses them

without further care, and leaves their examples to operate by chance. This fault the barbarity of his age cannot extenuate; for it is always a writer's duty to make the world better, and justice is a virtue independent on time or place.

In one way Johnson is justified, though few now could agree with him. Johnson was a devout Christian, as person and as writer. Whether Shakespeare was we do not know, but the plays are not Christian, and their audience is presumed such only as a social convention. Still, Johnson's wistful realization that Shakespeare does not seek to make us better is set aside by the critic's confession that "we owe everything to him." Those five words are massive and memorable; Johnson would not have said that of Homer or Pope.

I agree that we owe everything to Shakespeare, even if to say so invites scorn from the usual rabblement: comma counters, "cultural" materialists, new and newer historicists, gender commissars, and all the other academic impostors, mock journalists, inchoate rhapsodes, and good spellers. Without Shakespeare what would we know? We no longer recognize what we mean by "nature," unless it be Shakespeare's work. To appeal from reason to nature simply is to invoke Shakespeare.

Johnson had a nostalgia for the formalistic neoclassical rules of literature but discarded them whenever they did not fit Shakespeare, since Shakespeare alone gives copious sustenance to our "hunger of imagination." Brood on that Johnsonian phrase and summon up Falstaff, Hamlet, Iago, Cleopatra. All four are full-fed on imagination yet all of them hunger for more. However well you know the roles, you remain aware of Shakespeare's augmenting strangeness in representing them: they cannot be played *through,* they will not play out, which is not so true of Hal/Henry V, Othello, or Antony, grand figures who can be ransacked and exhausted. This is *strangeness* in its archaic sense of "foreign," but, again, it could as accurately be called "uncanny" in the Freudian mode of *Unheimlich,* the estrangement of the familiar which I discussed earlier. Johnson is highly aware of this Shakespearean phenomenon, though he avoids any particular naming of it. In the tradition of Longinus, he wants us to apprehend that Shakespeare is showing us much for the first time while making us feel we had truly known it all along but lacked awareness.

Citing this passage or that from Johnson's preface to his Shakespeare edition is a hopeless way of getting at its power of insight. Underlying it throughout is Johnson's sense of perilous balance, of falling into Swiftian madness rather

than imitating the supposedly Shakespearean "repose on the stability of truth."
For Johnson this is the value of Shakespeare; but reflect upon that massive
phrase, "the stability of truth." What can Johnson mean? Nothing, no one,
is stable in Shakespeare or in our lives; Johnson knows this too well. *It must
change* is the law of Shakespeare and of life; we have neither youth nor age but
a dreaming on both. In 1744 Johnson had composed a prologue for his onetime
student, the actor David Garrick, who was opening the theater in Drury Lane:

> When Learning's triumph o'er her barbarous foes
> First reared the stage, immortal Shakespeare rose;
> Each change of many-colour'd life he drew,
> Exhausted worlds, and then imagined new:
> Existence saw him spurn her bounded reign,
> And panting Time toil'd after him in vain.
> His powerful strokes presiding Truth impress'd,
> And unresisted Passion storm'd the breast.

Eighteen years before his preface, Johnson packs its essential teaching into
these eight lines, which convey Shakespeare's usurpation of reality by exhaust-
ing it. Shakespeare himself *is* change, and the bounds of existence are broken
and reformed because it is through Shakespeare that we are reminded that
the mind is a ceaseless activity. Human life is more than thought, and yet our
life also is thought as we follow Shakespeare in seeing. Wimsatt, when I was
his student listening to him on Johnson, liked to emphasize the great critic's
dislike of mere fact and love of elaboration. Hearing Wimsatt, I said once in a
seminar that his Johnson seemed to be a kind of baroque Neoplatonist, and my
teacher did not demur. That class was in the autumn of 1951; fifty-eight years
later I reflect back on it and wonder whether Johnson's Shakespeare is not a
Neoplatonic or Hermetic Demiurge, which is not a bad description of Prospero.

The preface's Shakespeare is remarkably close to the Bard of Hazlitt and
Coleridge, Lamb and Keats: the maker of a new reality in which—not altogether
consciously—we find ourselves more truly and more strange. Shakespeare
called out to the Romantic strain in Johnson, the mind through all its powers
seeking to exorcize the vileness of melancholy and assert itself against a universe of death.

The Skeptical Sublime

ANXIETIES OF EPICUREAN INFLUENCE

Dryden, Pater, Milton, Shelley, Tennyson, Whitman, Swinburne, Stevens

I treasure ruefully some memories of W. H. Auden that go back to the middle 1960s, when he arrived in New Haven to give a reading of his poems at Ezra Stiles College. We had met several times before, in New York City and at Yale, but were only acquaintances. The earlier Auden retains my interest, but much of the frequently devotional later poetry does not find me. Since our mutual friend John Hollander was abroad, Auden phoned to ask if he might stay with my wife and me, remarking on his dislike of college guest suites.

The poet arrived in a frayed, buttonless overcoat, which my wife insisted on mending. His luggage was an attaché case containing a large bottle of gin, a small one of vermouth, a plastic drinking cup, and a sheaf of poems. After being supplied with ice, he requested that I remind him of the amount of his reading fee. A thousand dollars had been the agreed sum, a respectable honorarium more than forty years ago. He shook his head and said that as a prima donna he could not perform, despite the prior arrangement. Charmed by this, I phoned the college master—a good friend—who cursed heartily but doubled the sum when I assured him that the poet was as obdurate as Lady Bracknell in *The Importance of Being Earnest.* Informed of this yielding, Auden smiled sweetly and was benign and brilliant at dinner, then at the reading, and as he went to bed after we got home.

The next day I told Auden I had to go off to teach Shelley's poetry. After saying I was "a dotty don" and that he liked dotty dons, he insisted on attending my class before he entrained back to New York City. I knew he did not care for Shelley and had extended this distaste to Whitman and Wallace Stevens, whom we had discussed at breakfast. All three were allied—for me—as Lucretian poets, but he did not esteem Lucretius either. I murmured that he would not enjoy the class, but along he came and then left silently afterward. I recall that never before had I taught even Shelley quite so ferociously.

It was consistent of Auden to condemn Shelley, Whitman, and Stevens, who were not Christian poets but Epicurean skeptics, metaphysical materialists, and above all High Romantics. Auden's celebrated *In Praise of Limestone* explicitly attacks Stevens. When I praised Shelley, Whitman, and Stevens as masters of nuance, Auden flatly said that none of the three had any ear for language. Discussing great poets he disliked was hardly Auden at his best, yet I grimly admired his surprising dogmatism. He was free of the Eliot-Pound virus of anti-Semitism, and immensely kind and considerate in most things, but he seemed rather proud of his critical limitations. I accepted his invitation to call upon him in New York City, but cannot remember ever seeing him again. I was still very young in the 1960s and was hopelessly passionate about the poets I loved best.

Wallace Stevens mentions both Shelley and Whitman by name in his poetry, and echoes them more widely and profoundly than critics have noted. The Shelleyan works that seem most inescapable for Stevens are the prose *Defence of Poetry* and the "Ode to the West Wind," but I find also allusions to or echoes of "Mont Blanc," *Alastor, Adonais,* "The Witch of Atlas," and the late Jane Williams's guitar love songs. In the anti-Marxist "Mr. Burnshaw and the Statue," Stevens saluted his High Romantic precursor's vision of change:

> In a mortal lullaby, like porcelain,
> Then, while the music makes you, make, yourselves,
> Long autumn sheens and pittering sounds like sounds
> On pattering leaves and suddenly with lights,
> Astral and Shelleyan, diffuse new day.

Commenting upon this, Stevens confirmed the tribute: "The astral and Shelleyan lights are not going to alter the structure of nature. Apples will always be apples, and whoever is a ploughman hereafter will be what the ploughman has always been. For all that, the astral and the Shelleyan will have transformed the world." Shelleyan transformation returns with extraordinary energy further on in "Mr. Burnshaw and the Statue":

> Mesdames, one might believe that Shelley lies
> Less in the stars than in their earthy wake,
> Since the radiant disclosures that you make
> Are of an eternal vista, manqué and gold
> And brown, an Italy of the mind, a place
> Of fear before the disorder of the strange,
> A time in which the poets' politics
> Will rule in a poets' world. Yet that will be
> A world impossible for poets, who
> Complain and prophesy, in their complaints,
> And are never of the world in which they live.

Auden rather weirdly condemned the conclusion of Shelley's *Defence*—"Poets are the unacknowledged legislators of the world"—by interpreting this as poets being absorbed into the Secret Police. Stevens gets it right in "an Italy of the mind," akin to Shelley's visionary exaltation of ancient Athens in his *Hellas*. A Lucretian atheism founds itself upon the necessity for change, in Stevens as in Shelley.

Walt Whitman is the precursor who looms largest in Stevens; his presence is so extensive that I can never come to the end of it. Of the greatest Whitmanian poems, only "Crossing Brooklyn Ferry," crucial for William Carlos Williams and Hart Crane, is relatively secondary for Stevens. His obsessions are with "Song of Myself," "The Sleepers," and "Out of the Cradle Endlessly Rocking," in that order. Just short of them come "As I Ebb'd with the Ocean of Life," "When Lilacs Last in the Dooryard Bloom'd," and "By Blue Ontario's Shore," again in that order. Whitman's Lucretianism is more metaphysical—that is to say, more anti-transcendental—than the High Romantic religion of Shelley, Keats, and Walter Pater, in which Stevens shares. The Montaigne-like intellectual skepticism of Epicurus is remote from Whitman, though not from Shelley or Stevens. I regret not asking Auden for his views on Montaigne, whom T. S. Eliot feared and rejected in the name of Pascal. A great lover of aphorism as a form, Auden almost certainly would have forgiven the inventor of the familiar essay his Lucretianism.

Stevens admired Shelley as an artist of metamorphosis, but there is both more warmth and more ambivalence in his lifelong agon with the bard of America. The ambivalence is most intense in regard to "Out of the Cradle Endlessly Rocking." My favorite Stevensian instance here is Crispin in the desperate "The Comedian as the Letter C," a poet

> too destitute to find
> In any commonplace the sought-for aid.
> He was a man made vivid by the sea,
> A man come out of luminous traversing,
> Much trumpeted, made desperately clear,
> Fresh from discoveries of tidal skies,
> To whom oracular rockings gave no rest.
> Into a savage color he went on.

But can Crispin get beyond "Out of the Cradle Endlessly Rocking"? Evidently not, since flight (repression) does not avail in "The Comedian as the Letter C." Walt's priority contributed to the authentic malaise that ended Stevens's poetry in the middle and later 1920s.

Lucretian tradition is not less anxious than Protestant continuity. Milton could subsume all anteriority except for Shakespeare. The Lucretians I discuss here—Shelley and Leopardi, Whitman and Stevens—were all strong poets, yet they lacked the rocklike egos of Dante, Milton, Goethe, and Wordsworth. Vergil, though a sincere Epicurean, seems uncomfortable with the overwhelming Lucretianism of his own epic. Ovid, equally captive to Lucretius, apparently rejoices in his poetic indebtedness. Akin to Shakespeare, the hierophant of metamorphosis is an incessant magpie, sensibly appropriating what he finds useful.

Lucretius does not thrive in British poetry until the later seventeenth century. Shakespeare never read him yet absorbed something of his skeptical naturalism through Ovid and Montaigne. One difference between Dante and Milton is that the Florentine master had never heard of Lucretius and so could consider Vergil an apt forerunner; a soul naturally Christian as it were, rather than the Epicurean materialist of mere actuality. Milton, knowing his poetic genealogy and determined to render both Lucretius and Vergil belated in regard to the Miltonic firstness, thus negated a tradition he did not care to entertain overtly, yet profited by nevertheless.

John Dryden, his ostensible Catholicism aside, seems to me the most Lucretian poet in the language before Shelley. A superb mistranslator, notorious for starting upon his rendition of the *Aeneid* before finishing a first reading of the poem, Dryden produced five fragments of Lucretius's *De rerum natura* that are still the best I know. Here is a passage of the latter part of book 3, "Against the Fear of Death":

What has this bugbear death to frighten man,
If souls can die, as well as bodies can?
For, as before our birth we felt no pain,
When Punic arms infested land and main,
When heaven and earth were in confusion hurl'd,
For the debated empire of the world,
Which awed with dreadful expectation lay,
Sure to be slaves, uncertain who should sway:
So, when our mortal frame shall be disjoin'd,
The lifeless lump uncoupled from the mind,
From sense of grief and pain we shall be free;
We shall not *feel*, because we shall not *be*.
Though earth in seas, and seas in heaven were lost,
We should not move, we only should be toss'd.
Nay, e'en suppose, when we have suffer'd fate,
The soul could feel in her divided state,
What's that to us? for we are only we
While souls and bodies in one frame agree.
Nay, though our atoms should revolve by chance,
And matter leap into the former dance;
Though time our life and motion could restore,
And make our bodies what they were before,
What gain to us would all this bustle bring?
The new-made man would be another thing.
When once an interrupting pause is made,
That individual being is decay'd.
We, who are dead, and gone, shall bear no part
In all the pleasures, nor shall feel the smart,
Which to that other mortal shall accrue,
Whom of our matter time shall mould anew.

Lucretius tells us not to fear death because we will never experience it: "We shall not *feel*, because we shall not *be*." Dryden admires Lucretian forthrightness, though he himself asserts a belief in the soul's immortality. Overtly a double man, Dryden thrives on contradictions, subsuming them by the vigor and clarity of both his verse and his prose. Toward Lucretius he manifests no ambivalence, unlike his stance in regard to his own precursors, Jonson and

Milton. His open love for Shakespeare and Chaucer is expressed with the pro-found passion of a great critic. No one has improved upon Dryden's praise: of all poets Shakespeare "had the largest and most comprehensive soul," while Chaucer's characters provoked "Here is God's plenty."

Lucretius's one poetic flaw is his tendentiousness, a quality of overpersuasion he shares with Sigmund Freud. But it scarcely bothers Dryden that Lucretius has too palpable a design upon the reader. Aptly, Dryden compares the Epicurean didact to Thomas Hobbes, the contemporary "magisterial authority" who communicates with "plain sincerity."

Milton, who allowed Dryden to "tag my verses" (to Marvell's merriment), cannot be called a Lucretian poet, just as he ought not to be called a Christian (or even a Protestant) poet, or a Platonist, or what you will. He is the most Miltonic of poets, however absurd that sounds. Dr. Johnson rightly observed that the closer Milton came to his precursors, the farther off he placed them. Yet there is a fascinating turn to his employment of Lucretius, who nearly becomes his guide through Chaos in *Paradise Lost*.

Lucretius, like Montaigne, rather subtly contaminates you unless you are wary. In a limited way, Lucretius was to Milton what Montaigne had been to Shakespeare: the moderating ecstasy of a skepticism. Shakespeare gave Hamlet to Shakespeare, but Montaigne helped. Milton gave Night to Milton, yet Lucretius proved a considerable resource. Whitman, Shelley, Leopardi, and Stevens would have been found by Night, Death, the Mother, and the Sea had they never read Lucretius, but the Epicurean exalter of the swerve was a marvelous stimulus to a Skeptical Sublime.

As a disciple of Walter Pater and his ephebe Oscar Wilde, I am an Epicurean literary critic, reliant upon sensations, perceptions, impressions. Pater, far more than has been realized, was the high priest of literary modernism: Yeats, Joyce, Pound, Eliot (who scoffed guiltily at the sublime Walter), and a wide panoply including Freud, Hopkins, Rilke, Proust, Valéry, Stevens, Crane, Woolf, and the last survivor, Samuel Beckett. In his beautiful but alas now un-read historical novel *Marius the Epicurean* (1885, 1892), Pater appropriated the Christian epiphany for aesthetic purposes:

> Through some accident to the trappings of his horse at the inn where
> he rested, Marius had an unexpected delay. He sat down in an olive-
> garden, and all around him and within still turning to reverie. . . . A
> bird came and sang among the wattled hedge-roses: an animal feeding

crept nearer: the child who kept it was gazing quietly: and the scene and the hours still conspiring, he passed from that mere fantasy of a self not himself, beside him in his coming and going, to those divinations of a living and companionable spirit at work in all things. . . .

In this peculiar and privileged hour, his bodily frame, as he could recognize, although just then, in the whole sum of its capacities, so entirely possessed by him—Nay! actually his very self—was yet determined by a far-reaching system of material forces external to it. . . . And might not the intellectual frame also, still more intimately himself as in truth it was, after the analogy of the bodily life, be a moment only, an impulse or series of impulses, a single process? . . . How often had the thought of their brevity spoiled for him the most natural pleasures of life. . . . To-day at least, in the peculiar clearness of one privileged hour, he seemed to have apprehended . . . an abiding-place. . . .

Himself—his sensations and ideas—never fell again precisely into focus as on that day, yet he was the richer by its experience. . . . It gave him a definitely ascertained measure of his moral or intellectual need, of the demand his soul must make upon the powers, whatsoever they might be, which had brought him, as he was, into the world at all.

This assimilation of Wordsworth's "Spots of Time" to the worldview of Lucretius corrects an idealizing naturalism with the most ancient of materialisms. Gerard Manley Hopkins, Pater's student at Oxford, restored this "peculiar and principled hour" to Christian epiphany, to be followed there by Eliot and Auden, but the Paterian skeptical secularization became more influential through Joyce's Stephen and Virginia Woolf (whose tutor was one of Pater's sisters). In American poetry the heirs of Pater were Wallace Stevens and Hart Crane, whose legacies endure in John Ashbery, now the poet of our climate.

I return from this Paterian digression to Milton and his Lucretian vision of Night and Chaos in books 2 and 3 of *Paradise Lost*. Satan, heroic voyager, beholds

> The secrets of the hoary deep, a dark
> Illimitable ocean without bound,
> Without dimension, where length, breadth, and height,
> And time and place are lost; where eldest Night
> And Chaos, ancestors of Nature, hold
> Eternal anarchy, amidst the noise
> Of endless wars, and by confusion stand.

For Hot, Cold, Moist, and Dry, four champions fierce
Strive here for mastery, and to battle bring
Their embryon atoms; they around the flag
Of each his faction, in their several clans,
Light-armed or heavy, sharp, smooth, swift or slow,
Swarm populous, unnumbered as the sands
Of Barca or Cyrenë's torrid soil,
Levied to side with warring winds, and poise
Their lighter wings. To whom these most adhere,
He rules a moment; Chaos umpire sits,
And by decision more embroils the fray
By which he reigns: next him high arbiter
Chance governs all. Into this wild abyss,
The womb of nature and perhaps her grave,
Of neither sea, nor shore, nor air, nor fire,
But all these in their pregnant causes mixed
Confusedly, and which thus must ever fight,
Unless the almighty maker them ordain
His dark materials to create more worlds,
Into this wild abyss the wary fiend
Stood on the brink of hell and looked awhile,
Pondering his voyage; for no narrow frith
He had to cross.

[2.891–920]

The foreboding phrase "His dark materials," splendidly appropriated by Philip Pullman, might be an apt title of this marvelous passage were it to be printed as an independent poem. Lucretius is translated precisely in "the womb of nature and perhaps her grave" (*De rerum natura*, 5.259). Miltonic scholars—John Leonard and David Quint, in particular—have explored Milton's use of Lucretius, a venture recently perfected in N. K. Sugimura's *Matter of Glorious Trial* (2009). Milton satirized the Lucretian *clinamen* (swerve) in Satan's fall, yet relied more on Lucretius than on Aristotle for a vision of Prime Matter. The Miltonic imagination rallied to the idea of a bottomless universe, which can be as suggestive as Shakespeare's bottomless dream on a midsummer's night.

In *De rerum natura*, 1.969–83, the universe famously is seen as unlimited and so ungoverned, a notion alien to the Hebrew Bible and to Christian tradition after it, which never welcome a return to the void. Sugimura argues that Milton does welcome, or at least countenance, it, but only to suggest that the dark material is itself spiritual, since Night and the abyss are Stoic figurations, not Epicurean. Newton's thought is an analogue, as Sugimura suggests. I would direct the question elsewhere: Why Lucretius? If you are Shelley, Leopardi, Whitman, Stevens—not Christian poets—then Lucretius is a true precursor. Though Milton, in his deepest being, was a sect of one, his choice of the atheist Lucretius as guide to the abyss is suggestive. Platonism and Neostoicism were as expedient for the blind Milton as Christianity was, yet his vision of poetry as simple, sensuous, and passionate is wholly Lucretian. The poet-as-poet in the Miltonic epics was attracted to Lucretius precisely as Shakespeare loved Ovid.

You can spend a lifetime reading the three major poets in the language—Chaucer, Shakespeare, Milton—and only gradually become aware that while they *may* have been Christians, their poetry resists baptism. Poetry at its strongest does not and cannot "believe" that something is so. Many scholars tell me that Montaigne, crown of all possible essayists, was a devout Catholic. What shall I do with this assertion? I will reread "Of Experience," last and greatest of the *Essays,* and wonder what room it reserves for faith. When it comes to holy dying, look to Jeremy Taylor or John Donne but stay apart from Montaigne, who splendidly tells you not to bother studying how to die because when the time comes, you will know how to do it well enough. With Lucretius, Montaigne knows that death is no part of experience even though dying is. Chaucer, Shakespeare, Milton—I would add Leopardi—are natural metaphysicians of materialism.

Shelley was not, yet his skeptical mind won the agon with his idealizing heart. He is a Lucretian poet yet hardly an Epicurean in his stance. Epicurus and Lucretius believed in mortal gods who had no concern for us. Calm and peaceful, the Lucretian divinities are not waiting for us in some future abode. Shelley, Leopardi, Whitman, and Stevens agreed, but did not follow Lucretius by excluding death from their imaginings.

Shelley, the Hamlet of lyric poets, joins the Prince of Denmark in what G. Wilson Knight called in *The Wheel of Fire* (1930) "the embassy of death." Lucretius gave Shelley his imagery of shadows in the unfinished last masterwork, *The Triumph of Life.* All objects, in Lucretius, emit a flow of replicas that pound against our senses. Such impact Lucretius calls "sensation," which Shelley renders into a sensory loss, shadows of nonrecognition. Lucretius, who denied a creation ab nihilo (as Milton did also), places more emphasis on insistence that material things never could be reduced to a nothingness. In Shelley's cosmos, things do emanate from nothing and can return to nonbeing again.

Lucretius and his tradition taught Shelley that freedom came from understanding causation. In his final phase, Shelley preceded Nietzsche by surmising that causes and effects alike were fictions. The grand tradition of naturalism moves from Lucretius on to Montaigne, Hume, and Freud. Shelley would belong to this tradition except that, like Nietzsche, he converted Epicurus's "the what is unknowable" into a quest for the imageless deep truth or mystery of things. Nietzsche urged the will's revenge against time and time's "it was," and yet "it was" remains part of the unknowable *what:* the will then would seek to revenge itself against a phantom or a fiction. Shelley, who in *Prometheus Unbound* had observed that the wise lack love and those who have love lack wisdom, went to his end in *The Triumph of Life* asking why good and the means of good were irreconcilable.

As your atoms fall downward into Lucretius' bottomless cosmos, they suddenly swerve, executing a clinamen at once gratuitous and crucial. The time and place are random, and the swerve is slight, merely a momentary tilt. All of our free will nevertheless is in that swerve, which is not a Lucretian irony, though his tonal complexities are difficult to judge. Yet precisely how are we to receive a theory of freedom that scarcely in itself seems free? Epicurus made only a few changes in the atomic theory of Democritus, and the swerve is the most notorious; indeed it was desperate. It has no causation, and can have none in a cosmos conceived as a vast mechanism. You cannot have a self-reliant person in a totally determined universe. Epicurus wanted both—absolute nondetermination and ethical choice—hence the unwilled swerve.

Freedom for Epicurus emanates from *ataraxia,* a kind of sublime indifference that renders you immune from anxieties and irrational fears. Is ataraxia the fruit of swerve? That seems grotesque, and something is always missing when we ponder the massive certitudes of Lucretius, endlessly eloquent as he is. Rather like Freud, Lucretius is incessant at the role-playing of a Great Explainer. Compared to Lucretius, Freud surprisingly is almost modest: he explained only that women are a mystery. Not for Lucretius, who regards sexual love as a calamity and a disease, and so no part of the grandeur of the way things are. The absurd attack of C. S. Lewis upon Milton's fallen angels—"What do you mean we have lost love? There's a perfectly good brothel around the corner!"— is merely the Lucretian stance. If you are miserable about love, grab the first trollop is the pragmatic counsel of the pious Epicurean.

Nothing could be less Shelleyan, however refreshing we may discover Lu-

cretius to be. Why then invoke Lucretius in reading and discussing the most
passionate celebrant of romantic love in the language? Invoking Freud in a
Shelleyan context makes me unhappy, even when these two luminaries of Eros
are brought together subtly and with skill by Thomas Frosch in his *Shelley and
the Romantic Imagination* (2007). Freud is well described by Philip Rieff as a Romantic rationalist, but Shelley is distinctly a highly rational High Romantic, who
exalts desire over any possible fulfillment. Ordinary unhappiness is an achievement for Freud and a fallback position in Lucretius. Shelley will not accept it
and urges us to refuse all desires that lack sublimity. Yeats, I ruefully concede
in my old age, indeed was Shelley's most authentic disciple and interpreter.

Can you be a Lucretian poet without being an Epicurean? The surprising
answer is an emphatic "Yes." Shelley, Whitman, and Stevens are the most Lucretian poets in the English language, and they were skeptics, unlike Pater,
whose Epicureanism crowds out his own considerable skepticism. What makes
Shelley, Whitman, and Stevens poets of the Lucretian sublime is their freedom
from banal religions, whether Olympian or pseudo-Christian. All that survives
of Epicureanism in them is a dialectic of cognition and sensation, for which
some brief remarks about the identity of cognition and seeing in Epicurus will
be necessary.

Epicurus asserts that the gods are visible as images that descend from space
and touch our minds by a curious kind of "seeing." The gods are perfectly useless unless they spur us to emulation of their sublime indifference. Is that
emulation an ethical activity, or is the tranquillity of the gods merely a shibboleth for Lucretius to translate into eloquence?

Here is Lucretius invoking Epicurus at the start of book 3:

> O glory of the Greeks, the first to raise
> The shining light out of tremendous dark
> Illuminating the blessings of our life,
> You are the one I follow; in your steps
> I tread, not as a rival, but for love
> Of your example. Does the swallow vie
> With swans? Do wobbly-legged little goats
> Compete in strength and speed with thoroughbreds?
> You, father, found the truth; you gave to us
> A father's wisdom, and from every page,
> O most illustrious in renown, we take,

As bees do from the flowery banks of summer,
The benefit of all your golden words,
The gold most worthy of eternal life;
For, once your reason, your divining sense,
Begins its proclamation, telling us
The way things are, all terrors of the mind
Vanish, are gone; the barriers of the world
Dissolve before me, and I see things happen
All through the void of empty space. I see
The gods majestic, and their calm abodes
Winds do not shake, nor clouds befoul, nor snow
Violate with the knives of sleet and cold;
But there the sky is purest blue, the air
Is almost laughter in that radiance,
And nature satisfies their every need,
And nothing, nothing, mars their calm of mind.
No realms of Hell are ever visible,
But earth affords a view of everything,
Below and outward, all through space. I feel
A more than mortal pleasure in all this,
Almost a shudder, since your power has given
This revelation of all nature's ways.

[Translated by Rolfe Humphries]

As gods go, these at least are harmless. Contrast Milton's God, a dreadful ogre rightfully blamed by William Empson for having caused all the trouble. Epicurus held on to his gods in defiance of the Skeptics, who urged total distrust of all the senses. That eliminated both the gods and all human feeling of pleasure and pain. In contrast, Epicurus and Lucretius might be termed *soft* empiricists. An Epicurean holds on to pure *sensations*, mental *perceptions*, and *feelings*, ideally of pleasure. Reflections are secondary, and are best kept close to sensation, perception, feeling, since to see *is* to think, according to Epicurus, a notion naturally attractive to poets from Lucretius until this moment. Ruskin and Pater, each initially under Wordsworth's influence, translated Epicurean perception into a critical impressionism, curiously moral in Ruskin but liberated by Pater into the dangerous freedom of the arts.

But I set aside Ruskin and Pater in order to return us to Shelley, a Lucretian only in regard to the sublime, redefined as the surrender of easier pleasures in exchange for pleasures so difficult that they seem painful to most human beings of whatever era. Uncompromising in his lifelong quest, Shelley had little or no hedonism in his nature. He translated, however, the odyssey of his soul, from the early *Alastor* on through *The Triumph of Life,* and the effect of that remorseless questing shaped more of literary history than has even yet been charted. Shelley's influence begins with his close friend and rival, Byron, and with Keats, who resisted and resented his would-be friend. In the next generation Shelley fostered doomed figures like Thomas Lovell Beddoes and George Darley, as well as the Cambridge circle of Arthur Henry Hallam, Alfred, Lord Tennyson, and their associates. Robert Browning was Shelley's principal heir as Tennyson was Keats's. After that, the sequence is remarkable: Swinburne, Shaw, Yeats, Hardy, Forster, Woolf, and, surprisingly, Joyce and Beckett. Shelley fuses with Hardy and Whitman in D. H. Lawrence's poetry, and then lives on in twentieth-century American lyrists as diverse as Elinor Wylie and Hart Crane.

Three remarkable critical essays—though they are both more and less than that—are crucial documents in the transmission of Shelley, aside from his now undervalued *A Defence of Poetry,* itself a major influence upon Wallace Stevens. In succession these are Hallam's review of Tennyson's *Poems, Chiefly Lyrical* (1831), Browning's "An Essay on Percy Bysshe Shelley" (1852), and Yeats's "The Philosophy of Shelley's Poetry" (1900). All three remain remarkably alive. I have just reread them in sequence, noting again that Browning and Yeats both are affected by Hallam's view of Shelley, and that Yeats clearly is indebted alike to Hallam and to Browning.

Hallam is remembered today as the lost love of Tennyson's life, and so as the elegiac subject of a marvelous array of poems: "Ulysses," "Tithonus," "Morte d'Arthur," and "In Memoriam," among others. Had Hallam lived—he died suddenly at twenty-two of a brain seizure—we might know him now as one of the major scholar-critics of the nineteenth century, whose work centered on the influence of Italian literature upon the English poets, and so as a precursor to the remarkable twentieth-century scholar-poet F. T. Prince, author of *The Italian Element in Milton's Verse* (1954). Hallam's critical gifts are best seen in his review of Tennyson, a remarkable performance for someone aged twenty-one.

Yeats, summarizing Hallam, repeated his distinction between poetry of sensation (Shelley and Keats) and of reflection (Wordsworth). Here is Hallam on Keats and Shelley: "So vivid was the delight attending the simple exertions of eye and ear, that it became mingled more and more with trains of active thought, and tended to absorb their whole being into the energy of sense." Expanding upon this, Hallam prophetically warned Tennyson against the societal pressures that eventually were to smother the laureate: "That delicate sense of fitness which grows with the growth of artist feelings, and strengthens with their strength, until it acquires a celerity and weight of decision hardly inferior to the correspondent judgments of conscience, is weakened by every indulgence of heterogeneous aspirations, however pure they may be, however lofty, however suitable to human nature."

Hallam's exemplary High Romanticism kindled the young Tennyson, whose response is sensitively charted in Cornelia Pearsall's study of his dramatic monologues, *Tennyson's Rapture* (2008). Perhaps Hallam's most remarkable gift, his oratorical eloquence, might have brought him into politics by William Gladstone's side, the two having been close friends at Cambridge. Pearsall shows that Hallam and Tennyson were politically archaic Whigs, throwbacks to an aristocratic conservatism that opposed both the crown and the masses. The Whig Reform Bill of 1832 brought about a carefully limited program of electoral reforms, fiercely supported by Tennyson and by Hallam, whose father was a major Whig historian.

Whiggism and the High Romanticism of Byron fit well together, but the revolutionary Shelley and the lower-class Keats were Hallam's poetic heroes, and through him became Tennyson's. Epicurean politics is a deliciously absurd notion. You would not know, reading my favorite nineteenth-century critic, the sublime Walter Pater, that he writes in the age of Gladstone and Disraeli, and I love Tennyson most when he shrugs off politics. Pearsall, though, subtly blends the Whiggism of Hallam and Tennyson to Hallam's poetic theory and its influence on his friend's work. Her sinuous fifth chapter, "'Tithonus' and the Performance of Masculine Beauty," is a model of what a historically grounded reading of a beautiful poem could yet be, and "Tithonus" is Tennyson's most beautiful poem, perhaps indeed the most beautiful in the language. I wish to add to Pearsall only the realization that Hallam's poetics are Epicurean-Lucretian, which explains Hallam's appeal to Pater and Yeats. It also helps in explaining the Vergilian beauty of "Tithonus," since tacitly Hallam and Tennyson understand that Vergil was an Epicurean and the anxious poetic heir of Lucretius. Tennyson's troubled reception of Lucretius gave him (and us) his magnificently extreme dramatic monologue "Lucretius," but I will postpone that until I can account for Hallam's welcome passion for Shelley's poetry.

Hallam's keen insight was that Shelley and Keats manifested "the energy of sense," which can *see* its thought and *think* its sensations. Eliot's somewhat misplaced praise of the Metaphysicals falls short of Hallam's recognition of unified sensibility in the younger High Romantics. Shelley more than Keats or perhaps any other poet in English is haunted by internalized images that possess the energy and vividness of direct sight. Yeats misnamed his essay on Shelley since it expounds the poet's imagery and not his philosophy, which is allied more to Hume than to Plato. I suspect that Shelley appealed to the writer in Hallam, who was fascinated by the flights of ascension to the high sublime.

> the one Spirit's plastic stress
> Sweeps through the dull dense world, compelling there,
> All new successions to the forms they wear;
> Torturing th' unwilling dross that checks its flight
> To its own likeness, as each mass may bear;
> And bursting in its beauty and its might
> From trees and beasts and men into the Heaven's light.

> [*Adonais*, 381–87]

Tennyson would have shuddered if a critic had described him as a Lucretian poet despite himself. But what else is he? It makes little sense to say that "against the Lucretian spirit Tennyson unfolds the Vergilian." I quote one of a score of Tennysonian scholars at random. Yes, Tennyson *labors* to assert the spirit and fears the Utilitarian renewal of Epicurean ethics and metaphysics, of which Lucretius is the oracle and Darwin and his bulldog Thomas Huxley the exemplars. Naturalism is the enemy for the Whiggish Tennyson, yet the enemy within is Tennyson's own vocation as a poet of sensation. Let us go further: as a poet.

"Lucretius" is a dramatic monologue of 280 lines, composed by Tennyson from October 1865 through January 1868. The poet was fifty-six when he began, more than thirty years on from the death of Hallam. In 1850 he had married and became poet laureate. Bereft of Hallam in 1833, he invented the dramatic monologue, thus anticipating Browning by about a year. When I think of this genre, Browning comes immediately to mind, since more than Tennyson he transmitted it, first to Dante Gabriel Rossetti and then to Ezra Pound and T. S. Eliot, from whom Randall Jarrell and Robert Lowell carried on, until Richard Howard returned to Browning in a remarkable feat of resurrection.

Tennyson's dramatic monologues swerve from Keats even as Browning's depart from Shelley, yet the lyrical element abides in both, a process brilliantly worked out by Herbert F. Tucker in *Browning's Beginnings* (1980) and *Tennyson and the Doom of Romanticism* (1988). There are no Lucretian elements in Browning, who took from Shelley neither doctrine nor style but something far more deeply interfused: an idea of the poet and the poem. Style is the Keatsian gift to Tennyson, whose extraordinary transmemberment of Keats into Vergil created an idiom later seized upon by T. S. Eliot, who gave it an American turn by an admixture of Whitman, much as Pound tempered Browning by the voice of an American bard at last. We need no longer believe the Eliotic and Poundian myths of their emergence into the sun by immersions into Provence and Paris.

Tucker reprints an 1832 notebook fragment that marks the start of Tennyson's dramatic monologues:

> I wish I were as in the days of old,
> Ere my smooth cheek darkened with youthful down,
> While yet the blessèd daylight made itself
> Ruddy within the eaves of sight, before
> I looked upon divinity unveiled
> And wisdom naked—when my mind was set
> To follow knowledge like a sinking star
> Beyond the utmost bound of human thought.

Two major monologues, "Tiresias" (1885) and the superb "Ulysses" (1842), are embedded here, and already the cadence of the great Vergilian monologue "Tithonus" (1864) is evident. "Lucretius" needs to be read against "Ulysses" and "Tithonus" since it is an involuntary palinode. Anyone experiencing Lucretius learns immediately that it manifests a return of the repressed, a displacement of the Vergilian Tennyson by the Lucretian within. Since Vergil—to repeat this truth—is an Epicurean in belief and an anxious poetic follower of Lucretius, this was hardly surprising.

Saint Jerome gathered together the Christian slanders against Lucretius and gave them permanent form in a myth that Tennyson inherited. Driven mad by an erotic elixir administered by his neglected wife, the Epicurean poet composed his epic in lucid intervals and then killed himself at forty-four, his wicked work left unfinished. Since Tennyson was so sophisticated, I doubt that he believed this legend, but either he wished to accept such nonsense or, more likely, saw how well it suited the outrageous dramatic monologue he composed.

Swinburne's sensational *Poems and Ballads* was published in 1866, and Tennyson had to feel the Shelleyan challenge of a younger lyric poet who revived Greek and Latin paganism, including the Epicurean philosophy. There was also the fierce provocation of his close friend Edward FitzGerald's *The Rubái-yát of Omar Khayyám*, a more than Epicurean poem slyly directed against the pieties of "In Memoriam" and carried to general fame by the enthusiasm of the Pre-Raphaelite infidels: D. G. Rossetti, Swinburne, William Morris, George Meredith. I suspect that a keener anxiety was induced by Browning, whose *Dramatis Personae* (1864) confirmed the lasting power of *Men and Women* (1855), in which Browning stole away forever Tennyson's prized invention, the dramatic monologue. On some level, by composing "Lucretius" the laureate cried out, "Take that!" to Swinburne, FitzGerald, and Browning.

I have been both enthralled by and resentful of Tennyson's tendentious monologue for more than six decades. It is outrageous that the sublime Lucretius speaks in Tennyson's voice and yet no translation of *De rerum natura* into English verse catches the sound of Lucretius as Tennyson does. I give Lucretius's description of a storm as eloquently rendered by Rolfe Humphries, and then a storm in Tennyson's "Lucretius":

> Sometimes, again, the violence of wind
> Hits from without on clouds already hot
> With a ripe thunderbolt, so fire erupts
> At once in any direction as the blast
> May make it go. And sometimes, also, wind
> Starts with no blaze at all, but catches fire
> As it speeds onward, losing in its course
> Large elements that cannot pass through air,
> Scrapes bodies infinitesimal in size
> From the same air, fire-particles—the way
> A leaden bullet in its flight will lose
> Its attributes of stiffness and of cold
> And melt or burn in air. The force of wind
> May even be cold, may be devoid of fire,
> And yet cause fire just from the violence
> Of impact, as we now and then observe
> When cold steel strikes cold stone. It all depends
> On timeliness; its own rush of energy

Converts the coldest of material,
Lukewarm to white-hot stuff, or chill to fire.

[*De rerum natura*, 6.281–92]

"Storm in the night! for thrice I heard the rain
Rushing; and once the flash of a thunderbolt—
Methought I never saw so fierce a fork—
Struck out the streaming mountain-side, and show'd
A riotous confluence of watercourses
Blanching and billowing in a hollow of it,
Where all but yester-eve was dusty-dry."

["Lucretius," 26–32]

Tennyson's economy adapts Lucretius, here and throughout the monologue, so as to augment the original's lucidity. This works to enforce the horror of madness in Tennyson's poet, as he alternates tormenting sexual visions with Epicurean hopes of tranquillity.

The erotic hallucinations are what is most memorable in the monologue, and one has to wonder, *Whose* obsessions are these, since they certainly are not those of *De rerum natura*?

"And here an Oread—how the sun delights
To glance and shift about her slippery sides,
And rosy knees and supple roundedness,
And budded bosom-peaks . . . "

[188–91]

Tennyson charmingly suggested to a magazine editor who cut this passage that it would do better in America, where readers were less squeamish. Yet this comes well after a much more engaging picture:

"I thought that all the blood by Sylla shed
Came driving rainlike down again on earth,
And where it dashed the reddening meadow, sprang
No dragon warriors from Cadmean teeth,
For these I thought my dream would show to me,
But girls, Hetairai, curious in their art,
Hired animalisms, vile as those that made

The mulberry-faced Dictator's orgies worse
Than aught they fable of the quiet Gods.
And hands they mixt, and yell'd and round me drove
In narrowing circles till I yell'd again
Half-suffocated, and sprang up, and saw—
Was it the first beam of my latest day?

   "Then, then, from utter gloom stood out the breasts,
The breasts of Helen, and hoveringly a sword
Now over and now under, now direct,
Pointed itself to pierce, but sank down shamed
At all that beauty; and as I stared, a fire,
The fire that left a roofless Ilion,
Shot out of them, and scorch'd me that I woke."

[47–66]

That overgoes Swinburne, as if to admonish the young man that he is not yet in the laureate's league. Tennyson's magnificently expressed erotomania lingers in my memory and dismisses the monologue's absurdly weak conclusion, when it breaks its form to become melodramatic narrative. After the Epicurean drives a knife into his side, his wife shrieks that she has failed her duty to him. At his nadir, the righteous Tennyson has Lucretius reply, "Thy duty? What is duty? Fare thee well!" Thus the laureate punishes his own daimon, the Hallam-inspired Keatsian poet of sensation.

"Ulysses" and "Tithonus" are stronger poems than "Lucretius" because they do not sabotage themselves at the close. After "Maud: A Monodrama" (1855), Tennyson declines, though "Tithonus" and "Lucretius" came after. The great style never abandoned Tennyson, and I began to see that it was Lucretian-Shelleyan as well as Vergilian-Keatsian. The death of Hallam was a tragedy for Tennyson's imagination, though it also gave him the elegiac intensity that his genius required.

Passing from Tennyson to Walt Whitman is to learn again the American difference that Emerson prophesied and that Hawthorne, Melville, Thoreau, Whitman, and Dickinson fulfilled. Curiously, only Whitman of those half-dozen had much admiration for Tennyson. Confronting the laureate's ghastly poem of 1886, "Locksley Hall Sixty Years After"—"Demos end in working its own doom"—Whitman replied, "We can well afford the warning calls . . . of such . . . voices as Carlyle's and Tennyson's." Charmingly, Walt anticipated our contemporary homage to Bruce Springsteen by frequently referring to Tennyson as "the boss of us all." In 1855, in the second of two anonymous reviews he accorded to *Leaves of Grass,* Whitman compared himself with Tennyson, scorned the spirit of gentility, yet admitted that "this man is a real first-class poet, infused amid all that ennui and aristocracy." British poetry, to Whitman, was Shakespeare, Sir Walter Scott, and Tennyson, his own exact contemporary. Tennyson read some of Whitman and reacted cautiously, though not as negatively as Matthew Arnold, the most overrated of all critics, ever. Swinburne, Hopkins, Wilde, Chesterton, and above all Lawrence are among the English appreciators of Whitman. It fascinates me to think of Tennyson reading the *Calamus* poems of overt male homoeroticism. Ambivalent always, would Hallam's beauty not have haunted him then?

Whitman emerged from Emerson's matrix, but with the strong sense of Epicurus and Lucretius working in him against Emersonian Idealism. Partly this was a family inheritance; the dissenting Quaker carpenter Walter Whitman, Sr., had been a follower of Thomas Paine and of Frances Wright, author of the Epicurean novel *A Few Days in Athens* (1829), dedicated to Jeremy Bentham. Walt told Horace Traubel he had heard Wright's antislavery and reform lectures in New York City in 1836 and 1838, and certainly he read *A Few Days in Athens,* which his father owned. Lucretius came later: Whitman owned a copy of the John Selby Watson translation of *De rerum natura* (1851) and took notes on the poem. In *Democratic Vistas* (1871) Whitman set forth a program that seems central to him: "What the Roman Lucretius sought most nobly, yet all too blandly, negatively to do for his age and its successors, must be done positively by some great coming literatus, especially poet, who, while remaining fully poet, will absorb whatever science indicates, with spiritualism, and out of them, and out of his own genius, will compose the great poem of death."

Lucretius composed the great poem that denies any concern for death, that refuses any anxiety with regard to dying. Whitman in 1865 had written the great American poem of death in "When Lilacs Last in the Dooryard Bloom'd." You could select out of *Leaves of Grass* an extraordinary ensemble of death poetry side by side with a cavalcade of poems urging and fostering more life. Stevens's Whitman is singing and changing the things that are part of him: "death and day." Here is a glory of the day, section 6 of "Song of Myself":

A child said *What is the grass?* fetching it to me with full hands;
How could I answer the child? I do not know what it is any more than he.

I guess it must be the flag of my disposition, out of hopeful green stuff
    woven.

Or I guess it is the handkerchief of the Lord,
A scented gift and remembrancer designedly dropt,
Bearing the owner's name someway in the corners, that we may see and
    remark, and say *Whose?*

Or I guess the grass is itself a child, the produced babe of the vegetation.

Or I guess it is a uniform hieroglyphic,
And it means, Sprouting alike in broad zones and narrow zones,
Growing among black folks as among white,
Kanuck, Tuckahoe, Congressman, Cuff, I give them the same, I receive them
    the same.

And now it seems to me the beautiful uncut hair of graves.

Tenderly will I use you curling grass,
It may be you transpire from the breasts of young men,
It may be if I had known them I would have loved them,
It may be you are from old people, or from offspring taken soon out of their
    mothers' laps,
And here you are the mothers' laps.

This grass is very dark to be from the white heads of old mothers,
Darker than the colorless beards of old men,
Dark to come from under the faint red roofs of mouths.

O I perceive after all so many uttering tongues,
And I perceive they do not come from the roofs of mouths for nothing.

I wish I could translate the hints about the dead young men and women,
And the hints about old men and mothers, and the offspring taken soon out
    of their laps.

What do you think has become of the young and old men?
And what do you think has become of the women and children?

They are alive and well somewhere,
The smallest sprout shows there is really no death,
And if ever there was it led forward life, and does not wait at the end to arrest it,
And ceas'd the moment life appear'd.

All goes onward and outward, nothing collapses,
And to die is different from what any one supposed, and luckier.

That is a long passage, more than thirty lines, but I do not know how to cut it.
Wholly Epicurean, it may have been started by the master's adage "The what is
unknowable." Starting from that truth, how could any of us answer the child?
Who among us could move as Whitman does, from not knowing to such vital
guesses? A master of metaphor, like his disciples Stevens, Eliot, and Crane,
Whitman accepts the Epicurean truth as against the Platonists (Emerson included). The *what* is unknowable because there are no ideal forms or arche-
types, but only the thing/phenomenon itself, like the grass. But *Leaves of Grass* is
a great composite trope of a title, drawing upon the biblical "All flesh is grass."
From the flag of hope through God's flirtatious handkerchief we go on to the
babe and the universal hieroglyphic, until we reach the all-but-Homeric trope:
"And now it seems to me the beautiful uncut hair of graves."

No two critics agree on what Whitman means by "death," but then neither do
any of the numerous Walts agree with one another. From "The Sleepers" (1855)
on, Death is part of a Whitmanian fourfold: Night, Death, the Mother, and the Sea.
That composite trope surges on in Federico García Lorca and Fernando Pessoa,
Robinson Jeffers and Conrad Aiken, Wallace Stevens and T. S. Eliot, until it receives its classical statement in Hart Crane. We are beyond Lucretius in this pro-
ductive trope, and perhaps return to Homer and the Bible, Milton and Coleridge,
as we quest for images of the power of the poetic mind over a universe of death.

What does Whitman mean by immortality? David Bromwich posits a trope
of otherness: "We continue in time only as an author's words continue in the
minds of his readers." Shrewd, but can that be the whole of Whitman's aspiration? Richard Poirier believes that, for Whitman, "art is an action and not the
product of an action," so that immortality simply would be the result of having
enjoyed a strong reception by one's readers. Closure, Kerry Larson suggests in
Whitman's Drama of Consensus (1988), never can be enacted in Whitman: "The
defiance of death and all terminations works to overdetermine indeterminacy."

Kenneth Burke, in conversation with me, suggested that the material imagery
of death in Whitman was so strong that nothing the poet wrote could escape its

shadows of ecstasy. Certainly that is true of the elegiac Whitman of 1860–65, but perhaps comes short of the mixed signals of "Song of Myself" (1855). Stevens had a particular admiration for the brief, late lyric of 1881, "A Clear Midnight":

> This is thy hour, O Soul, thy free flight into the wordless,
> Away from books, away from art, the day erased, the lesson done,
> Thee fully forth emerging, silent, gazing, pondering the themes
>   thou lovest best,
> Night, sleep, death and the stars.

The stars replace the maternal ocean, a refreshing change. Strength attracted Stevens, and Whitman's strength augments when he indulges his penchant for variety, his containment of multitudes. In the view of Schopenhauer, Wittgenstein's *Tractatus* utters the gnome "What the solipsist *means* is right but what he *says* is wrong." On death, what Whitman *means* is accurate but what he *says* is contradictory. His Lucretianism and his Idealism collided, and an extraordinarily sonorous cognitive music sometimes confounds itself.

With Whitman as with Tennyson, that scarcely matters; in "Experience," Emerson says, "The Daemon knows how it is done." Whitman's daimon, his dusky demon and brother, mocks him on the beach in "As I Ebb'd with the Ocean of Life":

O baffled, balk'd, bent to the very earth,
Oppress'd with myself that I have dared to open my mouth,
Aware now that amid all that blab whose echoes recoil upon me I have not
    once had the least idea who or what I am,
But that before all my arrogant poems the real Me stands yet untouch'd,
    untold, altogether unreach'd,
Withdrawn far, mocking me with mock-congratulatory signs and bows,
With peals of distant ironical laughter at every word I have written,
Pointing in silence to these songs, and then to the sand beneath.

I perceive I have not really understood any thing, not a single object, and
    that no man ever can,
Nature here in sight of the sea taking advantage of me to dart upon me and
    sting me,
Because I have dared to open my mouth to sing at all.

                                            [section 2]

When resolution comes in this poem of the breaking of the vessels, the un-
concerned gods of Lucretius are taken as final witnesses of the poet's crisis:

> We, capricious, brought hither we know not whence, spread out
>   before you,
> You up there walking or sitting,
> Whoever you are, we too lie in drifts at your feet.

The Iron Duke, Wellington, expired on September 14, 1852. As laureate,
Tennyson promptly brought forth his "Ode on the Death of the Duke of Wellington," a suitably ghastly performance, commencing:

> Bury the Great Duke
>   With an empire's lamentation,
> Let us bury the Great Duke
>   To the noise of the mourning of a mighty nation.

It was perhaps inevitable that Whitman, with his ambivalent admiration for the
Boss, slyly alludes to the Wellington ode in his own masterpiece of elegy, "When
Lilacs Last in the Dooryard Bloom'd" (1865). "Let the bell be tolled," Tennyson
keeps knolling, and Walt overgoes this: "With the tolling tolling bells' perpetual
clang." Though Tennyson assures us that the Iron Duke never lost a cannon, not
much else in the 281-line poem is memorable. With splendid tact, Whitman
avoids praising Lincoln's victory over his own countrymen, and creates an elegy of
206 lines worthy of comparison with Milton's "Lycidas" and Shelley's *Adonais*.

Like Eliot's *The Waste Land,* its unacknowledged descendant, "Lilacs" is an
elegy for the poet's own self. A Lucretian elegy is an oxymoron, yet Whitman—
with Shakespeare and Milton—defies all orderly forms and genres. Whitman
disliked being told that "Lilacs" was the height of his achievement. "Song of
Myself" has to be that since the supreme fiction of "Walt Whitman" is fully
achieved there and nowhere else. And yet "Lilacs" is the most fully worked-
through poem by any American down to this moment. Exquisite in its propor-
tions, it has the advantage of coming after "The Sleepers," "Crossing Brooklyn
Ferry," "Out of the Cradle," and "As I Ebb'd," all of them reprised in a finer
tone. Last year I lay five months in the hospital with a broken back and other
maladies, and lost myself day after day reciting "Lilacs" to myself soundlessly. I
possess it now by more than memory since in part it was the angel of my modest
resurrection. Is it altogether an illusion that it shares in the healing power that
Whitman exercised as a volunteer nurse and wound-dresser in the Civil War

hospitals of Washington, D.C.? I found and will go on finding an astonishing beauty in the quietude of section 3:

In the dooryard fronting an old farm-house near the white-wash'd palings,
Stands the lilac-bush tall-growing with heart-shaped leaves of rich green,
With many a pointed blossom rising delicate, with the perfume strong I love,
With every leaf a miracle—and from this bush in the dooryard,
With delicate-color'd blossoms and heart-shaped leaves of rich green,
A sprig with its flower I break.

This is the breaking of the tally. Whether Whitman knew the Sufi poetry of Persia I doubt, but he carried on its tradition of associating the lilac with masculine eroticism. The star Venus, the sprig of lilac, and the song of the hermit thrush fuse in a composite tally, an image of voice that *is* this poem. Lincoln's coffin, with its long procession from Washington, D.C., to Chicago, binds much of the text together, but the martyred president is hardly invoked until he is termed his nation's "sweetest, wisest soul" three lines from the poem's conclusion.

Whitman's most telling verb, here as elsewhere, is *passing,* and his superbly apt phrase, "retrievements out of the night," came to him as a revisionary afterthought:

Passing the visions, passing the night,
Passing, unloosing the hold of my comrades' hands,
Passing the song of the hermit bird and the tallying song of my soul,
Victorious song, death's outlet song, yet varying ever-altering song,
As low and wailing, yet clear the notes, rising and falling, flooding the night,
Sadly sinking and fainting, as warning and warning, and yet again bursting
    with joy,
Covering the earth and filling the spread of the heaven,
As that powerful psalm in the night I heard from recesses,
Passing, I leave thee lilac with heart-shaped leaves,
I leave thee there in the door-yard, blooming, returning with spring.

I cease from my song for thee,
From my gaze on thee in the west, fronting the west, communing with thee,
O comrade lustrous with silver face in the night.

Yet each to keep and all, retrievements out of the night,
The song, the wondrous chant of the gray-brown bird,

And the tallying chant, the echo arous'd in my soul,
With the lustrous and drooping star with the countenance full of woe,
With the holders holding my hand nearing the call of the bird,
Comrades mine and I in the midst, and their memory ever to keep, for the
    dead I loved so well,
For the sweetest, wisest soul of all my days and lands—and this for his dear
    sake,
Lilac and star and bird twined with the chant of my soul,
There in the fragrant pines and the cedars dusk and dim.

[section 16]

What—if he read it closely—would the Tennyson of 1866 have made of this
threnody? It challenges him in his own mode of Vergilian elegy, and the final
line so usurps his tone as to make him seem a belated imitator of Whitman.
Vergil, Tennyson, and Whitman are bound together by the Epicurean Lucretius. A step beyond Tennyson's sensibility and you are in the total thinking-
by-sensation of more radical Keatsians than Tennyson—the Pre-Raphaelites,
Pater and Wilde, and the young Wallace Stevens.

Since Swinburne, like Whitman, tends to fuse the elegiac and the celebratory, I
turn to the conclusion of "Ave Atque Vale," the (premature) elegy for Baudelaire:

> For thee, O now a silent soul, my brother,
>   Take at my hands this garland, and farewell.
>   Thin is the leaf, and chill the wintry smell,
> And chill the solemn earth, a fatal mother,
>   With sadder than the Niobean womb,
>   And in the hollow of her breasts a tomb.
> Content thee, howsoe'er, whose days are done;
>   There lies not any troublous thing before,
>   Nor sight nor sound to war against thee more,
> For whom all winds are quiet as the sun,
>   All waters as the shore.

[188–98]

Wallace Stevens's late "Madame La Fleurie" returns us to this solemn earth,
fatal mother and tomb:

Weight him down, O side-stars, with the great weightings of the
    end.
Seal him there. He looked in a glass of the earth and thought he
    lived in it.
Now, he brings all that he saw into the earth, to the waiting parent.
His crisp knowledge is devoured by her, beneath a dew.

The Pre-Raphaelite colorings in Stevens's early *Harmonium* poems probably
derive from Swinburne, in a curious assimilation of the British poet to Whitman, whom Swinburne had alternately admired and reviled. A common strain
of Lucretianism enabled the assimilation, though of the three poets it is Stevens who is the most Epicurean. Although Stevens declined to admit Pater's
influence, it is palpable enough. He would not owe to Pater, or to anyone, the
pleasures of priority in perception. Still, to think by seeing, to apprehend by
sensation, is to inhabit the imaginative cosmos of Epicurus and Lucretius,
where Shelley, Swinburne, and Whitman had moved and had their being before Stevens.

Rather than repeat elaborate commentaries that I have devoted to Stevens's
major long poems and sequences, I will look at his final swerve from a materialist metaphysic in his death poem "Of Mere Being," where the title's modifier
takes its archaic meaning of "pure" or unadulterated, with perhaps a touch
of its root, "flickering." The poem, possibly Stevens's last, was written just
before he left for hospital surgery in April 1954. Yeats's Byzantium poems, a
perpetual challenge to Stevens as to James Merrill after him, are being fended
off in Stevens's final vision:

> You know then that it is not the reason
> That makes us happy or unhappy.
> The bird sings. Its feathers shine.
>
> The palm stands on the edge of space.
> The wind moves slowly in the branches.
> The bird's fire-fangled feathers dangle down.

In a squib, "Memorandum" (1947), Stevens had intoned, not very elegantly:

> Say that the American moon comes up
> Cleansed clean of lousy Byzantium.

Much subtler at cleansing away Yeats, "Of Mere Being" "beyond the last thought" sees cognitively a phoenixlike bird rising in the palm tree, emblem of Stevens's Florida, "venereal soil." This also seems the "Palme" of Paul Valéry, a contemporary whom Stevens preferred to Yeats. Here are the final three of "Palme"'s nine stanzas, miraculously transported into English by James Merrill:

> These days which, like yourself,
> Seem empty and effaced
> Have avid roots that delve
> To work deep in the waste.
> Their shaggy systems, fed
> Where shade confers with shade,
> Can never cease or tire,
> At the world's heart are found
> Still tracking that profound
> Water the heights require.
>
> Patience and still patience,
> Patience beneath the blue!
> Each atom of the silence
> Knows what it ripens to.
> The happy shock will come:
> A dove alighting, some
> Gentlest nudge, the breeze,
> A woman's touch—before
> You know it, the downpour
> Has brought you to your knees!
>
> Let populations be
> Crumbled underfoot—
> Palm, irresistibly—
> Among celestial fruit!
> Those hours were not in vain
> So long as you retain
> A lightness once they're lost;
> Like one who, thinking, spends
> His inmost dividends
> To grow at any cost.

Stevens read this as the fable of reimagining a lifetime given to the slow maturation of his own poetic gift. The bird sings an out-of-doors song that perhaps
belongs to the Epicurean divinities, devoid of human meaning and feeling.
What matters is that "The bird sings. Its feathers shine." Approaching the end,
one hears and one sees, without reasoning. As in Valéry's "Palme," lightness is
the one appropriate response, a final patience:

> The palm stands on the edge of space.

And yet we are not out of nature:

> The wind moves slowly in the branches.

That might be Valéry or one of a number of Lucretians, but the last line is mere
Stevens:

> The bird's fire-fangled feathers dangle down.

That charming gaudiness of "fire-fangled" playing against "dangle down" suggests a final swerve from Whitman's sunrise glory of self-fabrication. Whitman and Stevens express again the American difference by their formulation
of a Lucretian poetics distinct from that of Dryden, Shelley, Swinburne, and
Pater. Call it a poetics of the American Sublime, which Emerson invented,
Whitman brought to a celebratory glory, and Wallace Stevens both mocked and
exemplified.

LEOPARDI'S LUCRETIAN SWERVE

Though his immediate agon was with Dante and Petrarch, the authentic Italian precursor of Giacomo Leopardi (1798–1837) was Lucretius, who for Dante did not exist. Amazingly erudite in nearly every Western language and literature, Leopardi valued Homer, Lucretius, and Rousseau over Dante, Petrarch, and Tasso. No Italian poet contemporary with Leopardi nor any since (not even Giuseppe Ungaretti, who revered Leopardi) is of his eminence. For another Romantic classicist one could turn to Walter Savage Landor as a worthy analogue, as he too could write like Simonides. In prose, Landor sometimes seems like Leopardi because they both derive from Lucian, but for poetry you need only the greatest of the Romantics as parallels: Friedrich Hölderlin, Victor Hugo, Wordsworth, Keats, Shelley. Of these, Shelley was the prime Lucretian, and he can exchange illuminations with Leopardi more fecundly than do Keats and Hölderlin. The Victorian poet James Thomson ("The City of Dreadful Night") fuses Shelley, Novalis, and Leopardi. I am surprised that Leopardi did not mean more to Stevens (who had studied with George Santayana), but the Stevensian Mark Strand compensates for that with his splendid poem "Leopardi":

> The night is warm and clear and without wind.
> The stone-white moon waits above the rooftops
> and above the nearby river. Every street is still

and the corner lights shine down only upon the hunched shapes
    of cars.
You are asleep. And sleep gathers in your room
and nothing at this moment bothers you. Jules,
an old wound has opened and I feel the pain of it again.
While you sleep I have gone outside to pay my late respects
to the sky that seems so gentle
and to the world that is not and that says to me:
"I do not give you any hope. Not even hope."
Down the street there is the voice of a drunk
singing an unrecognizable song
and a car a few blocks off.
Things pass and leave no trace,
and tomorrow will come and the day after,
and whatever our ancestors knew time has taken away.
They are gone and their children are gone
and the great nations are gone.
And the armies are gone that sent clouds of dust and smoke
rolling across Europe. The world is still and we do not hear them.
Once when I was a boy, and the birthday I had waited for
was over, I lay on my bed, awake and miserable, and very late
that night the sound of someone's voice singing down a side street,
dying little by little in the distance,
wounded me, as this does now.

This is both a close and yet very free version, inflected by the symbolist poet
Jules Laforgue, of "La sera del dì di festa," translated here by Jonathan Galassi:

The Evening of the Holiday

The night is soft and bright and windless,
and the moon hangs still above the roofs
and kitchen gardens, showing every mountain
clear in the distance. O my lady,
now every lane is quiet, and night lights
glow in the windows only here and there.
You sleep, for sleep came easily to you
in your still room. No worry

troubles you, [nor do you know or think]
of what a wound you opened in my heart
You sleep, but I come to my window
to salute this sky which seems so kind,
and eternal, all-commanding nature
who created me for suffering.
I deny you hope, she told me, even hope;
your eyes will never shine except with tears.
Today was a holiday. Tonight you rest
from play, and maybe in your sleep
you dream of all the men you pleased today,
and those who pleased you, too; but I don't come to mind,
not that I hoped to. So I ask myself
what's left in life for me,
and fall down on the ground and rage, and shake.
Horrific days at such a tender age! Ah, on the road
not far from me I hear the lonely song
of the workman, coming late
from his evening out to his poor home,
and my heart is stricken
to think how everything in this world passes
and barely leaves a trace. Look, the holiday
is gone, the workday follows our day of rest, and time makes off
with everything that's human. Where's the clamor
of those ancient peoples? Where is the renown
of our famed ancestors, and the great empire
of their Rome, her armies, and the din
that she produced on land and sea?
Everything is peace and quiet now,
the world is calm, and speaks no more of them.
In my young years, in the time of life
when we wait impatiently for Sunday,
afterwards I'd lie awake unhappy,
and late at night a song heard on the road
dying note by note as it passed by
would pierce my heart the same way even then.

The Homeric and Vergilian cadences of Leopardi's poem, caught by Galassi, soften into one of Strand's most poignant meditations, almost a Tennysonian dramatic monologue, Vergil-like in its dying fall. Leopardi's genius tends to isolate the Lucretian element in Vergil, the universal sorrows of human limitation confronting the way things are. Strand, a Lucretian largely through natural temperament yet also mediated by Whitman and Stevens, subtly reworks Leopardi into our native strain. Galassi implicitly demonstrates the Lucretian swerve of Leopardi's Homer and Vergil.

In an early entry in his enormous *Zibaldone* (I prefer *Mish-Mash* to *Hodge-Podge*), Leopardi mounted to his superbly negative idea of the sublime:

> Works of genius have this in common, that even when they vividly capture the nothingness of things, when they clearly show and make us feel the inevitable unhappiness of life, and when they express the most terrible despair, nonetheless to a great soul—though he find himself in a state of extreme duress, disillusion, nothingness, *noia,* and despair of life, or in the bitterest and *deadliest* misfortunes (caused by deep feelings or whatever)—these works always console and rekindle enthusiasm; and though they treat or represent only death, they give back to him, at least temporarily, that life which he had lost.
>
> And so that which in real life grieves and kills the soul, opens and revives the heart when it appears in imitations or other works of artistic genius (as in lyric poems, which are not properly imitations). Just as the author, in describing and strongly feeling the emptiness of illusions still retained a great store of illusions—which he proved by so intensely describing their emptiness—so the reader, no matter how disenchanted *per se* and through his reading, is pulled by the author into that very illusion hidden in the deepest recesses of that mind the reader was experiencing. And the very recognition of the irremediable vanity and falseness of all things great and beautiful is itself a great and beautiful thing which fills the soul, when the recognition comes through works of genius. And the very spectacle of nothingness presented seems to expand the soul of the reader, to exalt it, and reconcile it to itself and to its own despair. (A tremendous thing and certainly a source of pleasure and enthusiasm—this magisterial effect of poetry when it works to allow the reader a higher concept of self, of his woes, and his own depressed, annihilated spirit.)

Moreover, the feeling of nothingness is that of a dead and death-producing thing. But if this feeling is alive, as in the case I mean, its liveliness dominates in the reader's mind the nothingness of the thing it makes him feel; and the soul receives life (if only briefly) from the very power by which it feels the perpetual death of things and of itself. Not the smallest or least painful effect of the knowledge of great nothingness is the indifference and numbness which it almost always inspires about that very nothingness. This indifference and insensibility is removed by reading or contemplating such a work: it renders us *sensible* to nothingness.

["Z"].

I think this is the Lucretian sublime, necessarily Homeric but deeply colored by Epicurean metaphysics. Leopardi shares this with Shelley and Whitman, Stevens and Crane, and it is brilliantly present in Mark Strand and Henri Cole, heirs of the American strain of Romantic sublimity. Only Leopardi, in prose and poetry alike, has captured the precise note of the Lucretian fiercely somber exuberance in a modern language. Certainly the strongest of Italian poets since Dante and Petrarch, Leopardi, like Wordsworth, is the inaugurator of modern poetry. Something that went from Homer and the Hebrew Bible on to Goethe and William Blake changed forever with Wordsworth and Leopardi.

Two Romantic visionaries hardly could be more different than are Leopardi and Wordsworth in temperament, belief, and hope. And yet they share (with no knowledge of the other's existence) the fundamental patterns of the High Romantic crisis-poem, in which the poet saves himself from acedia if only to write the next poem, to make it possible.

The deepest difference between Leopardi and Wordsworth might be called one of hope, not only personal but for the historical persistence of poetry. More like Hölderlin and Shelley, Leopardi is engaged in composing what might be called "the last poem." In twenty years of writing, Leopardi brought forth only forty-one poems, as incredibly sparse and revised a body of work as Crane's. Galassi compares the *Canti* to *Leaves of Grass*, yet the close parallel is to just "Song of Myself," Whitman being so vast. Still, Whitman and Crane have nothing like the *Zibaldone*, grand rival to Emerson's *Notebooks*, which together are the Sage of Concord's masterpiece. The *Zibaldone*—it could be argued—is Leopardi's ultimate contribution, except that the *Canti* inaugurates modern Continental poetry in the same way that Wordsworth begins a new English poetry and that Whitman defines what will be American about our poetry. Leopardi renders Victor Hugo, Charles Baudelaire, and Heinrich Heine belated. All post-Wordsworthian British poets are his ephebes whether they know it or not, and after Whitman our poets can react only for or against him, as even such adversaries as Eliot and Pound finally come home to him, in *The Dry Salvages* and *The Pisan Cantos*.

Galassi terms Leopardi a European Romantic in spite of himself, but all High Romanticism depends upon self-negation with the outrageous exception of Victor Hugo, who spoke as a god. For Leopardi as for Keats and D. H. Lawrence, the moon is the trope for male self-negation. What Leopardi refuses is the rhetoric of those who would "start with the sun" (Lawrence) and thus evade a conscious belatedness. Lawrence turned to Whitman for that, while Stevens more covertly found his poetry's solar source in the bardic chanter who gave us *Leaves of Grass*. Whitman aspired to be both a new Homer and an American Bible. Leopardi enshrined Homer and Lucretius as the poetry of the past and explored his belatedness in relation to them. His ancient Greek and his Latin (indeed, his Hebrew) were as fresh to him as Italian, and his return to such heroic precursors helped him to see Dante and Petrarch as being as much latecomer poets as himself. I would suggest that this strong stance exposes a considerable anxiety of influence toward the greatest Italian poets yet also indicates his powerful abilities for revising them into his own songs, as he triumphantly does.

Galassi and the Italian critic Nicola Gardini emphasize the trope of falling in Leopardi. I would amend that to a Lucretian clinamen: the agile Leopardi takes care to *swerve* as he falls. The West, including Italy, in Leopardi's vista has gone downward and outward since the fall of the Roman Empire. But the Lucretian poet's freedom is to swerve, the inclination being his own art. Leopardi, like Milton's High Romantic Satan, "falls oblique," and this swerve in the *Canti* is crucial to modern poetry. Freud, profoundly consonant with Epicurus, in *Beyond the Pleasure Principle* remarks that each individuality wishes to die only in its own fashion.

Leopardi disliked his cold Christian mother, and his imagery for the maternal is antipathetic to the highest degree. Nature in Leopardi is close to Blake's Female Will and is not at all Wordsworthian or Keatsian. Passionately heterosexual and yet involuntarily celibate, Leopardi most certainly was a "poet of problems," as Galassi calls him. Iris Origo in her sympathetic biography, *Leopardi: A Study in Solitude* (1953), says his life was over at twenty-one. He lived on another eighteen years, with only aesthetic consolations. One doubts that for him any fulfillment could have fulfilled. What Thomas De Quincey said of his friend Coleridge is yet truer of Leopardi: "He wanted better bread than can be made with wheat."

Though the prose usefully contextualizes the *Canti,* I am a little distrustful of such exegesis, since the poet Leopardi is and is not the writer of the *Zibaldone* and the misleadingly named *Moral Essays.* Both prouder and more vulnerably, the lyric poet bets the house of his spirit on the *Canti.* He wins, at a huge human cost.

Burdened by self-consciousness, Leopardi like Shelley wanted to forsake "the dark idolatry of self," yet both High Romantic agonists discovered that this was not possible. Walt Whitman instinctively knew otherwise. If the United States itself was the greatest poem, why should not "Walt Whitman, one of the roughs, an American" sing "Song of Myself"? The songs of Giacomo Leopardi had an appropriate place in post-Napoleonic Italy, where they testified to the survival of a singularity so intensely individual that states and factions faded into the silence.

Lucretius urged an end to all unrealities, religious and erotic illusions among others. Partly Leopardi absorbed the lesson, but the erotic illusion expired slowly and painfully. Coleridge, an offended Christian sage, remarked that "whatever in Lucretius is poetry is not philosophical, whatever is philosophical is not poetry." That is not my experience of reading Lucretius, and it was not Leopardi's. Lucretius scorns consolations: by temperament Leopardi needed them, yet by intellect he knew better. He arrived before Nietzsche at the emancipation of realizing that we possess poetry lest we perish of the truth. And well before the Nietzschean Wallace Stevens, Leopardi told us that the final belief was to believe in a fiction with the nicer knowledge that what you believe in is not true.

The moral heroism of Leopardi when juxtaposed with his solitude compels wonder and veneration. Lucretius, Shelley, and Stevens were married men, though not particularly happy ones, and all were free of financial stress. Nietzsche had the academic benefits of a medical retirement. Leopardi had virtually nothing except his genius, which could not gain him either patronage or more than a minimal public. I think of William Blake, but he had his loving wife, Catherine. With only a few other exceptions, John Clare among them, Leopardi was naked to the storm of reality. Walt Whitman never had a permanent companion until the final phase in Camden, where Horace Traubel tended him, just as Antonio Ranieri watched over Leopardi's last two years in Naples. Yet even those years were dark.

Out of them came his strongest poem, "Broom, or the Flower of the Desert," which I had regarded as untranslatable, but Galassi surpasses himself and gives us Leopardi as if he wrote in our own language. My old acquaintance Donald Carne-Ross, whose brief book on Pindar should be regarded as a classic, said that Milton alone could have Englished Leopardi, in the idiom of "Lycidas" and *Samson Agonistes*. Here is the final, rather Miltonic stanza of "Broom":

> And you, too, pliant broom,
> adorning this abandoned countryside
> with fragrant blossoms,
> you will soon succumb
> to the cruel power of subterranean fire
> which, returning to the place it knew before,
> will spread its greedy tongue
> over your soft thickets. And unresisting,
> your blameless head will bend under the deadly scythe,
> but never having bowed in vain till then,
> abject supplicant before
> your future oppressor, and never raised
> by senseless pride up to the stars
> or above the desert, which for you
> was home and birthplace
> not by choice, but chance.
> No, wiser and much less fallible than man,
> in that you did not believe
> your frail generations were immortal,
> whether due to destiny or yourself.

Fifteen years before "Broom" was composed, Leopardi made a note that no good poetry had ever been written about religion except Milton's. Dante, truly menacing precursor, hovers in the highly Lucretian "Broom" since it is a purgatorial poem, with Vesuvius taking Mount Purgatory's place. This great poem is both an (unwilling) homage to Dante and a fierce resistance to him, under the banner of Lucretius and Epicurus.

In 79 C.E. an eruption of Vesuvius destroyed the cities of Pompeii and Herculaneum, burying them under fiery ash. In the volcanic desert, the broom flowers, its recalcitrance dear to Italians. Echoing the first canto of *Purgatorio* with considerable irony, Leopardi tells his century that it dreams of a freedom that actually means a return to enslavement. Benedetto Croce found the anti-aesthetic Leopardi's descent into political rhetoric in "Broom," but it works the way Milton's polemic against the church operates in "Lycidas," as a countersong to elegy.

Book 1 of *De rerum natura* is invoked as we are called upon to confront our mortal destiny as outlined by Epicurus. Nature is dismissed as a wonder not to be lauded: "the truly guilty: she who is mother of mortals / in giving us birth, stepmother in wishing us ill." Galassi, perhaps remembering Hamlet's "take up arms against a sea of troubles," introduces the Shakespearean trope to Leopardi, as it were. This moves me to observe how alien to Leopardi is the English Romantic stance, Miltonic and Coleridgean, of the power of the poet's mind over a universe of death, in which Night, Death, the Mother, and the Sea yield to the imagination's freedom.

For Leopardi there is only the swerve, the limited freedom of the atoms to execute a clinamen as they fall. He confronts an empty sky beneath which any one of us is a speck whose freedom can be only a slight caprice. "Broom"'s magnificent last stanza hesitates on the verge of identifying Leopardi himself with the "pliant" desert flower. The broom is less infirm than humankind, borne out sharply in Galassi's translation of "fallible" for *inferma*. Falling is our perpetual condition, in the Epicurean and not the Christian sense.

Perhaps the central impression, if you stand back from Leopardi's poetry, is how sane and normative his vision of everyday human reality becomes. For a High Romantic poet, that is rare; only John Keats is analogous. Despite his pessimism—a source for Schopenhauer—Leopardi ruggedly is humanistic, benign, compassionate, unhappily wise. Compared to the self-conscious grandeur of Dante and Petrarch, Leopardi's gentle pride of aesthetic self-realization is very winning.

That was the person-in-the-poet, but the poet proper was fierce, as strong poets have to be in their agon with tradition. Though addicted to the ancients, the phrase-drunk Leopardi was the highly conscious inheritor of the immensely rich vernacular poetry of Italy: Dante, Guido Cavalcanti, Petrarch, Jacopo Sannazaro, Torquato Tasso. The spirit of Ludovico Ariosto had no appeal for the somber Leopardi, suspended between history and pastoral but impatient of comedy, except for the satiric Lucian.

Anyone who arrives after Dante and Petrarch scarcely can hope to make a third with them, yet that was the achievement of Leopardi. His difference from those titans cannot be defined adequately merely by his pervasive Lucretianism. You could argue that Homer was his favorite poet and Rousseau as much a spiritual guide as Epicurus. And still Lucretius gave him the clue to his saving difference from Dante and Petrarch. Lucretius and Homer, and Vergil to a lesser degree, were for Leopardi not the poetry of the past (Dante and Petrarch) but of an ever-early recurrence, to which Leopardi assimilated himself. Poetry of the present was for Leopardi an oxymoron: for him there never was a present moment. Everything depended on how you fell, since falling was the human condition. And just there was Leopardi's Lucretianism: you must fall, but freedom is in the swerve, in falling with a difference.

Blake, Byron, and Shelley partly learned the clinamen from Milton's Satan, but there is no Prometheanism in Leopardi, whose apprehension of the limits to human illusion mark nearly all his prose and poetry. In many respects his is an anticipation of Freud's Romantic rationalism. With an inevitable eloquence, Leopardi teaches us reality testing: how to make friends with the necessity of dying.

The grandest poets tend to be the most allusive. Some years ago, one of my best students, a young woman from Ancona (Leopardi country), told me that Leopardi, like Thomas Gray and T. S. Eliot, relied too much upon consciously modulated echoes of prior poets, sometimes concealed. She was accurate except that she underappreciated his almost Shakespearean power to transmute his echoes into the purest Leopardi. Like the English Romantics—Shelley in regard to Milton and Wordsworth, Keats in response to Shakespeare—the rhetorician in Leopardi mounts a transumptive or metaleptic scheme in which Dante and Petrarch return from the dead wearing Leopardi's own colors. Homer, Lucretius and Epicurus, Vergil join Leopardi in what Stevens called an "ever-ready candor," while Dante and Petrarch augment in belatedness.

Leopardi is a poet of questions, not answers, as Dante was. That too distances Dante and yet again brings the lyrical Leopardi closer to the dramatic Shakespeare. The late A. D. Nuttall, in our correspondence, continually returned to his insight that Shakespeare declined to be a problem-solver for anyone. Leopardi poignantly could not resolve the dilemmas of his own problematic existence. He could not find an exit from the literary labyrinth in which he lived, and suffered extraordinary anguish. Out of that purgatorial flame he uttered and polished the *Canti* and emerges forever as a poet worthy of the company of Pindar and Milton, Keats and Shelley, Yeats and Crane.

SHELLEY'S HEIRS

Browning and Yeats

For many years now, the teaching of Robert Browning has been an immense joy to me, and to some of the best of my students. I first taught Browning in 1956, in a graduate course on Tennyson and Browning. After more than a half-century, I still recall the challenge that the poet of *Men and Women* and *The Ring and the Book* constituted for my students (many of them older than me) and for myself. A difficult poet, Browning is now in the shadows, the age of the reader being past. To apprehend Browning, you need a vitalism that approaches the daimonic. Yeats, perpetually fascinated by Browning, feared him as an influence, and cautiously did not assign him to any of his phases of the moon in *A Vision*, though he meets the criteria both of Phase 16, the Positive Man, and of 17, the Daimonic Man. Positive Men are Blake, Rabelais, Pietro Aretino, and Paracelsus; the Daimonic are Dante, Shelley, and Walter Savage Landor (and Yeats himself). Browning, in Yeatsian terms, is on the border between Blake and Shelley, while Yeats is more firmly in Shelley's realm of internalized quasi-romance.

Shelley's *Alastor; or, The Spirit of Solitude,* his first considerable longer poem, swerves away from Wordsworth's Solitary in *The Excursion,* and becomes a new kind of poem. I will go further: *Alastor* begins a new kind of poetry, still with us in our Age of Ashbery, particularly to be seen in the recent work of Henri Cole, the inheritor of Wallace Stevens and Hart Crane, both of whom wrote versions of *Alastor* in "The Comedian as the Letter C" and "Voyages," respectively.

Keats, who kept Shelley at an emotional distance, nevertheless struggled personally against him in *Endymion*, which has a negating relationship to *Alastor*. Browning's first major poem, "Pauline," is a loving imitation of *Alastor*, and never was readable. The Yeatsian longer poem in the *Alastor* mode is very fine and deserves more readers than it currently has. *The Wanderings of Oisin* is so durable that its time may yet come, though reading long poems is now a rare phenomenon. *Sigurd the Volsung*, the marvelous verse saga of William Morris, has few readers that I ever have met, but I go back to it every year or so. Yeats, a superb critic of poetry (when it did not menace him) cared most for Morris's prose romances, yet admired *Sigurd the Volsung*.

Browning, Yeats's fellow Shelleyan, caused Yeats considerable ambivalence. In the haunting essay "The Autumn of the Body" (1898), Yeats blames the decline and fall of poetry upon the formidable trio of Goethe, Wordsworth, and Browning. Supposedly their poetry "gave up the right to consider all things in the world as a dictionary of types and symbols and began to call itself a critic of life and an interpreter of things as they are." Matthew Arnold implicitly is thus blamed on Goethe, Wordsworth, and Browning, which is neither fair nor convincing. And yet Yeats admired Browning's dramatic lyrics and monologues. The dramatic monologue did not become a Yeatsian form, but there are remarkable affinities between "Abt Vogler" and "Byzantium" as dramatic lyrics, and "'Childe Roland to the Dark Tower Came,'" though an extraordinary monologue, illuminated the mystery of "Cuchulain Comforted."

Alastor's appeal to poets (including an unacknowledged attachment by the young T. S. Eliot) always was that it set a paradigm for what the eighteenth century called the incarnation of the poetic character. Shelley's young Poet (clearly a self-portrait) embarks alone on a symbolic voyage, questing for the visionary shape of a woman, a destructive muse of his own solipsistic creation. Nature takes its revenge on the Poet by stalking him with his *alastor* (ancient Greek for a hostile spirit), who in Shelley is the Poet's own principle of solitude, his shadow or daimon. Shelley's Poet wastes away and dies, a fate the young Shelley expected soon for himself from a tuberculosis that, in fact, he did not have. His friend, the classical ironist and satirical novelist Thomas Love Peacock, tells us that he cured the visionary poet by a diet of well-peppered mutton chops in defiance of Shelley's vegetarian faith.

Yeats, unlike Browning, did not need to deny a parent by his Shelley obsession. Indeed, he had been introduced to Shelley's poetry by his Bohemian painter father, John Butler Yeats. But Browning briefly was converted to Shel-

leyan "Atheism" until his fiercely Evangelical mother told him to choose between his hero-poet and herself. Mother love prevailed, and a sense of self-
betrayed integrity became a permanent feature of Browning's poetry from the
early *Alastor*-like "Pauline" on to his mature, supposedly objective dramatic
lyrics and dramatic monologues.

Browning wrote little critical prose. His most important effort was "An Essay
on Percy Bysshe Shelley," a foreword to an 1852 edition of spurious letters that
Shelley could not and would not have written. Nevertheless, Browning's essay
remains remarkable, and was an abiding influence upon Yeats, who echoed
three crucial passages:

> We may learn from the biography whether his spirit invariably saw and
> spoke from the last height to which it had attained. An absolute vision
> is not for this world, but we are permitted a continual approximation
> to it, every degree of which in the individual, provided it exceed the
> attainment of the masses, must procure him a clear advantage. Did the
> poet ever attain to a higher platform than where he rested and exhib-
> ited a result? Did he know more than he spoke of?
>
> [Browning, "An Essay on Percy Bysshe Shelley"]

> We write of great writers, even of writers whose beauty would once
> have seemed an unholy beauty, with rapt sentences like those our
> fathers kept for the beatitudes and mysteries of the Church; and
> no matter what we believe with our lips, we believe with our hearts
> that beautiful things, as Browning said in his one prose essay that
> was not in verse, have "lain burningly on the Divine hand," and that
> when time has begun to wither, the Divine hand will fall heavily on
> bad taste and vulgarity. When no man believed these things William
> Blake believed them.
>
> [Yeats, "William Blake and the Imagination" (1897)]

> The auditory of such a poet will include, not only the intelligences
> which, save for such assistance, would have missed the deeper mean-
> ing and enjoyment of the original objects, but also the spirits of a like
> endowment with his own, who, by means of his abstract, can forthwith
> pass to the reality it was made from, and either corroborate their im-

pressions of things known already, or supply themselves with new
from whatsoever shows in the inexhaustible variety of existence
may have hitherto escaped their knowledge. Such a poet is properly
the ποιητής, the fashioner; and the thing fashioned, his poetry, will
of necessity be substantive, projected from himself and distinct.

[Browning, "An Essay on Percy Bysshe Shelley"]

The first of these reflects Browning's sense of personal betrayal, in contrast
to Shelley's remorseless integrity, while the second gives the palm to Shelley's
subjectivity in preference to what Browning regarded as his own hard-won
objectivity. In the third passage, which is as knotty as a Browningesque poem,
we hear a defense of his own achievements in "objectivity," which Yeats was
too shrewd an *antithetical* quester altogether to believe. Browning's strongest
poems—"'Childe Roland to the Dark Tower Came,'" "Andrea del Sarto," "Fra
Lippo Lippi," among others—are as subjective as "Pauline." They too are fragments of a great confession.

Why did the exuberantly optimistic Browning, characterized by Gerard Manley Hopkins as "bouncing Browning," create a portrait gallery of self-ruined
monomaniacs, charlatans, voluntary failures, and suicidal grotesques? I once
believed that Browning, on some level of consciousness, was expiating for the
failure in will when he yielded to his mother's Evangelical outrage, but that now
seems simplistic. Browning inwardly was a daimon, in rather the way that Ibsen
was a troll. Preternatural energies surged in Browning, who was in many ways
far more subjective than was his beloved Shelley, an intellectual skeptic. Head
and heart opposed one another in Shelley; I am uncertain that I can distinguish
intellect from emotion anywhere in Browning's greater poems.

Shelley is the English lyric poet proper: his progeny—Browning, Yeats,
Thomas Hardy—cannot be characterized as lyricists, since even the early Yeats
aspired to write esoteric and occult scriptures. To find a Shelleyan lyric poet
of magnitude, I go to Hart Crane, a Pindaric rhapsode who conveys Shelley's
incantatory style into the twentieth century. Browning in that century was followed by Ezra Pound and the early T. S. Eliot as dramatic monologists. In my
own generation Browning's legacy was sustained by the late Edgar Bowers and
Richard Howard.

In teaching Browning these days, I frequently find that half my class falls
in love with his work while the other half remains puzzled by my passionate

insistence that Browning and Whitman are the major poets in the language after the High Romantics, surpassing even Yeats and Stevens. The resistance to Browning goes back to some of his contemporaries, including Hopkins, who was fascinated and frightened by Whitman, who seemed to the Jesuit poet his own self unmasked. For the ordinarily astute Hopkins, Browning was not even a poet. Oscar Wilde agreed, but added that Browning was "the most supreme writer of fiction, it may be, that we have ever had." As a creator of character, Browning approached Shakespeare. Wilde, being Oscar, could not forbear from going on to a famous observation: "The only man who can touch the hem of his garment is George Meredith. Meredith is a prose Browning, and so is Browning. He used poetry as a medium for writing in prose."

Character criticism in regard to Shakespeare went out of fashion after A. C. Bradley, despite a noble last stand by Harold Goddard and my own more recent efforts to revive the spirits of Maurice Morgann and Goddard. Even so I am surprised that the best Browning criticism these days retreats from his genius at creating men and women. Though I need to add that the grandest Shakespearean characters—Falstaff, Hamlet, Iago, Lear, Macbeth, Cleopatra—are of a different order from Browning's strongest: the Pope in *The Ring and the Book*, Fra Lippo Lippi, Andrea del Sarto, the voice that incants "'Childe Roland to the Dark Tower Came,'" and Caliban. The Browning personae are antiphonal voices, but not quite human beings. If that inevitably is a limitation, it also is so odd an originality as to defy immediate classification. We learn the nature of these voices but not their status on any scale of being.

The most troubling of them is the reciter of "'Childe Roland to the Dark Tower Came,'" who is never identified with Roland, but for convenience I will call him that. The poem has been an obsession for me since I was twelve, and nearly seven decades later I cannot speak it out loud to myself without freshly losing myself in becoming Roland. Part of the awesome power of this monologue that weirdly is also a quest-romance is the tension induced in the sensitive reader. It is difficult not to identity with Roland and yet we become skeptical of what he tells us he sees. If we rode by his side, would we observe what he says is there?

Any poem is a fiction of duration: what is the lapsed time from the start to the end of this trek to the Dark Tower? What is the distance the Childe (candidate for knighthood) traverses? Thirty-four six-line stanzas of controlled phantasmagoria in the present tense could chronicle a considerable journey, but not here. In stanza 8 Roland turns aside from highway to path and, without initial recognition, arrives at the Dark Tower in stanza 30. Through many years of reciting and meditating upon the poem one comes to understand that the reading time of 8 to 30 is longer than the duration of Roland's self-tormented trial by landscape. Distorting and breaking everything he believes he views, Roland also transforms a brief space-time continuum into something all but interminable.

No other poem by Browning is like this on its surface, except for the magnificent late chant "Thamuris Marching," which is a point-for-point undoing of Roland's self-mystification. "On its surface," because Roland has deep affinities with other monomaniac failed consciousnesses in Browning, ranging from the tomb-ordering Bishop to the masochistic perfectionist Andrea del Sarto and on to the self-exalter Cleon and the grotesque Caliban. No single classification embraces Browning's ruined psyches, but none is so remorseless, frightening, and yet at last triumphant as Childe Roland.

Everything about Roland's monologue is equivocal, including the dauntlessness with which it closes. Browning composed the poem in a single day, an adventure that goes on astonishing me. Was it a powerful return of the repressed, to utilize a classical Freudian trope? I am wary of interpreting the poem yet once more, since I have published half a dozen readings of it across the past thirty-five years, and time must have a stop. Another way into the poem is to ask myself for an explanation of why it continues to obsess me.

Like everyone I have known well, I tend to overprepare desired events, a praxis doomed never to work. The fortunate is a category that *happens,* by surprise, but Roland's career is a misfortune. Think of a friend or good acquaintance whose description of a journey or an encounter you have learned never to trust. Either she lives in a phantasmagoria or she lies against time and so is a poet, or both together.

Roland's first crisis is his vision of the blind horse in stanzas 13–14:

> As for the grass, it grew as scant as hair
>   In leprosy; thin dry blades pricked the mud
>   Which underneath looked kneaded up with blood.
> One stiff blind horse, his every bone a-stare,
> Stood stupefied, however he came there:
>   Thrust out past service from the devil's stud!
>
> Alive? he might be dead for aught I know,
>   With that red gaunt and colloped neck a-strain,

> And shut eyes underneath the rusty mane;
> Seldom went such grotesqueness with such woe;
> I never saw a brute I hated so;
> He must be wicked to deserve such pain.

The quester's reaction is that of a very young child left alone with a grievously injured kitten. Shutting his own eyes, Roland turns inward only to confront memories of two disgraced knights, his friends and companions. The Dead March resumed, its deformed imagery "breaks" in the Yeatsian sense of the word in "Byzantium" (both mar and create): "Break bitter furies of complexity, / Those images that yet / Fresh images beget." Roland's marred creation becomes his Gnostic heterocosm, an agonized intensity that precipitates the poem's second and final crisis of stanzas 30–31:

> Burningly it came on me all at once,
>> This was the place! those two hills on the right,
>> Crouched like two bulls locked horn in horn in fight;
> While to the left, a tall scalped mountain . . . Dunce,
> Dotard, a-dozing at the very nonce,
>> After a life spent training for the sight!

> What in the midst lay but the Tower itself?
>> The round squat turret, blind as the fool's heart,
>> Built of brown stone, without a counterpart
> In the whole world. The tempest's mocking elf
> Points to the shipman thus the unseen shelf
>> He strikes on, only when the timbers start.

Few lines in the world's strongest poetry reverberate with so much power as that rhetorical question: "What in the midst lay but the Tower itself?" At once commonplace and unique (to him), Roland's Dark Tower emanates from Shelley's *Prince Athanase,* which also brought forth Yeats's "The Tower," where the Archpoet comes to terms with himself. Browning here surpasses both Shelley and Yeats because Roland achieves a pitch of heroic self-acceptance unmatched except for Shakespeare's tragic hero-villains, Hamlet and Macbeth in particular. The final stanza is extraordinary, even for Browning upon his heights:

> There they stood, ranged along the hill-sides, met
>> To view the last of me, a living frame

> For one more picture! in a sheet of flame
> I saw them and I knew them all. And yet
> Dauntless the slug-horn to my lips I set,
>   And blew. *"Childe Roland to the Dark Tower came."*

The "sheet of flame," for readers informed by Romantic tradition, is stationed between Shelley's "the fire for which all thirst" in *Adonais,* and Yeats's Condition of Fire in *Per Amica Silentia Lunae* and *A Vision.* Addressing the elements in his "Ode to the West Wind," Shelley concluded by joining himself to the wind. "Be through my lips to unawakened earth // the trumpet of a prophecy!" Whether Childe Roland's "Dauntless the slug-horn to my lips I set, / And blew" alludes to Shelley is unknowable, but the two moments resemble one another more than either reflects the *Chanson de Roland*'s three blasts of the trumpet at Roncesvalles. Browning's desperate aspirant for knighthood is scarcely a poet-prophet. They are sparse in English—Milton, Blake, Shelley, Whitman, Lawrence, Crane. Browning, like Yeats and Stevens afterward, ironically dramatized himself out of so visionary a company.

Yet Childe Roland is neither an involuntary nor an intentional parody of Shelley. Browning has accepted himself too thoroughly for that, and the tense of his memorable nightmare of a poem pays overt homage to Shelley's "Ode" by maintaining itself in the present. If Childe Roland indeed is experiencing "the last of me," he is not so much dying as being caught up in the same "sheet of flame" his precursors are. Yeats mentions or echoes many poems by Browning, but I do not recall that "'Childe Roland to the Dark Tower Came'" is among them. Nevertheless I cannot meditate upon the Yeatsian Condition of Fire without thinking also of Browning's ruined and ruining candidate for knighthood.

In 1882, Yeats was seventeen, his consciousness a continual sexual reverie haunted by images from Shelley's quest romances *Alastor* and *Prince Athanase.* Yeats's own earliest poems, to be found now in the Variorum edition of his poetry, could be Shelley's. They employ Shelley's two prime figures, the Poet of *Alastor*/hero of *Prince Athanase,* and Ahasuerus the Wandering Jew of *Hellas.* In his *Autobiographies* the aging Yeats called these his two prime self-images: "In later years my mind gave itself to gregarious Shelley's dream of a young man, his hair blanched with sorrow, studying philosophy in some lonely tower, or of his old man, master of all human knowledge, hidden from human sight in some shell-strewn cavern on the Mediterranean shore."

These are Yeats's two *antithetical* questers. Yeats had borrowed *antithetical*, or the anti-natural, from Nietzsche by assimilating the German perspectivist to Blake. Shelley always remained Yeats's archetype of the lyric poet, and the Anglo-Irish reactionary, who was even quasi-fascist in his views, nevertheless went on identifying himself with the English visionary of the permanent left. Both poets turned every other literary mode into lyric, from the revolutionary drama *Prometheus Unbound* (the first of Yeats's "Sacred Books") to Yeats's beautiful misprision of the Noh plays in *At the Hawk's Well* and *The Only Jealousy of Emer.*

Theodor Adorno might have been thinking of Shelley and Yeats rather than of the so-called modernists when in his pungent "On Lyric Poetry and Society" he said of the lyric that it was both the (illusory) embodiment of perfected voice and also the consequence of the isolation of the artist in capitalist society. I myself think this Marxist myth of isolation, even in the subtle Adorno, can be dismissed through the dialectics of Schopenhauer and of the early Wittgenstein in the *Tractatus,* in his observation that what the solipsist *says* is irony but what he *means* is right. The Shelleyan-Yeatsian, Whitmanian-Stevensian poet, who was best embodied in the twentieth century by Hart Crane rather than by T. S. Eliot, intended a realism beyond philosophical idealism, Platonic or Hegelian, despite his only apparent solipsism. Adorno, still a lingering Hegelian, like all Marxists, was interested (as R. Clifton Spargo noted) in contemporary socio-political exclusions by the lyric cry. What matters more is the lyrical protest against time and time's "it was," in Nietzsche's plangent formulation. The lyric of Yeats takes up a stance *within* Shelley's stance but turned against the precursor. Yeats played at an idealist system in his Hermetic *A Vision,* but his grim accuracy in calibrating the loss and gain of relying upon Romantic tradition validates Shelley's own precision in realizing the profit and loss of inheriting from Milton and from Wordsworth.

Shelley's identification with Shakespeare's Ariel was a wistful gesture at escaping his historical dilemma. Yeats, unwilling to accept belatedness, troped history and the dead poets into his occult symmetries in *A Vision.* Despite its frequently beautiful Paterian prose, *A Vision* matters mostly because it gave Yeats metaphors for the great mythopoeic poems of his strongest volumes, *The Tower* and *The Winding Stair.* Though scholarship sometimes lags in seeing and saying this, both books are Shelleyan in mode, though hardly in political attitudes.

What Yeats always owed to Shelley was the idea of the poem: not the lyric cry but the cry of the human. Though Wallace Stevens may have been unaware of how much he took from Shelley and Whitman, *his* "fiction of the leaves" fuses together both prime precursors. In *A Vision,* Yeats oddly places together in his Phase 17 three rather different poets: Dante, Shelley, and Walter Savage Landor. Unmentioned but evident, this is the poet Yeats's own place, so that he makes a fourth with them. The place is the daimon's, and Yeats regards Dante, Shelley, Landor, and himself as instances of "the *Daimonic* Man," who at his best possesses a Paterian imagination—"simplification through intensity"—but who courts the aesthetic disaster of "Dispersal." When such a man's mind works with true creativity, it is "through *antithetical* emotion," but the biographical consequence is likely to be the enforcement of self-realization by loss of love.

Landor, a poet of classical restraint, is there as personal puzzle since unlike Yeats he did "invite a marmoreal Muse." Dante doubtless had been in the place where the daimon is, but Yeats's description of his own phase keeps Shelley in mind throughout. As was appropriate, Yeats's misreading of Shelley (and of Blake) became progressively stronger, and resulted in some of the most powerful (if sometimes incoherent) poems of the twentieth century. The most famous is "The Second Coming," which set the style for an age that still continues.

Despite its closing line, this should be called "The Second Birth" since it celebrates the Second Coming of the Egyptian sphinx and not of Christ. Ultimately Yeats's starting point had to be Shelley's rugged sonnet "Ozymandias":

> I met a traveller from an antique land
> Who said: Two vast and trunkless legs of stone
> Stand in the desert . . . Near them, on the sand,
> Half sunk, a shattered visage lies, whose frown,
> And wrinkled lip, and sneer of cold command,
> Tell that its sculptor well those passions read
> Which yet survive, stamped on these lifeless things,
> The hand that mocked them, and the heart that fed:
> And on the pedestal these words appear:
> "My name is Ozymandias, king of kings:
> Look on my works, ye Mighty, and despair!"
> Nothing besides remains. Round the decay
> Of that colossal wreck, boundless and bare
> The lone and level sands stretch far away.

Ozymandias is another name for Ramses II of Egypt (thirteenth century B.C.E.), whose colossal tomb at Memphis was in the shape of a male sphinx, a lion body with the head of a man. The Theban sphinx, Riddler and Strangler, overcome by Oedipus, had the head of a woman. Yeats, a late Pre-Raphaelite, followed Swinburne and Wilde in seeing the Oedipal female sphinx as the muse of sado-masochistic self-destruction. This was the sphinx of Yeats's Tragic Generation, his friends the poets of the 1890s: Ernest Dowson, Lionel Johnson, Arthur Symons, Victor Plarr. But Yeats's vision of Oedipus is unlike any other I know. Contrary to his few peers in twentieth-century poetry in English—Wallace Stevens, D. H. Lawrence, Hart Crane—Yeats had no interest in the Freudian version of Oedipus. Indeed, I have never found even a single mention of Freud in Yeats's vast writings, though there are curious analogues between Yeats's uncanny system and Freud's. Evidently, the founder of psychoanalysis never encountered the work of the great Anglo-Irish poet and occultist, but Freud's obsession with telepathy and the paranormal would have been gratified by the supposedly nonrational Yeats. Admirers of Yeats who idolize him chide me for my skepticism, but redundantly. I am delighted by Yeats's canniness, and after some resistance he has opened me to his varieties of Gnosticism. Above all, he thinks magnificently in images, which he called picture-thinking, but which ought to be named, more traditionally, rhetorical thinking, akin to Shakespeare's—and Shakespeare, more than Hume or Wittgenstein, remains the greatest of thinkers.

A Vision, in its final version, begins with "A Packet for Ezra Pound," in which Yeats addresses Pound directly with marvelously new mythmaking concerning Oedipus:

> I send you the introduction of a book which will, when finished, pro-claim a new divinity. Oedipus lay upon the earth at the middle point between four sacred objects, was there washed as the dead are washed, and thereupon passed with Theseus to the wood's heart until amidst the sound of thunder earth opened, "riven by love," and he sank down soul and body into the earth. I would have him balance Christ who, crucified standing up, went into the abstract sky soul and body, and I see him altogether separated from Plato's Athens, from all that talk of the Good and the One, from all that cabinet of perfection, an image from Homer's age. When it was already certain that he must bring himself under his own curse did he not still question, and when an-swered as the Sphinx had been answered, stricken with the horror that is in *Gulliver* and in the *Fleurs du Mal,* did he not tear out his own eyes?

He raged against his sons, and this rage was noble, not from some
general idea, some sense of public law upheld, but because it seemed
to contain all life, and the daughter who served him as did Cordelia
Lear—he too a man of Homer's kind—seemed less attendant upon an
old railing rambler than upon genius itself. He knew nothing but his
mind, and yet because he spoke that mind fate possessed it and king-
doms changed according to his blessing and his cursing. Delphi, that
rock at earth's navel, spoke through him, and though men shuddered
and drove him away they spoke of ancient poetry, praising the boughs
overhead, the grass under foot, Colonus and its horses. I think that
he lacked compassion, seeing that it must be compassion for himself,
and yet stood nearer to the poor than saint or apostle, and I mutter to
myself stories of Cruachan, or of Crickmaa, or of the road-side bush
withered by Raftery's curse. What if Christ and Oedipus or, to shift
the names, Saint Catherine of Genoa and Michael Angelo, are the two
scales of a balance, the two butt-ends of a seesaw? What if every two
thousand and odd years something happens in the world to make one
sacred, the other secular; one wise, the other foolish; one fair, the
other foul; one divine, the other devilish? What if there is an arithme-
tic or geometry that can exactly measure the slope of a balance, the dip
of a scale, and so date the coming of that something?

"The Second Coming" (1919) was composed almost a decade before this, and
seems to inform those "two scales of a balance, the two butt-ends of a seesaw."
Yeats's Oedipus is hard to comprehend without intensely rhetorical thinking,
because Yeats projects him as a kind of poet's poet. Phase 15, a state of complete
beauty—"nothing is apparent but dreaming *Will* and the *Image* that it dreams"—
concludes more mysteriously than any other passage in *A Vision:* "Even for the
most perfect, there is a time of pain, a passage through a vision, where evil
reveals itself in its final meaning. In this passage Christ, it is said, mourned
over the length of time and the unworthiness of man's lot to man, whereas his
forerunner mourned and his successor will mourn over the shortness of time
and the unworthiness of man to his lot; but this cannot yet be understood."
The unnamed "successor" to Christ, the "new divinity," is Yeatsian Oedipus as
opposed either to Sophoclean Oedipus or the Hamlet-like Freudian Oedipus.
Curiously akin to Freud in this regard, Yeats was resentful and equivocal toward
Shakespeare. Yeats, in *A Vision,* follows Joyce in an Irish protest; he wishes for

the lost plays of Sophocles, and yet gives the struggle up when he admits that Shakespeare's personages are "more living than ourselves." Rightly, Yeats sees that in Shakespeare "human personality . . . burst like a shell." Nevertheless, Yeats selects Oedipus as the new God over Shakespeare's vitalists: Hamlet, Falstaff, Iago, Cleopatra.

There is no Yeatsian delusion that Oedipus was a historical personage: the incoming savage god, heralded by the rebirth of the Egyptian sphinx, is literary and mythological, as he should be. Yeats felt, with William Blake, that anything possible to be believed was an image of truth. But when Yeats said that Christ "went into the abstract sky," he also is being Blakean. The sky god is Jehovah-Urizen, the limiter with the compasses. Oedipus, who goes down into the earth to become an oracular god, is an ideal emblem of Phase 15: he is heroic, divine, tragic, and a supreme instance of gnosis. He is what the aged Yeats would have wished to be, an incarnate poem.

Yeats had, in the Freudian sense, an Oedipal relation to his own father, the Pre-Raphaelite painter John Butler Yeats, who taught his son the concept of Unity of Being. But how do you rebel against a Bohemian father who exiles himself to New York City, who cannot abide John Milton, and who urges you to preserve your creative freedom above all else? There is some recalcitrant, negative emotion in "The Second Coming," and it may be related to Yeats's divination of Oedipus.

I return to this shattering poem that more than triumphs over its own incoherence, and indeed exploits such sacred disorder. Why the Egyptian sphinx rather than the Greek? Because Yeats is thinking of Oedipus as he drafts what will become "The Second Coming," yet he strongly desires to exclude his "new divinity" from the poem. The motive may have been personal and familial, but it is also part of the fascination with what's difficult, endemic in Yeats's work. Oedipus and his Theban sphinx were too familiar in Yeats's ambiance because of Wilde and the Tragic Generation. Always in the wake of Pater's definition of Romanticism as "adding strangeness to beauty," the seer of "The Second Coming" turns instead to the sphinx of "Ozymandias," remembering that Shelley's "the hand that mocked them" plays upon two meanings of mocked: imitated by art and disdained. Shelley is interested in Rameses II as the type of tyranny, and the lion body is neglected. Though Yeats represses Oedipus, the lion moving his slow thighs intimates the sexual menace of the male sphinx, rough beast answering the seductiveness of the Tragic Generation's female Oedipal sphinx.

"The Second Coming," composed in January 1919, belatedly was regarded by

Yeats as a prophecy of fascism, whose representatives in Mussolini and Franco the poet was to support. There is a fascist flavor to Yeats's theology of his Oedipus, who is Western Man, free of Asiatic formlessness, and divinized so as to become free of our family romances. Like Christ, Oedipus is God's Son, though unlike Christ, the self-blinded Son need undergo no crucifixion.

No one should expect that Yeats's excursions into religion and history had any function beyond bringing him more audacious metaphors for his poems and plays. Goethe remarked that all poets, as poets, were polytheists, and Yeats never could have too many gods. Shelley the atheist perhaps made Eros his god, but *The Triumph of Life,* his death poem, catalogues the death of love for all of us. Blake insisted that all deities resided within us, and at life's end identified himself with "the Real Man, the Imagination," which is more suggestive of Wallace Stevens than of Yeats.

Announcing the advent of a new divinity was perpetually a Yeatsian pleasure, which is why the Archpoet is so much in his own place when he composes "The Second Coming," "Leda and the Swan," and "The Gyres." Influx of daimonic divinity into nature and the human tells us that we are in the Yeats country, which he finally named Byzantium. Yeats is a religious poet, but he professes the religion of poetry, in the allied modes of Shelley and Blake. The elite of the Western world dwell now in Yeats's country; the Evening Land is now as much Enlightened Europe as it is the New World. Only religion and metaphysics that have been made into great imaginative literature can now reach our remnant of deep readers.

"The Second Coming," however, is not religion made into strong poetry but poetry (Shelley and Blake) transfigured into Yeats's own apocalyptic genre. "The centre cannot hold" is Shelley's: "the stubborn centre must / Be scattered, like a cloud of summer dust" ("The Witch of Atlas"). Shelley's Witch *is* Imagination bidding farewell to love, since the dying generations are rejected by her and must perish with the earth.

I cannot think of another twentieth-century poem in any Western language that rivals "The Second Coming" in rhetorical power. Yeats's poem of violent annunciation is as fearfully relevant now as it was in January 1919, when it was composed. Many, myself included, meditated upon "the best lack all conviction, while the worst / Are full of passionate intensity," when the Twin Towers crumbled, killing three thousand innocents. We commit our own misprision upon Yeats, who would not have shared our horror. "The Second Coming" is a celebration of the rough beast, not a lamentation. Neither a Christian nor a humanist, Yeats was an apocalyptic pagan, who would have looked on and laughed in what he called "tragic joy." Like Shakespeare, and in another way like Blake and Shelley, Yeats renders all moralizing irrelevant to the aesthetic apprehension of reality. In *A Vision* we are told that "all imaginable relations may arise between a man and his God." Politically, Yeats was refreshingly outrageous, and hardly asked to be held responsible for his outbursts. His essay *On the Boiler* (1939) is a wild absurdity in which "the drilled and docile masses," if they do not submit, are to be rolled over by "the skilful, riding their machines as did the feudal knights their armoured horses." That is Yeats twenty years after "The Second Coming," yet the spirit is the same.

The occasion that provoked this apocalyptic poem was the 1918 Allied-sponsored invasion of Poland by the German Freikorps, intent upon breaking through Trotsky's Bolshevik army and ending the Russian Revolution. Eventually Trotsky won, and the outnumbered Freikorps fell back into Germany, where in time they supplied cadres for Hitler. Yeats's manuscript of "The Second Coming" begins with "The Germans are now to Russia come," which is revised out of the text. Inserted into the poem was its decisive change from "The Second Birth" of the Egyptian sphinx to its "Second Coming." This revision augments the poem's power at the cost of reducing its coherence, since the Second Coming of Jesus Christ is essentially irrelevant to it. Blake's Urizen, who will awaken from his "stony sleep" (Blake's phrase), is Yeats's reborn male sphinx. More subtly, Yeats transposes the lament of Shelley's Prometheus into a mordant observation from the right as against the Shelleyan left:

> The good want power, but to weep barren tears.
> The powerful goodness want: worse need for them.
> The wise want love; and those who love want wisdom;
> And all best things are thus confused to ill.

> [*Prometheus Unbound*, 1.625–28]

> The best lack all conviction, while the worst
> Are full of passionate intensity.

> ["The Second Coming," 7–8]

Shelley and Blake are utilized for a political vision they would have abhorred. But who can quarrel with Yeats's sublime misprision of his two prime precursors? His audaciously creative misreading *works*.

*   *   *

Precisely what Shakespeare thought of Marlowe's supposed atheism we never will know, yet surmise is possible and useful. Marlowe's God was rhetoric, the "pathetical persuasion" of his Tamburlaine. The poet-dramatist Shakespeare had no God and did not require one. He had a muse of fire, even as Yeats had a Condition of Fire. Shelley wrote of "the fire for which all thirst," and Blake's Los the Artificer molded his Forms in the Furnace of Affliction. The Yeatsian Condition of Fire counts all of these, and recasts them in the occult mode of the Cambridge Platonists, Henry More and Ralph Cudworth. In the most beautiful of his prose writings, *Per Amica Silentia Lunae,* Yeats gave a permanent voice to his transmemberment of his traditions: High Romanticism, with its aesthetic twilight in Walter Pater, and the rich but irrational esoteric doctrines of the spiritual alchemists of Neoplatonic and Hermetic lore. In the friendly silence of the moon, Yeats is free to approach a nearly total self-revelation, rendered with superb clarity and unencumbered by the harsh intricacies of *A Vision.*

I owe fundamental speculations on poetic influence to a sustained reading of *Per Amica Silentia Lunae* carried on as part of the long labor (1963–69) of writing a large exegesis, *Yeats* (1970). To this day I possess by memory most of Yeats's poetry as well as *Per Amica Silentia Lunae.* Meditating upon Yeats's reveries on Shelley and Blake crystallized for me the realization that the most fruitful poetic influence was a creative misreading or misprision. Today there is an unsettling mix of an estranged familiarity and a shock of the new in coming back to three poets I read and wrote about extensively from sixty to thirty years ago.

For Yeats the daimon was the "ultimate self" of each of us. This followed ancient tradition of which the daimon of Socrates was the culmination. Only Goethe, of the major Western poets, was as obsessed with the daimon as Yeats was. E. R. Dodds, in *The Greeks and the Irrational,* traces the idea of the daimon, or occult self, to Scythian shamanism, coming into Greece through Thrace. In European literary tradition, the daimon was understood to be the poet's alter ego, or genius. Yeats, eclectic and esoteric, followed Nietzsche's idea of the antithetical and employed it in conjunction with the daimonic to characterize poetic or anti-natural creation. The antithetical self simplifies through intensity, a mark of the Romantic imagination, particularly in Pater's reformulation of it.

Per Amica Silentia Lunae, more than *A Vision,* is Yeats's Book of the Daimon. A beautiful, original twist is given by Yeats to daimonic lore. The poet's daimon, or opposing self, is also his muse, the unattainable Irish beauty Maud Gonne. One can precisely call her Yeats's Genius, perpetually frustrating him into poetic greatness. As Yeats ruefully came to realize, nothing could have been worse for his poetry than marriage to Gonne. The desire that is satisfied never would have been authentic desire for the Shelleyan Yeats. I suspect that most of us, as we pass into old age, brood on lost love and unfulfilled desire. If we are not a Yeats or a Hart Crane, we merely study the nostalgias, and cannot compose "A Dialogue of Self and Soul" or "Voyages."

The grandest of all Yeatsian moments for me comes in *Per Amica Silentia Lunae:* "I shall find the dark grow luminous, the void fruitful when I understand I have nothing, that the ringers in the tower have appointed for the hymen of the soul a passing bell." Here the natural man, William Butler Yeats, and the antithetical quester perfectly fuse, as they rarely do even in his most magnificent poems. Yeats had remarked that the tragedy of sexual intercourse was the perpetual virginity of the soul. Touching the universal, Yeats unexpectedly becomes a wisdom writer, hardly his usual mode. What is it about the creation of *Per Amica Silentia Lunae* that liberated the poet into such austere clairvoyance?

The central trope of all of Yeats's writing is what he calls the Condition of Fire, a blend of Shelley, Blake, Pater, and esoteric traditions. As a metaphor, the Condition of Fire is almost too large to analyze into its components. Shelley's "the fire for which all thirst" is an exemplary instance of a conceptual image at the center of Neoplatonic speculation. The Condition of Fire is analogous to what Yeats calls "the place of the *daemon,*" which again embraces the universal: "I am in the place where the daemon is, but I do not think he is with me until I begin to make a new personality, selecting among those images, seeking always to satisfy a hunger grown out of conceit with daily diet; and yet as I write the words 'I select,' I am full of uncertainty not knowing when I am the finger, when the clay." This long, beautiful sentence, marked by a Paterian hesitancy, can be judged the culmination of the tradition of daimonic thought. Empedocles names our occult self as our daimon, "the carrier of man's potential divinity and actual guilt" (E. R. Dodds). Yeats's revisionary daimon returns to Empedocles, circumventing Socrates and Goethe, and transmutes the daimonic into the opposing self, in league with the destructive muse. The quest of Yeats increasingly becomes to be "in the place where the daemon is," a place usually occupied by the prime precursor, Shelley, from *Alastor* on to *Adonais.*

Yeats has so many permanent dramatic lyrics that no single one stands above scores of others. Still, it is not arbitrary to choose "Byzantium" as a signal triumph for Yeats in his endless, loving struggle with the composite influence upon him of Shelley and of Blake.

Four years separate the composition of "Sailing to Byzantium" and "Byzantium," utterly different poems about a city of the mind, caught in two visions, historically more than four centuries apart. "Sailing to Byzantium" seeks the Condition of Fire but only precariously attains it. "Byzantium" takes place wholly *within* the Condition of Fire, and in some respects celebrates it as an occult victory over nature.

"Sailing to Byzantium" indicates something of Yeats's poignant inability to free thought of its sexual past. Freud thought that the strongest psyches, guided by his principles, could get beyond moody broodings. Freud, I think, idealized: even the greatest poets—Dante, Shakespeare, Chaucer, Milton, Goethe—experienced no such liberation, which indeed would have beggared the *Commedia* and the best plays ever written.

In his sixties, Yeats is in the early autumn of the body, and in a prose draft reviews the sexual lovers of his lifetime, vowing to voyage from the country of the young and of his own ebbing vitality to a realm of ageless perfection. Yet he discovers that a flight from nature to Byzantium is not an *escape* from nature, since the "artifice of eternity" continues to depend upon natural forms. "Byzantium" is a very different and awesome poem, a kind of "Kubla Khan" for the twentieth century, together with Wallace Stevens's "The Owl in the Sarcophagus" and Hart Crane's "Voyages II." Like Coleridge's incantatory fragment, these are poems of an absolute cognitive music. We go to them for an aesthetic sensation we scarcely can find elsewhere.

The one time I met Wallace Stevens, he startled me by quoting from memory the stanza beginning "Men scarcely know how beautiful fire is," one of the glories of Shelley's most visionary long poem, "The Witch of Atlas." Yeats knew the poem at least as well as Stevens did, and "Byzantium" is an exalted misprision of Shelley's highly sophisticated mythopoeia, as well as of *Adonais* and certain apocalyptic passages of Blake.

In the terms of *A Vision,* Yeats places his poem in both Phase 1 and Phase 15, neither of them a human incarnation. The starlit dome is in the dark of the moon of Phase 1; the moonlit dome is in Phase 15, a state of complete beauty, even as Phase 1 features complete plasticity. Stationing "Byzantium" both as an aesthetic phenomenon of poetic images and as an emblem of an occult death-before-life gives Yeats an uncomfortable advantage over us, his readers. We simply cannot know where we are, and so we don't really know what the poet is talking about, and perhaps Yeats does not really know either. The rhetoric of "Byzantium" is pitched so high, its rhythms so wonderfully modulated, that we don't much care. With a poem so rich beyond measure, incoherence is no more a burden here than it need be in "The Second Coming."

Yeats was warming himself back into life after a severe illness. He hardly intended to write a premature elegy for his poetic self, but that edge gets into the poem. Willed phantasmagoria, on the part of a lesser poet, might annoy us, but the greatest poet since the High Romantics, Whitman, and Browning can do with us what he wants. Where else could such ecstatic cadences be uttered with audacity and authority, breaking though our rational skepticism and carrying us into the madness of art?

I remember remarking somewhere that Yeats was neither humane nor humanistic, unlike Stevens, his nearest rival in the past century. The human condition is savagely denigrated in "Byzantium." We are mere complexities of fury and mire, a rabblement scorned by Yeatsian artifices. This does not render "Byzantium" any less powerful as rhetoric or as vision, but it matters to me and perhaps to many other readers. Poetry need not be what Stevens called one of the enlargements of life, but the disparagement of the only existence we have may not be a legitimate aim of the sublime imagination.

The fascination of "Byzantium" is partly its difficulty. Read very closely and repeatedly, it also seems to me one of the modern triumphs of creative misreading, primarily of Shelley, whose voice and example never abandoned Yeats or Browning before him: Yeats's famous "official" death poem, "Under Ben Bulben," returns us to Shelley's "Witch of Atlas," and to a stanza that haunts "Byzantium."

> By Moeris and the Mareotid lakes,
>   Strewn with faint blooms like bridal chamber floors,
> Where naked boys bridling tame water-snakes,
>   Or charioteering ghastly alligators,
> Had left on the sweet waters mighty wakes
>   Of those huge forms—within the brazen doors
> Of the great Labyrinth slept both boy and beast,
> Tired with the pomp of their Osirian feast.

[505–12]

The Witch—who after all is not Shelley but the visionary consciousness as such—is close enough to Yeats's deprecation of human blood and mire. I recall observing that she gazes outward and downward to our cosmos from her Byzantium-like dome, whereas Yeats's perspective is inward and upward. She dwells perpetually in the Condition of Fire, akin to the burning fountain of *Adonais*. Her coldness seems to have fascinated Yeats, who cultivated her dispassionate attitude toward human suffering, particularly when he excluded the World War I poet Wilfred Owen from his *Oxford Book of Modern Verse*.

Stand back from "Byzantium" and you gain a perspective different from Yeats's Shelleyan vision, which is so consuming that it ironically naturalizes you in a poem that rejects nature. Yeats himself inhabits the poem only in the second of its five stanzas. Why? For that stanza's duration, "Byzantium" becomes a dramatic lyric rather than a doctrinal one of an esoteric variety. Yeats finds himself in the cathedral square confronting a floating image, presumably a Vergil to his Dante, but this appearance is not elaborated in the three remaining stanzas. Again I want to know why, and cannot find any persuasive answer.

Presumably that makes little difference since the remaining stanzas are breathtakingly brilliant, resembling in this passages abounding in *A Vision*, as in the description of Phase 15: "Now contemplation and desire, united into one, inhabit a world where every beloved image has bodily form, and every bodily form is loved." Whether we are in this Plotinian Phase 15, or in the plasticity of Phase 1, Yeats contrives to keep us in a wonder-wounded state of mind. How else to react to the sublime assault upon us of the fourth stanza:

> At midnight on the Emperor's pavement flit
> Flames that no faggot feeds, nor steel has lit,
> Nor storm disturbs, flames begotten of flame,
> Where blood-begotten spirits come
> And all complexities of fury leave,
> Dying into a dance,
> An agony of trance,
> An agony of flame that cannot singe a sleeve.

The now classical critical question concerning this is, "Are we contemplating the image in a poet's mind or are we being granted a vision of the life-before-birth?" Somehow both at once, Yeats desired us to believe. Composing this at sixty-five, with eight more years to live, Yeats was recuperating slowly from lung and Malta fever complications, and personal mortality necessarily became one of his major themes. "Byzantium," with beautiful indirection, becomes an elegy for the poetic self, following the example of *Adonais*, which vies with "The Witch of Atlas" as the direct precursors Yeats engages. Forty years ago, I was uncertain as to the poetic success of the engagement, but now at eighty, after several approaches to death, I do not hesitate to find "Byzantium" a victory of poetic misprision.

Yeats's explicit death poems can be said to begin with the heartening "At Algeciras—A Meditation upon Death" in *The Winding Stair*. They continue marvelously with "Vacillation" and culminate in two majestic meditations, "The Man and the Echo" and "Cuchulain Comforted." "The Black Tower" and the famous "Under Ben Bulben" are unworthy of the major poet of the twentieth century.

"Cuchulain Comforted" is an enigmatic masterpiece by any standard. It is difficult partly because it defiantly utilized the strict mythology of *A Vision* in contemplating the life after death. Cuchulain, the hero, encounters his opposites in the cowards, who like him are moving between death and eventual rebirth. Book 3 of *A Vision* divides this into six periods:

1) The Vision of the Blood Kindred
2) Meditation
3) Shiftings
4) Beatitude
5) Purification
6) Foreknowledge

The Vision of the Blood Kindred is simply a farewell to "the unpurged images of day." More complexly, the Meditation is divided in three: the Dreaming Back, the Return, the Phantasmagoria. In the Meditation the dead are granted a coherent image of their completed life. Yet this image emerges only through the Dreaming Back of the turbulent past. Phantasmagoria is followed by the Shiftings, in which all morality vanishes. This marriage of good and evil (in a rather weak misreading of Blake's *Marriage of Heaven and Hell*) leads on to the paradoxical Beatitude, at once unconsciousness and a consciously privileged moment. Perfection of the Spirit is the work of Purification, in which all complexities are dispelled. In the Foreknowlege, the timorous Spirit can delay its own rebirth, but only for a time, however lengthened.

In "Cuchulain Comforted" the cowardly Spirits approach the end of the Shiftings and enter Beatitude only in the famous last line of the poem: "They had changed their throats and had the throats of birds." Cuchulain, barely behind them, is passing out of the Meditation into the Shiftings. The spokesperson for the Shrouds or Spirits, who already are birdlike, urges Cuchulain to make his own shroud, and tells the hero that they are afraid of the rattle of the weapons he still bears. They know that rebirth is coming, when they will continue to be cowards.

Marvelously, Yeats does not permit Cuchulain to speak at any moment in the poem. The hero simply takes up the linen proffered him, and begins to sew his shroud. He thus joins himself to the community of cowards, whose fear of his notorious violence may be a prolepsis of their own loss of comradeship in the solitude of rebirth. That here, and in his uncompleted final drama, *The Death of Cuchulain,* Yeats merges into his hero is palpable and persuasive. What remains mysterious is his own stance toward his own cowardice, analogous to the silence of Cuchulain throughout the poem. "They had changed their throats and had the throats of birds" is certainly a subtle allusion to Dante's Brunetto Latini, who somehow is among the victors and not the defeated. But why does Yeats conclude his greatness with this surprising death poem?

There are no explicit allusions to the composite precursor Shelley-Blake in "Cuchulain Comforted," but Yeats's masters hover at its borders. Shelley would have admired this poem because, as he had urged Yeats, it is necessary to cast out remorse, and that is part of "Cuchulain Comforted"'s burden. Blake I think would have turned away from it because for him, death was just going out from one room into another, and mythologizing mortality was therefore alien to him.

I am not certain that even Yeats has a more impressive dramatic lyric than "Cuchulain Comforted." After glorifying violence throughout his later years, and flirting with Irish and European fascism, Yeats parts with Homeric and Old Irish heroism in this skilled and chastened Dantesque vision of judgment. Shelley, in his *Triumph of Life,* ended his poetic career at twenty-nine with an indirect critique of the *Commedia.* Blake, dying at seventy, had made his own searching critique in his remarkable illustrations of Dante. Yeats, at the end, had no quarrel with Dante, though the Irish Archpoet never was a Christian. "Cuchulain Comforted," to me, is one of the triumphs of the influence relationships between Yeats and the two poets he had absorbed most fully.

WHOSE CONDITION OF FIRE?

Merrill and Yeats

Some critics form fours, as Northrop Frye did in *Anatomy of Criticism* and elsewhere, following William Blake. Dante dealt in nines: Beatrice was the Lady Nine and the perfect human age was nine nines, the eighty-one years that her poet sought to attain—then, at last, he would have comprehended everything. He lived to finish the *Commedia,* Shakespeare's only true rival, but died, alas, at fifty-six, a quarter-century short of the age when, he believed, Jesus' body would have assumed eternal form in *this* life had he not been crucified at thirty-three.

Six, traditions say, is a "perfect" number, as is twenty-eight. I am unhappy with perfect numbers but cannot evade them. Six days of creation, via their Kabbalistic interplays, gave me six tropes I called "revisionary ratios" and turned into *A Map of Misreading* more than a third of a century ago. Starting with irony, considered as a Lucretian swerve or clinamen, I went on to synecdoche as the *tessera* (desire for recognition) of mystery cults and clearly Whitman's most characteristic rhetorical figure. The metonymy/metaphor division of Roman Jakobson, I rewrought as *kenosis/askesis,* the first an undoing measure and the second a perspectivizing maneuver. Between them came hyperbole, but conceived as a daimonic assertion of individual genius. To conclude the sequence I summoned metalepsis, or the metonymy of a metonymy, which I called by the ancient Athenian word *apophrades,* the unlucky (dismal) days when the dead returned momentarily to repossess their former homes.

My esoteric sixfold does have an odd way of showing up in a fair number of ambitious poems in the Romantic tradition, but, like all exegetical instruments, it is subject to abuse, and I have ceased to recommend it to my students or to anyone else. I regard it now as a purely personal dialectical dance, part of the Kabbalah of Harold Bloom. Possibly it reflects again my own copious anxieties of influence: Jewish traditions, Freud, Gershom Scholem, Kafka, Kierkegaard, Nietzsche, Emerson, Kenneth Burke, Frye, and above all the poets. In the labyrinth of *this* book it cannot provide a wished-for thread, since only Shakespeare and Whitman can do that for me.

In old age one wants to write the criticism of our climate, and this seems my last chance to do that. I take my lead from Walter Pater in his essay "Aesthetic Poetry" in his exemplary volume of criticism *Appreciations* (1889). The subject is William Morris, the poet of *The Defense of Guenevere* (1858) and *The Earthly Paradise* cycle. *Appreciations* also contains an essay on Dante Gabriel Rossetti's *Poems* (1870). Unsurprisingly, it neglects Swinburne, whose *Poems and Ballads* (1866) had received far more notice (much of it scandalized) than the work of Morris or Rossetti, but Swinburne's prose and judgments induced in Pater an intense anxiety of influence. By "aesthetic poetry" Pater, the "aesthetic critic," meant the genuine poetry of *his* generation, which came after Tennyson and Browning. Pre-Raphaelite poetry thus acquired in Pater its authentic critic.

The poets of my generation of the highest order are John Ashbery, A. R. Ammons, and James Merrill. Since I discuss Ashbery and Ammons later in this book, primarily in their relation to Whitman and Stevens, I will center here upon Merrill. He had no connection to Whitman, but subsumed Stevens and Auden in his epic *The Changing Light at Sandover*. His prime precursor was Yeats, an anxious relationship admirably chronicled in Mark Bauer's *The Composite Voice* (2003). Nobody can assert credit for raising in Merrill's "dreambeds / Hideous Blooms to stir up rivalry at high levels" (wickedly I omit all but two capital letters), since Yeats-in-Merrill did the work. The daimon knows how it is done.

In our conversations Merrill avoided all discussions of poetic influence, a restful precaution I was happy to share. One gathers that he overtly took up a benign stand on this matter, like his wonderful "Mirror" in the poem of that title: "to a faceless will, / Echo of mine, I am amenable." Yeats's will, however, never could be faceless. Merrill began to read him at the age of sixteen, and then studied Yeats's "system," *A Vision,* from 1955 on under the impact of Ouija-board conversations with his "angel" Ephraim.

In *Braving the Elements* (1972) the poem "Willowware Cup" is an imitation and implicit critique of Yeats's superb "Lapis Lazuli," which was written in 1938, the year before the Irish Archpoet's death. A sublimely lunatic rhapsody, making light of the impending Second World War, "Lapis Lazuli" insists that Hamlet and Lear somehow are buoyant: "Gaiety transfiguring all that dread." On the lapis lazuli carving Yeats beholds two Chinese sages serenaded by their musician-servant:

> Every discolouration of the stone,
> Every accidental crack or dent,
> Seems a water-course or an avalanche,
> Or lofty slope where it still snows
> Though doubtless plum or cherry-branch
> Sweetens the little half-way house
> Those Chinamen climb towards, and I
> Delight to imagine them seated there;
> There, on the mountain and the sky,
> On all the tragic scene they stare.
> One asks for mournful melodies;
> Accomplished fingers begin to play.
> Their eyes mid many wrinkles, their eyes,
> Their ancient, glittering eyes, are gay.

In the gentle "Willowware Cup," Merrill reads not tragic joy but sexual love's pathos: "something warm and clear." Unfortunately Yeats wins this agon through firepower, and Merrill absorbed the lesson. His epic, *The Changing Light at Sandover,* could be subtitled "Answer to Yeats," on the model of Jung's *Answer to Job.* Merrill greatly admired that book, and was a touch saddened when I told him I disliked it, and indeed the rest of Jung. Like Jung, Merrill valued the Prometheus archetype for the theft of fire, which the poet of *Sandover* steals from Yeats's Condition of Fire, as expounded in *A Vision*'s forerunner, the Paterian reverie *Per Amica Silentia Lunae.*

Mark Bauer accurately traces the stolen fire in Merrill's Yeatsian *The Country of the Thousand Years of Peace* (1959), as well as its continuous presence as a prevalent trope thereafter. The major critical study of Merrill, Stephen Yenser's *The Consuming Myth* (1987), also treats the Yeatsian element in the mature Merrill. Had only the lyrical element in Merrill prevailed, then Yeats would have been contained as transmuted by the later poet. *Sandover*'s ambitions strained all that, and I regret my own inability to agree with Merrill's exegetes as to his success in chastening Yeats in the cosmological domain.

An esoteric reader by training and disposition, I read and teach *The Changing Light at Sandover* with enormous pleasure yet with imperfect sympathy. Partly I am unredeemed in my involuntary resistance to the extended angelic passages in capital letters that dominate the second and third parts of Merrill's epic. Am I the only reader who desires less of this and more of J.M.? "The Book of Ephraim" benefits vastly by being all in Merrill's voice, and my students share my relief when later we are given the lovely canzone "Samos" and the sublime epilogue, "The Ballroom at Sandover." Yeats's aesthetic tact had severely excluded his wife's spirit communications. Defiantly, Merrill played at allowing the spirit world a more direct access to us.

Merrill himself was exquisitely tactful and gentle, unfailing in his personal goodwill. That Yeats, in contrast to Stevens and Auden, is treated rather rudely in *Sandover* is all the more surprising. As the most formidable poet since Robert Browning, he is an influence all but impossible to absorb. Merrill, a formal master, had no choice but to wrestle Yeats, whose great style essentially is aggressive. Of all twentieth-century poets of true eminence, Merrill had the largest debt to Yeats, surpassing even the effect of the seer of *A Vision* upon such Irish poets as Seamus Heaney and Paul Muldoon. Mark Bauer precisely indicates that Merrill was the principal heir of Pater's aesthetics, mediated by Yeats and by the Ruskinian Proust. What I love best in Merrill is his unflinching advocacy of the religion of Art.

But nothing is got for nothing, and Yeats can be an expense of spirit. There is a sadomasochistic strain in Merrill's work, yet he is free of Yeats's brutality. Power as Emerson defined it in *The Conduct of Life* is what strong poetry is all about. This is not political control but the potential for more life. Even as Ashbery and Ammons derive uncanny power from Whitman, Merrill taps it through Yeats. Whitman is not a character in the poetry of Ashbery or Ammons, but Yeats is a person or being in *Sandover,* a presence not at all in the benign mode of Auden and Stevens. He is a disturbance who requires correction or effacement, and he simply will not go away, despite Merrill's outrageous ingenuity in seeking to exorcise the real father of his life's work.

Bauer has demonstrated this comprehensively, and I do not need to repeat him here. My favorite part of *Sandover* is the glorious canzone, and I turn now to the agon with Yeats that forms its hidden plot. All voyages, in Merrill, sense the burden of *not* being to Yeats's Byzantium, since in Merrill you sail always to the City of Art to find Yeats already there upon your arrival. Fire binds together Merrill's five twelve-line stanzas and five-line envoi. Whose fire is it? "The dream-fire / In which . . . each human sense / burns," "prismatic fire / . . . of sea's dilute sapphire," "noon's pulsing ember raked by fire," "timeless, everlasting fire," "a fire / escape . . . ," "we've . . . taken fire"—all of these and more embellish the canzone until the envoi strikingly concludes:

> Samos. We keep trying to make sense
> Of what we can. Not souls of the first water—
> Although we've put on airs, and taken fire—
> We shall be dust of quite another land
> Before the seeds here planted come to light.

Yeats's Byzantium is an idealized vision of the city of Justinian in about 550 C.E., and owes as much to Shelley as Merrill does to Yeats. "God's holy fire" in "Sailing to Byzantium" is a mode in which the artwork has absorbed the artist's whole being into itself. Merrill wants to *be* Samos, a natural place rather than a city of the mind, but a spot equally caught up in Yeats's Paterian Condition of Fire.

Yeats defined his version of Romantic imagination by the formula "Simplification through intensity." Merrill was uneasy with this High Romanticism and avoided Yeatsian colorings insofar as he could, mostly by comic distancings. Such self-deflations, on Merrill's part or of *his* Yeats, work only hit or miss, even in "Samos," though I am a little chagrined at finding any fault with the gorgeous "Samos." Who but Merrill, at the height of his powers, could have composed it? Samos, in Merrill, is a paradisal island: "the imagined land," as Wallace Stevens would have called it, "the ultimate elegance." In a dialectic best caught by Stephen Yenser, Merrill wants at once to be in nature and out of it. The conflict stems from Yeats's "Sailing to Byzantium," and Merrill abides in it.

Most informed common readers as well as astute literary critics would regard Yeats as the strongest of twentieth-century poets in any Western language. Eliot and Stevens, Auden and Heaney acknowledge him, not without rue. Merrill is unique in the scale and stance of his struggle with Yeats. It was necessary because Yeats found him early and stayed with him until the end. There is a shattering of the vessels shared by Yeats and Merrill. They agreed with Blake that anything possible to be believed was an image of truth.

I recall only two or three occasions when I was alone with Merrill. He would phone sometimes for information, sometimes about Yeats or Blake or Gnosticism, once or twice about Freud. Conversation, whether face to face or via phone, was never easy because of temperamental differences. Walt Whitman, central to Ashbery and to Ammons, is so absent from Merrill that I asked once, when we were alone, why he considered the best and most American of our poets so peripheral to him. Merrill mused a moment or two, affirmed Whitman's place among the greatest poets and expressed puzzlement. Yeats also was untouched by Whitman, whose freedom from mythologies helped make Stevens the antimythological poet deprecated by Auden's "In Praise of Limestone."

Yeats's idea of the poem and his sense of the poet were essentially Shelleyan, and became Merrill's. Elinor Wylie, an enthusiasm of the adolescent Merrill, had a Shelley obsession that bordered upon total identification. The archetypal Shelleyan poem is a dramatic lyric, mythological and remorseless, that reads like an episode in a great romance. What Shelley's *Alastor* and *Prince Athanase* had been to Yeats, the Byzantium poems, "Lapis Lazuli," "The Second Coming," and "Vacillation" became to Merrill. The ontological pattern of self and soul in dialogue with one another is Yeatsian in Merrill, Whitmanian in Ammons and Ashbery. Ammons, who set Ashbery over even himself, did not sympathize with my conversion to Merrill when I read and reviewed *Divine Comedies* (containing "The Book of Ephraim") in 1976, nor did Robert Penn Warren, who expressed surprise. The revelation of Merrill's challenge to Yeats on communal occult ground overcame my long blindness in regard to Merrill's achievements.

Standing back from Merrill and Yeats can help one develop a deeper understanding of the influence process. I note that Bauer is not free of the misconception that *The Anxiety of Influence* argues a "masculine" and "heterosexual" speculation as to literary reception, supposedly founded on an "Oedipal" account of family romances. This declaration is self-refuting. Bauer's admirable study of Yeats and Merrill allows itself these shibboleths, but then gives a long, detailed demonstration of Merrill's lifetime struggle with Yeats's fathering force.

William Butler Yeats's actual father was the delightful painter John Butler Yeats, who abandoned British respectability for a Bohemian existence in New York City. The later correspondence between painter and poet shows a role reversal, with W.B. giving fatherly advice to the genial scamp. In human terms that relationship defines an important distance between Yeats and Merrill: What could John Butler Yeats and Charles Edward Merrill, co-founder of Merrill Lynch, have said to one another had Manhattan ever brought them together?

Fathers aside, contemporary critical fashion has an obsession with sexual orientation, and would insist that Yeats's passionate heterosexuality and Merrill's consistent homoeroticism provided a difference that sheltered the later poet from the precursor's fire.

Once again, influence anxiety, as I have seen it, takes place between poems, and not between persons. Temperament and circumstances determine whether or not a later poet *feels* anxiety at whatever level of consciousness. All that matters for interpretation is the revisionary relationship between poems, as manifested in tropes, images, diction, syntax, grammar, metric, poetic stance. In their introduction to the beautiful *Selected Poems* (2008), the editors, J. D. McClatchy and Stephen Yenser, ask how the typical Merrill poem works, and they answer: the dialectic of metaphor and the affirmation of form. That is also the Yeats poem, even more metaphorical and formal.

Kimon Friar, Merrill's teacher and lover at Amherst College, was a catalyst in deepening the poet's relationship to Yeats, particularly through Friar's over-estimation of *A Vision,* which he regarded as a masterpiece and hoped Merrill would "translate" into a long poem. Merrill's skepticism in regard to *A Vision* was a prelude to his dialectical attitude toward his own Ouija-board spooks. In the summer of 1955, with his partner David Jackson playing the part of Mrs. Yeats, Hand to his Scribe, Merrill first contacted Ephraim, Greek Jew and muse of *Sandover.* Immediately, he returned to reading *A Vision.*

Friar was almost as invested in Hart Crane as he was in Yeats, and I wondered why Merrill was not cathected onto Crane. Happily this was something Merrill and I discussed. The impacted density and rhapsodic word-consciousness of Crane, combined with the Whitmanian aspirations of *The Bridge,* rather alienated Merrill, as he told me. I recall an exchange in which I said that at his best Crane seemed to fuse a Lucretian element (learned from Shelley, Whitman, Stevens) into his aspiration to be a Pindar of the Machine Age. Respecting Crane, but at a distance, Merrill wrinkled his nose and intimated that he himself had little desire to be a celebratory poet. He was, and was not, divided in this also.

Hart Crane's agonistic relationship to T. S. Eliot is parallel to the Merrill-Yeats tangle, but differs because Crane contested Eliot's worldview. Allen Tate, Crane's close friend, was Eliot's disciple in all things. That cannot be said of Merrill in regard to Yeats, though Yeats's occultism was a firm connection. The calculated barbarism of late Yeats, allied to a repression concept of civil society, is happily lacking in the humane Merrill. Why then did Yeats become the prime precursor? Strong poets do not choose but are found by the imaginative register of blood kindred. Merrill's early dramatic lyric "Medusa" takes much of its delicious decadence from the most famous and influential of all Yeats's poems, "The Second Coming." Here is "Medusa"'s fifth and final stanza:

> The blank eyes gaze past suns of no return
> On vast irrelevancies that form deforms,
> The maladies of dream
> Where the stone face revolves like a sick eye
> Beneath its lid: so we
> Watch through the crumbling surfaces and noons
> The single mask of stone
> And the dry serpent horror
> Of days reflected in a doubtful mirror
> With all their guileful melody, until
> We raise our quivering swords and think to kill.

"A gaze blank and pitiless as the sun" emanates from Yeats's rough beast, the second birth of the one-eyed Egyptian male sphinx of Memphis, sacred to the sun god, which portends a new antithetical annunciation, contrary to the Christian First Coming. A subtle sadomasochism in Yeats's poem becomes more explicit in "Medusa" as it will throughout Merrill.

"Medusa" is apprentice Merrill. "About the Phoenix," from *The Century of a Thousand Years of Peace*, bravely attempts to revise "Sailing to Byzantium," again Yeats at his most universal. In regard to contesting Yeats, Merrill remained foolhardy, a stance difficult to maintain in the occult realm of *Sandover*. There Yeats's strength could not be evaded, and Merrill's resort was to bestow upon himself and us a parody of Yeats, in a few places dismissed with little dignity. That mars Merrill's own aesthetic dignity, and would be strange (he was the most courteous of men) but that it reveals further how anxious Yeats made him, unlike Stevens and Auden, who could be more readily assimilated.

"About the Phoenix" mutes allusions to "Sailing to Byzantium," and yet they hover. Tired of the Yeatsian "high-flown," Merrill rejects Byzantium's golden bird, which he transmogrifies into the Phoenix, "between ardor and ashes." The fire is *Per Amica*'s Condition of Fire, which burns on throughout Merrill, who never quite yielded to Yeats's passionate conviction that poetic imagination involved "simplification through intensity," the Paterian declaration that persuasively redefines simplicity as what Yeats wanted to call "Unity of Being."

Early and late, Merrill doubted his own personal unity. Like Byron, an increasing alternative to the visionary Yeats, Merrill found his aesthetic freedom as a parodist. *Don Juan* follows Pope's *Dunciad* as the epic of parody, and Merrill in *Sandover* sought to add a sublime third to this tradition. Parody in some regards defends against influence; it allowed Pope and Byron to exploit Milton without yielding to him. Amazing mimic as he was, Merrill remained only a mixed success at parody. Pope and Byron can be savage; Merrill was too gentle.

Free of epic ambitions, Merrill after *Sandover* perfected himself as a parodist of Yeats, particularly with "Santorini: Stopping the Leak" in *Late Settings* (1985). That marvelous volume has two other major poems, "Clearing the Title" and "Bronze," but "Santorini" is a rare masterwork, even for late Merrill. It opens as overt parody of Yeats:

> —Whereupon, sporting a survivor's grin
> I've come by baby jet to Santorin.

Even as "Santorini" perfects aspects of Merrill's personal mythmaking, it audaciously opens itself to both of Yeats's Byzantium poems. This is an agon only Yeats could win, yet Merrill is too shrewd for a wrestling match with Yeats cast as the Angel of Death. Writing an ottava rima suspended halfway between Byron and Yeats, Merrill knowingly composes one of his finest elegies for himself, deceptively light as he always can be. The late Anthony Hecht and I once agreed in conversation, rather fancifully, that listening to Mozart's G Minor Quintet made us think of Merrill at his frequent best.

Yeats temperamentally had little in common with Merrill and might have been impatient with him had they met in an afterworld not designed by the American visionary. But then I wonder whether personality and character are much involved in being elected by a precursor. Walt Whitman, who found Oscar Wilde too effusive when the Irish aesthete came to Camden, New Jersey, hardly could have handled Hart Crane or D. H. Lawrence, had either of these disciples also arrived to offer homage. Yeats admired men of action but at a sufficient distance. Byron liked the Cornish adventurer Edward Trelawney, who came to loathe Byron and remained loyal to Shelley's memory throughout a long life, now remembered only because of his association with both poets.

"Santorini" forges itself upon Merrill's ambivalence toward Yeats, though an assured insouciance conveys the later poet's achieved freedom to sport with the precursor's fierce rhetoric:

We must be light, light-footed, light of soul,
Quick to let go, to tighten by a notch
The broad, star-studded belt Earth wears to feel
Hungers less mortal for a vanished whole.
Light-headed at the last? Our lives unreal
Except as jeweled self-windings, a deathwatch
Of heartless rhetoric I punctuate,
Spitting the damson pit onto the plate?

Lighter indeed these tonalities than characteristic Yeats, yet for all the Merrillian mastery, who sets the terms? The Byzantium poems, the "Vacillation"
sequence, and the prose *Per Amica Silentia Lunae* have scriptural status in Merrill. More than Auden and Proust, Stevens and Dante, they stand for poetry
and all its perpetual possibilities. Yeats's primacy is unlike the role of Eliot in
Crane's struggle with tradition, or Stevens in Ashbery's development. Whitman
is mediated by Eliot and Stevens for Crane and Ashbery, and as the later poets
developed they found fecund sanctuary in Whitman's stance and idiom. A. R.
Ammons was fascinated by Stevens and fond of William Carlos Williams, yet
from the start came out of Whitman. Merrill attempted to use Auden as a screen
for Yeats, and had clear relations both to Stevens and to Elizabeth Bishop, but
the poet's family romance for him always remained Yeatsian.

Except for the brilliant "Book of Ephraim," I prefer Merrill's achievement in
his lyrics and meditations to the epic *Sandover,* but time may give the preference
to the occult journey. Yeats, both before and after *Sandover,* does not vex Merrill
nearly as much as he does in the epic. Bauer charts, fully and accurately, Merrill's campaign to distance himself from Yeats in "Ephraim," where the Irish
Archpoet is *not* allowed to speak, as though Merrill desires, above all else, not
to age into the magus of *A Vision.* Proust instead is evoked as a safer forerunner,
to be lovingly saluted but never parodied.

Merrill was a stunning mimic, as anyone who heard him perform would
remember. Like Byron, a growing presence in late Merrill, the artist of parody
triumphs throughout *Sandover.* Linda Hutcheon's *A Theory of Parody* (1985) pith-
ily calls the parodic mode an "ironic signaling of distance." Much of *Sandover* is
a signal station ceaselessly sending out reports of W. B. Yeats's dwindling into
the distance. Incessant signals work against themselves: the farther Merrill
exiles him, the closer Yeats approaches.

Bauer gallantly notes Merrill's parodistic performance in regard to Yeats's verse prologue to *A Vision,* the somewhat inadequate "The Phases of the Moon." Imbuing himself with otherness, the subjective early Merrill, up to and in "Ephraim," thus embraces his New Science of angelology in *Mirabell* and *Scripts.* I am put off by lists, even Merrillian ones, and doubtless Yeats's bat-cries incited Merrill's, but to what poetic ends? Parodic bat-angels, more Popean than Byronic, throng *Mirabell,* and transmutation into a peacock or two does not make them less chaotic. I was properly reproved by Merrill in correspondence for begging for more J.M. lowercase and less Yeatsian uppercase, an aesthetic plea on my part. With Blakean dignity, he replied that the Authors were in Eternity and his role was faithfully to take dictation. A Johnsonian respect for the common reader is not relevant to *Sandover,* which calls for readers uncommon indeed. The line where superb manners cross over into mannerism wavers, and the aesthetic question is not easily resolved. I recall my own passion for the fictions of Ronald Firbank, who was more a fantasist than a parodist. Firbank alas is not for the common reader. Is it a question of genre? Can an epic, of all forms, be inaccessible to the literate public? Blake's brief epics never will have a general audience, nor do Wallace Stevens's longer poems and Crane's *The Bridge.* But then, the *Commedia* no longer does either, to which you can add *Paradise Lost* and *The Dunciad.* Byron's *Don Juan* could, if only readers can be persuaded to turn again to long poems. *Sandover* is in excellent company as parodistic epic, in some regards worthy of Pope and Byron, but its Yeatsian "science," however distanced, weighs it down.

It is dangerous to usurp a great poet and then to tame him into passivity as a character in one's own poem. That could of course be an admonition to any exegete whosoever. Blake just about manages it in his brief epic *Milton,* in contrast to the success of Dante in his total appropriation of Vergil. Correcting the precursor can seem high-handed in Blake, and I am uneasy when Dante outrageously negates Vergil's Epicureanism. Vergil is wholly Lucretian and hardly a wistful forerunner to Dante's Christian triumphalism.

Merrill, for all his courteous comedy, treats Yeats unkindly as an actor in *Sandover,* with mixed results. Employing Auden to demean Yeats is unworthy of Merrill, particularly since Auden's "In Memory of W. B. Yeats" is a rather inadequate poem. Merrill adapts T. S. Eliot's "continual extinction of personality" to his own kenosis of stripping away the self. This reduction can work for Merrill and his Auden yet sours in cutting down the High Romantic personality of Yeats. I get suspicious when Merrill's spirit communicators attack the singularity of the poetic self. They dislike Yeats, condescend to Stevens, and would have rebelled against Lawrence and Crane. For all his own endearing uniqueness, Merrill joins an occult crusade against the High Romantic self, which is triumphant in Byron, Whitman, and Yeats. Here, on pages 486–87 of *Sandover,* is the debacle Merrill's Yeats cannot sustain:

Pla. MOTHER, WHAT USE FOR THAT ONE OF OUR BAND
        MOST PUT UPON, OUR HAND?
DJ.   (Hand poised but trembling from the strain) Who? Me?
Nat. HA, FROM WITHIN IT DO NOT I
        A CROUCHING ELDER SCRIBE ESPY?

        As in *Capriccio* when poor *Monsieur Taupe*
        Emerges from the prompter's box (of course
        In this case *DJ's* hand) there scrambles up
        Stiffly at first a figure on all fours.
        He straightens as one wild cadenza pours
        Through the rapt house; whips out pince-nez and page.
        A deep, sure lilt so scores and underscores
        The words he proffers, you would think a sage
        Stood among golden tongues, unharmed, at center stage.
WBY. O SHINING AUDIENCE, IF AN OLD MAN'S SPEECH
        STIFF FROM LONG SILENCE CAN NO LONGER STRETCH
        TO THAT TOP SHELF OF RIGHTFUL BARD'S APPAREL
        FOR WYSTAN AUDEN & JAMES MEREL
        WHO HAVE REFASHIONED US BY FASHIONING THIS,
        MAY THE YOUNG SINGER HEARD ABOVE
        THE SPINNING GYRES OF HER TRUE LOVE
        CLOAK THEM IN HEAVEN'S AIRLOOM HARMONIES.
Nat. NOT RUSTY AFTER ALL, GOOD YEATS.
        (The record ends.) NOW BACK INSIDE THE GATES
        OF HAND. BUT FIRST MARK WHAT I SAY:
        YOU ARE TO TAKE THAT HAND ON 'JUDGMENT DAY'
        AND PLEAD ITS CASE
        WITH YOUR OWN ELOQUENCE IN A HIGH PLACE,
        THAT IT NOT BE DIVIDED FROM
        OUR SCRIBE IN ANY FUTURE SECULUM.
        Bowing, Yeats crawls back under DJ's palm.

Bauer sees this for what it is, but understandably refrains from judgment. To repeat myself, anxiety of influence as an affect of the belated poet scarcely interests me. The impingements of one poem upon another is my concern, and I cannot pretend not to see an absurd diminishment of the strongest poet of the twentieth century by an heir of genius who knew better. Whose Condition of Fire was it anyway?

Whitman and the Death of
Europe in the Evening Land

EMERSON AND A POETRY YET TO BE WRITTEN

B egetter of much (if not most) of American literature and thought for some six generations now, Emerson liked to think of himself as an end-less experimenter with no past at his back. A great poet in prose, and a very good one in verse, he invested himself in his journals, lectures, and essays because Wordsworth's giant form blocked the New England seer from achiev-ing a full voice in verse. Walt Whitman and Emily Dickinson, partly through Emerson's effect upon them, finally gave the United States poets who could rival Wordsworth.

All the cultural past actually *was* at the erudite sage's back, but he denied that history existed. There was only biography. The distinguished historian C. Vann Woodward, no admirer of Emerson, vigorously assured me that Waldo (the name preferred by Emerson) was responsible for all the excesses of the cultural revolution of the late sixties and the seventies. An equally distinguished friend, the poet-novelist Robert Penn Warren, told me repeatedly that Emerson's true legacy was all of American violence from John Brown to the present!

I myself worked my way out of a middle-of-the-journey crisis by immersing myself in Emerson from 1965 on. The commentary that helped me most was Stephen Whicher's *Freedom and Fate* (1953), still in my judgment the most use-ful book on the endlessly metamorphic Waldo. The famous outcry of Emerson's disciple Henry James, Sr., remains pertinent: "O you man without a handle!" Try to grasp the American prophet and Proteus slips away.

Emerson's reading of literary culture—Plato, Montaigne, Shakespeare—is always an extraordinarily creative misreading. Cheerfully, Emerson turns Plato into Montaigne and Montaigne into Plato. Skepticism and Absolute Idealism can be held together as an emulsion (at best), but in Emerson's essays all things flow to all as rivers to the sea. Shakespeare, hailed first as Waldo's central poet, ebbs into the master of the revels for mankind. All poetry already written, all thinking already thought is audaciously deprecated in contrast to what yet will be. That is why Emerson's major achievement is his *Journal,* unbounded and exuberantly at home in the optative mood. Purchase a complete set of the *Journal,* preferably in an older edition rather than in the elaborately over-edited Harvard version, and read in it every evening across a few years until you have finished it. You will learn the mind of America, which remains to a disturbing extent Ralph Waldo Emerson's mind.

Reading Emerson is sometimes bewildering, partly because he is an aphorist who thinks in isolated sentences. His paragraphs frequently are spasmodic, and his essays (except for "Experience") can be read back-to-front without too much loss. I have a preternatural memory and recall hundreds of Emersonian apothegms verbatim, but frequently am stumped at locating them in his essays or precisely where in the *Journal.* He defined freedom as wildness, and his never-resting mind is always at a crossing, shooting a gulf, and darting to a new aim. You can read Waldo by ambushing him, but generally he has gone forward when you make your move.

If all that's past is your antagonist then no tradition whatsoever can make you an offer you can't refuse.

Kerry Larson observes that justice, in the abstract, was a topic Emerson simply failed to master, thus opening him to Melville's satire in *The Confidence-Man.* Though Larson admirably defends Emerson's law of compensation—"Nothing is got for nothing"—I prefer to take Emerson's American Religion rather more seriously than most of his defenders or his resentful critics tend to do. His discontinuous rhetoric is designed to break down conventional responses, as any original religious discourse has to do. It is useless going to Emerson with your preconceived notions of morality and social justice, as Larson emphasizes. Emerson's spirit is agonistic, and he wants you to wrestle with him, a frustrating demand on the reader because Waldo is too slippery to hold.

History, which for all of us is what it seemed to Joyce's Stephen, a nightmare from which we want to awake if only we could, was no burden for Emerson, who willed it out of existence. That has to be regarded as a religious action, not at all to be confused with what resenters of Emerson call "religiosity," of which he possessed none. Self-Reliance is his American religion, but at our moment we are likely to find this formulation difficult. The Emersonian trope of Self-Reliance has been literalized and trivialized by popular culture, and so its Hermetic implications are lost.

A suggestive reading of the essay "Self-Reliance" by David Bromwich explores its indisputable links to Wordsworth's "Ode: Intimations of Immortality from Recollections of Early Childhood." Subtly, Bromwich analyzes Emerson's rejection of Wordsworth's myth of memory:

> Emerson for his part believed that individual power tends to harden soon enough into just such a repose; but he wants us to believe that the opposite is always possible; and his departure from Wordsworth is connected with his own violent hatred of memory. To the conspicuous faith of the ode, that our memories leave the deposit from which our profoundest thoughts derive, Emerson replies in "Self-Reliance": "Why should you keep your head over your shoulder? Why drag about this corpse of your memory, lest you contradict somewhat you have stated in this or that public place? Suppose you should contradict yourself; what then?" We are once again at the point where natural piety, consistency of opinion, and a respect for duties laid upon oneself as actor in the spectacle of social morality, come to seem names for the same thing. Wordsworth, however reluctantly, is responsive to their call, and Emerson is not.

> ["From Wordsworth to Emerson" (1990)]

Bromwich is detached enough not to take sides, yet implicitly he favors Wordsworth, as I do Emerson. Though Bromwich sees that Self-Reliance can be read as a religious term, he seems to prefer a social interpretation of it. But I follow Emerson by insisting it is a religious naming, which establishes our unacknowledged national faith, the American Religion. This relies upon Emerson's invention of what could be called a purely daimonic American unconscious:

> The magnetism which all original action exerts is explained when we inquire the reason of self-trust. Who is the Trustee? What is the aboriginal Self, on which a universal reliance may be grounded? What is the nature and power of that science-baffling star, without parallax, without calculable elements, which shoots a ray of beauty even into

trivial and impure actions, if the least mark of independence appear?
The inquiry leads us to that source, at once the essence of genius, of
virtue, and of life, which we call Spontaneity or Instinct. We denote
this primary wisdom as Intuition, whilst all later teachings are tui-
tions. In that deep force, the last fact behind which analysis cannot
go, all things find their common origin.

Bromwich reads this by despiritualizing it, but that will not work, though he
sees clearly enough that Emerson pugnaciously dismisses all myths of anteriority: "When we have new perception, we shall gladly disburden the memory
of its hoarded treasures as old rubbish." Against Coleridge, an early influence
upon him but now discarded, Emerson sublimely snaps: "In the hour of vision
there is nothing that can be called gratitude, or properly joy."

Emerson's religious stance was best set forth by Stephen Whicher in *Freedom
and Fate* (1971):

> The lesson he would drive home is man's entire independence. The
> aim of this strain in his thought is not virtue, but freedom and mastery.
> It is radically anarchic, overthrowing all the authority of the past, all
> compromise or coöperation with others, in the name of Power present
> and agent in the soul. . . .
>
> Yet his true goal was not really a Stoic self-mastery, nor Christian
> holiness, but rather something more secular and harder to define—
> a quality he sometimes called *entirety,* or *self-union.* . . .
>
> This self-sufficient unity or wholeness, transforming his relations
> with the world about him, is, as I read him, the central objective of
> the egoistic or transcendental Emerson, the prophet of Man created
> in the 1830's by his discovery of the extent of his own proper nature.
> This was what he meant by "sovereignty," or "mastery," or the striking
> phrase, several times repeated, "the erect position."

Indeed neither a Stoic nor a Christian, Emerson was an American Orpheus,
and thus as shamanistic as Empedocles. His disciples Walt Whitman and Hart
Crane are imbued with Emerson's Orphism, which descended to the Concord
seer via the Cambridge Platonists Henry More and Ralph Cudworth. Orphism
is the doctrine of the occult self, not the psyche but the daimon. Emerson cus-
tomarily alters everything he receives, and his Orphism is free both of any
notion of reincarnation and of purification. Orpheus in Emerson is what the

Kabbalists called Adam Kadmon, the Divine Man of the Hermetic corpus as Primal or Central Man. He precedes the Creation-Fall, and is prophesied as an American-More-Than-Christ, who has not yet proclaimed his Kingdom of Man over Nature.

Emersonian Orphism augments power, or *potentia,* and is close to Giambattista Vico's dialectics of divination, at once god-making ("We only know what we ourselves have made") and warding off dangers—internal and societal—to the self, via accurate prophecy. One should expect Emerson to out-Vico Vico, as it were, and he transmits every luster into something he himself has made. Hence the magnificent and perhaps most Emersonian of sentences, from the first paragraph of "Self-Reliance": "In every work of genius we recognize our own rejected thoughts; they come back to us with a certain alienated majesty."

If you discard all history, then literary historians join the rubbish heap with the chronicles of empire. We tend not to absorb how fiercely extreme Emerson was. My late friend Bart Giamatti, president of Yale and later baseball commissioner, charmed me with his outburst: "Emerson is as sweet as barbed wire." Stephen Whicher more gently got this right.

Founding another academic industry upon Emerson betrays him, since self-union is not a social enterprise. The prophetic Waldo sought what Stevens was to call a time in which majesty was a mirror of the self. You will not become a better or more moral citizen by reading Emerson, whose purposes were directed at freeing minds capable of freedom. In the pure good of theory, he annihilated all influence, his own included. Myself a disciple of Emerson from 1965 to the present moment, I am properly disconcerted by Emerson on influence. Contradicting himself is not a problem; a natural Emersonian, I am capable of contradicting myself in consecutive sentences. But influence *is:* you don't abolish it by denial. Cheerfully, Emerson affirms and negates it, paragraph by paragraph.

The crisis comes in the marvelously vexed "Shakespeare; or, The Poet" in *Representative Men* (1850). No Bloomian Bardolatry can match Emerson's observation "He wrote the text of modern life." We thus become his characters, even if he could not come round to us. Emerson says that Shakespeare was "the father of the man in America," the best expression I know of our national reliance upon much the greatest of writers:

> Shakespeare is as much out of the category of eminent authors, as he
> is out of the crowd. He is inconceivably wise; the others, conceivably.

A good reader can, in a sort, nestle into Plato's brain, and think from thence; but not into Shakespeare's. We are still out of doors. For executive faculty, for creation, Shakespeare is unique. No man can imagine it better. He was the furthest reach of subtlety compatible with an individual self,—the subtilest of authors, and only just within the possibility of authorship. With this wisdom of life, is the equal endowment of imaginative and of lyric power. He clothed the creatures of his legend with form and sentiments, as if they were people who had lived under his roof; and few real men have left such distinct characters as these fictions. And they spoke in language as sweet as it was fit. Yet his talents never seduced him into an ostentation, nor did he harp on one string. An omnipresent humanity co-ordinates all his faculties. Give a man of talents a story to tell, and his partiality will presently appear. He has certain observations, opinions, topics, which have some accidental prominence, and which he disposes all to exhibit. He crams this part, and starves that other part, consulting not the fitness of the thing, but his fitness and strength. But Shakespeare has no peculiarity, no importunate topic; but all is duly given; no veins, no curiosities: no cow-painter, no bird-fancier, no mannerist is he; he has no discoverable egotism: the great he tells greatly; the small, subordinately. He is wise without emphasis or assertion; he is strong, as nature is strong, who lifts the land into mountain slopes without effort, and by the same rule as she floats a bubble in the air, and likes as well to do the one as the other. This makes the equality of power in farce, tragedy, narrative, and love-songs; a merit so incessant, that each reader is incredulous of the perception of other readers.

This power of expression, or of transferring the inmost truth of things into music and verse, makes him the type of the poet, and has added a new problem to metaphysics. This is that which throws him into natural history, as a main production of the globe, and as announcing new eras and ameliorations. Things were mirrored in his poetry without loss or blur; he could paint the fine with precision, the great with compass; the tragic and comic indifferently, and without any distortion or favor. He carried his powerful execution into minute details, to a hair point; finishes an eyelash or a dimple as firmly as he draws a mountain; and yet these, like nature's, will bear the scrutiny of the solar microscope.

In short, he is the chief example to prove that more or less of production, more or fewer pictures, is a thing indifferent. He had the power to make one picture. Daguerre learned how to let one flower etch its image on his plate of iodine; and then proceeds at leisure to etch a million. There are always objects; but there was never representation. Here is perfect representation, at last; and now let the world of figures sit for their portraits. No recipe can be given for the making of a Shakespeare; but the possibility of the translation of things into song is demonstrated.

To be wise without emphasis or asserting: we cannot say that of Plato or of Emerson himself. I can think of no one except Shakespeare and Montaigne who has such wisdom beyond tendentiousness. I rejoice that Emerson praises Shakespeare more accurately than does the entire tradition of Shakespearean commentary.

But then comes the most peculiar reversal in all of the Sage of Concord's writings, when Shakespeare is indicted for sharing the "the halfness and imperfection of humanity." What does Emerson want? As I noted earlier, Thomas De Quincey remarked of his friend Coleridge that he wanted better bread than could be made with wheat. Shakespeare is said by Emerson to have "converted the elements, which waited on his command, into entertainments." One wants to ask Emerson: Are *King Lear* and *Macbeth* entertainments? Something obscure and dark for once blinds Emerson as he deprecates the best comedies ever written—*Twelfth Night* and *A Midsummer Night's Dream*—as just "another picture more or less." Does Emerson really desire Shakespeare to have written another Qur'an? No, he glumly admits that religious founders render life ghastly and joyless. Of all Emersonian yearnings for the Central Man who shall come, this is the least persuasive: "The world still wants its poet-priest, a reconciler, who shall not trifle with Shakespeare the player."

What has happened to capsize Emerson? We rightly shudder when exegetes Christianize *King Lear* and *Macbeth*, as if to give us as poet-priest Shakespeare the reconciler. Plainly, Emerson cannot mean that. But what can he mean? He would have had no patience with historicizers of Shakespeare, Old style or New. I enjoy his likely wonderment at French Shakespeare, feminist Shakespeare, homosexual poetic Shakespeare, Marxist Shakespeare, postcolonialist Shakespeare, and all the rest of our current academic pieties. Simple enough to say what Emerson did not mean, but how shall we fathom what reconcilement is to replace Shakespearean trifling?

We shall not. But we can stand back and ask what led Emerson to this lapse. His nature at once admitted and repelled all influence, by his own accounts. Eloquence was his strength, and perhaps his truest ambition was to achieve preternatural eminence in eloquence. No other American writer is so skilled in eloquence except for his disciple Whitman, who largely burned out after a great decade, 1855–65. But Emerson, Whitman, Francis Bacon, Thomas Browne, Robert Burton, Thomas De Quincey, Walter Pater, and W. B. Yeats all together cannot compete in eloquence with Falstaff, Hamlet, Iago, Cleopatra, Lear, and Macbeth.

Then the additional question arises of whether eloquence is enough. When most himself, Emerson was easy with that conviction. If you are surpassing eloquent, influence seems a secondary matter:

> His health and greatness consist in his being the channel through which heaven flows to earth, in short, in the fulness in which an ec-statical state takes place in him. It is pitiful to be an artist, when, by forbearing to be artists, we might be vessels filled with the divine over-flowings, enriched by the circulations of omniscience and omnipres-ence. Are there not moments in the history of heaven when the human race was not counted by individuals, but was only the Influenced, was God in distribution, God rushing into multiform benefit? It is sublime to receive, sublime to love, but this lust of imparting as from *us,* this desire to be loved, the wish to be recognized as individuals,—is finite, comes of a lower strain.

> ["The Method of Nature" (1841)]

I have just reread this a dozen or so times, and am fascinated and bewildered by it, as always I have been. That "fulness" (as Emerson doubtless knows) was the Gnostic pleroma, the place of rest to which we long to return. Ecstasy is antithetical here to the labor of being an artist. Any individual artist or agonist has forsaken a humanity that was "the Influenced, was God in distribution, God rushing into multiform benefit." This ecstasy never altogether abandoned Emerson, but how do you write a poem or an essay or any aesthetic venture if you value being "Influenced" as a divine condition?

Shakespeare implicitly is the counterstatement to this worship of Influx. Emerson, a great critic, saw and said how Shakespeare transcended even the strongest writers: Homer, Dante, Chaucer, Cervantes. But where is "God in distribution" in the most individual of all literary artists? *The Tragedy of King Lear* is the sublime of imaginative literature, and is a profound negation of any received ecstasy. Self-Reliance in Emerson depends upon his experience that in his highest moments *he* is a vision. Those moments do not stem from reading Shakespeare but do provide a basis for the American Religion. Doubtless reading *Twelfth Night* is not a path to ecstasy, yet the play can be evaded only by a weak misreading, unworthy of the great Emerson. His mistake was a failure in misprision. Those he inspired, however dialectically, were no better able to make use of Shakespeare. *Moby-Dick* cannot win when Melville enters into an agon with *King Lear,* but the engagement helps confer a tragic dignity upon Ahab's defeat.

Emerson's lifelong obsession was with a poetry *yet to be written,* and which never could be written. That carries prospectiveness to the border of madness. *King Lear* has been written, even if we no longer seem capable of reading it. A superb reader, Emerson was a figure of capable imagination, when he wanted to be. Theologian of our American Religion, Emerson knew only the God within. That knowing waned slowly with the decades of the *Journals.* Shakespeare also never abandoned him. Here is a journal entry for April 1864:

> When I read Shakespeare, as lately, I think the criticism and study of him to be in their infancy. The wonder grows of his long obscurity; how could you hide the only man that ever wrote from all men who delight in reading? Then, the courage with which, in each play, he accosts the main issue, the highest problem, never dodging the difficult or impossible, but addressing himself instantly to that,—so conscious of his secret competence; and, at once, alike an aeronaut fills his balloon with a whole atmosphere of hydrogen that will carry him over Andes, if Andes be in his path.

A marvelous tribute, this is a good last word on Emerson and Shakespeare.

WHITMAN'S TALLY

Universal forerunner of nearly all who came after him, Shakespeare nevertheless is not often thought to have Whitman among his progeny. Many years ago, walking around the Battery at Manhattan's tip with Kenneth Burke, my critical mentor and I conducted a long, rambling conversation as an experiment in bringing Whitman and Shakespeare together. I remember the year as being 1975 or '76, and that the spry Burke, at seventy-eight or so, tired less in our perambulating than I did. Burke had written a splendid centenary essay in 1955, "Policy Made Personal: Whitman's Verse and Prose-Salient Traits," in which he argues that Whitman has three key terms: *vistas, leaves, lilacs.* I would add one more, *tally,* but Burke's triad all are instances of the tally, as he pointed out to me. "Policy Made Personal" quotes Whitman on Shakespeare, but this is Whitman at his defensive weakest, in the rather mixed prose work *Democratic Vistas* (1871): "The great poems, Shakespeare included, are poisonous to the idea of the pride and dignity of the common people." Shakespeare was "rich" (also James Joyce's judgment) but "feudal." Whitman's "vistas" are not broad or general views, but prospects, as when we look through a cleared clump of trees and, in the open space, fancy that we behold future time. I take Whitman here on Shakespeare to be not far from Emerson in *Representative Men,* where Shakespeare is first a god who writes the text of life, and then is dispatched in favor of the poet-of-poets who will come, and will instruct as well as entertain us.

Whitman keeps count of his vistas; he tallies them, as he does with his fiction of the leaves and his sprigs of lilac. For Burke this was a personalizing of policy, since rhetoric, psychology, and cosmology fused for Whitman. Burke advised me to ask what a poet was trying to do for him- or herself *as a person* by writing his or her poem. But I told him I wanted to ask what a poet was attempting to do for him- or herself *as a poet* by composing a particular poem.

With Whitman, we always are free to start anywhere, and somewhat less arbitrarily than may appear, I choose the wonderful cluster of twelve poems, *Live Oak, with Moss.* Possibly written in late 1859 and early 1860, *Live Oak, with Moss* enabled Whitman to create the superb homoerotic sequence *Calamus,* of the "deathbed edition." *Calamus,* together with the two great *Sea-Drift* elegies—"Out of the Cradle Endlessly Rocking" and "As I Ebb'd with the Ocean of Life "—is the new glory of the third edition of *Leaves of Grass* (1860). Add the "Lilacs" elegy for Lincoln, and a dozen or so shorter poems and fragments, and you have the best of Whitman, though in the next chapter I will place a particular emphasis upon "Vigil Strange I Kept on the Field One Night" from *Drum-Taps* (1861) and the "Lilacs" threnody (published that autumn).

Live Oak, with Moss is hardly a homoerotic manifesto but something closer to Michael Moon's useful surmise that it is a miniature of Shakespeare's Sonnets, which were also, of course, addressed to a fair young man. Several dozens of the Sonnets are among the best shorter poems in the English language, but so too are Whitman's twelve poems (most easily found now in the Norton Critical Edition of *Leaves of Grass,* edited by Moon). Shakespeare's Sonnets seem to haunt Whitman in certain movements, as at the start of poem VI: "What think you I have taken my pen to record?" or, in VIII, "I am what I am." Against the negative capability of Shakespeare, as formulated by John Keats, Whitman opposed the "powerful press of himself," the American bard or heroic personality, democratic policy translated into acute individuality. As a cluster (Whitman's own term) *Live Oak, with Moss* is remarkably varied, possibly in competition with any dozen or so of Shakespeare's Sonnets.

The masterpiece of Whitman's cluster is the famous second poem, "I saw in Louisiana a live-oak growing," one of the major lyrics in the American language:

I saw in Louisiana a live-oak growing,
All alone stood it, and the moss hung down from the branches,
Without any companion it grew there, glistening out joyous leaves of dark
    green,

And its look, rude, unbending, lusty, made me think of myself;
But I wondered how it could utter joyous leaves, standing alone there
    without its friend, its lover—For I knew I could not;
And I plucked a twig with a certain number of leaves upon it, and twined
    around it a little moss, and brought it away—And I have placed it in sight
    in my room,
It is not needed to remind me as of my friends, (for I believe lately I think
    of little else but them,)
Yet it remains to me a curious token—I write these pieces, and name them
    after it;
For all that, and though the live-oak glistens there in Louisiana, solitary in a
    wide flat space, uttering joyous leaves all its life, without a friend, a lover,
    near—I know very well I could not.

In response to this grand lyric meditation, I have spent much time staring at the evergreen oaks of Louisiana and Florida, strange for me because I am not much of a lover of nature. Yet the live-oak is as excessive among trees as Falstaff is amid Shakespeare's other characters; for Whitman, and his readers, the live-oak is an emblem of how meaning gets started rather than merely deferred or repeated. When printed in the fourth edition of *Leaves of Grass* (1867), the poem's tenth line read, "Yet it remains to me a curious token, it makes me think of manly love." The central line certainly is "And I plucked a twig with a certain number of leaves upon it, and twined around it a little moss," for that is the tally that is Whitman's central image.

Burke remarks that Walt's southern vistas are perfumed, but so are the tallies, whether sprigs of lilac or of live-oak moss. Calamus, the water-grass or rush called "sweet flag," might be termed Whitman's northern vista (to be Burkean again) since Walt wrote to William Michael Rossetti emphasizing its "fresh, aquatic, pungent bouquet," and implying that it had the shape of masculine genitalia (as in "Song of Myself," section 24, where it is part of a narcissistic, auto-erotic celebration).

Whitman's "leaves," for Burke, are related to "grass" as individuals are to groups. Eschewing the (finely) obvious, Kenneth remarked that everyone would recognize the classical and biblical allusions involved: the metaphor of Whitmanian "leaves" starts (for me) with Homer and then continues through Pindar, Vergil, Dante, Spenser, Milton, and Shelley before "Song of Myself" appropriates it, passing on to Wallace Stevens, T. S. Eliot, and a host of Americans. The autumnal individual death is fused by Whitman with the biblical figuration "All flesh is grass."

Subtler even than Burke, John Hollander indicates the ambiguity of the title: *Leaves of Grass.* How do we read that rich *of?* Palpably not literal, does the phrase primarily signify that Whitman's grass-book has its affinity with the leaves of Shakespeare's Sonnets, and other authorial offerings that Walt read as homoerotic intimacies, from Vergil to the nineteenth century? Hollander's emphasis properly gives primacy to the *grass* of the American Bible's title. The wounded and dying young men Whitman attended in the Washington, D.C., war hospital became his authentic leaves; their maimed flesh his grass. Just ten years earlier, he had a Pisgah-sight of the wasted richness of their lives and flesh: "the beautiful uncut hair of graves."

Burke found in Whitman's *leaves* this poet's very American propensity for sudden and constant departures: Walt is always passing by us, though his leavings are never final. In common with Hart Crane, Burke traces Whitman's bridge between substantives and verbs, passages to America and to more than America, if there can be what is more than America in Whitman's vision of the leaves, which are "blades" in multiple senses, including the gay blades of the poet's perpetual yearnings.

Burke's third term, *lilacs,* is the dialectical synthesis of *vistas* and *leaves.* The sprig of lilac, the tally, haunts Whitman's readers, whether Hart Crane in *The Bridge* or the doomed Jean Verdenal, T. S. Eliot's lover, who met him at a Paris rendezvous bearing a sprig of lilac, emblem of a heroic sacrifice to come in the Dardanelles campaign. The scent of lilacs pervades both Whitman and Eliot. A Burkean excursus into sublimely wild criticism obscured the connection, but it has been taken up by many of us in the wake of Burke. A not-un-Burkean cadenza on the tally is intended by me as yet another tribute to Kenneth, our leading American sage since Emerson and William James.

Upward from the dead, Hart Crane rhapsodized, Walt brought "tally" and its new bond of love between the greatest poets. Like Crane, I would add to the latter Emily Dickinson, whose mastery of the Emersonian intransigent blank is even more nuanced than Wallace Stevens's. Very subtly, Crane, in his final, truncated phase, covenants both with Dickinson and with Whitman, an imaginative fusion that sets itself against what Crane feared *The Waste Land* had done to American poetry. Whitman brings tally, at once the emblem of erotic surrender and of affirmed continuity. Dickinson brings a qualified triumph over our dread of mortality, not a fear for ourselves but the ongoing loss of our beloved dead.

I have written about the Whitmanian tally many times, and want now to make a fresh approach to this central image of voice in American literature. When we speak of a poet's "voice," we are compelled to be metaphorical, since we are transferring from the auditory to the visual, or, in transcendental terms, to the visionary. Whitman's tally was nothing but erotic: it invokes masturbation. Is this literal self-gratification or is it, as an entire school of homoerotic scholars insist, a screen for gay close encounters?

Tally still is part of vernacular usage in the American Southwest and in parts of England. Both verb and noun, it means a counting up (keeping score, as by notches on a twig) and a counting down, or final total. When Whitman relies strongly upon the word, as in "Lilacs," it is taken to the very edge of possible meanings and blends vistas, leaves, and lilacs into a fresh troping of Whitman's transcendental yearnings for the beloved dead.

The tally presents itself as an unforgettable manifestation in "Song of Myself," section 25:

Dazzling and tremendous how quick the sun-rise would kill me,
If I could not now and always send sun-rise out of me.

We also ascend dazzling and tremendous as the sun,
We found our own O my soul in the calm and cool of the day-break.

My voice goes after what my eyes cannot reach,
With the twirl of my tongue I encompass worlds and volumes of worlds.

Speech is the twin of my vision, it is unequal to measure itself,
It provokes me forever, it says sarcastically,
Walt you contain enough, why don't you let it out then?

Come now I will not be tantalized, you conceive too much of articulation,
Do you not know O speech how the buds beneath you are folded?

Waiting in gloom, protected by frost,
The dirt receding before my prophetical screams,
I underlying causes to balance them at last,
My knowledge my live parts, it keeping tally with the meaning of all things,
Happiness, (which whoever hears me let him or her set out in search of this
    day.)

My final merit I refuse you, I refuse putting from me what I really am,
Encompass worlds, but never try to encompass me,
I crowd your sleekest and best by simply looking toward you.

Writing and talk do not prove me,
I carry the plenum of proof and every thing else in my face,
With the hush of my lips I wholly confound the skeptic.

Walt's internalized sunrise *is* voice, which the poet tropes as a new kind of balance:

My knowledge my live parts, it keeping tally with the meaning of all things.

The line is one of the poet's most astonishing, since it brings together knowledge and the genitalia, whose function is to tally every possible meaning. How shall we translate this? One prose reduction would lead us to see this as auto-eroticism, and certainly there is such an implication whenever Whitman keeps tally, as in "Spontaneous Me" or more abstractly in "Chanting the Square Deific." As to Whitman's desires, the poetry and the record overtly proclaim homo-eroticism. But Whitman's powerful account of his self-explorations seems an equally exultant celebration of orgasm brought about by masturbation.

As a screen for homoerotic activities this is not convincing. There is very little celebratory poetry devoted to self-gratification. I can think only of Goethe, who ends each of the five acts of *Faust, Part 2* with metaphoric masturbations, and of Theodore Roethke, writing under Whitman's influence. Now, in the early years of the twenty-first century, we are accustomed to homosexual literature but not to the solipsistic ecstasy of masturbation. Whitman, always outdoing our creeds, breaks the new road here also. But why is he so insistent upon telling us more than we need to know?

I have added *tally* to Kenneth Burke's *vistas, leaves,* and *lilacs* so as to catalogue Whitman's four master tropes and finally to see that the four fictions of the self all are forms of one another. Only Whitman would see that leaves are prospects, lilacs (even in bloom) remain leaves, tallies are lilacs, and round the cycle endlessly we go. Whitman chooses the lilac because it blooms so early, but he absorbs in it the fall of the leaf, glimpses into the clearing, and above all the tally, his signature.

In "When Lilacs Lost in the Dooryard Bloom'd," Whitman's soul, concerning which he knows as little as we do, tallies the voice of the hermit thrush. Is this because Whitman now associates his soul with the need to die an individual death, which he calls "sane and sacred"? Rhetorically impressive, this yet may be the largest flaw in an extraordinary elegy for the self (rather than for President Lincoln).

"Lilacs" seems to me the greatest American poem *because* its largeness of vision is inevitably expressed by a metric of which the poet had become a master. There is a biblical reverberation to Whitman's elegy, and not only because the hermit thrush's song of death echoes the erotic intensity of the Song of Songs.

The best text of Whitman currently and generally available is *Leaves of Grass and Other Writings,* the Norton Critical Edition, superbly re-edited by Michael Moon (2002), who gives us the eight lines excised from the 1860 "You Felons on Trial in Courts":

O bitter sprig! Confession sprig!
In the bouquet I give you place also—I bind you in,
Proceeding no further till, humbled publicly,
I give fair warning, once for all.

I own that I have been sly, thievish, mean, a prevaricator, greedy, derelict,
And I own that I remain so yet.

What foul thought but I think it—or have in me the stuff out of which it is
    thought?
What in darkness in bed at night, alone or with a companion?

The bouquet is the complete *Leaves of Grass,* the sprig serves as the tally, and the confessional bitterness had hovered in Whitman since the 1855 "Song of Myself." Since we cannot know what in Whitman is figurative and what literal, I assume that the concealed experience here is some kind of homoerotic debacle in the winter of 1859–60, a crisis whose most perfect expression is "As I Ebb'd with the Ocean of Life." The impulse to surrender the twig or tally is a kind of castration motif that will culminate in the "Lilacs" elegy.

When I think of Whitman's tally I come first to the lilac, but the calamus and its sibling weeds never are far distant. All are emblems of the male genitalia and of a pact between poets, however separated by time. In a mediocre 1860 poem, Whitman says to us that we "tally all antecedents," which is his widest use of his signature trope. What can a figuration refer to except perhaps another metaphor, particularly in Whitman? Since *tally* is both noun and verb—unlike *vista, leaf, lilac*—one sees why Whitman falls in love with the word. In itself, it both binds and counts. Because of Whitman's influence, overt *and* concealed, in

Pound and Eliot, Hart Crane and D. H. Lawrence, William Carlos Williams and the ever-evasive Wallace Stevens, one could say that the tally could be treated as the central image of much of post-Whitmanian American poetry.

Whitman, on whatever level of literalness, associated the composition of his poems, through masturbation, with an idealized homoeroticism, a strong or creative misreading of Emerson's Platonism. Actualities—whether heterosexual or homosexual—tend to defeat idealizations. Crane, Whitman's prime heir, testifies to that by his life and work, and still Crane found in Whitman what he needed: "Upward from the dead / Thou bringest tally." Pound condescended to Whitman and yet gave voice to a grand return of the poetic father in *The Pisan Cantos*. In Canto 82 we again confront the tally, and in a Whitmanian context: "man, earth: two halves of the tally / but I will come out of this knowing no one / neither they me." Here the Pisan earth replaces the waters that surround Long Island, and the estrangement prevails. What seems clear is that Pound's sense of Whitman was far deeper than his own prose ever intimates.

The triumph of Whitman's tally is the Lincoln elegy. There seem finally two grand modes in Whitman: celebration and lamentation. The longer one stays with him, the more difficult it becomes to separate the two. "Song of Myself" has an elegiac undersong, and "Lilacs," by the scandalous eloquence and sonorous beauty of its close, can seem more a celebration of itself than a self-elegy.

Our national poet, like the national poets of Europe, mysteriously does not so much reflect as project us. Shakespeare is so vast that England domesticates him by revising even the great tragedies into hopefulness, and sometimes I am left staring at a Christian (even a Catholic) Shakespeare irrelevant to *Othello, King Lear,* and *Macbeth*. Whitman, after we stopped neglecting him, has been weakly misread as a rebel, an antiformalist, and a sexual pioneer. I am always misunderstood when I ask what would be the consequence if it were discovered that Robert Browning was in the closet (with Henry James) while Walt cavorted with whores. Neither sexual orientation had any cognitive or aesthetic value in itself.

The tally is at once the poem, the icon, and the man or woman. Shakespeare and Whitman are icons of universal appeal who transcend the interests of any nation-state of whatever era. You can pluck patriotic speeches out of their contexts in Shakespeare, but within the plays they are qualified by ironies too large to be seen. The persona of Walt Whitman, an American, scarcely is available to us any more in sociopolitical terms, since the United States becomes more and more a plutocracy, theocracy, and oligarchy.

* * *

Where shall we refind Shakespearean and Whitmanian vistas? The great critic G. Wilson Knight remains the best guide to the spiritual problematics of Shakespeare, out of fashion as Knight now is. Whitman has found one such guide in Angus Fletcher, but the criticism afforded Walt is mostly inadequate. Hart Crane remains his precursor's best prophet. *The Bridge* is an epic tally, summing up the American past until 1930, and like Whitman mingling together the elegiac and the celebratory. Brooklyn Bridge stands in for "Crossing Brooklyn Ferry," as Crane also finds emblems. Whether a "steeled Cognizance" is an apt replacement for leaves of grass is a question I myself cannot answer. The American Sublime is shared by Whitman and Crane; between them they all but define it but only by example. Here are the final sections of "Song of Myself" in juxtaposition with the last poem of Crane's "Voyages":

The spotted hawk swoops by and accuses me, he complains of my gab and my
     loitering.

I too am not a bit tamed, I too am untranslatable,
I sound my barbaric yawp over the roofs of the world.

The last scud of day holds back for me,
It flings my likeness after the rest and true as any on the shadow'd wilds,
It coaxes me to the vapor and the dusk.

I depart as air, I shake my white locks at the runaway sun,
I effuse my flesh in eddies, and drift it in lacy jags.

I bequeath myself to the dirt to grow from the grass I love,
If you want me again look for me under your boot-soles.

You will hardly know who I am or what I mean,
But I shall be good health to you nevertheless,
And filter and fibre your blood.

Failing to fetch me at first keep encouraged,
Missing me one place search another,
I stop somewhere waiting for you.

                              ["Song of Myself," section 52]

               Where icy and bright dungeons lift
               Of swimmers their lost morning eyes,

And ocean rivers, churning, shift
Green borders under stranger skies,

Steadily as a shell secretes
Its beating leagues of monotone,
Or as many waters trough the sun's
Red kelson past the cape's wet stone;

O rivers mingling toward the sky
And harbor of the phoenix' breast—
My eyes pressed black against the prow,
—Thy derelict and blinded guest

Waiting, afire, what name, unspoke,
I cannot claim: let thy waves rear
More savage than the death of kings,
Some splintered garland for the seer.

Beyond siroccos harvesting
The solstice thunders, crept away,
Like a cliff swinging or a sail
Flung into April's inmost day—

Creation's blithe and petalled word
To the lounged goddess when she rose
Conceding dialogue with eyes
That smile unsearchable repose—

Still fervid covenant, Belle Isle,
—Unfolded floating dais before
Which rainbows twine continual hair—
Belle Isle, white echo of the oar!

The imaged Word, it is, that holds
Hushed willows anchored in its glow.
It is the unbetrayable reply
Whose accent no farewell can know.

["Voyages VI"]

Writing so perfectly as he does here, Whitman lulls us into not immediately seeing the disintegration of his persona. Crane, after five "Voyages" of erotic celebration, invokes a muse in the mode of Pater's description of Botticelli's Venus. I will begin here with "Voyages," and then make my way back to "Song of Myself."

Crane addresses *his* sea, the Caribbean, which he knew as a child summering with his mother and where he was to choose suicide three months before his thirty-third birthday. This invocation of the sea has a Shakespearean sureness to its phrasing, even as it, like Whitman's "Song of Myself," section 52, courts disintegration, though Whitman's departure is Epicurean-Lucretian, and Crane's is Orphic-Platonic. There is no transcendence in Whitman's leaving; Crane occultly joins himself to the oldest (and most violent) of ancient Greek transcendences.

Both Crane and Whitman are toning down: these are not instances of the tally. Crane's stanzas are unlike any others he wrote, though they share his usual firmness at quatrains. Nor can I discover elsewhere in Whitman the quiet persuasiveness of section 52 of "Song of Myself." Crane, pitched very high in the first five "Voyages," seeks and finds another kind of eloquence.

Whitman and Crane alike are poets of the sublime, but the likeness does not extend far. Whitman frequently is in ambush; Crane is as knowing in the agonistic mode as Pindar was. Crane can be charmingly relaxed, as when he speaks of "peonies with pony manes" or salutes Whitman as being both Pan and the heavenly bread of everyday existence. Whitman's descents to the communal, his lists of everyday glories, commends even the chaff of the shoreline. Crane's parallel vision comes in the first stanza of "Voyages VI":

> Where icy and bright dungeons lift
> Of swimmers their lost morning eyes,
> And ocean rivers, churning, shift
> Green borders under stranger skies,

Both poets had difficult relations with their fathers: "As I Ebb'd with the Ocean of Life" will show an impulse toward reconcilement on Whitman's part. Dead at thirty-two, Crane has no similar turning, or perhaps it was contained in his death ode, "The Broken Tower." In "Lilacs," Abraham Lincoln replaces Walter Whitman, Sr., with magnificent results, since the broken nation awaits restoration. "The Broken Tower" speaks of "the broken world," hardly to be restored by any poet. Crane's quest is to "trace" the visionary company of love, a lost enterprise from the start. As in "Proem: To Brooklyn Bridge," Crane addresses a stranger God, beyond our world.

A transcendence that cannot be named is the consequence. Whitman, at his most transcendental, holds back with Epicurean naturalistic reservations: "The what is unknowable." Crane, a kind of natural Gnostic, keeps trying to name what can restitute the broken world. Two-thirds of a century after I first read Crane's "Atlantis," I remain stunned by its power.

> Migrations that must needs void memory,
> Inventions that cobblestone the heart,—
> Unspeakable Thou Bridge to Thee, O Love.
> Thy pardon for this history, whitest Flower,
> O Answerer of all,—Anemone,—
> Now while thy petals spend the suns about us, hold—
> (O Thou whose radiance doth inherit me)
> Atlantis,—hold thy floating singer late!

The "Thou" is the bridge, but how has Crane transformed Brooklyn Bridge? Certainly into a Shelleyan-Platonic daimon, "the many twain," yet the metamorphosis is beyond that. Whitman in his most exalted moments becomes a god or the sun as god, sending forth sunrises at will. He did not need Jesus because he had himself been crucified *and* resurrected in "Song of Myself," section 38. Crane, with only the Christian Science of his mother as a spiritual heritage, was from the start a natural Catholic, heterodox because of his Gnosticism. And yet there is no more powerful gathering of religious yearning than in Crane's poetry, which like Oscar Wilde sees Jesus as essentially a poet. Crane seeks to lend a myth to God, who needs a fresh start himself, and whose Word is imaged by Crane with a dazzling procession of figurations. I once remarked to my late friend, the poet John Frederick Nims, whose version of Juan de la Cruz's "Dark Night of the Soul" is deeply engrained in me, that "To Brooklyn Bridge" is an American companion poem to John of the Cross's sublimity. Nims, himself a Catholic, admired "To Brooklyn Bridge," but was wary of the comparison.

Crane specified that the "Proem" was to be printed in italics, so as to stand apart from *The Bridge*. At the conclusion, "To Brooklyn Bridge" acquires a deeper resonance, unmatched in American poetry since Whitman and Dickinson.

> *Again the traffic lights that skim thy swift*
> *Unfractioned idiom, immaculate sigh of stars,*

Beading thy path—condense eternity:
And we have seen night lifted in thine arms.

Under thy shadow by the piers I waited;
Only in darkness is thy shadow clear.
The City's fiery parcels all undone,
Already snow submerges an iron year . . .

O Sleepless as the river under thee,
Vaulting the sea, the prairies' dreaming sod,
Unto us lowliest sometime sweep, descend
And of the curveship lend a myth to God.

There is the precarious closeness to a Pietà in *"And we have seen night lifted in thine arms."* An extraordinary pair of quatrains follows:

Under thy shadow by the piers I waited;
Only in darkness is thy shadow clear.
The City's fiery parcels all undone,
Already snow submerges an iron year . . .

O Sleepless as the river under thee,
Vaulting the sea, the prairies' dreaming sod,
Unto us lowliest sometime sweep, descend
And of the curveship lend a myth to God.

Throughout Crane has celebrated Brooklyn Bridge's "curveship," its "vaulting" or agile "leap." That is still to be seen, from both shores, but any one of us would be regarded as very odd if we were to express religious sentiments while admiring it. Crane's bridge *is* Crane, as Whitman's bridge is his body. Both vault to transcendence, and then fall broken upon the broken fragments of love.

In "Cape Hatteras," a brilliant but uneven section of *The Bridge*, Crane directly confronts Whitman as what Blake would have called the Angel of America:

"—Recorders ages hence"—ah, syllables of faith!
Walt, tell me, Walt Whitman, if infinity
Be still the same as when you walked the beach
Near Paumanok—your lone patrol—and heard the wraith
Through surf, its bird note there a long time falling . . .
For you, the panoramas and this breed of towers,

> Of you—the theme that's statured in the cliff.
> O Saunterer on free ways still ahead!
> Not this our empire yet, but labyrinth
> Wherein your eyes, like the Great Navigator's without ship
> Gleam from the great stones of each prison crypt
> Of canyoned traffic . . . Confronting the Exchange,
> Surviving in a world of stocks,—they also range
> Across the hills where second timber strays
> Back over Connecticut farms, abandoned pastures,—
> Sea eyes and tidal, undenying, bright with myth!

The labyrinth is Crane's America, slouching toward disaster. Earlier in "Cape Hatteras" we are shown an even darker evocation of the labyrinth:

> What whisperings of far watches on the main
> Relapsing into silence, while time clears
> Our lenses, lifts a focus, resurrects
> A periscope to glimpse what joys or pain
> Our eyes can share or answer—then deflects
> Us, shunting to a labyrinth submersed
> Where each sees only his dim past reversed . . .

* * *

Unlike most legatees of Whitman, Crane never *sounds* like his visionary precursor. Part of Hart Crane's splendor is his invocation of the ambience of Whitman's free verse in the formal idioms of Christopher Marlowe, Arthur Rimbaud, Herman Melville, Emily Dickinson, and T. S. Eliot. *The Bridge* breaks loose in certain sections from Crane's characteristic quatrains and octaves. His last major poem, "The Broken Tower," is in rhymed quatrains, which work to bind together the ecstasy and anguish of the poet's elegy for himself.

Poetic influence is a labyrinthine process, and at its deepest is remote from echo and allusion, though it does not exclude them. Robinson Jeffers writes in a version of Whitman's open form, though his vistas are never Whitmanian, while D. H. Lawrence breaks from Thomas Hardy's metrics to engulf himself in Whitmanian innovation, yet only rarely reminds us of Whitman, even in the liberating chants of *Look! We Have Come Through!*

When Whitman tallies he takes measure of all things, implicitly including the measure of his own poetry. In his very different way, Whitman is as formalist a poet as were our late contemporaries James Merrill and Anthony Hecht, who usefully may be contrasted to the late A. R. Ammons and to John Ashbery, both of them strongly influenced by the poet of *Leaves of Grass*. Ammons and the versatile Ashbery can be far freer in form than Whitman ever is. The King James Bible is the largest influence upon Whitman's style, and the Hebrew *parallelism* breaks through in the strongest of the translators, William Tyndale and Miles Coverdale.

There is no single measure to Whitman's songs, just as his huge enlargements transcend all previous notions as to what can constitute materia poetica. To hold together the vastness of his topics and the fluid dissolves of his tropes Whitman had to discover a master metaphor and found it in the tally, at once his "confession sprig" and his incanted warbles for lilac-time.

The Whitmanian tally is the binding agent for "When Lilacs last in the Dooryard Bloom'd," the sonorous elegy for the martyred Abraham Lincoln. Together with "As I Ebb'd with the Ocean of Life," "Lilacs" is the most formally measured of Whitman's poems. I have a passion for "Lilacs," though the epic "Song of Myself" is certainly the center of the Whitmanian poetic cosmos. Henry and William James, T. S. Eliot (belatedly), and Wallace Stevens all associated "Out of the Cradle Endlessly Rocking" with "Lilacs" because there is a clear affinity between the mockingbird's song and the song of death warbled by the hermit thrush. The boy Whitman first beholds the mockingbird "when the lilac-scent was in the air." The crucial difference between "Out of the Cradle" and "Lilacs" seems to me that the sea in the first poem lisps the low and delicious word *death,* which becomes the burden of the hermit thrush's song in "Lilacs." In the earlier poems, the male mockingbird sings of bereavement but not of death, though that is implied.

Why did Whitman choose the word *tally* for what I judge to be his comprehensive vision of poetic voice? The word has a curious history. It derives from the Latin *talea,* which means a cutting, rod, or stick, on which you record payments and the sum still owed. In English, it transmuted into the idea of a duplicate or other half. It then became associated with illicit love. To live "tally" was to dwell together without marriage. In time the word expanded to become *tally-whacking, tally woman,* and *tally-wags* (for the male genitalia).

Only surmise is possible for why Whitman employed it so extensively. On one level it is a count of his "thousand responsive songs at random," which seems to be related to onanism, though as I have noted the bevy who profess a homosexual poetics prefer to ignore the palpable auto-eroticism and see him as enjoying a free life of gay encounters and relationships. That would please me if it were so, but little evidence can attest it. Sprigs of lilacs were important to Whitman, as was the calamus, or sweet flag; both represented male genitalia to him. His earliest use of *tally*, so far as I can tell, is in section 25 of "Song of Myself": "My knowledge my live parts, it keeping tally with the meaning of all things." That is, even for Walt, a very ambitious line, bringing together knowledge, the Whitmanian genitalia, and *all* things that are meaningful. Pragmatically that suggests auto-eroticism, once described by the late Norman Mailer as "bombing oneself," and still taboo.

Late in his life, Whitman wrote of his choice "to tally greatest bards," and insisted he preferred nature to them, Shakespeare included. In a strange poem of 1866, "Chanting the Square Deific," he strikingly says, "All sorrow, labor, suffering, I, tallying it, absorb in myself." *All* and *tally* seem deeply connected for him. Perhaps that accounts for the way in which tally and tallying bind together "When Lilacs Last in the Dooryard Bloom'd."

There, at the end of section 7, giving up his sprig of lilac to Lincoln's coffin, Whitman surrenders the tally to the work of mourning. I feel the awe and poignancy of this surrender. It is a decade since "Song of Myself," and the incarnation of the poetic character in Walt ebbs, more than he could have realized in 1865. In the marvelous section 14, the tally enters first before the death carol of the hermit thrush: "And the voice of my spirit tallied the song of the bird." That "tallied" is intricate. Does it mean "doubled" or "keeping score"? Either way, Whitman is the full partaker of the carol of death, which taps into the Eros of the Song of Solomon but surpasses it by suggesting an incestuous union between death and the bard:

> Lost in the loving floating ocean of thee,
> Laved in the flood of thy bliss O death.

I find it stunning, every time I recite "Lilacs," that the first line of the following section, 15, should be "To the tally of my soul." Is this the unknown soul of "Song of Myself"? Yes and perhaps no, because the great decade between 1855 and 1865 has transformed the soul's mystery into what can be known: the tally. How are we to read that? There has to be an erotic element in that tally. Does it represent Whitman's perpetual homosexual longing, a desire perhaps never fully gratified?

The tally returns in the astonishing final verse-paragraph of "Lilacs," where Whitman cries forth, "And the tallying chant, the echo arous'd in my soul." That is clearly a transmuted soul, having little in common with "Song of Myself."

The aroused echo of birdsong returns Walt to the mockingbird's song of loss in "Out of the Cradle," yet the effect is very different, since the "Cradle" elegy concludes with the triumph of death, which is not "Lilacs"'s resolution. Whitman's tally, being erotic, ambivalently embraced both life and death and points the path out of death-in-life. The reader tallies the sprig of lilac, the carol of the hermit thrush, and the achieved form of the elegy for Lincoln, so that they become a composite of the image that is Whitman's poetic voice.

It is immensely moving that the deathbed edition of *Leaves of Grass* has a title-page epigraph, signed by Whitman, of a brief poem evidently written by him in 1876. So far as I can tell, this is the final use of *tallying* by the seer of *Leaves of Grass:*

> Come, said my Soul,
> Such verses for my Body let us write, (for we are one,)
> That should I after death invisibly return,
> Or, long, long hence, in other spheres,
> There to some group of mates the chants resuming,
> (Tallying Earth's soil, trees, winds, tumultuous waves,)
> Ever with pleas'd smile I may keep on,
> Ever and ever yet the verses owning—as, first, I here and now,
> Signing for Soul and Body, set to them my name,
> > Walt Whitman

"My Soul" here is closer to Emerson's "Oversoul" than ever before, and is a culmination of the evolution of "My Soul" from the unknowability of "Song of Myself" through the *Sea-Drift* elegies and "Lilacs." Resuming his chants, in whatever sphere, Whitman gives us one of the most powerful of his parentheses: "(Tallying Earth's soil, trees, winds, tumultuous waves,)."

It was in the early eighteenth century that *tally* and *tallying* moved from the commercial to the erotic sphere. Here, at his formal conclusion, Walt's "tallying" abandons both these spheres for an ultimate, which is necessarily unnamable. For his devoted readers, "tallying" here has an immensely rich metaphoric scope. The earth, trees, winds, and waves, by having been tallied, become irradiated images of bardic voice. The truly undiscovered Whitman is the master of trope, defensively distancing himself from his prime precursor, Emerson. Walt's triumph finds its emblem in the tally, itself a resource in American poets still to come, as it was for Ezra Pound and Hart Crane.

DEATH AND THE POET

Whitmanian Ebbings

That influence, as transmission from earlier to later, can be benign is hardly interesting. And between languages it never induces anxiety; Stevens could be fascinated by Paul Valéry without any fear of contamination. Whitman, who *had* composed the greatest poems of our climate, possessed Stevens, prompting formidable ambivalences. No other poems he read so haunted Stevens as did "Out of the Cradle Endlessly Rocking" and "When Lilacs Last in the Dooryard Bloom'd." What found him about those two in particular?

I keep coming back to Walt Whitman's most comprehensive trope: Night, Death, the Mother, and the Sea. As a fourfold metaphor this is traditional, reflecting both Yahweh's battle with Tiamit and Homer's oceanic vision. What Whitman changed was the Mother's role and identity, since she draws Night, Death, and the Sea away from a monstrous chaotic motif and closer to an image of fostering, though not always benign.

I have learned to locate the ultimate clue to Whitman's vision in the extraordinary "The Sleepers," which shared greatness in the original 1855 *Leaves of Grass* with "Song of Myself," and which seems to me the most authentically difficult of Whitman's six masterpieces of the long poem, each of which should always be read as it first was printed. Initially the high hazard of the poet's potential loss of identity to Night and the Sea was violently stressed. Sleep becomes the composite form that unites Death and the Mother with Night and the Sea, and it is only in and through the distortions of sleep and dream that Whitman discerns his unknown and forever unknowable soul, as contrasted with his fictive self, Walt Whitman, and his poignant "real me," or the "me myself."

What does it mean to regard one's own soul as *the* unknown aspect of nature? Whitman's metaphysical naturalism, his Epicureanism, can be studied in Frances Wright's Epicurean novel *A Few Days in Athens,* which we know he had read and studied, perhaps even under Wright's direct tutelage. With Shelley and Stevens, Whitman is a Lucretian poet, though unlike them he came late to *De rerum natura.* But from Wright he had learned the Epicurean principle that "the what is unknowable." If the soul is unknowable, then so also is sleep, our submerged life populated by Death and the Mother, Night and the Sea.

The famous conclusion to "The Sleepers" is overconfident in tone, and is less interesting than the rugged Epicurean twenty-seven-monosyllable line preceding it:

> I know not how I came of you and I know not where I go with you, but I
>   know I came well and shall go well.

Up to the "but" that is Epicurean eloquence; the known is less persuasive than the "know not." As a Lucretian poet, Whitman can be as sophisticated as Shelley and Stevens. Whenever he joins Emerson's "Optative Mood" he can seem uneasy. Perhaps, more than Emerson, Whitman was the prompter of pragmatism in William James, whose love for Whitman became a celebration of the American bard's "healthy-mindedness." Henry James evolved into an idolator of the elegiac Whitman, while his philosopher-psychologist brother wanted to accept affirmative Walt as the ideal voice of the nation.

I read Whitman one way in my youth, in quite another during my middle years, and now in old age tend to concentrate mostly upon his amazing artistry. In my twenties, he was the Central Man of American Romantic literature. Later I saw him as prophet of the American Religion. At eighty I value Walt most for his rhetorical skill, his titanic innovations in what John Hollander teaches me to call "the trope of form." Verse is unbound, not free, in Whitman. James Wright, himself a superb Whitmanian poet, refreshingly stressed Walt's "delicacy," a term Whitman would have welcomed. Randall Jarrell, emerging from New Critical cant to be surprised by Whitmanian mastery of form and diction, interests me less than James Wright's subtler responses, particularly to the invention of what Paul Fussell first called the Shore Ode, America's answer to the Wordsworthian crisis-poem.

In Wordsworth and what became *his* tradition, experiential loss was compensated by imaginative gain. Emersonians follow a grimmer law of compensation: "Nothing is got for nothing." After the twilight magnificence of the "Lilacs" elegy for Abraham Lincoln, Whitman ceased his reception of "retrievements out of the night." He would not allow anyone to judge "Lilacs" the greatest of his poems, but it was and is not only the sublime of his personal achievement but to this day is unsurpassed by anything else written in this hemisphere, in any language: English, Spanish, Portuguese, French, Yiddish. This ultimate elegy has become the New World's permanent prophecy of our fate as the Evening Land of Western literary culture. "Lilacs" is Whitman's sunset glory—"More life," the Hebrew blessing, is hardly its burden but is a fit motto for the epic of himself, Whitman's "dazzling and tremendous" sunrise and primary poem. To this day Whitman is aesthetically undervalued. He cannot stand with Chaucer and Shakespeare, who repopulated a world, but his place is with Milton, Blake, Wordsworth, and Shelley, poets of the sublime.

In the twentieth century, I find those poets in Yeats, Stevens, Crane, and the now neglected D. H. Lawrence. Stevens defensively deprecated Whitman, yet is flooded by him, as is Lawrence. Crane's idiom has nothing of Whitman's, but spiritually he asserts sonship to Walt. Yeats is the exception: the remarks on Whitman in *A Vision* are silly. Lost in Phase 6, where the *Will* is "Artificial Individuality," the New World's greatest writer "created an Image of vague, half-civilised man, all his thought and impulse a product of democratic bonhomie." More than Yeats's lifelong hatred of democracy is needed to explain this collapse of judgment in so major a literary consciousness.

James Merrill, a profoundly Yeatsian poet, once remarked to me that he could not absorb Whitman but judged this to be his own limitation. Robert Frost, Marianne Moore, Robert Penn Warren, Elizabeth Bishop, and Merrill seem to be the only twentieth-century American poets of authentic eminence untouched by Whitman. One could add John Crowe Ransom and Allen Tate, southern traditionalists and New Critics. Robert Penn Warren, wise and wary, would placate me by saying that his distaste for Emerson was so intense that he could not accept the clearly Emersonian Whitman.

The poets of my own generation frequently came back to Whitman by way of Stevens and Crane, or of William Carlos Williams and Poundian disciples like Charles Olson. In old age, it seems to me an astonishingly rich generation, born between 1923 and 1935: Anthony Hecht, Edgar Bowers, Jack Gilbert, Gerald Stern, A. R. Ammons, John Ashbery, W. S. Merwin, James Wright, Philip

Levine, Alvin Feinman, John Hollander, Irving Feldman, Gary Snyder, Allen Grossman, Mark Strand, Charles Wright, Jay Wright, and others. If that history appears motivated by male preferences, I will observe only that Elizabeth Bishop, Jean Garrique, Muriel Rukeyser, May Swenson, and Amy Clampitt came a touch earlier, and Grace Schulman, Louise Glück, Vicki Hearne, Jorie Graham, Gjertrud Schnackenberg, Rosanna Warren, Thylias Moss, Susan Wheeler, and Martha Serpas later.

The most widely read of our poets in that now senior (or, alas, deceased) group probably include Ammons, Ashbery, Merwin, James Wright, Levine, and Strand. Hollander is an immensely learned writer, as was Hecht, and they have become poets' poets, which saddens me. I will center upon Ammons, Ashbery, Merwin, Charles Wright, and Strand in their relationships to Whitman in a later chapter. Sometimes those are direct (Ammons, Ashbery, Wright) and sometimes mediated (Merwin by Pound and Eliot, Strand by Stevens). Whitman is an undersong in Pound, and emerges again in *The Pisan Cantos.* In Eliot, Whitman is the corpse planted in the garden, and resurrects in *The Waste Land,* and *Four Quartets,* while in Stevens the American bard is a drowned swimmer who rises up to break the water's surface so often that the reader learns to expect him. Taken together, Eliot and Stevens constitute a paradigm for realizing how poetic influence need not be an affair of stylistics. It works in the depths of image and idea, and produces intricate evasions that nevertheless bud and bloom.

James Wright died at fifty-two. I met him only a few times in New York City and can recall only one conversation, in which I expressed admiration for his strong book, *Shall We Gather at the River* (1968). Like many other readers I was particularly moved by "The Minneapolis Poem" with its plangent invocation of Whitman:

> But I could not bear
> To allow my poor brother my body to die
> In Minneapolis.
> The old man Walt Whitman our countryman
> Is now in America our country
> Dead.
> But he was not buried in Minneapolis
> At least.
> And no more may I be
> Please God.

Seven years before I had heard Wright lecture on "Whitman's Delicacy" and met him afterward for the first time. We talked briefly about Paul Fussell's fine notion of "the American Shore Ode," upon which I had heard Fussell lecture the year before, and Wright reminded me of his own very powerful Shore Odes, "At the Slackening of the Tide" in *Saint Judas* (1959) and "The Morality of Poetry," printed just before it in that book. Ever since, I have tended to fuse memories together, and more than once wrongly credited Wright with the formulation of the American Shore Ode, of which he was one of the masters, together with Ammons, Clampitt, Stevens, Bishop, Swenson, Eliot (*The Dry Salvages* in *Four Quartets*), and Crane. In the "Voyages" sequence and the Key West poems, Crane is second only to Whitman of *Sea-Drift* as the American genius of the shore.

Paul Fussell outlined some of the characteristics of the "American Shore Ode" (1962): "It is a lyric of some length and philosophic density spoken (usually at a specific place) on an American beach; its theme tends to encompass the relationship of the wholeness and flux of the sea to the discreteness and fixity of land objects. This kind of poem does more than simply engage in transcendental meditations about the sea: the important thing is the dissimilarity between shore and sea, sand and water, separateness and cohesiveness, analysis and synthesis—a dissimilarity which explains and justifies their paradoxical marriage." Allied to the Shore Ode is the old, more inclusive genre of the "Promenade Poem," described in the late Thomas Greene's *Calling from Diffusion: Hermeneutics of the Promenade* (2002). Greene describes two remarkable Shore Odes, Amy Clampitt's "Beach Glass" and A. R. Ammons's famous "Corson's Inlet," and then proceeds to the masterpiece of the subgenre, Whitman's "As I Ebb'd with the Ocean of Life."

Clampitt's "Beach Glass" is in the mode of Elizabeth Bishop's shoreline reveries, while "Corson's Inlet" manifests the characteristic deep relation to Whitman's *Sea-Drift* pieces of Ammons's meditations. I wrote on "Corson's Inlet" many years ago, and here will center on "Beach Glass," which has its own subtle awareness of Walt at the waterline. The Shore Ode, as I now suggest, is the American counterpart of the Greater Romantic Ode that my mentor M. H. Abrams initially established as a subgenre. Long ago I converted that into the antithetical crisis-lyric I analyzed in *A Map of Misreading*. English inland reverie and American shoreline poem ultimately descend from Petrarch's beautifully harrowing Canzone 129, a descent that Greene eloquently terms the discovery of the Promenade Poem.

Here is the opening of "Beach Glass":

> While you walk the water's edge,
> turning over concepts
> I can't envision, the honking buoy
> serves notice that at any time
> the wind may change,
> the reef-bell clatters
> its treble monotone, deaf as Cassandra
> to any note but warning. The ocean,
> cumbered by no business more urgent
> than keeping open old accounts
> that never balanced,
> goes on shuffling its millenniums
> of quartz, granite, and basalt.

The opening irony juxtaposes her companion's metaphysical "turning over concepts / I can't envision" to the "honking" and "clatters" of the water's edge. This irony plays against the synecdoche of the ocean's millennial shufflings "of quartz, granite, and basalt." *Shuffling,* as Clampitt was aware, is a rich Shakespearean word employed three times in *Hamlet.* The Prince, in his most famous soliloquy, broods on shuffling off this mortal coil. As Claudius tries to pray in his closet we hear the usurper say of heaven, "There is no shuffling there," but later we experience Claudius teaching Laertes to exchange blades "with a little shuffling." Whether the ocean possesses two touches of Claudius to one of Hamlet, we just don't know. I jocularly asked Amy Clampitt that once when out walking with her and Harold Korn, her husband and my old friend from undergraduate days. Always reticent, Clampitt replied only with a smile.

> It behaves
> toward the permutations of novelty—
> driftwood and shipwreck, last night's
> beer cans, spilt oil, the coughed-up
> residue of plastic—with random
> impartiality, playing catch or tag
> or touch-last like a terrier,
> turning the same thing over and over,
> over and over. For the ocean, nothing
> is beneath consideration.
> The houses

of so many mussels and periwinkles
have been abandoned here, it's hopeless
to know which to salvage. Instead
I keep a lookout for beach glass—
amber of Budweiser, chrysoprase
Of Almadén and Gallo, lapis
by way of (no getting around it,
I'm afraid) Phillips'
Milk of Magnesia, with now and then a rare
translucent turquoise or blurred amethyst
of no known origin.

The first verse-paragraph here generally empties out the beach world with our contemporary version of Whitman's sea-drift:

Chaff, straw, splinters of wood, weeds, and the sea-gluten,
Scum, scales from shining rocks, leaves of salt-lettuce, left by the tide . . .

This poverty is redressed by the charming discovery of a miniature sublime of beach glass: amber, chrysoprase, lapis, turquoise, amethyst. A superb final movement both confirms and undoes this sublimity:

The process
goes on forever: they came from sand,
they go back to gravel,
along with the treasuries
of Murano, the buttressed
astonishments of Chartres,
which even now are readying
for being turned over and over as gravely
and gradually as an intellect
engaged in the hazardous
redefinition of structures
no one has yet looked at.

The metaphor, sand to beach glass to gravel, is an aesthetic one and leads on to the wonderful Venetian glass of Murano and the stained glass of the cathedral at Chartres that alike must return to gravel also. That constitutes a kind of return of the dead artisans, not so much as an emblem of mutability but of the limited yet real triumph of Clampitt's shore poem over time, and in a modest way its winning a place in the shadow of Whitman's "As I Ebb'd with the Ocean of Life."

The gifted Irish novelist John Banville judges Henry James to be the ultimate master of the art of the novel in English. Such an estimate is provocative, since it sets James above Jane Austen, Charles Dickens, and George Eliot. I assume that Banville sees Joyce as a writer of prose epics in *Ulysses* and the *Wake,* which belong to a category that might include *Moby-Dick, War and Peace, In Search of Lost Time,* and *The Magic Mountain,* among other works. I myself, if I could reread yet once more only a single novel in English, would choose Samuel Richardson's *Clarissa* (1747–48). No single character in James, not even Isabel Archer, has the Shakespearean richness of Clarissa Harlowe. But reading through Henry James's twenty novels, you absorb so large a consciousness in prose narrative that in English only Dickens seems a true rival. James unsurprisingly gave no unqualified praise either to Dickens or to George Eliot, whose magnificent *Middlemarch* he dismissed as "an indifferent whole." Balzac, safely different in language and in mode, moved James to critical ecstasy, whereas James granted Jane Austen "her narrow *unconscious* perfection of form" (emphasis mine).

No other American novelist, from Hawthorne on to Faulkner and beyond, is of James's eminence. His American agonist, as he perhaps sensed in 1865 with a ghastly review of *Drum-Taps,* was and is Walt Whitman. The elegiac Whitman he came to love, more perhaps than the work of any other poet except Shakespeare. Barely twenty-two when he outrageously reviewed Whitman, as an older man James would chant "When Lilacs Last in the Dooryard Bloom'd" and "Out of the Cradle Endlessly Rocking" to William James and Edith Wharton, among others. I bring Whitman and Henry James together here as an experiment in tracing a different kind of influence from any of the modes upon which I have meditated.

When James died in London early in 1916, just more than a half-century had passed since the most unfortunate of all his many book reviews. I review the review rather closely, aided by my long acquaintance with would-be demolitions. Commencing with his "melancholy" as a reader of Whitman, James allows us no uncertainty as to his own aim: "It exhibits the effort of an essentially prosaic mind to lift itself, by a prolonged muscular strain, into poetry." Let us call this the Native Strain, since after all the prosaic mind is that of Walt Whitman, who *is* American imaginative literature. Angus Fletcher remarks that the review tells us much more about the twenty-two-year-old Henry James than it does about *Drum-Taps,* which James either did not *read,* or could not. Whether James in

1865 would have rejected the "Lilacs" elegy for Lincoln we cannot know, since it was not in the first issue of *Drum-Taps*, but was bound into a second printing later in 1865. Even had James encountered it then, it might not have changed the young master's conviction that "this volume is an offence against art."

Drum-Taps did include the extraordinary "Vigil Strange I Kept on the Field One Night":

Vigil strange I kept on the field one night;
When you my son and my comrade dropt at my side that day,
One look I but gave which your dear eyes return'd with a look I shall never
    forget,
One touch of your hand to mine O boy, reach'd up as you lay on the ground,
Then onward I sped in the battle, the even-contested battle,
Till late in the night reliev'd to the place at last again I made my way,
Found you in death so cold dear comrade, found your body son of responding
    kisses, (never again on earth responding,)
Bared your face in the starlight, curious the scene, cool blew the moderate
    night-wind,
Long there and then in vigil I stood, dimly around me the battlefield
    spreading,
Vigil wondrous and vigil sweet there in the fragrant silent night,
But not a tear fell, not even a long-drawn sigh, long, long I gazed,
Then on the earth partially reclining sat by your side leaning my chin in
    my hands,
Passing sweet hours, immortal and mystic hours with you dearest comrade—
    not a tear, not a word,
Vigil of silence, love and death, vigil for you my son and my soldier,
As onward silently stars aloft, eastward new ones upward stole,
Vigil final for you brave boy, (I could not save you, swift was your death,
I faithfully loved you and cared for you living, I think we shall surely meet
    again,)
Till at latest lingering of the night, indeed just as the dawn appear'd,
My comrade I wrapt in his blanket, envelop'd well his form,
Folded the blanket well, tucking it carefully over head and carefully under
    feet,
And there and then and bathed by the rising sun, my son in his grave, in his
    rude-dug grave I deposited,

Ending my vigil strange with that, vigil of night and battle-field dim,
Vigil for boy of responding kisses, (never again on earth responding,)
Vigil for comrade swiftly slain, vigil I never forget, how as day brighten'd,
I rose from the chill ground and folded my soldier well in his blanket,
And buried him where he fell.

I quote this poem complete because it cannot be understood otherwise, so perfect is its art. Kenneth Burke once remarked to me that Whitman's artistry was not yet fully revealed to his critics, an understatement by the best of twentieth-century rhetoricians. Since "Vigil Strange" clearly is a homoerotic elegy, and James in 1865 had experienced a single night's union with Oliver Wendell Holmes, Jr., himself a war hero, I surmise one of the origins of the reviewer's discomfort with Whitman. An exasperation is present throughout the review, but is expressed only by hyperbolical disdain for the poet's supposed pretensions.

"Vigil Strange" has been called "a monologue both lyrical and dramatic" by Michael Moon. Robert Browning separated the two subgenres; Whitman fuses them in "Vigil Strange" and elsewhere in *Drum-Taps.* Since this monologist is an idealization of Whitman himself, in what role does he speak? Transgressively this soldier Whitman (who was involved in the Civil War only as a volunteer unpaid nurse) is presented as the lover-father of a young boy-combatant, thus merging an incestuous element into the "love of comrades." So persuasive is the poem's rhetoric that few of its readers have been offended by the apparently metaphorical relationship that is celebrated and mourned. The word *vigil* is used twelve times in the twenty-five lines, constituting a kind of refrain. The Latin *vigilia* means "wakefulness," and *vigil* began in English as a devotional watching. Whitman's "Vigil Strange" is striking because the strangeness consists in the monologist's refusal either to weep or to lament his double grief for son and lover. R. P. Blackmur, despite his reservations about Hart Crane, remarked on Crane's absolute flair for producing meaning by rhythm, and Crane's feeling for "the heart of words." The praise was precise, and applies equally well to Whitman, whose rhythm here is revived in the Lincoln elegy "When Lilacs Last in the Dooryard Bloom'd," and whose feeling for the heart of the word *vigil* is so uncanny. Crane, who battled against Eliot's stylistic influence upon him, never employs a Whitmanian metric but learns from Whitman to quest for the heart of words.

Though "Vigil Strange" is probably the best poem in the first printing of

Drum-Taps, there is no record of how James reacted to it, either in 1865 or later. Some critics have suggested that James's homosexual relationships were a displacement of his lifelong love of his brother William, one year older than the novelist. I once found this notion puzzling, but now accept some plausibility in it. "Vigil Strange," if he had read the poem closely, must have aroused in Henry James a powerful ambivalence. And yet the overt proclamation of homoeroticism by Whitman evoked only a repressed or evaded rejection by the young James, who centered upon the Whitmanian temerity in usurping American bardhood. The self-revelatory sentence in the review is near its close: "You must be *possessed,* and you must strive to possess your possession." That was to be James's own striving, yet was first nature to Whitman, totally possessed in his poetic mission and, at his greatest, wonderfully possessing his possession. James eventually joined brother William in judging Whitman the master of American poetry.

Why did the James family, and Henry in particular (in his maturity), come to prefer "Out of the Cradle Endlessly Rocking" and "When Lilacs Last in the Dooryard Bloom'd" to all other American poems? An aesthetic answer certainly would be sufficient. If "Song of Myself," "Crossing Brooklyn Ferry," "The Sleepers," and "As I Ebb'd with the Ocean of Life" were added, then in my judgment you would have the half-dozen essentials of American poetry. And yet Henry's sonorous recitations of "Out of the Cradle" and "Lilacs" had the effect of a religious ecstasy for the Jameses and their circle. Something of the preternatural closeness of all the Jameses, especially William and Henry, is rather like the aura of Whitman's greatest elegies. That precisely these poems had a lasting effect on Wallace Stevens makes me wonder at what seems to be the universality of Whitman's Shore Ode and his threnody for Abraham Lincoln, our nation's martyr in removing the curse of African American slavery.

A lifelong student of influence in the life of the arts, literature most of all, I too have become an obsessive rereader and chanter of Whitman's greatest poems. There is a baroque splendor to the orchestration of Whitman's masterworks that demands more formalist analyses than are currently fashionable. *The Anatomy of Influence* is in part a study of Walt Whitman but since I cannot give full readings here, I desire to show aspects of the high art of these endlessly elaborating splendors. The late Anthony Hecht and I, each time we met, discussed what we both regarded as the complex inventions of our greatest formalist poet, evoker of the archetypal American songs of the mockingbird and the hermit thrush.

"Out of the Cradle," first titled "A Child's Reminiscence" (Christmas 1859) and described by its poet as his "curious warble," was subsequently called "A Word out of the Sea" (that word being *death*) until Whitman decided to employ the hypnotic opening line as the ultimate title. Of the ode's 183 lines, about 70 constitute the aria sung by the mockingbird.

Whitman, one of the most metaphorical of poets, has little in him of Ezra Pound's distrust of trope. Life is metaphorical; death, literal. Any poem's treatment of death must be metaphorical: death our death in itself is not a poem:

> There is no life in thee, now, except that rocking life imparted by a gently rolling ship; by her, borrowed from the sea; by the sea, from the inscrutable tides of God. But while this sleep, this dream is on ye, move your foot or hand an inch; slip your hold at all; and your identity comes back in horror. Over Descartian vortices you hover. And perhaps, at mid-day, in the fairest weather, with one half-throttled shriek you drop through that transparent air into the summer sea, no more to rise for ever. Heed it well, ye Pantheists!

I owe to the long-departed Stephen Whicher the juxtaposition of this passage from "The Masthead" chapter of *Moby-Dick* with "Out of the Cradle Endlessly Rocking." Knowing Whicher only slightly before that, I discussed with him the links between Melville, Whitman, Stevens, and Crane on the fourfold trope of Night, Death, the Mother, and the Sea in the winter of 1960–61, in Ithaca, New York, when I returned to my alma mater to give some lectures, and my undergraduate adviser, M. H. Abrams, re-introduced us. I was thirty and Whicher forty-five or so, and I greatly admired his study of Emerson, *Freedom and Fate* (1953). There was time for only one rather extended conversation, which could not be repeated, for he ended his own life soon afterward. I remember his insights with gratitude. He seemed abstracted but not agitated or troubled, and I have never had the heart to ask Abrams, who was close to him, about this death.

I had attended Whicher's September 1960 lecture on "Out of the Cradle" but did not read it while he was still alive. It read nearly half a century ago as a prelude to his own final days. Rereading it now I am both moved and puzzled. Writing a century after Whitman composed the "Cradle" pre-elegy, Whicher called his essay "Whitman's Awakening to Death."

In the winter of 1859–60, Whitman seems to have gone through a crisis, presumably caused by a homoerotic failure, the defeat of a relationship. "As I Ebb'd" and "Out of the Cradle" took their origin in that crisis. The solar vitalism of the Whitman of 1855–58 diminished after a bad winter. The major *Calamus* poems all cluster in 1859, and are followed by the two great *Sea-Drift* elegies. Whicher interprets these last as an Oedipal trespass, which seems more clearly to characterize "As I Ebb'd." Yet he is accurate in tracing Whitman's path "from passion to perception," until the poet accepts the mother's voice out of the sea as the "sane and sacred" word *death,* thus replacing the winter comrade who had deserted him or whom he had fled.

All explanations based on sexual orientation seem useless to me in the context of imaginative literature. Many great and good poets have been bisexual or homoerotic or heterosexual or none of the above. Even more, many more weak poets, also were of all possible orientations. I pick up a copy of a large anthology lying near to hand, *Best Poems of the English Language,* which I brought out in 2004, confining it to poets born in the nineteenth century or earlier. It ends thus with Hart Crane, born in 1899. Without counting I see that it contains more than a hundred men and women. I could work through them to speculate on how many were of other sexual persuasions, but it would be absurd. Walt Whitman and Hart Crane are not "homosexual poets" and Lord Byron was not a "bisexual poet." Nothing in such namings can help us to estimate and appreciate the aesthetic value of Whitman, Crane, and Byron. There is no "homoerotic tradition" of authentic poetry, and it is useless to assume that there must be one.

Whitman awakens to a different imaginative meaning of death because of a homoerotic encounter of 1859–60, while John Keats awakened to a new sense of death because of his unfulfilled desire for Fanny Brawne. Melville, whatever early experiences he went through as a young mariner in the South Seas, endured an agonizing marriage that did not suit him, but Thomas Hardy suffered much the same, with desires that were much less equivocal. The thwarting of desire matters far more than the name and nature of the desire. It was Yeats who wrote: "The desire that is satisfied is not a great desire."

NOTES TOWARD A SUPREME FICTION
OF THE ROMANTIC SELF

W hat Western tradition has termed the "subject" or the "self" always has been a fiction, a saving lie to assuage anxieties. Heidegger and his Franco-American disciples move me not at all when they de-construct the self. Unless she is a poetic figure overtly telling a story of the self, the strong writer would have little to tell us. Virginia Woolf, disciple of Walter Pater, followed the great aesthete in elaborating conscious fictions of the self. Whether such consciousness is an aesthetic advantage seems dubi-ous to me. Mr. Pickwick inspired me to love and delight in him; Mrs. Dalloway fascinates me, but rather coldly. D. H. Lawrence dissolves even Birkin's self; Michael Henchard appears to be a rock until tragedy splits him. *Women in Love* is a permanent novel, but *The Mayor of Casterbridge* has Shakespearean mo-ments. Thomas Hardy was better off not doubting the relative stability of the self.

The contrast is strongest for me between Joseph Conrad's *Nostromo* and Henry James's *The Wings of the Dove*. In late James, the self is overtly problemati-cal. Conrad knows what James does, but chooses to work with antique notions of fatal flaws, which helps account for his influence upon William Faulkner, F. Scott Fitzgerald, Ernest Hemingway. Without the destructive element, Conrad could not have composed his masterpieces: *Under Western Eyes, The Secret Agent, Victory,* and best of all, *Nostromo*. Despite James and Joyce, Kafka and Proust, Conrad has his own unique eminence. He has now turned unfashionable and is excluded from the academy for his "colonialist" sins. He will return, as superior literature always does, burying its academic undertakers.

To speak of the self, human or literary, as a fiction is already a wearisome platitude. Insofar as it is true, it also is trivial. In life and in letters, it is a difference that makes little or no difference. Its day is over. Subjectivity required no defense. Difficult to attain, once earned it is a value if a commonplace. These are American remarks, doubtless reflecting the influence of my much lamented friend Richard Rorty. "Theory," though hanging on in the boondocks, was and will be alien to American literature and its most useful criticism.

"Naming" (as in Theodor Adorno and Walter Benjamin) is closer to the real concerns of literature. I am moved here by my own splendid name of "Bloom," particularly since my personal favorite among Whitman's poems is "When Lilacs Last in the Dooryard Bloom'd." Charmed as I also am by Stevensian derivatives ("stopped / In the door-yard by his own capacious bloom" and "Our bloom is gone. We are the fruit thereof"), it seems to me the most literary of names, though a price is paid. Whenever I teach Joyce's *Ulysses* I refer to the hero as Poldy, since my name has been confiscated—for a time. I never feel that my name comes from the outside. In the cold April in which I write any snatch of fresh bloom cheers me. There is little logic to a self-delighting name, but I gasp when told this is a creation by catastrophe.

The missing name in *Paradise Lost* is Lucifer, the unfallen form of Satan. Shakespeare shows us Macbeth, Othello, Antony, Lear, and other tragic protagonists before and after their taking the way down and out, but Milton is not Shakespeare. We barely behold a prelapsarian Satan, yet already he is Satan. As a Milton idolator, I don't enjoy finding flaws in him, but I go on wondering why he did not show us a sublime Lucifer. We are given Adam and Eve before *their* fall, and we deserve Lucifer, foremost of the angels. Surmise is all we have, so I allow myself to suspect a Miltonic achieved anxiety in relation to Shakespeare.

As a name, Milton knew that "Satan" meant the accuser of sin, God's prosecuting attorney. "Lucifer" is the light-bearer, or Morning Star, a grand appellation. Did Milton fear that was too grand for Satan? One step onward and we would have the angelical C. S. Lewis advising us that the proper way to read *Paradise Lost* is to start with a good morning's hatred of Satan. Milton, a great poet and member of his own party-of-one without knowing it, certainly would not have agreed with his dogmatic exegetes. He does not like Satan, but he certainly molds an energetic hero-villain in the tradition of Elizabethan-Jacobean drama. Whether Hamlet, in one of his myriad aspects, can be categorized as a hero-villain is disputable, but I think Hamlet informs Satan in his single most challenging declaration:

> who saw
> When this creation was? Rememberst thou
> Thy making, while the maker gave thee being?
> We know no time when we were not as now;
> Know none before us, self-begot, self-raised
> By our own quickening power.

[5.856–51]

I recall first reading these lines two-thirds of a century ago and brooding hardest on "our own quickening power." In Satan, that is an anti-natural vitalism, in ultimate defiance of Saint Augustine. Would not John Milton, proudest and most ambitious of poets since Dante and a lifelong evader of Shakespeare, have endorsed Satan's "self-begot" *as a poet,* though not necessarily as a person? More broadly, I go on taking Satan as a source for all High Romantic poets, from William Blake to Hart Crane, who assert their paradoxical dependence/independence of precursors. Yeats, in so many ways the apogee of High Romanticism, adopted Vico's maxim: "We only know what we ourselves have made." Yet he also said that we go to the poets to make our souls.

Milton is subtle and long delayed in naming Satan (which is ancient Hebrew for "adversary"). Once the twenty-six lines of the first invocation are completed, Milton turns to his hero-villain (lines 27–83), who first is called "the infernal serpent" and is not named as Satan until line 82. After all, the poet does not fear the name. Akin to this fifty-five-line gap in naming is Milton's refusal to use the unfallen name, "Lucifer," even once in the poem. Again, it is not until book 5 that the loss of the abrogated name is noted:

> but not so waked
> Satan, so call him now, his former name
> Is heard no more in heaven.

[5.658–60]

The significance of the censored name is enhanced by Milton's refusal to allow it into his poem. It can be seen as the opposite to Jacob's name changed to "Israel," or Enoch's to the Kabbalistic "Metatron." Is there not a personal shading for Milton, whose blindness may recoil from the image of light-bearer or

Morning Star? After all, Milton regards most of his countrymen as being more fallen than himself since they had chosen "a captain back *for* Egypt," rejecting the memory of Oliver Cromwell, the poet's "chief of men."

Names are magical for all great poets, who seek immortality for their own: Shakespeare, Milton, Wordsworth, Whitman. What is there not in a name, when it is one of those? For these are the strongest poets in the English language of the past four centuries. *Strong,* as I employ it, translates the German *streng,* and perhaps should be rendered "strict." The strength or strictness is a paradox, a fantastic assertion of the will that both accepts the weight of tradition and battles against it by misreading, at once breaking and remaking, as Milton's Satan accepts too much in God for any freedom to follow.

Satan is not allowed by Milton to assert the relatively autonomous self of Lucifer. He must resist God and the unfallen angels in the weaker self of the adversary, Satan. The *history* of Satan, in *Paradise Lost,* is written by the poem's true god, the Holy Spirit that inspires Milton, rather than the irascible schoolmaster of souls called God. To be self-begot by your own quickening power is of course an untruth, whether in or out of the poem. But what is truth for Satan or for us? Death—and poetry exists to postpone death, to hold it off. Reality-testing is the Freudian ethic, but this is precisely where Shakespeare and Milton, much his favorite poets, brush Freud aside. Time is death, God's history. Poetry lies against time. Nietzsche speaks of the will's revenge against time and time's "it was."

Satan is heroic because for him all is agon. Hopelessly weak in regard to divinity, nevertheless he strives as though there is nothing that matters except not to be overcome. He is—to me—the inevitable paradigm for the strong poet who strictly meditates a muse who is thankless, having known too many before him.

But how can we distinguish between the grandiose and the great, since both are telling lies about themselves and the past? Here I enter upon the vexations of the canonical, where one scarcely can intimate prophecies as to survival without giving offence. No critic can hope to receive more than a passing grade here. Samuel Johnson, critic-of-critics, brilliantly canonized Oliver Goldsmith but blundered in regard to the marvel of Laurence Sterne. Few days go by without my saying that such-and-such a work is just another period piece, but that was what the Grand Cham of literature meant when he said, "*Tristram Shandy* did not last."

*   *   *

The strictest reply a master poet can make to time's "it was" is to propound a supreme fiction of the self, where the crucial word is *fiction*. In the United States that means Whitman and his major progeny: Wallace Stevens, William Carlos Williams, Marianne Moore, Ezra Pound, T. S. Eliot, Hart Crane, and John Ashbery. Add Emerson as Whitman's master and the progeny includes Robert Frost. From Emily Dickinson, an Emersonian with a difference, you can go on to Elizabeth Bishop, May Swenson, Amy Clampitt. Of all those (and you can add as you will) the most overt re-weavers of the self as supreme fiction are Emerson, Whitman, and the appropriator of American supreme fictions, Wallace Stevens.

On the European side, Goethe contrived himself, "genius of happiness and astonishment," as a supreme fiction. His closest descendant in Britain, Thomas Carlyle, is now neglected, but Goethe also touched Emerson, Byron, and Shelley. Wordsworth pugnaciously would have denied he made a fiction of himself, but what else in *The Prelude* matters compared to the poet himself as the most supreme of all fictions? Emerson calls his saving lie against time "the Central Man," while Whitman names him as the rough Walt, the self of "Song of Myself." Wallace Stevens, with both the advantages and displeasures of knowing himself to be a latecomer, writes his romance of the self in *Notes Toward a Supreme Fiction* (1942). One of the many prologues to this vitalizing song of the self is Stevens's "A High-Toned Old Christian Woman" (1922):

> Poetry is the supreme fiction, madame.
> Take the moral law and make a nave of it
> And from the nave build haunted heaven.

However supreme, a fiction remains a fiction. The phrase "supreme fiction" emanates from Oscar Wilde, whose "De Profundis" shows him entertaining one fiction too many, in which the imprisoned wit becomes Christ. That too was part of Whitman's fiction. Stevens, whose sensibility was not religious, has no interest in such an identification, but still attempts to define "the fictive hero."

The emblems of the Emersonian quest for the Central Man are scattered throughout the diffident transcendentalism of *Notes:* "vivid transparence," "major man," "man-hero." Like Whitman, his hidden master, Stevens essentially is a celebratory poet, but as a poet he is even more evasive than the rough but delicate Walt. From Shakespeare, Stevens had learned a stance of disinteredness and disengagement, so that *Notes* sometimes gives the impression of qualifying all of its assertions. As I remember once arguing with the formidable and admirable Helen Vendler, a qualified assertion is not an asserted qualification. *Notes* distinctly is in Emerson's Optative Mood.

All three cantos and thirty-one blank terza rima versicles of *Notes* work joyously at expounding the three necessities of a supreme fiction: it must be abstract in Paul Valéry's sense of *abstractus,* withdrawn from a stale pseudo-reality to an ever-early freshness. It must change since an unchanging fiction ceases to give pleasure. And indeed it must give pleasure, for why else lie against time?

I have published several commentaries on *Notes,* though more than thirty years ago, and I revisit now only the poem's visionary flight into the sublime, versicles V–IX of "It Must Give Pleasure." These are the Canon Aspirin passages, in which that amiably Firbankian personage dreams an angel, merges with it, and thus inspires Stevens to stand back and declare himself free of his own fiction's fiction, the Canon Aspirin's angel. There is an analogue here to Blake's disengagement from his Tyger, and perhaps an echo of that Song of Experience: "On what wings dare he aspire?" The Canon's absurd name, "Aspirin," is a defense of Stevens's cheerful investment with his partial identity of a figure. The High Romantic poet, Stevens's composite precursor (Whitman, Wordsworth, Keats, Shelley), receives an affectionate if somewhat ironical portrait in the Canon, who dreams he had become a Miltonic angel: "Forth then with huge pathetic force / Straight to the utmost crown of night he flew."

When the Canon-Angel descends to impose illusory ideas of order, Stevens urges him to silence so as to "hear / The luminous melody of proper sound":

> What am I to believe? If the angel in his cloud,
> Serenely gazing at the violent abyss,
> Plucks on his strings to pluck abysmal glory,
>
> Leaps downward through evening's revelations, and
> On his spredden wings, needs nothing but deep space,
> Forgets the gold centre, the golden destiny,
>
> Grows warm in the motionless motion of his flight,
> Am I that imagine this angel less satisfied?
> Are the wings his, the lapis-haunted air?
>
> Is it he or is it I that experience this?
> Is it I then that keep saying there is an hour
> Filled with expressible bliss, in which I have

No need, am happy, forget need's golden hand,
Am satisfied without solacing majesty,
And if there is an hour there is a day.

Responding to his own challenge, Stevens achieves his American Sublime, beyond irony. His Romantic fiction had failed, but a new Romantic replaces an older one. This marvelous declamation invokes and surpasses crucial moments in Wordsworth, and in Whitman. In *The Prelude*, 14.91–120, Wordsworth gives us his poetic self-recognition:

Like angels stopped upon the wing by sound
Of harmony from Heaven's remotest spheres.

In "By Blue Ontario's Shore," section 18, Whitman apprehends his own glory:

I will confront these shows of the day and night,
I will know if I am to be less than they,
I will see if I am not as majestic as they,
I will see if I am not as subtle and real as they,
I will see if I am to be less generous than they,
I will see if I have no meaning, while the houses and ships have meaning,
I will see if the fishes and birds are to be enough for themselves, and I am
     not to be enough for myself.

The passion of both Wordsworth and Whitman allows them momentarily to forget that they propound fictions of the self. Stevens knows that his difference is in the realization that the self and poetry *are* fictions, a sadness never more to be evaded. However supreme, they are lies against time and against nature. A vitalizing, anti-naturalistic untruth is more than valuable when time and nature spell out the truth of death our death.

NEAR THE QUICK

Lawrence and Whitman

The strongest adversary for deep reading is neither "theory and cultural studies," nor the prevalence of the visual (television, motion pictures, computer screens), but the extraordinary profusion and speed of information. There is an authentic link between American gnosis, our all-but-universal national religion (masking as Christianity) and our desire for information, be it scandal or body counts. D. H. Lawrence, ambivalently in thrall to Whitman, found in him the greatest and (to Lawrence) most obscene of American *knowers*. Walt would have been amused; one of my favorite literary games is to guess what the American bard might have thought of Lawrence's *Studies in Classic American Literature,* where the two grandest essays are on Melville and Whitman, with the latter receiving the most accurate accolades yet accorded him.

There are, these days, several major writers who are neglected, for various reasons. Robert Browning has been supplanted by his wife, Elizabeth Barrett Browning, doubtless an estimable human being and now yet one more heroine of feminist literary critics, but except in snatches I find her scarcely readable. Lawrence, whose every phrase is alive with spirit, has sustained me in wonder and in thought since first I read him sixty years ago.

It is a curiosity that Lawrence's exuberant *Studies in Classic American Literature* (1923) devotes two chapters to Fenimore Cooper but none to Emerson. In the final version of "Whitman," which concludes the book, Emerson rather oddly is stigmatized as maintaining a tiresome "superiority" of the soul above the flesh. Lawrence, an insatiable reader, could not absorb Emerson, for reasons I can only surmise. From Lawrence's perspectives (there is never just one) Emerson may have seemed a nihilist, as indeed the author of *The Conduct of Life* accurately can be described. Yet though his insights concerning Melville and Whitman remain fresh and useful, Lawrence regarded Emerson as a kind of namby-pamby moralist. Perhaps it needed the visionary homoeroticism of Melville and Whitman to propel Lawrence into a Paterian-Yeatsian Condition of Fire.

Studies in Classic American Literature, despite its blindness toward our Central Man, remains the most vitalizing work on what makes the American imagination American. Whether or not Lawrence recalls Goethe and Nietzsche's emphasis upon *it writes, not I write,* he finds the United States to be the unique land that exalts IT, the "whole soul" as opposed to the will: "American consciousness has so far been a false dawn. The negative ideal of democracy. But underneath, and contrary to this open ideal, the first hints and revelations of IT. IT, the American whole soul." One aspect of Lawrence's emphasis is distressing: the authoritarian politics of such later novels as *Aaron's Rod, Kangaroo,* and *The Plumed Serpent* seem foreshadowed in this dismissal of American democracy. Still, it is not useful to name Lawrence a fascist, a term perfectly applicable to Pound, Eliot, and even some violent moods of the aging Yeats. Like Yeats, Lawrence was an esotericist, though not in the Irish Archpoet's systematic occultism. By shunting aside the American ideology of democracy, Lawrence faced a crisis in his extraordinary passion for Whitman, to whom he owed his own rebirth as a poet.

Lawrence's relationship to Whitman vies as ambivalence with Hart Crane's attitude toward T. S. Eliot, or Whitman's own troubled sonship to Emerson. An explosive writer, Lawrence worked from draft to draft of the Whitman essay in *Studies in Classic American Literature,* an enigmatic shuttle. Better to start earlier, though, with "Poetry of the Present," the introduction to the American edition of Lawrence's *New Poems* (1918). Readers generally find it odd that Lawrence divides his work into "Rhyming Poems" (influenced by Thomas Hardy) and "Unrhyming Poems" (Whitman). The three great volumes—*Look! We Have Come Through!* (1917), *Birds, Beasts and Flowers* (1923), *Last Poems* (1932)—are all markedly Whitmanian.

"Poetry of the Present" contrasts Shelley and Keats, supposedly poets of the past, to Whitman as the bard of "the instant moment": "Because Whitman put this into his poetry, we fear him and respect him so profoundly." Lawrence's greatness is in that "we fear him." The swerve from Whitman in *Look! We Have Come Through!* is that the unmarriageable Walt is implicitly evoked in a series of poems of marital strife and reconciliation, the perpetually over-intense love of Frieda and Lawrence. The superb "Song of a Man Who Has Come Through" fuses Shelley's "Ode to the West Wind" with Whitmanian exaltation: "The rock will split, we shall come at the wonder, we shall find the Hesperides."

Lawrence's joy, which he makes into aesthetic gratification, presumably was enabled by overcoming prior sexual overexcitement through the agency of anal intercourse. It is good to note this and then marvel at Lawrence's art of celebration, clearly founded upon Whitman's:

> Not I, not I, but the wind that blows through me!
> A fine wind is blowing the new direction of Time.
> If only I let it bear me, carry me, if only it carry me!
> If only I am sensitive, subtle, oh, delicate, a winged gift!
> If only, most lovely of all, I yield myself and am borrowed
> By the fine, fine wind that takes its course through the chaos
>   of the world.
> Like a fine, an exquisite chisel, a wedge-blade inserted;
> If only I am keen and hard like the sheer tip of a wedge
> Driven by invisible blows,
> The rock will split, we shall come at the wonder, we shall find
>   the Hesperides.

The fourfold repetition of "if only" echoes Shelley's prayer to the West Wind: "if I were" and "If even / I were." Both poets welcome the wind, but Shelley sees it as creator and destroyer. Lawrence, beyond ambivalence, salutes the wind with Whitmanian exuberance, until an extraordinary knocking intervenes:

> What is the knocking?
> What is the knocking at the door in the night?
> It is somebody wants to do us harm.
>
> No, no, it is the three strange angels.
> Admit them, admit them.

Lawrence is not Abraham at Mamre receiving Yahweh-as-Angel accompanied by the Angels of Death and Destruction, but rather Lot at Sodom saving the three strange angels from rape by the lustful Sodomites. Why are the angels in Lawrence's poem? English Nonconformist in his religious background, Lawrence broke away into his own vitalistic religion making, earning scorn from churchwarden T. S. Eliot in *After Strange Gods: A Primer of Modern Heresy* (1934). Eliot condemned Thomas Hardy and Lawrence as Inner Light heretics, which is accurate enough and more refreshing than current fashions of condemnation, in which Hardy and Lawrence are dismissed as supposed misogynists.

What explains the intrusion of Lot's saga into Lawrence's celebration? Proust invokes the Cities of the Plain to create the beautiful myth of the descendants of Sodom and Gomorrah suffering their pleasures and sorrows in the cosmos of *In Search of Lost Time.* Lawrence, repressing his homoeroticism, associates finding the Hesperides or lost paradise with heterosexual sodomy (to call it that) and seems shadowed by the biblical parable of the overthrow of Sodom and Gomorrah. Anxious to disengage from that shadow, he surprisingly concludes "Song of a Man Who Has Come Through" by incorporating the Angels of Death and Destruction into his poem.

Lawrence wrote ceaselessly, and as a self-revisionist tended to write entirely new versions of his own poems and fiction. In particular, he could not stop writing drafts of his essay on Whitman, from 1917 to 1923. No one else before or since has written on Whitman with anything like Lawrence's insight, eloquence, love, and exasperation. At moments Walt drives Lawrence to a kind of madness. Alternatively hilarious and luminous, Lawrence's observations necessarily reveal more about the English writer than the American bard, but the drama of influence and its discontents rarely is as rich and valuable as in Lawrence's agon with his American original.

At times Lawrence darts off into his own phantasmagoria, as in this brilliant, insane Eskimo rhapsody:

> As soon as Walt *knew* a thing, he assumed a One Identity with it. If he knew that an Eskimo sat in a kyak, immediately there was Walt being little and yellow and greasy, sitting in a kyak.
>
> Now will you tell me exactly what a kyak is?
>
> Who is he that demands petty definition? Let him behold me *sitting in a kyak.*
>
> I behold no such thing. I behold a rather fat old man full of a rather senile, self-conscious sensuosity.
>
> DEMOCRACY. EN MASSE. ONE IDENTITY.

The universe, in short, adds up to ONE.

ONE.

I.

Which is Walt.

His poems, *Democracy, En Masse, One Identity*, they are long sums in addition and multiplication, of which the answer is invariably MYSELF.

He reaches the state of ALLNESS.

And what then? It's all empty. Just an empty Allness. An addled egg.

Walt wasn't an Eskimo. A little, yellow, sly, cunning, greasy little Eskimo. And when Walt blandly assumed Allness, including Eskimoness, unto himself, he was just sucking the wind out of a blown eggshell, no more. Eskimos are not minor little Walts. They are something that I am not, I know that. Outside the egg of my Allness chuckles the greasy little Eskimo. Outside the egg of Whitman's Allness too.

There is no Eskimo and no kayak anywhere in *Leaves of Grass*. Lawrence is as lunatic here as Carlyle was in his outrageous pamphlet *The Nigger Question*, contemplating imaginary West Indians demolishing ripe pumpkins with their gleaming teeth. Carlyle compensates for this somewhat in *Sartor Resartus* (if I remember rightly) when he suggests that the British Parliament would improve if at all their sessions the peers and M.P.'s went buck naked. How often I fantasize an ordinance requiring our senators and representatives to meet and deliberate in the reality of the body and its decay!

Lawrence could chant of as many nonexistent kayaks as he liked because of his extraordinary transition to celebrating Whitman as "the first white aboriginal":

Whitman, the great poet, has meant so much to me. Whitman, the one man breaking a way ahead. Whitman, the one pioneer. And only Whitman. No English pioneers, no French. No European pioneer-poets. In Europe the would-be pioneers are mere innovators. The same in America. Ahead of Whitman, nothing. Ahead of all poets, pioneering into the wilderness of unopened life, Whitman. Beyond him, none. His wide, strange camp at the end of the great high-road. And lots of new little poets camping on Whitman's camping ground now. But none going really beyond. Because Whitman's camp is at the end of the road, and on the edge of a great precipice. Over the precipice, blue distances, and the blue hollow of the future. But there is no way down. It is a dead end.

Pisgah. Pisgah sights. And Death. Whitman like a strange, modern, American Moses. Fearfully mistaken. And yet the great leader.

The essential function of art is moral. Not aesthetic, not decorative, not pastime and recreation. But moral. The essential function of art is moral.

But a passionate, implicit morality, not didactic. A morality which changes the blood, rather than the mind. Changes the blood first. The mind follows later, in the wake.

Now Whitman was a great moralist. He was a great leader. He was a great changer of the blood in the veins of men.

Abashed, I bow down to Lawrence for that, reserving only the dissent that a triumphant aesthetic creation validates Whitman's promise to us:

> You will hardly know who I am or what I mean,
> But I shall be good health to you nevertheless,
> And filter and fibre your blood.
>
> Failing to fetch me first keep encouraged,
> Missing me one place search another,
> I stop somewhere waiting for you.
>
> ["Song of Myself," section 52]

Lawrence was obsessed with leadership, to the degree that his later novels such as *Aaron's Rod, Kangaroo,* and *The Plumed Serpent* edge toward hysteria and fascism. Whitman's idea of leadership was Abraham Lincoln. Politically, Lawrence and Whitman are irreconcilable, but as a poet Lawrence became almost wholly Whitmanian, though he leaves unclear his attitude toward his precursor's homoeroticism. What he inherited primarily was Whitman's mythology of modern death.

I write these pages in 2009, when Lawrence is not much read. And yet only W. B. Yeats and James Joyce among English-language contemporaries seem his artistic equals, which is to value Lawrence even more highly than Hardy, Conrad, Woolf, or T. S. Eliot. On the Continent one adds Proust, Kafka, Mann, Beckett (since he writes in French and English) to Yeats and Joyce. American peers include Stevens, Crane, and Faulkner. My sense of Lawrence's reception by current students is that he again appeals to an elite, after an odd time when he was obscured by the sociopolitics of feminist academics and journalists.

Lawrence's splendor partly is his versatile mastery of nearly all literary genres: poems, stories short and longer, novels, essays, tracts, plays, letters, prophecies, literary criticism, history and travel writing. Primarily his originality and canonical persistence are founded on a new vision of how to represent human consciousness, one that goes beyond Henry James's and Conrad's, and clashes with Joyce's, if only because Lawrence lacks an authentic comic component in his genius. Both Lawrence and Joyce inherited the High Romantic exaltation of will and desire from Blake, Wordsworth, and Shelley. Blake and Joyce shared an affinity with Rabelais, but Wordsworth, Shelley, and Lawrence decidedly did not.

Wordsworth and Joyce were able to persist in a heroic naturalism, but Lawrence joined himself to an apocalyptic tradition that goes, in its more modern phase, from Joachim of Flora through Blake and Shelley on to Yeats, who admired Lawrence. The keenest judgment rendered of Walt Whitman is that of Wallace Stevens, whose Walt chants, "Nothing is final," "No man shall see the end." Lawrence tried to turn Whitman into the Gnostic Melville, but that strong misreading just does not work. Whitman only rarely writes out of bitterness: "Respondez!" "A Hand-Mirror," and only a few other poems. But after *The Rainbow* (1915), too sublime for bitterness, even *Women in Love* (1920) falls into it, to my aesthetic unhappiness. At his strongest, Lawrence like Whitman was too large for bitterness, too deeply imbued by compassion for suffering humans.

After too many years, I have just reread Lawrence's two major novels. *The Rainbow* moves me to awe and wonder. It might have shocked Tolstoy, but he could have found something of his own uncanny powers of representation in it. Whitman also might have admired it. *The Rainbow* could be compared to several of Hardy's truest novels taken together. I think of *The Woodlanders, The Return of the Native, The Mayor of Casterbridge. Women in Love* is unforgettable and flawed, but even the flaws have greatness, as do Hardy's greatly imperfect *Tess of the D'Urbervilles* and *Jude the Obscure*. Schopenhauer was too close to Hardy; with Nietzsche he hovers near in Lawrence yet finally is evaded.

Gershom Scholem liked talking to me about Whitman, whom he read with approving gusto, observing that the poet of "Song of Myself" was an original Kabbalist, owing nothing to Jewish esoteric tradition. Lawrence's own analogues to Kabbalah are traced by Charles Burack in *D. H. Lawrence's Language of Sacred Experience* (2005). Burack argues for Lawrence's access to the Zohar through such dubious sources as Madame Blavatsky; I myself tend to consider Whitman's effect upon Lawrence. On Schopenhauerian lines, it seems possible that Lawrence, like Whitman, was a kind of natural Kabbalist. Whitman's vision of himself as "Adam early in the morning" establishes him as Primal Man-God, androgynous and unfallen. The first generation of Brangwens in *The Rainbow* seem to approximate that exalted state of being, one that Lawrence himself struggles to regain in the poems of *Look! We Have Come Through!*

One of the crowns of that volume is "New Heaven and Earth," in some respects the most profoundly Whitmanian poem not written by Walt, despite Lawrence's skilled efforts at distancing himself from his titanic forerunner. Lawrence's varied stances toward Whitman remind me of Baudelaire's similar strategies pursued in regard to that force of nature, Victor Hugo. Arriving in a new poetic world is made precarious by giants who appropriated all of the space for themselves:

> And so I cross into another world
> shyly and in homage linger for an invitation
> from this unknown that I would trespass on.
>
> I am very glad, and all alone in the world,
> all alone, and very glad, in a new world
> where I am disembarked at last.
>
> I could cry with joy, because I am in the new world, just ventured in.
> I could cry with joy, and quite freely, there is nobody to know.

Lawrence might have insisted he was all alone in the new world because entrance depended upon an achieved sexual harmony with a woman, hardly a Whitmanian aspiration. The insistence, however dignified, would be irrelevant since Whitman celebrates both heterosexuality and "the love of comrades." Still there is a poignancy in the *Calamus* poems utterly unlike those gathered as *Children of Adam*. Lawrence's reluctance to acknowledge Whitman's authentic sexual orientation may reflect the repressive force of his own homoeroticism, so powerfully exemplified by the Birkin-Gerald relationship, plangently still echoed in the closing moments of *Women in Love*.

There is an attempted turn away from Whitman in sections of II–III of "New Heaven and Earth" but it is too palpable to work. "Everything was tainted with myself," Lawrence laments, but this mode is Whitman at his strongest, the poet who could write, "I am the man. I suffered. I was there," and "agonies are one of

my changes of garments." In recoil, section IV impressively invokes the horror
of World War I battles, yet the mode again is Whitman, the seer of *Drum-Taps.*
Even Lawrentian death and resurrection, a section later, repeats Whitman's
pattern, and the transitional section VI probably unconsciously brings us to
the beach scene of "As I Ebb'd with the Ocean of Life":

> The unknown, the unknown!
> I am thrown upon the shore.
> I am covering myself with the sand.
> I am filling my mouth with the earth.
> I am burrowing my body into the soil.
> The unknown, the new world!

Section VII at last fights free of Whitman, since it beautifully chants Lawrence's renewal of relations with Frieda. Yet whose accent opens the poem's
final section?

Green streams that flow from the innermost continent of the new world,
what are they?
Green and illumined and travelling for ever
dissolved with the mystery of the innermost heart of the continent
mystery beyond knowledge or endurance, so sumptuous
out of the well-heads of the new world.—

Again this is the best Whitman Walt never composed. A majestic chant of the
new world hardly can be wrested away from the poetic inventor of newness.
Lawrence's dilemma explains the ambivalence of his visions and revisions of
Whitman in *Studies in Classic American Literature.* "Manifesto," another sequence of great exuberance, tries to get free both of Shelley and of Whitman:

> We shall not look before and after.
> We shall *be, now.*
> We shall know in full.
> We, the mystic NOW.

That is too strenuous, and falls short of Lawrence's two poetic masters. The
final poem of *Look! We Have Come Through!* is "Craving for Spring," and it seems
to answer the closing question of Shelley's "Ode to the West Wind." Lawrence
applies a Shelleyan ardor against the Whitmanian tally or image of voice:

Oh, if it be true, and the living darkness of the blood of man is purpling
    with violets,
if the violets are coming out from under the rack of men, winter-rotten
    and fallen,
we shall have spring.
Pray not to die on this Pisgah blossoming with violets.
Pray to live through.

I think here Lawrence uncovers a further poetic strength in himself that will
make possible the greater post-Whitmanian poems of *Birds, Beasts, and Flowers,* including "Medlars and Sorb-Apples," "Snake," and the "Tortoise" series.
Last Poems, published posthumously in 1932, adds the death poems: "Bavarian
Gentians," "The Ship of Death," and the superb "Shadows," and my personal
favorite, the stunningly original "Whales Weep Not!," which Whitman would
have envied Lawrence. I want, though, to close this juxtaposition of Whitman
and Lawrence with the last two squibs in *Nettles* (1930). "Leaves of Grass, Flowers of Grass" questions Whitman's central metaphor:

> Leaves of grass, what about leaves of grass?
> Grass blossoms, grass has flowers, flowers of grass,
> dusty pollen of grass, tall grass in its midsummer maleness,
> hay-seed and tiny grains of grass, graminiferae
> not far from the lily, the considerable lily.

Obliquely Lawrence contrasts his flowers of grass to Whitman's *Leaves of Grass,*
but his "tall grass in its midsummer maleness" is the purest Whitman. Lawrence's point, which is to reject Whitmanian democracy, clarifies with his squib
as coda, "Magnificent Democracy":

> Oh, when the grass flowers, the grass
> how aristocratic it is!
> Cock's-foot, fox-tail, fescue and tottering-grass,
> see them wave, see them wave, plumes
> prouder than the Black Prince,
> flowers of grass, fine men.
>
> Oh, I am a democrat
> of the grass in blossom,
> a blooming aristocrat all round.

Two authentic, strong poets scarcely could differ as much in temperament as Whitman and Lawrence; Fernando Pessoa and Jorge Luis Borges were far closer to Whitman in their personalities. Lawrence was *found* by Whitman for the inescapable quest they shared, best expressed by Lawrence in "Poetry of the Present":

> This is the unrestful, ungraspable poetry of the sheer present, poetry whose very permanency lies in its wind-like transit. Whitman's is the best poetry of this kind. Without beginning and without end, without any base and pediment, it sweeps past forever, like a wind that is forever in passage, and unchainable. Whitman truly looked before and after. But he did not sigh for what is not. The clue to all his utterance lies in the sheer appreciation of the instant moment, life surging itself into utterance at its very well-head. Eternity is only an abstraction from the actual present. Infinity is only a great reservoir of recollection, or a reservoir of aspiration: man-made. The quivering nimble hour of the present, this is the quick of Time. This is the immanence. The quick of the universe is the *pulsating, carnal self,* mysterious and palpable. So it is always.
>
> Because Whitman put this into his poetry, we fear him and respect him so profoundly. We should not fear him if he sang only of the "old unhappy far-off things," or of the "wings of the morning." It is because his heart beats with the urgent, insurgent Now, which is even upon us all, that we dread him. He is so near the quick.

He is so near the quick. Lawrence says that truly of Whitman, and at his best we can say that of him. Who else? Certainly Shakespeare, whose Hamlet appropriates the quick as no one else can. Many great poets—Milton, Wordsworth, Shelley, Yeats, Crane—have most other gifts but not the newness, the Now declaring itself. Formalist criticism always fails with Lawrence: witness the debacle of R. P. Blackmur, who dismissed Lawrence's poems as "work written out of a tortured Protestant sensibility and upon the foundation of an incomplete, uncomposed mind." Dogma also misses Lawrence: T. S. Eliot is driven to hysteria by Lawrence's religion making. It may be that Lawrence, for all our current neglect, will prove to be Walt Whitman's best apostle.

HAND OF FIRE

Hart Crane's Magnificence

I t is seventy years since I first fell in love with Hart Crane's poetry in early summer 1940, as I approached my tenth birthday. I taught *The Bridge* yesterday to a receptive Yale undergraduate discussion group and went home exhausted, since emotional and cognitive engulfment is Crane's continued effect upon me. Crane is a difficult poet who requires extraordinarily close reading—word by word, phrase by phrase, line by line. Add to that the rarely acknowledged nature of his work: he is a religious poet without even a faithless faith. An admirer of Wallace Stevens's *Harmonium,* he did not live to read *Notes Toward a Supreme Fiction,* composed a decade after his death by water. Stevens's final belief is in a fiction, with the nicer knowledge of knowing that what you believe in is not true. That leaves untouched the truth of what you *know.*

The Bridge (1930) is Crane's Word, a Blakean Hand of Fire. Weakly misread, it was judged a "splendid failure" by the sometime New Critics (Allen Tate, Yvor Winters, R. P. Blackmur, Cleanth Brooks) and their ongoing more-or-less followers in and out of the academy. In my experience, it surmounts such rivals as *Paterson,* the *Cantos,* and *The Waste Land,* which tend to garner more praise. Neo-Christianity, a literary disease of which Thomas Stearns Eliot was the Vicar of Academies, was a kind of academic faith during the 1950s and 1960s but barely exists at the dawn of the second decade of the twenty-first century. In Eliot's disciple Tate, it found an early spokesman even when Tate wrote a foreword to his friend Crane's *White Buildings* (1926), a work that rivals

Stevens's *Harmonium* as the preeminent "first volume" by any American poet since *Leaves of Grass* (1855):

> There is the opinion abroad that Crane's poetry is, in some indefinite
> sense, "new." It is likely to be appropriated by one of the several eso-
> teric cults of the American soul. It tends toward the formation of a state
> of mind, the critical equivalent of which would be in effect an exposure
> of the confusion and irrelevance of the current journalism of poetry,
> and of how far behind the creative impulse the critical intelligence, at
> the moment, lags. It is to be hoped, therefore, that this state of mind,
> where it may be registered at all, will not at its outset be shunted into
> a false context of obscure religious values, that a barrier will not be
> erected between it and the rational order of criticism.

The "rational order" means Eliot's *The Sacred Wood* (1920), a primer for
neoclassical modernism. Crane is as High as a High Romantic ever could be:
his peers are Shelley, Blake, Lawrence, and Yeats, all of them questing after
strange gods, which is also the quest of *The Bridge,* published in 1930, the year
of Lawrence's early death at forty-four. Traces of *The Rainbow* and *The Plumed
Serpent* found their way into Crane's work, though it is hard to surmise what
Lawrence would have made of Crane, a fellow Whitmanian yet one who did not
write as Lawrence did, in Whitmanian cadences, but in Elizabethan-Eliotic
quatrains and octaves. I recall discussing affinities between Crane and Lawrence with Tennessee Williams, who revered both precursors and tended to
compose Cranean lyrics and Lawrentian stories before breaking free in his
plays, haunted as they still are by these forerunners.

I do not want to repeat my account of the American Religion here, but refer
any interested reader to my book of that title (1992, 2006) and to my introduction in the Library of America *American Religious Poems* (2006). The literary aspect of the American Religion begins with Emerson's doctrine of Self-
Reliance, formulated by the Sage of Concord in response to the bank panic of
1837. Yet the popular faith preceded Emerson by a generation and started at
the great Cane Ridge, Kentucky, revival, an enormous anti-Calvinist upsurge
of religious (and sexual) enthusiasm that bubbled on throughout the second
week of August 1801 at which twenty-five thousand renegade Presbyterians
melted together with Baptists, Methodists, and other sectaries in an ecstasy
of oneness with the American Jesus—a figure possessing nothing in common
with the European Theological Christ.

Hart Crane's mother, Grace Hart Crane, was a Christian Scientist, an eccentric mode that never affected the young poet, who had no interest in any creeds, nor in politics either. His spirituality has been best defined by the admirable British poet Elizabeth Jennings in *Every Changing Shape* (1961): "Crane employed many Christian words, signs and symbols. But, as with Rilke, he removed these things from the realm of strict orthodoxy and gave them a free life of their own. His imagination unyoked them from the bondage of dogma."

Crane's version of the American Religion stems from a fusion of William Blake with the native tradition of Emerson, Whitman, Melville and Dickinson. He read S. Foster Damon's still useful *William Blake: His Philosophy and Symbols* (1924) and worked out a spiritual vision of classic American literature. Reading Lawrence's *The Man Who Died* in 1931–32 had a complex effect upon Crane's last major poem, "The Broken Tower," bestowing an image of resurrection upon the sea-change of his initial (and final) heterosexual relationship, similar to that of Lawrence's Jesus in the novella, who resurrects as a sexual being in the spirit of Blake's vision.

Lawrence's apocalyptic vitalism had esoteric sources, including the cloudy P. D. Ouspensky, whom Crane also read, or tried to read. Yet neither Lawrence nor Crane became Theosophists, as did Yeats, at once the supreme twentieth-century poet and the most credulous. Lawrence was somewhat susceptible to cosmological quackeries, particularly in *The Plumed Serpent,* which interested Crane. Nevertheless Crane's skeptical intellect finally resisted sacred occultism just as it declined all dogmas in religion or politics. Crane's deepest affinity may be with Emily Dickinson: his Word, like hers, is a "Loved Philology" and not the Logos of the gospel of John.

Dickinson's secret lover, who perhaps became her husband, Judge Otis Phillips Lord, died in 1884. In a letter to Lord, she stated their joint stance: "We both believe and disbelieve a hundred times an Hour, which keeps Believing nimble." Her disbelieving was nimbler, but her fictive God remained personal. Crane's unknown God is neither personal nor impersonal. Like Blake, Crane was a man without a mask, and his transcendental confrontations seek to persuade only in the name of his poetry. Is Dickinson or very late Stevens different?

Whatever else we might term Crane's work, it is distinctly *not* devotional poetry, nor is "Song of Myself," nor the work of Frost, Stevens, William Carlos Williams, or Marianne Moore. Eliot, Tate, Auden, and the earlier Robert Lowell intended devotion in a number of celebrated lyrics and meditations. I cannot read these without remembering once again Dr. Samuel Johnson's strictures: the good and evil of Eternity are too ponderous for the wings of wit. The mind sinks under them, content with calm belief and humble adoration.

That can produce poignant prayer but only weak poetry.

Crane, a Pindaric celebrant of Eros, necessarily would not divide flesh from spirit. His first notable religious poem is the difficult "Lachrymae Christi," which has never found me, despite its intricate slain numbers. Christ's tears evoke the sweet red wine of Naples, so named for them, and thus introduce the wine god Dionysus into the poem. Nietzsche is invoked throughout, and becomes an implicit triad with Jesus and Dionysus.

In a grand passage of Yeats's Paterian reverie *Per Amica Silentia Lunae,* which Crane never mentions but which haunts the American's days and works, the Irish seer uttered his credo: "I shall find the dark grow luminous, the void fruitful when I understand I have nothing, that the ringers in the tower have appointed for the hymen of the soul a passing bell." It is Nietzschean also but not in his Dionysiac mode, where the smiles of the ravished god create the Olympian divinities and his tears form humans. Dionysus is caught up in his own rapture, but has nothing and no one, fated like Nietzsche and Crane to the passing bell of those who never will marry. The crisis of "Lachrymae Christi," densest of all Crane lyrics, comes in a fierce parenthesis:

> (Let sphinxes from the ripe
> Borage of death have cleared my tongue
> Once and again; vermin and rod
> No longer bind. Some sentient cloud
> Of tears flocks through the tendoned loam:
> Betrayed stones slowly speak.)

Borage is both a purgative medicine and a wine drunk as a cordial. Here it belongs to death and to resurrection. Harshly paraphrased, this parenthetical stanza declares that "let" (hidden) sphinxes (in the Kabbalistic or Hermetic sense of riddles that the Adam Kadmon, or Divine Man, will solve) repeatedly free Crane's poetic voice from bondage and punishment (vermin and rod). Nature raises herself to weep human tears, and Blakean stones slowly achieve utterance.

Why does Crane so strenuously insist upon our unpacking him? The doctrine here is Nietzschean as well as esoteric; how shall he make it his own

as well as ours? His agon is not only with the heroic precursors—Whitman,
Nietzsche, Yeats—but with the stylistic forerunner Eliot, and also with William
Carlos Williams, older by sixteen years and a rival claimant of the American
poetic heritage as against Pound and Eliot. Crane found Williams useful as a
contestant, while Williams followed Crane's career with considerable anxiety.
I do not know any readers who set *Paterson* and *The Bridge* equally high, because the two epics are antithetical. Williams's "No ideas but in things" was
answered by Stevens's "The first idea is an imagined thing." Visionary Crane
answers more fully.

In his letters, Crane deprecates the "casual" in Williams, though with great
respect. After Crane's self-destruction, Williams displayed more agonistic
anxiety than sympathy. The passionate apostle of a New World Naked was not
about to proclaim a belated High Romantic visionary:

> I cannot grow rhapsodic with him . . . evangel of the post-war, the
> replier to the romantic apostle of *The Waste Land*.

The recognition that Crane and Eliot both were Romantic is shrewd, yet Williams's resentment of Crane clearly was defensive. He loathed "Atlantis," but it
was the culmination of Shelley's invocatory strain, while Williams was a lifelong
lover of Keats.

I now turn to *The Bridge,* since Crane's "Voyages" were my subject earlier in
this labyrinth. I will confine myself to "Proem: To Brooklyn Bridge" and "Atlantis," with only glances at the rest of the poem. This discussion guides me on
to the conclusion of closely reading Crane's death poem, "The Broken Tower."

The odd judgment that Crane was a "failure"—if sometimes a "splendid"
one—that prevailed when I began teaching him at Yale in 1955 was founded
upon essays by Tate, Blackmur, and Winters, all of whom abhorred Emerson
and Whitman. Fifty-five years later, the authority of these rather limited scho-
liasts has waned, and there are distinguished studies of Crane by John Irwin,
Sherman Paul, and Lee Edelman, among others. Critical dogma, frequently a
disguised Neo-Christianity (Eliotic) or social morality (homophobic), blinded
Tate and Blackmur. Winters, an endless moralizer, like Blackmur was a minor
poet. Tate, a more considerable poet, could not overcome the joint influence
of Eliot and Crane.

The Bridge doubtless is uneven, but whole cantos of it are perfect, and
throughout Crane's language lives, moves, breathes. Nearly eighty years after its

publication it is possible to read the poem accurately even if you greatly prefer Eliot, Pound, or Williams to Crane, as I of course do not. Reading Crane across seventy years makes me initially incapable of seeing how difficult he remains for many. His greatest strength, his rhetorical originality, disconcerts because in this crucial regard he has as precursors only Marlowe and Shakespeare, who fulfilled the relation between classical rhetoric and memory by developing further Ovid's vision of ceaseless metamorphoses. (Edelman's brilliant 1987 rhetorical study *Transmemberment of Song* is immensely helpful on Crane's relationship to Marlowe, Shakespeare, Shelley, Whitman, and Eliot.) Tropes cross over incessantly in Marlowe, and Shakespeare vastly enlarges the change. Great celebrants of desire, Marlowe and Shakespeare dissolve the synchronic, static elements of rhetoric into a flow through time. Marlowe's "Hero and Leander" (which Crane read appreciatively) and Shakespeare's "Venus and Adonis" both work tropologically to make themselves fresh and early, and their forerunner Ovid late, as though *he* is imitating them.

Word-consciousness is a deliberate intoxication throughout Marlowe, and is subdued to a multiplicity of purposes by Shakespeare. Unlike Marlowe, Shakespeare delighted in making up new words—eighteen hundred of them, two-thirds still in use. Crane also invents words, two at least to be found now in other poets and in critics: "*transmemberment* of song" from "Voyages" and *curveship* from "Proem: To Brooklyn Bridge." A transmutation that dismembers is Crane's Orphic destiny, while lending a myth to God is "of the curveship"—the leap or vaulting of Brooklyn Bridge.

Shakespeare is everyone's precursor, but favorite plays differ from writer to writer. Eliot weirdly chose *Coriolanus,* while Stevens perhaps owed most to *A Midsummer Night's Dream.* Crane responded most fervently to *The Tempest,* where Ariel's songs affected him as they had Shelley. His sonnet "To Shakespeare" contrasts Prospero's serenity and Ariel's song with Hamlet's complex dialectic of tears and laughter, and "Voyages" alludes to Ariel's "Full fathom five" song in rivalry with *The Waste Land*'s citation. Crane's Orphic transmemberment is Shakespeare's "sea-change."

The Bridge has so much local life that its design can be obscured by dwelling too happily on eloquences likely to break forth anywhere. Like all Crane's readers, I encounter trouble trying to state his epic subject. The simplest and best answer is Brooklyn Bridge itself, but that opens more vistas than can be studied. As a great Romantic poet, Crane perpetually confronts the central theme of that tradition: the power of the poet's mind over a universe of death.

Brooklyn Bridge manifests the power of its engineer-architect John Roebling's vision over natural limitations, including his own crippled condition.

Crane constantly rethought *The Bridge:* this imparts vibrancy but at moments threatens coherence. It was for him a "Bridge of Fire" always in danger of narrowing into a "Hand of Fire." As befits a Nietzschean, Crane seems to follow a poetics of memorable pain, akin to Yeats and Stevens. His quest is not for solace, not until the momentary peace at the close of his death poem, "The Broken Tower." Ecstasy is chosen over wisdom in *The Bridge*. One mark of the American Religion is the identification of freedom with solitude, an equation painfully tutored by "Voyages" and offset again only by the resolution of "The Broken Tower," a resolution that proved ephemeral, as evidenced by Crane's suicide.

One way of apprehending *The Bridge*'s splendor is to dwell upon its central trope, the "vaulting" or "leap" fused into the bridge by John and Washington Roebling, father and son. The Longinian ascent to the heights of the sublime, to a pleasure so difficult as to make us impatient with simpler pleasures, creates a threshold experience. Angus Fletcher, the Orphic exegete of poetic thresholds, locates them between labyrinth and temple. As "The Tunnel" section demonstrates, Crane is an authority on labyrinths. He salutes Brooklyn Bridge as temple fused with threshold but the apostrophe is brilliantly precarious. Perhaps his truest vista is comprised by the final four stanzas of the "Proem":

> *O harp and altar, of the fury fused,*
> *(How could mere toil align thy choiring strings!)*
> *Terrific threshold of the prophet's pledge,*
> *Prayer of pariah, and the lover's cry—*
>
> *Again the traffic lights that skim thy swift*
> *Unfractioned idiom, immaculate sigh of stars,*
> *Beading thy path—condense eternity:*
> *And we have seen night lifted in thine arms.*
>
> *Under thy shadow by the piers I waited;*
> *Only in darkness is thy shadow clear.*
> *The City's fiery parcels all undone,*
> *Already snow submerges an iron year . . .*
>
> *O Sleepless as the river under thee,*
> *Vaulting the sea, the prairies' dreaming sod,*

Unto us lowliest sometime sweep, descend
And of the curveship lend a myth to God.

There are only limited moments in American poetry this beautiful: epiphanies in Whitman, Dickinson, Stevens, and elsewhere in Crane. Here the awesome Pietà—"*and we have seen night lifted in thine arms*"—redeems the shadows yet not "*an iron year.*" Crane's Jerusalem, his bridge to the Atlantis, is more his Nineveh, the city to which Jonah was sent in the little prophetic book that is read aloud in Jewish temples on the afternoon of the Day of Atonement.

The "Proem" recapitulates an American tradition that goes from William Cullen Bryant through Whitman to William Carlos Williams and gathers up also visual perspectives derived from El Greco and William Blake. Eliot necessarily is an absence; even his "Preludes," which haunted Crane, are set aside by the invocation to Brooklyn Bridge, though *The Waste Land* will return in "The Tunnel."

So perfect is the initial apostrophe "To Brooklyn Bridge"—it vies with "Voyages II" and "The Broken Tower" as perhaps Crane's best poem—that one is prone to underappreciate "Ave Maria," a sonorous and moving soliloquy of Columbus aboard ship bound for the New World. Beneath the soliloquy's surface is a dialogue between Hart and Walt founded upon Whitman's "Passage to India" and "A Prayer of Columbus." Edelman shrewdly points to Crane's audacity, in the "Cape Hatteras" canto of *The Bridge,* of ascribing to the precursor the fundamental emblem of the later poet's life and work: "Our Meistersinger, thou set breath in steel, / And it was thou who on the boldest heel / Stood up and flung the span on even wing / Of that great Bridge, our Myth, whereof I sing!"

That is not precisely Crane upon the heights, loaded down as it is with implicit anxiety, but the disciple needs to take the Great American Original at his divine word. In *The Bridge,* the Roeblings' masterpiece, God, and Whitman are three-in-one. To be the son of Whitman indeed is to be God's Son, but this God is a living labyrinth, as Crane knew himself to be. All of Crane's poetry, like Whitman's, is labyrinthine, a single poem, leaves of grass transmembered into one song, one bridge of fire.

Fire is not one of Whitman's prime elements, in contrast to earth, air, water: one does not think of "Song of Myself" as a Promethean poem, unlike *The Bridge* or so much of Blake, Shelley, Yeats—even Stevens and, rather curiously, Eliot. Milton avoids any mention of Prometheus in *Paradise Lost,* while Shakespeare reduces "the right Promethean fire" to what the brilliant narcissist Berowne in *Love's Labor's Lost* tells us men seek in women's eyes. For Stevens, "Fire is the symbol: the celestial possible."

Crane's element was death by water, neither Walter Pater's hard gemlike flame nor Yeats's Paterian Condition of Fire. The one time I met Stevens, he quoted to me the stanza in Shelley's "Witch of Atlas" that begins, "Men scarcely know how beautiful fire is." Shelley and Stevens, both prophetic of Hart Crane, threw away the lights, the definitions, and said of what they saw in the dark that it was this or that but refused to use the rotten names. Emersonians re-name first by unnaming—Whitman and Dickinson—and Crane culminated his tradition by insisting that the truth is nameless. Confronting the auroras of autumn, Stevens attempted the heroic destruction of rendering this named thing nameless, but opened the door of his spirit's house "upon flames." Of all the American poetry composed after him, I wish Crane had survived to read *The Auroras of Autumn*. In "The Broken Tower" he is haunted by *Harmonium*'s "Sunday Morning"; had he gone on, his talisman might have become Stevens's realization that the auroras were not a sign or symbol of malice but rather an innocence of earth, a vision recalling Whitman and Keats.

Poetic thought is always a mode of memory. Primarily this is the memory of prior poems. Social theories and historicizing of the arts alike founder on the rock of memory, since a great poem, to realize itself, must begin by remembering another poem. If a societal context or historical event disturbs a woman or man into poetry, it tends to be treated as though already it was a poem. These obvious truths—which I helped set forth half a century ago—have been obscured by forty years of counterculture and its discontents. Yes, *The Tempest* is a social fact and a historical event, but it *matters* because it is a dramatic poem and stage drama that will not go away. Neither will *The Bridge*.

Who has the authority to proclaim what is or is not a permanent poem? From Arthur Rimbaud to John Ashbery, great poets tend to deprecate the critics, but without critical authority (never centered in any single consciousness) we drown in tidal waves of sincere bad verse. The English economist Thomas Malthus, more than Darwin, Marx, or Freud, is the figure who truly terrifies the literary world. Overpopulation daunts the imagination. What is there left to say? How many can any one of us hear?

Only prodigious gifts can now re-invent poetry for us. Since Shakespeare, belatedness governs; no one else is going to re-invent us. After Hart Crane, Gerard Manley Hopkins, and Dylan Thomas, impacted density of rhetoric, metric, affective intensity cannot increase without sacrificing coherence. Keats and Shelley, developing out of Shakespeare and Marlowe, were the direct ancestors of Hopkins and Crane. A rhetoric that breaks the vessels—a Gnostic and Kabbalistic trope—is necessarily a kind of creation-by-catastrophe. Crane's breaking of the vessels is most intense in the "Atlantis" canto that now formally concludes *The Bridge* but actually was the first part of the epic to be composed.

Like Shelley, Crane had a complex relationship to Plato, not easy to grasp. For both Highest Romantics, Plato is the ancestral mythmaker, directly apprehended by Shelley (whose ancient Greek was as superb as Swinburne's), but mediated for Crane by Emerson and Pater. What the *Symposium* was to Shelley, *Critias* and *Timaeus* were to Crane, the first for the legend of Atlantis, the second for the demiurgical creation myth.

Emerson, writing on Plato, gave Crane what may have been a starting point: "He has reason, as all the philosophic and poetic class have: but he has also, what they have not,—this strong solving sense to reconcile his poetry with the appearance of the world, and build a bridge from the streets of cities to the Atlantis." The sea god Poseidon created the realm of Atlantis in the ocean we still call the Atlantic. Atlas, Poseidon's son, founds the capital of Atlantis. His initial project is bridge building:

> First, they constructed bridges joining the rings of sea, which sur-
> rounded the ancient metropolis, making a road out from the palace
> and in to the palace. Their first project was to build a palace in the
> dwellings of the god and of their ancestors. One king inherited the
> project from his predecessor, and, as he improved on the beauty
> of what had already been improved, he would surpass to the extent
> of his resources what his predecessor had been able to achieve.
> They continued this progress until they had created for themselves
> a dwelling astonishing in size and in its manifold beauty.
>
> [Plato, *Critias*, translated by Diskin Clay]

Crane's "Atlantis" evolved from February 1923 through late 1926, when what had been called "Bridge: Finale" at last was given its Platonic title. As is so frequent with Crane, an endless self-revisionist, the first fragment of the poem vanishes utterly:

> And midway on that structure I would stand
> One moment, not as diver, but with arms

> That open to project a disk's resilience
> Winding the sun and planets in its face.
> Water should not stem that disk, nor weigh
> What holds its speed in vantage of all things
> That tarnish, creep, or wane; and in like laughter,
> Mobile, yet posited even beyond that time
> The Pyramids shall falter, slough into sand,—
> And smooth and fierce above the claim of wings,
> And figured in that radiant field that rings
> The Universe:—I'd have us hold one consonance
> Kinetic to its poised and deathless dance.

At the end of some 1,926 worksheets the poem's true beginning manifests:

> O Bridge, synoptic foliate dome:
> Always through blinding cables to our joy
> —Of thy release, the square prime ecstasy.
> Through the twined cable strands, upward
> Veering with light, the flight of strings,
> Kinetic choiring of white wings . . . ascends.

That "synoptic foliate dome" suggests Shelley's in *Adonais,* the paradigm for "Atlantis" rather in the way *Alastor* had set the patterns of "Voyages." Shelley, more even than Whitman and Eliot, may in time seem Crane's most authentic forerunner. Both poets go *through* Plato as Montaigne and Emerson did so as to arrive at a Lucretian metaphysical stance, also prevalent in Whitman, Melville, and Stevens. Both in Shelley and in Crane there is perpetual conflict between the way things are and the vaunting power of poetic vision—things as they might be. Difficult to describe, a tension between how it is and the high urge to invoke transcendence renders peculiarly valuable the style of apostrophe in the two poets. *Adonais* ostensibly is pastoral elegy while "Atlantis" concludes an American brief epic, yet genre falls away when we bring the poems together. Whitman's "bridge" and Keats's "star" perform a common work for Crane and Shelley. Perhaps we can think of *The Bridge* as an extended elegy (partly pastoral) for Walt Whitman, though Crane would not have welcomed this notion. *Adonais*'s fifty-five Spenserian stanzas are capable of being read as yet another variant on Shelleyan quest romance founded upon his *Alastor.*

Shelley and Crane both tend to transfigure every genre into the condition of lyric. Of "Atlantis" Crane observed that in it the bridge becomes a ship, a world, a woman but crucially a tremendous Aeolian harp. That is Shelley's trope in *A Defence of Poetry*, in which all of us, but poets in particular, form

> an instrument over which a series of external and internal impressions are driven, like the alternations of an ever-changing wind over an Aeolian lyre.

In *Adonais* that wind, identified with the fierce spirit invoked in the "Ode to the West Wind," descends upon the poet in a triumphantly suicidal conclusion. "Atlantis," despite its dialectical negativity, exalts hope even though the bridge-harp becomes daimonized into an unknown god. This is consistent with the desperate eloquence of the "Proem: To Brooklyn Bridge," where the "curveship" is called on "to lend a myth to God." Sherman Paul once remarked that for Hart Crane *bride* and *bridge* are cognate. I recall Kenneth Burke half-mischievously telling me, as we were driven across the bridge from Brooklyn Heights to Manhattan, that Brooklyn Ferry for Whitman and Brooklyn Bridge for Crane were crossings or benedictions, tropes to restitute their inability to love women.

Whitman's "Song of the Universe" is cited by Paul as a presence in "Atlantis." Put together in 1874, long into a poetic decline that went from 1866 until the poet's death in 1892, it nevertheless possesses considerable pathos as Whitman strains to recapture his departed daimon. That is hardly the burden of "Atlantis," whose daimonic force seems to touch no limit, even when its final line begins with a Whitmanian "Whispers." In Whitman, they are "whispers of heavenly death," recalling "Out of the Cradle Endlessly Rocking," where the sea whispers and lisps "the low and delicious word death." Crane chooses to end his masterwork with "Whispers antiphonal in azure swing," knowing that the informed reader must recall Whitman's "The sea whisper'd me." If together Whitman and Crane constitute "One Song, one Bridge of Fire!" then Crane's antiphonal whispers also lisp to us of death. Crane, I think, would have demurred: the Bridge of Fire is a sunset vision but also a dawn kindling.

"Atlantis" is certainly not Crane's finest poem, yet it is his most representative, in vision and in impact. I was one of many young readers swept away by it at my first reading at age ten. Already deep in Blake and Shelley, Whitman and Shakespeare, I was prepared for its ecstasy, though I could not quite apprehend just how it worked its intricate cognitive music so magically upon me. Dimly I recall my early sense that it was steeped in *Moby-Dick* and *The Tempest*, both of which already had flooded me. Crane made some boys and girls among my friends into poets, but after absorbing him I began tentatively to become an exegete, an enterprise first fostered in me by Blake. With Blake and to some degree with Whitman, I assimilated understanding the poetry to my background in biblical commentary, but Crane, like Shakespeare, Shelley, and Melville, started me on the path to Pater's appreciation of "the finer edge of words."

"Atlantis" seems word-drunk, yet that is illusive; Crane revised with a meticulous precision. The drafts marvelously display his artistry, moving on with agility from an initial fragment that concludes, "I'd have us hold one consonance / Kinetic to its poised and deathless dance." At once dome and dance, Brooklyn Bridge kindles its seer to a visionary breakthrough in lines sent to the photographer Alfred Stieglitz on Independence Day 1923:

> To be, Great Bridge, in vision bound of thee,
> So widely straight and turning, ribbon-wound,
> Multi-colored, river-harboured and upbourne
> Through the bright drench and fabric of our veins,—
> With white escarpments swinging into light,
> Sustained in tears, the cities are endowed
> And justified, conclamant with the fields
> Revolving through their harvest in sweet torment.

When most ecstatic, "Atlantis" also is wonderfully restrained. There is a rhetorical reserve always kept apart even as Crane works his rhetoric to its apparent limits. Whitman at once is the great resource and the abiding problem for *The Bridge,* strangely more pervasive in "Atlantis" than in "Cape Hatteras," where the American bard is the overt subject. Nothing is more consistent in post-Whitmanian American poetry than Whitman himself. Only a handful of our central poets—Dickinson, Frost, Marianne Moore, Elizabeth Bishop, James Merrill—are free of *Leaves of Grass.* Walt bubbles up where he is not wanted— in Stevens's "The Rock," Eliot's *Burnt Norton,* Pound's *The Pisan Cantos*—and surfaces as the return of the repressed. In *The Bridge* he is desired, invoked, welcomed, yet does not always come just where and when he is called.

Whitman is and always will be not just the most American of poets but American poetry proper, our apotropaic champion against European culture. He warned that he could not be tamed or contained, and to reject him is to reject all hope for an American culture that has brought any authentic new values into the world. For what have we given the world that is of supreme aesthetic splendor and newness? Whitman and jazz, I would have to judge, and *Leaves of Grass* goes beyond even the joy and wisdom of Louis Armstrong. Crane, as attuned to jazz as he was to Whitman, so far has proved to be too difficult to join to that panoply, but after Dickinson and Whitman he is our major poet. Giving up at thirty-two in his desperation, he kept us from a final harvest of his gifts for vision and rhetoric, which surpassed all his American forerunners and those who have come after in the Age of Ashbery.

"Atlantis" is a rhetorical experiment in much the same way that the 1855 *Leaves of Grass* was what Whitman called a language experiment. Rhetoric is an art of persuasion, of defense, of discovery, but above all else of appropriation. American rhetoric, from its fountainhead, Emerson, on, appropriates in order to *know* Self-Reliance, the American Religion. This is a knowing in which the knower also is known by the God within. The two central American poems of that gnosis are now "Song of Myself" and *The Bridge,* neither of which is quite equaled by such wonders as *Notes Toward a Supreme Fiction, Paterson,* and more recently Ammons's *Sphere,* Ashbery's *Flow Chart,* and Merrill's "Book of Ephraim."

Plato's mythic Atlantis fuses with Shelley's "mirrors of / The fire for which all thirst" in Crane's Chant of Cathay. Crane's Plato was quarried from Walter Pater's *Plato and Platonism* (1893), where the harmony and system of Eros is emphasized:

> Just there, then, is the secret of Plato's intimate concern with, his power over, the sensible world, the apprehensions of the sensuous faculty: he is a lover, a great lover, somewhat after the manner of Dante. For him, as for Dante, in the impassioned glow of his conceptions, the material and the spiritual are blent and fused together. While, in that fire and heat, what is spiritual attains the definite visibility of a crystal, what is material, on the other hand, will lose its earthiness and impurity. It is of the amorous temper, therefore, you must think in connexion with Plato's youth—of this, amid all the strength of the genius in which it is so large a constituent,—indulging, developing, refining, the sensuous capacities, the powers of eye and ear, of the fancy also which can refashion, of the speech which can best respond to and reproduce, their liveliest presentments. That is why when Plato speaks of visible things it is as if you saw them.

As a virtual elegy for Whitman, "Atlantis" hymns Socratic love, as is wholly appropriate for what was the inception and the finale of *The Bridge.* I recall Allen

Ginsberg remarking to me that despite our aesthetic disagreements, we met in our mutual love for the poetry of Hart Crane, always referred to by Ginsberg as our "distinguished Platonist."

The composition of "Atlantis" was a perpetual labor for Crane, stretching from February 1923 to December 1929. Its twelve octaves were burnished by the poet into his most formidable rhetorical performance, packed with allusions and deliberately rescuing and rehabilitating the tropes of *White Buildings*. The spirits of Marlowe, Shelley, and Melville join Whitman and *The Tempest* in these ninety-six lines, which aggressively encompass a range we might expect in a poem ten times its length. "Atlantis" is Crane's most ambitious poem, and it is a synecdoche for *The Bridge*, just as *Adonais* partakes in all of Shelley's previous poetry. Sadly, *Adonais* also prophesies Shelley's unfinished death poem, *The Triumph of Life*, even as "Atlantis" prefigures "The Broken Tower."

Sibylline voices flicker through the opening octave, heralding the bridge as Aeolian harp begetting an unknown god, possibly the myth lent to God by the "Proem." As readers we are where Crane is, neither observing Brooklyn Bridge nor walking across it but part of its structure, forced into its leap, its vaulting song at midnight, lit by the moon and "veering with light, the flight of strings." As in Whitman's "Crossing Brooklyn Ferry," we have merged with the poet and his poem.

In the second octave the fusion becomes "synoptic": all tides, all ships at sea, all oceans answer the one Platonic call: "Make thy love sure—to weave whose song we ply!" And suddenly—bridge, poem, poet, reader—we are to-gether within the dream:

> And on, obliquely up bright carrier bars
> New octaves trestle the twin monoliths
> Beyond whose frosted capes the moon bequeaths
> Two worlds of sleep (O arching strands of song!)—
> Onward and up the crystal-flooded aisle
> White tempest nets file upward, upward ring
> With silver terraces the humming spars,
> The loft of vision, palladium helm of stars.

Shakespeare himself might have admired "white tempest nets" as a kenning for "sails." Crane explicitly describes his poem—"New octaves"—as part of the bridge's structure, "harp and altar of the fury fused." As "the loft of vision, pal-ladium helm of stars," the bridge, structure and poem, stands in place of the domain of heroic poets of antiquity and those they celebrated. What this third octave clarifies is the upward sweep of Crane's imaginative vision, qualified by the paradox of all his poetry, the perpetual downward gaze of his actual eyes. It is as though the Marlovian intensity of his desire is tempered by his sense of being lost in the mundane world he scarcely bears to see. That dichotomy of desire and sight does not undermine vision's validity but enforces Crane's characteristic acknowledgment of the limits of figuration. As Stevens was to formulate this a decade after Crane's death, the final belief is to believe in a fiction while knowing that what you believe is not true. Whitman's America and Crane's bridge are knowing fictions, giant images of unfulfilled desire.

That is the prelude to the fourth octave, which opens with a superb reprise of the "Proem":

> Sheerly the eyes, like seagulls stung with rime—
> Slit and propelled by glistening fins of light—

Lee Edelman rightly points to Crane's poetic negativity here. As late Romantic, the seer of *The Bridge* confesses that he simultaneously moves through life as though it were dream or nightmare and yet is able to read the "cipher-script of time" as we cannot. In solving the cipher, the Shelleyan-Cranean poet turns "Tomorrows into yesteryear," the metaleptic reversal of earliness and lateness that makes Crane the forerunner of Shelley and Whitman, Eliot and Stevens, and not their belated heir. Negativity governs the admission of ambivalence toward ancestors, who must be consumed in "smoking pyres of love and death."

Crane's Word, his poetic Logos, gathers in his forebears, but at the high cost of his own Orphic splintering. In the two following octaves—"Like hails, farewells" and "From gulfs unfolding"—I hear the intensifying drive of the last seventeen stanzas of Shelley's *Adonais*, which haunts all of "Atlantis." Crane at sixteen read Shelley, and repeatedly returned to the High Romantic lyrist throughout the 1920s. *Alastor*, Shelley's early quest romance, is embedded in "Voyages," and *Adonais* increasingly provided a model for "Atlantis." In retrospect it is difficult not to associate Shelley's early death at twenty-nine with Crane's at thirty-two. Shelley's drowning could have been accidental or suicidal; we do not know. Is it altogether fanciful to find in the relationship between *Alastor* and "Voyages" or *Adonais* and "Atlantis" an implicit covenant of death by water?

There is a crossing at the halfway point of "Atlantis," from "O Love, thy white, pervasive Paradigm . . . !" to "We left the haven hanging in the night." After six octaves remorselessly leaping upward there is a lateral movement westward, across the Pacific, to arrive at Cathay four lines from the poem's end. "Psalm of Cathay!" Crane's voyager chants exultantly just before the invocation of Love's white pervasive paradigm, Brooklyn Bridge, as the knowledge of Platonic Eros in harmony and system. With the second movement of "Atlantis" launched westward, Crane addresses the bridge as knower and known:

> O Thou steeled Cognizance whose leap commits
> The agile precincts of the lark's return;
> Within whose lariat sweep encinctured sing
> In single chrysalis the many twain,—
> Of stars Thou art the stitch and stallion glow
> And like an organ, Thou, with sound of doom—
> Sight, sound and flesh Thou leadest from time's realm
> As love strikes clear direction for the helm.

From childhood on this stanza has been a poetic touchstone for me, and it can be considered a summit of Crane's art. "Commits" connects or places a promise as well as leaps, the vaulting built into the bridge by John Roebling's art of design. Shelley, in *Adonais*'s most famous stanza, had contrasted the Neoplatonic One with the mutable many who include all of us:

> The One remains, the many change and pass;
> Heaven's light forever shines, Earth's shadows fly;
> Life, like a dome of many-coloured glass,
> Stains the white radiance of Eternity.
> Until Death tramples it to fragments.—Die,
> If thou wouldst be with that which thou dost seek!
> Follow where all is fled!—Rome's azure sky,
> Flowers, ruins, statues, music, words, are weak
> The glory they transfuse with fitting truth to speak.

"Stains" takes the duel meaning of "defiles" and "colors" in this magnificently equivocal display of Shelley's ambivalence toward personal survival. Crane echoes this: "In single chrysalis the many twain." "Encincture" necessarily means "belted" or "circled," but Crane enriches the word by playing it against "the agile precincts" which both encircle and pare down into divisions. The Marlovian hyperbole "Of stars Thou art the stitch and stallion glow" bestows upon the bridge a male desire that invokes Helen in both poets' versions of the

Faust story and prepares for the transmutation of wind-harp into organ as the great bridge changes sex from woman to man. What follows is a difficult and continuous ecstasy:

> Swift peal of secular light, intrinsic Myth
> Whose fell unshadow is death's utter wound,—
> O River-throated—iridescently upborne
> Through the bright drench and fabric of our veins;
> With white escarpments swinging into light,
> Sustained in tears the cities are endowed
> And justified conclamant with ripe fields
> Revolving through their harvests in sweet torment.

That octave had been a long time evolving in Crane's drafts. In its final form it salutes Brooklyn Bridge as an unsponsored spirituality with an ambiguous relation to death. "Unshadow" is a Cranean coinage and opposes itself to a marvelous image in the "Proem":

> *Under thy shadow by the piers I waited;*
> *Only in darkness is thy shadow clear.*

There the shadow is the shape sought by the mystical lover, and so implies life and value. The "fell unshadow" is the reverse: an unclear falling away into death and chaos. Poignantly the bridge answers day with a harvest marked by tears and torment but sweet though in sadness, as in Shelley's "Ode to the West Wind." In the next octave "glittering," "white," "silver," and then "white" again mount up to "Deity's young name," a Dionysian resurrection ending strongly in "ascends."

The final octaves require being taken up together, as they culminate not only *The Bridge* but also the arc of Hart Crane's work and life:

> Migrations that must needs void memory,
> Inventions that cobblestone the heart,—
> Unspeakable Thou Bridge to Thee, O Love.
> Thy pardon for this history, whitest Flower,
> O Answerer of all,—Anemone,—
> Now while thy petals spend the suns about us, hold—
> (O Thou whose radiance doth inherit me)
> Atlantis,—hold thy floating singer late!

> So to thine Everpresence, beyond time,
> Like spears ensanguined of one tolling star
> That bleeds infinity—the orphic strings,
> Sidereal phalanxes, leap and converge:
> —One Song, one Bridge of Fire! Is it Cathay,
> Now pity steeps the grass and rainbows ring
> The serpent with the eagle in the leaves . . . ?
> Whispers antiphonal in azure swing.

This is Crane's equivalent of Shelley's voyage to death and Eternity in the final stanza of *Adonais,* another unsponsored flight of the Alone to the Alone. Walt Whitman is the Answerer, as John Keats was for Shelley. The sea flower, whitest Anemone, is heraldic here in regard to Whitman and to Blake, and astonishingly subdues the bridge to the idea of love, Shelley's "white radiance of Eternity." "Terrific threshold" as the bridge is, the white temple rises beyond it. The "Anemone" takes its name from ancient Greek: it is the wind's daughter, and as such replaces the Aeolian harp of the bridge. I agree with Edelman that Crane intends a figuration for Whitman in this sea blossom, but I don't see how that feminizes Walt Whitman, one of the roughs, an American. As Adam early in the morning, Walt is the unfallen God-Man, an androgyne.

Marvelously imagining Brooklyn Bridge's final leap as a converging with his own poem, *The Bridge,* Crane is able to summon the voice that is great within us to a sublime rising: "—"One Song, one Bridge of Fire!" The answer to "Is it Cathay . . . ?" depends on the reader's own perspective, or perhaps on events to come, as modern Cathay daily comes closer. Whitman is subtly present in *The Bridge*'s closing lines:

> Now pity steeps the grass and rainbows ring
> The serpent with the eagle in the leaves . . . ?
> Whispers antiphonal in azure swing.

Leaves of grass linger here, as does rainbow, mark of a covenant newly cut between Whitman and Crane. The serpent of time and eagle of space are Shelleyan and Nietzschean emblems and repeat the ending of "The Dance" section of *The Bridge.* Whispers are a mark of Whitman's voice, whether out of the sea or of heavenly death. The antiphon blends Crane's and Whitman's voices, properly since "Atlantis" rather than "Cape Hatteras" is Crane's worthy elegy for Whitman.

I want to stand back from "Atlantis" and render a suitable appreciation for it, since I am unlikely ever to write about Hart Crane again once I thread my way out of this particular labyrinth. There are more perfect poems by Crane than "Atlantis"—"Proem: To Brooklyn Bridge," "Voyages II," "Repose of Rivers," "The Broken Tower"—but "Atlantis" is the quintessence of America's Orphic poet. This is his icon: the poem, the icon, and the man. All of his dangerous gifts come together here: high conceptual rhetoric, preternatural sensitivity to the hearts of words, a dithyrambic ecstasy finding inevitable wisdom through rhythmical origination. "Atlantis" is his incarnate Word, at once a gathering, a splintering, and something more. Call it an unfulfilled and never to be realized prophecy, a United States of America that yet would be a sublime presence in itself and to the world.

If that rings of pretension and desperation, then I urge: "Back to Emerson!" The Optative Mood passed from Emerson to Whitman and then concluded with Crane. Two of the most intelligent of Crane's personal friends, Allen Tate and Yvor Winters, became his critical enemies because American Romanticism— Emerson, Whitman and their progeny—was anathema to them. Kenneth Burke, more gifted than either, told me that full appreciation of Crane's poetry came to him only after the poet's death, though his own informed love of Emerson and Whitman always was prodigal.

Judging *The Bridge* a "failure," however "splendid," prompts me to the question, What twentieth-century American long poem is a "success"? Time reveals that Crane—more than Frost, Stevens, Eliot, Pound, Williams, Moore—was the legitimate heir of Emerson, Whitman, Melville, and Dickinson, the central imaginative tradition of our nation. "Atlantis," and *The Bridge,* of which it was both inception and formal conclusion, grow more luminous with time. Eighty years after its publication, it more fully finds a readership deeply receptive. What seemed too difficult for students decades ago now is almost totally available to them. It helps that roughly half of my current Yale young women and young men are Asian Americans who have a fresh perspective upon original formulations of the myth of America. Like Whitman, Crane is altogether an American poet. T. S. Eliot, who made every effort to become English, remained a Whitmanian poet, despite all his evasions of Whitman. Absent in *East Coker* and *Little Gidding,* where Yeats stands in for Walt, the voice of the American bard is clear in *The Dry Salvages* and bruised but present in *Burnt Norton.* Teaching *The Waste Land* and "When Lilacs Last in the Dooryard Bloom'd" together is startlingly revelatory, as the texts keep merging. Crane was touched by Rimbaud and tormented by his own agon with Eliot, but Whitman never left him. Nor could Wallace Stevens and Eliot free themselves of Whitman. In style, Crane owed Whitman nothing, which was equally true of Stevens and Eliot. But Walt's poetic stance, rather than form or style, is difficult to escape for any major American poet after Whitman. *Leaves of Grass* is an atmosphere, a vision, above all an image of voice and of voicing. Perhaps best of all it is what Whitman called a vista.

Crane was blessedly free of politics—including our currently tiresome sexual politics—even as he was free of European or received religion. Yet he is, like Whitman, a poet of the unformulated American Religion, the faithless faith of Emersonian Self-Reliance. Criticism as yet lacks the analytical instruments that could illuminate the spiritualities of Whitman and Crane. Despite the eloquence of his letters, Crane never ventured a religious formulation in regard to *The Bridge*. And he was consistently wary of saying too much about his own conception of the myth (or dream) of America. *The Bridge* does not say it for him but instead embodies it. The structures of Crane's poem and of Brooklyn Bridge hardly can fuse, yet it is Crane's fiction that they do. In that metaphoric interlacing Crane gives us an allegory of American possibilities.

"The Broken Tower" is Crane's farewell to the art of poetry which was his life. I do not know another poem like it, despite its packed allusiveness. There are parallels of equal distinction: Donne's "A Nocturnal upon Saint Lucy's Day," Milton's "Lycidas," Blake's "The Mental Traveller," Shelley's "Ode to the West Wind," Whitman's "As I Ebb'd with the Ocean of Life." Crane desperately needed reassurance that he was still a poet, but it was not forthcoming. His suicide perhaps would have come even if he had been persuaded that his great gifts were intact. He had been doom-eager all his life.

The literary sources and analogues for "The Broken Tower" are so numerous that I wonder how even so singular a poem can suggest and contain them and yet be strengthened rather than diffused. Thomas Gray's "Elegy Written in a Country Churchyard" probably remains the most popular poem in the language, with Edward FitzGerald's *The Rubáiyát of Omar Khayyám* a close second. Both poems have become structures of allusive commonplaces and survive gloriously because of that. "The Broken Tower," difficult rather than popular, resembles the "Elegy" and the *Rubáiyát* only by powerfully usurping its forerunners. Crane's poem alludes to Spenser and Milton by way of their descendants Shelley, Longfellow, Melville, Browning, Pater, Stevens, Yeats, and Eliot, a heritage shared in part by his friend Léonie Adams, whose lyric "Bell Tower" (1929) was another starting point:

> And these at length shall tip the hanging bell,
> And first the sound must gather in deep bronze,
> Till, rarer than ice, purer than a bubble of gold,
> It fill the sky to beat on an airy shell.

Crane began to compose "The Broken Tower" in Taxco, Mexico, during the Christmas season 1931, and completed the poem at Easter 1932. Before that he absorbed D. H. Lawrence's novella *The Man Who Died,* in which a resurrected Jesus rejuvenates after making love to a woman associated with the sun as god. That is one reading—not necessarily Crane's—of his surprising love-affair with Peggy Baird Cowley, divorced wife of his old friend Malcolm Cowley. However "The Broken Tower" might be interpreted, "resurrection" of its chanter is beyond hope.

Crane had read more widely and deeply than his critics acknowledge. His "logic of metaphor" implicitly is also a history of metaphor, as Kenneth Burke remarked to me. The trope of a ruined or broken tower is endemic in English poetry and begins properly with Chaucer's Saturn in the Knight's Tale:

> Min is the ruine of the high halles,
> The falling of the toures and of the walles.

Crane may also have encountered an evocative line by Edmund Spenser quoted by some later poet:

> The old ruines of a broken toure.

In Milton's "Il Penseroso" there is the famous image of the Hermetist-Platonist in his tower of contemplation:

> Or let my lamp at midnight hour,
> Be seen in some high lonely tower,
> Where I may oft outwatch the Bear,
> With thrice great Hermes, or unsphere
> The spirit of Plato to unfold
> What worlds, or what vast regions hold
> The immortal mind that hath forsook
> Her mansion in this fleshly nook.

In the fragmentary *Prince Athanase* (1817) Shelley returned to the mode of his
Alastor:

> He had a gentle yet aspiring mind;
> Just, innocent, with varied learning fed;
> And such a glorious consolation find
>
> In others' joy, when all their own is dead:
> He loved, and laboured for his kind in grief,
> And yet, unlike all others, it is said
>
> That from such toil he never found relief.
> Although a child of fortune and of power,
> Of an ancestral name the orphan chief,
>
> His soul had wedded Wisdom, and her dower
> Is love and justice, clothed in which he sate
> Apart from men, as in a lonely tower.

The image of "the lonely tower" was captured by Yeats and became his own,
illuminated by Samuel Palmer's engraving of Milton's "Il Penseroso." Another
Shelleyan tower became more darkly influential upon Browning, Melville, and
Yeats, and through them on Crane. In Shelley's *Julian and Maddalo,* Lord Byron
(Count Maddalo) urges Shelley (Julian) to confront a dark tower based upon
the story of the poet Torquato Tasso's madness:

> "Look, Julian, on the west, and listen well
> If you hear not a deep and heavy bell."
> I looked, and saw between us and the sun
> A building on an island; such a one
> As age to age might add, for uses vile,
> A windowless, deformed and dreary pile;
> And on the top an open tower, where hung
> A bell, which in the radiance swayed and swung;
> We could just hear its hoarse and iron tongue:
> The broad sun sunk behind it, and it tolled
> In strong and black relief.
> . . . .
> "And such,"—he cried, "is our mortality,
> And this must be the emblem and the sign

Of what should be eternal and divine!—
And like that black and dreary bell, the soul,
Hung in a heaven-illumined tower, must toll
Our thoughts and our desires to meet below
Round the rent heart and pray—as madmen do."

Browning, obsessed by Shelley all his life, returned to this tower in his mono-logical quest-romance, "'Childe Roland to the Dark Tower Came'":

What in the midst lay but the Tower itself?
    The round squat turret, blind as the fool's heart,
    Built of brown stone, without a counterpart
In the whole world. The tempest's mocking elf
Points to the shipman thus the unseen shelf
    He strikes on, only when the timbers start.

Not see? because of night perhaps?—why, day
    Came back again for that! before it left,
    The dying sunset kindled through a cleft:
The hills, like giants at a hunting, lay,
Chin upon hand, to see the game at bay,—
    "Now stab and end the creature—to the heft!"

Not hear? when noise was everywhere! it tolled
    Increasing like a bell. Names in my ears
    Of all the lost adventurers my peers,—
How such a one was strong, and such was bold.
And such was fortunate, yet each of old
    Lost, lost! one moment knelled the woe of years.

There they stood, ranged along the hill-sides, met
    To view the last of me, a living frame
    For one more picture! in a sheet of flame
I saw them and I knew them all. And yet
Dauntless the slug-horn to my lips I set,
    And blew. *"Childe Roland to the Dark Tower Came."*

Crane's shadows are also in the tower, the lost adventurers his peers: Mar-lowe, Shelley, Melville, Baudelaire, Rimbaud, and others. Yeats, who said he feared Browning's influence, wrote his own version of "'Childe Roland'" many times, culminating in "The Tower." I do not know whether Crane, who read most of Pater, ever absorbed Yeats's Paterian reverie *Per Amica Silentia Lunae*, but his own early poems show traces of Yeats, and he regularly associated the Irish Archpoet with Joyce, Pound, and Eliot as the major modernists. The best motto for "The Broken Tower" would be the most famous sentence in *Per Amica*, which I shall cite one last time: "I shall find the dark grow luminous, the void fruitful when I understand I have nothing, that the ringers in the tower have appointed for the hymen of the soul a passing bell."

Widely read in American poetry from William Cullen Bryant to William Carlos Williams, Crane may have been aware of Longfellow's plangent lyric "The Bells of San Blos," but he certainly knew Melville's *Piazza Tales.* He alludes to "The Encantadas" in "Repose of Rivers" and "O Carib Isle!" but owed most to "The Bell-Tower." There the Promethean Bannadonna builds a bell tower three hundred feet tall and designs a mechanical monster, Haman, as sexton-slave to ring the massive bell: "So the blind slave obeyed its blinder lord; but, in obedience, slew him. So the creator was killed by the creature. So the bell was too heavy for the tower. So the bell's main weakness was where man's blood had flawed it. And so pride went before the fall."

Fierce self-revisionist as always, Crane greatly improved "The Broken Tower" in his final version. The drafts help clarify the poem's relationship to its precursors:

> Haven't you seen—or ever heard those stark
> Black shadows in the tower, that drive
> The clarion turn of God?—to fall and then embark
> On echoes of an ancient, universal hive?
>
> The bells, I say, the bells have broken their tower!
> And swing, I know not where . . . Their tongues engrave
> My terror mid the unharnessed skies they shower;
> I am their scattered—and their sexton slave.
>
> And so it was, I entered the broken world—
> To hold the visionary company of love, its voice
> An instant in a hurricane (I know not whither hurled)
> But never—no, to make a final choice! . . .

All the antithetical questers, from Marlowe to Melville, are "those stark / Black shadows in the tower." In terror and *scattered* (unlike God, who is *gathered* at dawn by the bell rope) the last High Romantic visionary nears conclusion.

"The visionary company of love" echoes (or alludes to) Pater's first chapter of
Gaston de Latour (1896), a fragmentary tale of a fictive young poet, disciple of
Ronsard and Du Bellay.

One can make a cento of some supreme moments in the poetry of Hart
Crane, adding to two I quoted previously— from "Proem: To Brooklyn Bridge"
and "Atlantis"—these four:

> And so, admitted through black swollen gates
> That must arrest all distance otherwise,—
> Past whirling pillars and lithe pediments,
> Light wrestling there incessantly with light,
> Star kissing star through wave on wave unto
> Your body rocking!
>   and where death, if shed,
> Presumes no carnage, but this single change,—
> Upon the steep floor flung from dawn to dawn
> The silken skilled transmemberment of song;
>
> Permit me voyage, love, into your hands . . .
>
>   ["Voyages III"]

> Down, down—born pioneers in time's despite,
> Grimed tributaries to an ancient flow—
> They win no frontier by their wayward plight,
> But drift in stillness, as from Jordan's brow.
>
> You will not hear it as the sea; even stone
> Is not more hushed by gravity . . . But slow,
> As loth to take more tribute—sliding prone
> Like one whose eyes were buried long ago
>
> The River, spreading, flows—and spends your dream.
> What are you, lost within this tideless spell?
>
>   ["The River"]

> Whose head is swinging from the swollen strap?
> Whose body smokes along the bitten rails,
> Bursts from a smoldering bundle far behind
> In back forks of the chasms of the brain,—

Puffs from a riven stump far out behind
In interborough fissures of the mind . . . ?

And why do I often meet your visage here,
Your eyes like agate lanterns—on and on
Below the toothpaste and the dandruff ads?
—And did their riding eyes right through your side,
And did their eyes like unwashed platters ride?
And Death, aloft,—gigantically down
Probing through you—toward me, O evermore!

["The Tunnel"]

The bells, I say, the bells break down their tower;
And swing I know not where. Their tongues engrave
Membrane through marrow, my long-scattered score
Of broken intervals . . . And I, their sexton slave!

Oval encyclicals in canyons heaping
The impasse high with choir. Banked voices slain!
Pagodas, campaniles with reveilles outleaping—
O terraced echoes prostrate on the plain! . . .

And so it was I entered the broken world
To trace the visionary company of love, its voice
An instant in the wind (I know not whither hurled)
But not for long to hold each desperate choice.

My word I poured. But was it cognate, scored
Of that tribunal monarch of the air
Whose thigh embronzes earth, strikes crystal Word
In wounds pledged once to hope—cleft to despair?

["The Broken Tower"]

These are six permanent touchstones for American Romantic poetry, comparable to the sublime in the world's expression, ancient and modern. At such
moments, Crane is beyond argument. He himself judged "Proem: To Brooklyn
Bridge," to be his best work. After a lifetime's reading, I award the palm to "The
Broken Tower." Why? The bells, Crane's lyric gift, have been too strong for the
tower of his consciousness, and he has been destroyed, not by society or by

family romance but by his own greatness in his most beautiful poems. He is not saying, with his belated admirer William Empson, that it is the poems he has lost, the ills, the missing dates that cause his heart to expire. His best poems *have* found him; they are the appointments he had kept (without having made them), and they end his life and poetic career.

That tribunal monarch of the air who scored Crane's Word (in every sense of *scored*) is at once Satan and Apollo, the fallen angel Apollyon of ancient tradition, who reappears in Browning's Dark Tower quest-monologue. What generally is misread in "The Broken Tower" are its two final stanzas:

> And builds, within, a tower that is not stone
> (Not stone can jacket heaven)—but slip
> Of pebbles,—visible wings of silence sown
> In azure circles, widening as they dip
>
> The matrix of the heart, lift down the eye
> That shrines the quiet lake and swells a tower . . .
> The commodious, tall decorum of that sky
> Unseals her earth, and lifts love in its shower.

"Slip" is neither a pier nor a woman's undergarment. "Slip / Of pebbles" refers to the semi-liquid material of finely ground clay used in ceramics and pottery making. Crane's new inner tower is not stone but an intermixture of male and female sexual fluids, and so returns to the clay from which we were fashioned. The poem's closing image is drawn from *Paradiso,* canto 14:

> Qual si lamenta perchè qui si moia,
>   per viver colà su, nor vide quive
>   lo rifigerio dell'etterna ploia.

"Whoever laments that here we must die in order to live up above does not see that the refreshment of the eternal shower is here."

Hart Crane was not a Christian but—like Whitman, Melville, Dickinson—a poet of the American Religion, our strange fusion of Gnosticism, Orphism, and Self-Reliance. His wonderful closing trope wistfully relies upon Dante's figure of the resurrection of the body by an eternal shower of divine love. It is an effective closure for "The Broken Tower" but not fully consonant with the tragic splendor of most of the poem. There is deep pathos in that imported Dantesque resolution. It is a borrowing rather than a lending of a myth to God.

WHITMAN'S PRODIGALS

Ashbery, Ammons, Merwin, Strand, Charles Wright

For a long time now I have mused upon Walt Whitman's relationship to poets who are my direct contemporaries, several of them personal friends: John Ashbery, W. S. Merwin, A. R. Ammons, Mark Strand, and Charles Wright, among others. Whitman's influence upon that generation is even wider: Allen Ginsberg, Philip Levine, Galway Kinnell, James Wright, the later John Hollander are clear instances. But five in a generation will suffice, whether for the American bard's direct influence or for mediation through Stevens, Eliot, Pound, and William Carlos Williams.

Starting with Ashbery today is the right procedure, for he has been the poet of his era since the publication of *Some Trees* (1956), and will be till he ends his song. Wallace Stevens died in 1955, and I still recall purchasing *Some Trees* in the old Yale Co-op on the book's publication day. I stood in the bookstore reading it through with a rising sense of joy that what had been lost with the death of Stevens and of Hart Crane before him had been recovered. Another great poet had emerged as one of Walt Whitman's prodigals.

I made too much of Stevens's influence in the early years of my knowing Ashbery and his poetry. With the passage of decades I sense Whitman as the strong precursor for Ashbery, while Stevens transmitted certain nuances of Whitman that Ashbery absorbed while studying Stevens with F. O. Matthiessen as a Harvard undergraduate. On the basis of conversations with Matthiessen, I do not think he was fully aware of the Whitmanian strain in Stevens. The poet-in-Ashbery picked up this recognition, on some level of consciousness, by reading Whitman for himself.

"Hoon is the son of old man Hoon," Stevens wrote to Norman Holmes Pearson of Yale. When Pearson, honoring me with his gift of *Poems of Samuel Greenberg* (a hidden source for Hart Crane), told me of Stevens's letter, I replied, "Yes, Walt Whitman is the son of the alcoholic Quaker carpenter Walter Whitman, Sr." There are diverse poets rambling about in Ashbery's many mansions, and some of them are not for me: let the L=A=N=G=U=A=G=E Poets take them away! Yet there is a primary Ashbery (or Ashberys), and he sings his own songs of myself and compiles his own leaves of grass.

About two months ago, Ashbery and his partner David Kermani called upon my wife and me at our Greenwich Village loft, where they had not visited before. I asked Ashbery to inscribe copies of *Flow Chart* and the new Library of America first volume of his *Collected Poems.* We had been discussing Whitman, and rather slyly John, in his inscription, quoted from *Flow Chart:* "We're interested in the language, that you call breath." In the *Collected Poems* he wrote, from "Finnish Rhapsody": "And it will be but half-strange, really be only semi-bizarre." Both passages are clues to Whitman-in-Ashbery:

The one who runs little, he who barely trips along
Knows how short the day is, how few the hours of light.
Distractions can't wrench him, preoccupations forcibly remove him
From the heap of things, the pile of this and that:
Tepid dreams and mostly worthless; lukewarm fancies, the majority of them
    unprofitable.
Yet it is from these that the light, from the ones present here that luminosity
Sifts and breaks, subsides and falls asunder.
And it will be but half-strange, really be only semi-bizarre
When the tall poems of the world, the towering earthbound poetic utterances
Invade the street of our dialect, penetrate the avenue of our patois,
Bringing fresh power and new knowledge, transporting virgin might and
    up-to date enlightenment
To this place of honest thirst, to this satisfyingly parched here and now,
Since all things congregate, because everything assembles
In front of him, before the one
Who need only sit and tie his shoelace, who should remain seated, knotting
    the metal-tipped cord

For it to happen right, to enable it to come correctly into being
As moments, then years; minutes, afterwards ages
Suck up the common strength, absorb the everyday power
And afterwards live on, satisfied; persist, later to be a source of gratification,
But perhaps only to oneself, haply to one's sole identity.

["Finnish Rhapsody"]

We're interested in the language, that you call breath,
if breath is what we are to become, and we think it is, the southpaw said.
    Throwing her
a bone sometimes, sometimes expressing, sometimes expressing something
    like mild concern, the way
has been so hollowed out by travelers it has become cavernous. It leads to
    death.
We know that, yet for a limited time only we wish to pluck the sunflower,
transport it from where it stood, proud, erect, under a bungalow-blue sky,
    grasping at the sun,
and bring it inside, as all others sink into the common mold. The day
had begun inauspiciously, yet improved as it went along, until at bed-
time it was seen that we had prospered, I and thee.
Our early frustrated attempts at communicating were in any event long
    since dead.
Yet I had prayed for some civility from the air before setting out, as indeed
    my ancestors had done
and it hadn't hurt them any. And I purposely refrained from consulting *me*

[*Flow Chart,* canto V]

The magic of the possible *apophrades,* the days of the dead when (unluckily)
the ancestors return to occupy their former thresholds, was available to Ashbery from the beginning. I no longer can reread, chant, or teach section 4 of
"Song of Myself," without *hearing* Ashbery, who has usurped forever one mode
of Whitman's voicing:

Trippers and askers surround me,
People I meet, the effect upon me of my early life or the ward and city I live
    in, or the nation,
The latest dates, discoveries, inventions, societies, authors old and new,

My dinner, dress, associates, looks, compliments, dues,
The real or fancied indifference of some man or woman I love,
The sickness of one of my folks or of myself, or ill-doing or loss or lack
    of money, or depressions or exaltations,
Battles, the horrors of fratricidal war, the fever of doubtful news, the fitful
    events;
These come to me days and nights and go from me again,
But they are not the Me myself.

Apart from the pulling and hauling stands what I am,
Stands amused, complacent, compassionating, idle, unitary,
Looks down, is erect, or bends an arm on an impalpable certain rest,
Looking with side-curved head curious what will come next,
Both in and out of the game and watching and wondering at it.

Backward I see in my own days where I sweated through fog with linguists
    and contenders,
I have no mockings or arguments, I witness and wait.

There is the positive mode of "Finnish Rhapsody" and of *Flow Chart,* Ashbery's own "Song of Myself." Having taken over the ball, Ashbery runs with it, though he runs little, barely trips along. The lesson however is more that of Valéry's "Palme" than of Whitman himself. Dreams, fancies:

Yet it is from these that the light, from the ones present here that luminosity

Sifts and breaks, subsides and falls asunder.

Not so strongly or bizarrely, as the honest thirst ("poverty" as Emerson and Stevens called honest hunger or need for poetry) is assuaged memorably by the tall poems of the world, by Whitman, Stevens, Ashbery, though modestly the last demurs, "But perhaps only to oneself, haply to one's sole identity."

    Ashbery's "sole identity" has some clearly defined traits: wistful, tentative, hesitant, imbued with a far-seeing quality best called nobility. On the grayer side, there is a restrained aversion to our public discourse and exaltation of mindlessness. In the twenty-first century, Ashbery personally can seem a final dignified survivor of late-nineteenth-century imaginative culture, resembling Harvard poets of that era: Trumbull Stickney, George Cabot Lodge, the young Wallace Stevens. Effortlessly he is the perpetual advance guard of experimental American poetry, and by paradox he incarnates archaic values.

Angus Fletcher illuminates what can be called "the Ashbery phrase" or "the Whitman phrase," reliant upon the image of a wave. If that image, in poetry, is a fault then the fault is of nature itself. Though all of *Flow Chart* can be read as a giant elegy for Ashbery's mother, unlike Whitman, Stevens, and Crane he shies away from the fourfold trope that brings together Night, Death, the Mother, and the Sea. He writes in waves but attempts to live a freedom from overdetermination by an external muse.

The consequence is that he breaks with the Miltonic-Wordsworthian tradition that seeks to assert the power of the poet's mind over a universe of death. This great theme is still embodied by "As I Ebb'd with the Ocean of Life," "The Idea of Order at Key West," and "Voyages," but is avoided in *Flow Chart* and *A Wave*. In choosing vulnerability, Ashbery allies himself with Swinburne, a poetic master who has been absurdly underrated from T. S. Eliot down to the present moment. Thomas Lovell Beddoes, uncanny Romantic lyrist, is an Ashbery favorite, as another instance of forsaking the antithetical stance against nature that goes from Blake and Shelley on to William Butler Yeats. Nietzsche, patron of antithetical thought, is not a presence in Ashbery.

There is loss as well as gain in forsaking the antithetical stance against nature. Poetry may relax too much and appear to come too easily if you abandon yourself to phrasal waves and ride with them.

You wonder as you wander in later Ashbery how you can hope to apprehend an underground stream of poetry that goes on inside him all the time. He almost always can bring poetry back up but not always the poem. As Whitman ebb'd with the ocean of life, the language kept flowing, but the poetry became diffuse and the strong poems infrequent. Ashbery, apparently asking less, fares better. No reader is happy with Walt in his dreariest cataloguings, his Songs of the Answerer, Joys, the Broad-Axe, the Exposition, the Redwood-Tree, Occupations, Rolling Earth—on and on and on. There are eight hundred pages of Whitman, and about one hundred or so remain the best work of any American writer ever, including Dickinson, Melville, Emerson, Hawthorne, Henry James, Stevens, Faulkner, or whoever you most favor. A thousand pages of Ashbery can be found in the Library of America *Collected Poems, 1956–1987*, and the second volume is like to be as capacious. I am grateful, I remain in love with this poetry, yet there is a problem of absorption with such florabundance.

And yet there are entire books of Ashbery without a flat or a resting-place, and they are too numerous to list. The lesson of Whitman was learned wisely by Ashbery, as by Stevens before him. Not every poem can be "Song of Myself" or

The Auroras of Autumn or *A Wave*. These three are grand instances of what Angus Fletcher in *A New Theory for American Poetry* (2004) calls the environment-poem, founded on the Whitman "*phrase*":

> I. Whitman, known for inventing free verse, even more radically invented a new kind of poem, which we must call the *environment-poem*. His poems are not *about* the environment, whether natural or social. They *are* environments. This generic invention, though not entirely without precedent, and not without affinities in certain nature writings, is a strange idea. Stranger than one might at first imagine.
>
> II. The principle of order, form, expressive energy, and finally of coherence for such environment-poems is the *phrase*, which I mean in a grammatical and in an extended gestural sense. The paramount use of phrase accounts for the Whitman style, and more important for his poetics, for the way he arranges the boundaries and the innards of his poems.
>
> III. The phrase, as it controls the shaping of the environment-poems that are required if he is to express any truths about a Jacksonian world—whether pragmatic, political, mystical, aesthetic, or otherwise—takes its physical correlate and its metaphysical function from Whitman's obsessive analysis of wave motions. To put it iconically: when John Ashbery wishes to overgo his own Whitmanian prose-poem, "The System," or his vastly complex *Flowchart*, he simply writes "A Wave."

American Romanticism, from Emerson to Ashbery, is seen by Fletcher as a return to the eighteenth-century English tradition of "descriptive" and "picturesque" poetry rather than to the High Romantic sublime of Wordsworth and Shelley, who alternated transcendental visions with their own versions of descriptive and picturesque precursors, James Thomson's *The Seasons* in particular.

Partly I differ from Fletcher, if only because I distrust the genre of "environment-poem." Why would not *Paradise Lost* and Blake's *Milton* also be environment-poems, or the *Commedia* for that matter? Leopardi similarly could be regarded as a master of environment-poetry. What is most useful about Fletcher's new theory is his formulation of that wavelike entity "the Whitman phrase," as fecund in Stevens and Crane as in Ashbery, and splendidly applicable to Swinburne also, and even, at moments in *Prometheus Unbound,* to Swinburne's heroic precursor, the revolutionary Shelley. Wavelike, "the Swinburne phrase" gives an absolute coherence to one of my favorites, the sequence "By the North Sea":

> A land that is thirstier than ruin;
> A sea that is hungrier than death;
> Heaped hills that a tree never grew in;
> Wide sands where the wave draws breath;
> All solace is here for the spirit
> That ever for ever may be
> For the soul of thy son to inherit,
> My mother, my sea.

Incongruously the son of an admiral, and brought up on the Isle of Wight, Swinburne thought of himself as emergent from the waves, and of the pagan sun as his true father. Ashbery turns to him in *Flow Chart* as a model for the extraordinary double sestina in canto V, commencing with "we're interested in the language, that you call breath." Taking his material from the *Decameron*, 10.7, Swinburne in November 1869 composed "The Complaint of Lisa," a bravura display of his stunning skill at versification, which Dante Gabriel Rossetti dubbed a "dodicina." Beautifully facing this challenge, Ashbery overgoes Swinburne's model in a virtuoso performance matched only by Merrill's sestina "Samos" in *Scripts for the Pageant*.

Fletcher, the Orphic literary theorist of America even as Crane is its Orphic poet, has an emphasis throughout his work on three images: labyrinth, threshold, temple. Ambivalently the labyrinth can image panic or a delight in wandering. Between labyrinth and the temple, image of centrality, intervenes a threshold, almost identical with the questing poet-hero. Hart Crane is a poet of all three conditions—labyrinth, threshold, temple—but his threshold is Brooklyn Bridge more than his fragile existence as a doomed Orpheus.

Ashbery always is on a threshold, poised between a labyrinthine Eros and a templar Thanatos. Perilous beauty is his reader's reward, particularly in the longer or long poems, *A Wave* and *Flow Chart*. As elsewhere the seminal precursor text, rarely overt in echo, is "Song of Myself," though Whitman's suave nuances are evaded with even subtler diffusions by his prodigal grandson—the composite, intervening poetic father being T. S. Eliot/Wallace Stevens. Perceptive readers, striding ahead of scholars, learn quickly to trace Whitman in Eliot, who only toward the end confessed his American indebtedness. Though necessarily ambivalent, Stevens made explicit his deep relationship to "Out of the Cradle Endlessly Rocking" and the "Lilacs" elegy in particular. Reading Ashbery, "Song of Myself" now comes first to mind, and then "Crossing Brooklyn Ferry," where Ashbery joins Crane and William Carlos Williams as legatees. *The Bridge* and *Paterson* are Whitmanian in very different ways from *The Waste Land* and *Notes Toward a Supreme Fiction*. Ashbery, knowingly an inheritor of all this richness, finds yet another path out of Whitman and Stevens to his marvelous "All we know / Is that we are a little early."

A critic who founds himself upon belatedness is not a good fit for Ashbery, as both the poet and "Goofus" (or "the old guy") are well aware. Yet that must be why I fell in love with *Some Trees* and the multitude of Ashbery volumes since, as well as those I expect to live to welcome. Fletcher wisely observes, "Whitman is always waiting, peering ahead, testing his own expectancy," and so is Ashbery. Like Wordsworth, the inaugurator of modern poetry, he celebrates "something evermore about to be." I like a parallel observation by Fletcher:

> On this account Ashbery writes with a special way of paying close attention. You will say, all serious activities, including the activity in and around a poem, are surely attentive. But in fact most poetry is deliberately inattentive. It dwells in memorized formulas (ballads); it dwells in romantic exaggerations and hyperboles ("My love is like a red red rose"); it dwells in the great generalized traditions of myth, those stories appearing everywhere as the loosely ordered *structures* of poetry and literature; it dwells in a studied indirectness and obliquity which are the very opposite of attentively observed reality. Poems seem to be elsewhere, as booksellers know. Inspired, the poets' minds drift or fly to the horizon. . . . Even neoclassic poets like Ben Jonson or John Betjeman are less haunted than might be expected by their societal facts; they are playing with societal principles. So it seems that a strictly attentive poetry is unusual, and will need a proper definition. But again, attentive in what sense? If there is something measuring and medical as well as meditative about Ashbery's verse, then there would have to be an underlying order to it, something like a search for health, or the self-examination of a body that is working well or not, perhaps the first stages of a diagnosis. Some rule of order operates here, albeit mainly hidden from sight.

> [*A New Theory for American Poetry*]

The measuring-medical-meditative sequence is Ashberian, and so is Fletcher's Montaigne-inflected "to discover the scene is to discover the self." *Flow Chart* (December 8, 1987–July 28, 1988) in its two hundred pages discovers neither, nor does that lessen this long poem. "Song of Myself" ends by dissolving Whitman's strong identity into air and earth, while *The Bridge*, like *The Waste Land*, finally yields the self to fire and water. Ashbery, allowing the tradition to choose him while refusing to be late in it, writes "Anybody's Autobiography," in John Shoptaw's phrase from *On the Outside Looking Out* (1994). That would seem to free the poet from inner evasion, yet Ashbery is as severely harassing a master of intricate evasions as are Whitman and Stevens.

For all his notorious penchant for "impersonality" as a poet, Eliot actually is idiosyncratic, more like Tennyson than Whitman, if less thorny than Browning and Pound. Ashbery still tells me he admires early Auden, who shied away from personality. If I miss anything in Ashbery's poetry it is the incantatory music of self in Shelley and his heirs: Beddoes, Yeats, Crane. Ashbery is imbued with them but stays apart from the Orphic voices, marvelously played with in his own "Syringa."

If there is a progression in the wavelike movement of *Flow Chart*, it emerges after repeated readings through a sense of attaining an epiphany in the double sestina of canto V. Retrospectively the poem seems to gradually well up to that illumination and then subside. This works rather unlike "Song of Myself," which moves through two crises (sections 28 and 38) before its surpassingly beautiful resolution in sections 51–52. And yet *Flow Chart* and the earlier *A Wave* are the most Whitmanian of Ashbery's poems, in movement and cognitive music—perhaps I should say, in breathing.

In Fletcher's eminently useful chapter on the Whitman phrase, he remarks that this phrase "is itself modeled on the virtually infinite translation of the wave—in nature, art, thought, and human experience." Is there an Ashbery phrase? His thoughts are invariably cadenced, as are Whitman's, and Fletcher's description of how Whitman thinks instantly evokes much of Ashbery for me:

> To say that Whitman thinks intransitively, veering always toward the middle voice, is to claim that he sees rather than narrates, taking the word *see* in its prophetic sense. It is also to claim that he finds this seeing a sufficient index to a possible action implied in the gesture, a Neapolitan gesture, caught by the instant photo of what is seen. We do

not forget that when he put his own engraved photograph opposite the
1855 title page of his book, he meant to suggest to the readers to read
his book in a new way. Besides the wide format permitting the long
lines to remain long on the page, he meant us to follow those lines as a
picture-taker follows a subject. Everything is a brilliant sketch, almost
a cartoon (and again his journalism is an influence). We are invited
to catch glimpses of outlines, and that requires us not to be trammeled
by ideas of logical or material concatenation. To read Whitman aright,
we have to remain perpetually intransitive, like the vast majority of
his middle-voicing verbs, his verbs of sensation, perception, and
cognition.

[*A New Theory for American Poetry*]

I hear Lucretius hovering in that last sentence, and Ashbery is another Epicurean or Lucretian poet. I am aware that he is an Episcopalian, but only as Walt
was a Quaker. In procedure as in ultimate ethos, Ashbery instructs his reader
to be perpetually intransitive. Whitman intends this to pertain also to Eros,
but here Ashbery is sly and noncommittal.

Whitman kept revising his one book, *Leaves of Grass.* Ashbery, a poet of many
books, is too copious to allow us ever to speak of "The Book of John Ashbery"
and prefers to keep his separate volumes in print, if he can. Where Whitman,
tentative and delicate in style, surprisingly sought totalization, Ashbery seems
to equate it with death. Probably we will have no last poem by him, which is
why the first poem in *A Wave*, "At North Farm," fascinates many of his readers
(myself included).

The amplitude of *Flow Chart* requires summary to be readily grasped, and
I recommend my readers to employ Shoptaw for a full account, or Fletcher's
meditation on Ashbery, which offers a dazzling and speculative interpretation.
My own mode is to study misprision, here the wonderfully creative misreading
of Whitman that *Flow Chart* ventures, implicitly and persuasively. Ashbery's
Walt is transumed into a different earliness by another maternal mourner
whose elegiac stance carries a new freshness into the ancient mode of Bion and
Moschus, Theocritus and Vergil, Spenser and Milton, Shelley and Swinburne.

Somewhere in *A Wave,* Ashbery recalls an epiphany:

There are moments like this one
That are almost silent, so that bird-watchers like us

> Can come, and stay awhile, reflecting on shades of difference
> In past performances, and move on refreshed.

The "shades of difference" between Whitman and Ashbery are more wavering than those between Whitman and Stevens. Though Stevens also is much given to wave imagery, his Lucretian swerves are abrupt, rather in Milton's manner than in the suave shadings shared by Whitman and Ashbery. Guided by Ashbery I return to "Finnish Rhapsody," one of his favorites in his vast canon, and we Ashberians can be grateful for the clue. The poem's title amicably acknowledges the Finnish national epic, the *Kalevala,* whose metrics first were brought over into English by Longfellow in his "Song of Hiawatha," still a highly readable work and personally dear to me because I first read it, as a small boy, in the eloquent Yiddish translation of Yehoash (Solomon Bloomgarden). "At North Farm" is a more enigmatic Ashberian allusion to the *Kalevala;* "Finnish Rhapsody" is beautifully funny until it raises itself into sublimity in the final verse paragraph, quoted above, which Whitman would have celebrated. Superbly balanced between ecstasy and sorrow, this affirms, with Whitman and Stevens, that the words of the world are the life of the world: "One's sole identity," however it yields, remains author of more than a few of "the tall poems of the world," the towering earthbound poetic utterances.

So large and shapely is the Ashberian achievement that I will condense it here as though *Flow Chart*'s double sestina of canto V could represent all of it. Doubtless that is unfair to someone who—in my judgment—has been our national poet for more than a half-century, yet the double sestina is as canonical a poem as Ashbery ever composed. As with its Swinburnean model, the formal, intricate elegance of this later double sestina always startles me.

Fletcher thinks Ashbery uses his double sestina to get away from problems of identity. If that is so, such a strategy gorgeously does not work:

Yet I had prayed for some civility from the air before setting out, as indeed
    my ancestors had done
and it hadn't hurt them any. And I purposely refrained from consulting *me,*
§
the *culte du moi* being a dead thing, a shambles. That's what led to me.
Early in the morning, rushing to see what has changed during the night,
    one stops to catch one's breath.
The older the presence, we now see, the more it has turned into thee

with a candle at thy side. Were I to proceed as my ancestors had done
we all might be looking around now for a place to escape from death,
for he has grown older and wiser. But if it please God to let me live until
    my name-day
I shall place bangles at the forehead of her who becomes my poetry, showing
    her
teeth as she smiles, like sun-stabs through raindrops. Drawing with a finger
    in my bed,
she explains how it was all necessary, how it was good I didn't break down
    on my way
to the showers, and afterwards when many were dead
who were thought to be living, the sun
came out for just a little while, and patted the sunflower

on its grizzled head. It likes me the way I am, thought the sunflower.
Therefore we all ought to concentrate on being more "me,"
for just as nobody could get along without the sun, the sun
would tumble from the heavens if we were to look up, still self-absorbed,
    and not see death.

To say that "the sun / would tumble from the heavens if we were to look up, still
self-absorbed, and not see death" is analogous (in a lesser key) to the ancestor
Whitman's grand defiance:

Dazzling and tremendous how quick the sun-rise would kill me,
If I could not now and always send sun-rise out of me.

["Song of Myself," section 25]

    I do not suppose Ashbery ever will give up evading Ashbery, and since this
helps his poetry, why should one care? Still even though the self is a fiction,
the waning away of self is a fiction also, and in general a rather tiresome one (at
least to me). As it should, Ashbery's double sestina concludes with a six-line
envoi, invoking the poet's mother:

The story that she told me simmers in me still, though she is dead
these several months, lying as on a bed. The things we used to do, I to thee,
thou to me, matter still, but the sun points the way inexorably to death,
though it be but his, not our way. Funny the way the sun

can bring you around to her. And as you pause for breath,
remember it, now that it is done, and seeds flare in the sunflower.

The sunflower is finally life, flaring with seeds. This will lead on to the final lines of canto V, resting upon "this vantage point, so / deeply fought for, hardly won." That proud, deserved phrasing is not at all Whitmanian. Nowhere will Walt admit the long foreground of his apprenticeship to Emerson and the King James Bible, which led to his visionary breakthrough of 1854–55. But then it is also unlike Ashbery to proclaim a triumph over difficulties in order to achieve stance, tone, voice. He always will remain Whitman's true grandson, whom the American bard would have welcomed.

It is intensely sad for me to begin writing again about Archie Randolph Ammons (1926–2001), as I keep resisting the realization that he is dead. We were very close from 1968 until he departed, a third of a century later, a friendship that refuses to end.

Ammons indulges sometimes in pretending to be affected by William Carlos Williams, but that seems a light matter to me. There was a more substantial influence of later Stevens upon the later Ammons, but that also seems peripheral. What I heard earliest in Ammons was present to the end: Walt Whitman. Emerson and Dickinson, even Wordsworth, were differences that made a difference to Ammons, but Whitman is almost always there. Walt and Archie both are sly: they *look* easy, but they are evasive and offer difficult pleasures. Both are comic celebrants of Emerson's American Sublime. They don't mock it while relying upon it, as Stevens did, yet unlike Hart Crane's, their allegiance to it is ambivalent.

Of all his contemporaries, Archie valued Ashbery most, not the Ashbery of throwaway eloquences but the poet of *The Double Dream of Spring;* the two men shared something rather like the mutual esteem for each other's work of Edwin Arlington Robinson and Robert Frost. I cannot recall ever being present when Ammons and Ashbery met, but they did on several occasions and even gave a joint reading. I remember telling Ashbery of my unhappiness at the exclusion from his *Selected Poems* of essentials like "Evening in the Country," "Fragment," and "The One Thing That Can Save America," and I recall also Ammons's laconic agreement over the telephone. But Archie understood that he and Ashbery were co-heirs of Whitman, more overtly than were Stevens, Eliot, Pound, and Williams.

Ammons never went far away from the *Sea-Drift* elegies. I once said to Archie that "Sea-Drift" would be an admirable title for a complete *Collected Poems of A. R. Ammons*—but he shook his head and answered with the single word: "Dunes."

Like Whitman's water edges, Ammons's dunes keep reforming. Once, hearing my wife admonish me for my bad habit of saying, "I am just oozing along," Archie advised, "Just drift along, Harold." I mention this because I translate much of Ammons as drifting the American Sublime. In "Song of Myself," section 25, Whitman wrote,

Dazzling and tremendous, how quick the sun-rise would kill me,
If I could not now and always send sun-rise out of me.

We also ascend dazzling and tremendous as the sun,
We found our own O my soul in the calm and cool of the day-break.

I remember chanting these lines aloud to Archie, doubtless too often, during the academic year 1968–69 at Cornell. His subtle answer to Whitman's challenge arrives initially at the close of the superb "The Arc Inside and Out" in the final pages of *Collected Poems, 1951–71:*

> . . . neither way to go's to stay, stay
> here, the apple an apple with its own hue
> or streak, the drink of water, the drink,
>
> the falling into sleep, restfully ever the
> falling into sleep, dream, dream, and
> every morning the sun comes, the sun.

An even grander reply to Whitman concludes the late, unpublished "Quibbling the Colossal":

> . . . so,
> shine on, shine on, harvest moon: the computers
>
> are clicking, and the greatest dawn ever is
> rosy in the skies.

CAST THE OVERCAST

I myself quibble with Archie about the word *quibbling*. We use it now in the Evening Land to mean an evasion or a denial, and that might suit Stevens, but not

Ammons. I take it then that Archie meant the archaic sense, a Latin pun upon *qui,* the "who" or "what" of legal documents. "Colossal" goes back to *colossus,* a huge statue or something that in significance and proportion can be likened to so large a figure. Perhaps Walt Whitman, himself a magnificent quibbler, was the American Colossal, our Sublime. With an insouciance worthy of Walt himself, Ammons lets fresh light in, and goes on giving many of us more room to breathe and stretch.

Ammons was almost as prolific as Ashbery, but here I will confine myself mostly to the readily available *Selected Poems* (expanded edition, 1986) and *Sphere* (1974). A North Carolina hill man, Ammons from the start voiced an uncanny music, unlike Whitman's yet related to one of its modes of indirection:

> so I look and reflect, but the air's glass
> jail seals each thing in its entity:
>
> no use to make any philosophies here:
> > I see no
> god in the holly, hear no song from
> the snowbroken weeds: Hegel is not the winter
> yellow in the pines: the sunlight has never
> heard of trees: surrendered self among
> > unwelcoming forms: stranger,
> hoist your burdens, get on down the road.

> ["Gravelly Road"]

That *knowing* is a mark of what I have learned to call the American Religion, our Native Strain or gnosis, of which Emerson was the theologian and Whitman and his prodigals the Orphic seers, down to the contemporary Charles Wright. Ammons is more traditional, even Shelleyan, than Whitman in relying upon an inspiriting wind:

> Guide
>
> You cannot come to unity and remain material:
> in that perception is no perceiver:
> > when you arrive
> you have gone too far:
> > at the Source you are in the mouth of Death:

you cannot
　　turn around in
the Absolute: there are no entrances or exits
　　　no precipitations of forms
to use like tongs against the formless:
　　no freedom to choose:

to be
　　you have to stop not-being and break
off from *is* to *flowing* and
　　this is the sin you weep and praise:
origin is your original sin:
　　　the return you will long for will ease your guilt
and you will have your longing:

　　the wind that is my guide said this: it
should know having
　　given up everything to eternal being but
direction:

how I said can I be glad and sad: but a man goes
　　from one foot to the other:
wisdom wisdom:
　　to be glad and sad at once is also unity
and death:
　　wisdom wisdom: a peachblossom blooms on a particular
tree on a particular day:
　　unity cannot do anything in particular:

are these the thoughts you want me to think I said but
　　the wind was gone and there was no more knowledge then.

The totality of this surrender of self remains startling: the only parallel in Whitman comes in the final section of "Song of Myself":

I depart as air, I shake my white locks at the runaway sun,
I effuse my flesh in eddies, and drift it in lacy jags.

Walt disintegrates, like Rocketman in *Gravity's Rainbow*. Ammons hears no more from the wind after its word "longing." Years later, in the dedicatory lines to the long, Whitmanian *Sphere: The Form of a Motion*, the wind and Ammons are alienated from one another:

> I went to the summit and stood in the high nakedness:
> the wind tore about this
> way and that in confusion and its speech could not
> get through to me nor could I address it:
> still I said as if to the alien in myself
>   I do not speak to the wind now:
> for having been brought this far by nature I have been
> brought out of nature
> and nothing here shows me the image of myself:
> for the word *tree* I have been shown a tree
> and for the word *rock* I have been shown a rock,
> for stream, for cloud, for star
> this place has provided firm implication and answering
>   but where here is the image for *longing*:
> so I touched the rocks, their interesting crusts:
> I flaked the bark of stunt-fir:
> I looked into space and into the sun
> and nothing answered my word *longing*:
>   goodbye, I said, goodbye, nature so grand and
> reticent, your tongues are healed up into their own
> element
> and as you have shut up you have shut me out: I am
> as foreign here as if I had landed, a visitor:
> so I went back down and gathered mud
> and with my hands made an image for *longing*:
>   I took the image to the summit: first
> I set it here, on the top rock, but it completed
> nothing: then I set it there among the tiny firs
> but it would not fit:
> so I returned to the city and built a house to set
> the image in
> and men came into my house and said
>   that is an image for *longing*
> and nothing will ever be the same again

This was Ammons's summa. He went on writing for another twenty-eight years with continued power of inventiveness, but he could not surpass this nor did he need to, for even Ashbery has nothing this exalted.

Is "I went to the summit and stood in the high nakedness" a palinode in regard to "Guide" or essentially a clarification? "Longing" ebbs to an image for "*longing*"; in Whitman, "adhesiveness" ebbs with the ocean of life, and the love of comrades generalizes yet further into the wound-dresser's dirge for all the veterans. Ammons's image for longing is fully akin to Whitman's image of voice, the tally. I remarked that once to him, and he silently nodded—but then, we had worked out Whitman's trope of the tally together across a number of years. He had read Whitman early and continuously; while we agreed as to which were the best poems, Ammons was intimately attached to "The Sleepers" above even "Song of Myself" and the major elegies.

Of Whitman's ambitious poems, "The Sleepers" seems to me the most difficult, and counts among its progeny not only much of Ammons but also Wallace Steven's "The Owl in the Sarcophagus," an elegy for the poet's friend Henry Church, and perhaps a more demanding work than anything else by Stevens. When I said once to Ammons that the surrealistic "The Sleepers" seemed not his mode he recited section 43 of *Sphere:*

> home at night and go to bed like a show folding: it's
> great to get back in the water and feel time's underbuoys,
> the cradling saliences of flux, re-accept and rock me off;
>
> then, in nothingness, sinking and rising with everyone not
> up late: the plenitude: it's because I don't want some
> thing that I go for everything: all the people asleep with
>
> me in sleep, melted down, mindlessly interchangeable,
> resting with a hugeness of whales dozing: dreams nudge us
> into zinnias, tiger lilies, heavy roses, sea gardens of
>
> hysteria, as sure of sunlight as if we'd been painted by
> it, to it: let's get huzzy dawn tangleless out of bed,
> get into separateness and come together one to one

The resemblance is clear, though the affect is opposite. Some decades ago the poet-critic Richard Howard named Ammons's great theme, "putting off the flesh and taking on the universe." The second part of that formula is Whitmanian, the first not, except in moments when Walt ebbed in despair. Ammons, like any comprehensive poet who expresses the fully human, has his American and universal darknesses, and he weathered his early (rather impressively scary) transcendental impulses and desires, his *longing.*

And yet most of his more devoted readers think of him as a poet of radiances, some in a Whitmanian epiphanic mode, but some surprisingly constant. A late longer poem, "Religious Feeling" (not included in the final volume, *Bosh and Flapdoodle*), is tentative, even for Ammons, yet seems to carry on from the admirable "Easter Morning," the major poem added to the expanded *Selected Poems.*

"Easter Morning" is several poems in one, yet at its center is mourning for the poet's little brother, who died young. Walking in his native North Carolina hills in late middle age, mourning all his familial dead, Ammons is granted a vision:

> Though the incompletions
> (& completions) burn out
> standing in the flash high-burn
> momentary structure of ash, still it
> is a picture-book, letter perfect
> Easter morning: I have been for a
> walk: the wind is tranquil: the brook
> works without flashing in an abundant
> tranquility: the birds are lively with
> voice: I saw something I had
> never seen before: two great birds,
> maybe eagles, blackwinged, whitenecked
> and -headed, came from the south oaring
> the great wings steadily; they went
> directly over me, high up, and kept on
> due north; but then one bird,
> the one behind, veered a little to the
> left and the other bird kept on seeming
> not to notice for a minute: the first
> began to circle as if looking for
> something, coasting, resting its wings
> on the down side of some of the circles:
> the other bird came back and they both

circled, looking perhaps for a draft;
they turned a few more times, possibly
rising—at least, clearly resting—
then flew on falling into distance till
they broke across the local bush and
trees: it was a sight of bountiful
majesty and integrity: the having
patterns and routes, breaking
from them to explore other patterns or
better ways to routes, and then the
return: a dance sacred as the sap in
the trees, permanent in its descriptions
as the ripples round the brook's
ripplestone: fresh as this particular
flood of burn breaking across us now
from the sun.

I might have expected to find this in one of Robert Penn Warren's later poems (he immensely admired Ammons) or in Whitman, and was surprised to find it when Ammons mailed me a typescript of "Easter Morning." Helen Vendler sees a Wordsworthian solace in the poem, but I am not persuaded. As I go on aging I keep going back to Lucretius; and I remember conversations about Lucretius with Archie in which we delighted in a common tracing of the Epicurean poet in Shelley, Whitman, Stevens, and himself. I am preceded here by Donald Reiman and others, and I am glad to see that this true aspect of Ammons is recognized.

Lucretius tempers and I think finally nullifies any religious yearnings, as a poet or person, that Ammons possessed. In our post-Freudian era, a diffused version of psychoanalysis continues the Lucretian strain. There are hints in Ammons's poetry of a recoil from his own father, of whom he found no good to mention in recalling childhood.

However hopeful a reader judges "Easter Morning" to be, Ammons himself begins "Religious Feeling" by invoking his concern with hierarchy. Rapidly this modulates to a curiously Neoplatonic One, who does not abide for any space, as ambivalence soon prevails, though Ammons is ambivalent about ambivalence. The best poem in his final volume is "In View of the Fact," a straightforward confrontation of the increasing loss of friends to death. At eighty I read it with resignation and recognition:

now, it's this that and the other and somebody
else gone or on the brink: well, we never

thought we would live forever (although we did)
and now it looks like we won't: some of us

are losing a leg to diabetes, some don't know
what they went downstairs for, some know that

a hired watchful person is around, some like
to touch the cane tip into something steady,

so nice: we have already lost so many,
brushed the loss of ourselves ourselves

As I read late Ammons I miss without regret something like Stevens's Whitmanian "mythology of modern death." In that regard Stevens is closer to Whitman than Ammons was. If you said to Archie that his early transcendental experiences had failed him, he tended to grow silent though once at least he said to me, "No, Harold, I failed them."

Sphere is not as widely read as it should be, even by Ammons enthusiasts. Perhaps it will be again, in two or three years, when a massive *Complete Collected Poems* finally emerges. Currently the poem divides its critics, except for the dedicatory chant, which many consider his finest short poem. *Sphere* aims too high, some say, and certainly it is an overtly agonistic work, the contest being with the meditative Stevens upon a ground that Ammons fails to usurp. And yet his own splendors keep breaking the vessels he hopes will contain them:

I am not a whit manic
to roam the globe, search seas, fly southward and northward
with migrations of cap ice, encompass a hurricane with

146

a single eye: things grown big, I dream of a clean-wood
shack, a sunny pine trunk, a pond, and an independent income:
if light warms a piney hill, it does nothing better at the

farthest sweep of known space: the large, too, is but a
bugaboo of show, mind the glittering remnant: things to do
while traveling: between entrance and exit our wheels

contact the ribbon of abstract concrete: speed-graded curves
destroy hills: we move and see but see mostly the swim of
motion: distance is an enduring time: here, inside, what

have we brought: between blastoff and landing, home and
office, between an event of some significance and another
event of some significance, how are we to entertain the time

147

and space: can we make a home of motion

The form of a motion for Ammons almost always leads to tropes of exile, as one
might expect from a Bible-soaked secularist. I remember telling him that the
crucial injunction of Yahweh, whether to Abraham, Moses, or Israel-in-Egypt
was *yetziat,* "get you up and go," which reverses exile. Ammons at his most
characteristic speaks to the place that the god has vacated, to what the Gnostics
called the kenoma.

He responded to Whitmanian expressions not of the fullness of being but
of the emptiness:

Of the turbid pool that lies in the autumn forest,
Of the moon that descends the steeps of the soughing twilight,
Toss, sparkles of day and dusk—toss on the black stems that decay in
    the muck,
Toss to the moaning gibberish of the dry limbs.

["Song of Myself," section 49]

Of "The Sleepers" he cited section 3 as a favorite, where a courageous swimmer
dies hard, and oddly mentioned his own brief lyric "Offset," as thematically
comparable:

Losing information he
rose gaining
view
till at total
loss gain was
extreme:
extreme & invisible:
the eye

> seeing nothing
> lost its
> separation:
> self-song
> (that is a mere motion)
> fanned out
> into failing swirls
> slowed &
> became continuum.

I thought once that I read so many books because I could not know enough people, but I remain puzzled whether knowing so many poets has made me need or want poems more or less. The last time I saw Anthony Hecht, who died in 2004, was just before he read at Yale (I cannot recall the year). I went up to see him before he came down to read, hugged him, and whispered "Magister Ludi" in his ear. He and Ammons had no affinities whatsoever, yet I found myself reading side by side this morning a "last poem" by each; Ammons's "In View of the Fact" (quoted above) and Hecht's final poem in his last book, *The Darkness and the Light,* whose last stanza resonates with my own answering spirit:

> Like the elderly and frail
> Who've lasted through the night,
> Cold brows and silent lips,
> For whom the rising light
> Entails their own eclipse,
> Brightening as they fail.

*   *   *

I pass to a living poet and friend, William Stanley Merwin. The Proteus of American poetry, Merwin has migrated through a dozen phases or so, starting in 1952 with *A Mask for Janus* and still continuing with *The Shadow of Sirius* (2008). I began to read him in 1952, and have been a constant admirer on to this moment, when he seems to me at his best. Here is his recent version of "Animula," attributed to the Emperor Hadrian, who destroyed the better part of Jewry in crushing the insurrection of Bar Kochba and the great Rabbi Akiba, founder of normative Judaism:

> Little soul little stray
> little drifter

> now where will you stay
> all pale and all alone
> after the way
> you used to make fun of things

Whoever wrote it, and to whose soul, it is finer even in Merwin than in the original. But then I think of William Merwin as a revivalist of lost originals, as a maker of "unframed originals," the title of one of his prose works (1982). A perpetual translator, Merwin has avoided the academies except as a jongleur performing his own poetry. Sometime in the early 1960s (perhaps 1961?) I recall introducing a Yale reading in which he exquisitely spoke "Departure's Girl-Friend," a poem I memorized at first hearing. I have loved it ever since:

> Loneliness leapt in the mirrors, but all week
> I kept them covered like cages. Then I thought
> Of a better thing.
>
> And though it was late night in the city
> There I was on my way
> To my boat, feeling good to be going, hugging
> This big wreath with the words like real
> Silver: *Bon Voyage.*
>
>   The night
> Was mine but everyone's, like a birthday.
> Its fur touched my face in passing. I was going
> Down to my boat, my boat,
> To see it off, and glad at the thought.
> Some leaves of the wreath were holding my hands
> And the rest waved good-bye as I walked, as though
> They were still alive.
>
> And all went well till I came to the wharf, and no one.
>
> I say no one, but I mean
> There was this young man, maybe
> Out of the merchant marine,
> In some uniform, and I knew who he was; just the same
> When he said to me where do you think you're going,
> I was happy to tell him.

But he said to me, it isn't your boat,
You don't have one. I said, it's mine, I can prove it:
Look at this wreath I'm carrying to it,
Bon Voyage. He said, this is the stone wharf, lady,
You don't own anything here.
                                    And as I
Was turning away, the injustice of it
Lit up the buildings, and there I was
In the other and hated city
Where I was born, where nothing is moored, where
The lights crawl over the stone like flies, spelling now,
Now, and the same fat chances roll
Their many eyes; and I step once more
Through a hoop of tears and walk on, holding this
Buoy of flowers in front of my beauty,
Wishing myself the good voyage.

This was published in *The Moving Target* (1963): it is original, plangent, and unlike almost anything else by Merwin. Possession of a poem by memory across nearly a half-century performs tricks of the mind: whose girl-friend is she anyway? A once forlorn splendor of a woman who identifies herself with Merwin's text (she has never met him) told me some years back that she read the title as though "Departure" was one of a series of vanishing lovers. That is not my reading but seems valid enough, particularly since I am happily bewildered by the plethora of interpretations "Departure's Girl-Friend" seems to welcome.

Each time I encounter something else by Merwin, this poem changes for me. Recently I read the beautiful prose meditation *The Mays of Ventadorn* (2002), which I had overlooked until the poet kindly sent it to me. A reader of his first volumes—*A Mask for Janus, The Dancing Bears* (1954), *Green with Beasts* (1956), poems of which are collected in *Migration* (2005)—had to hear in them the accents of T. S. Eliot and Ezra Pound:

A falling frond may seem all trees. If so
We know the tone of falling. We shall find
Dictions for rising, words for departure;
And time will be sufficient before that revel
To teach an order and rehearse the days
Till the days are accomplished: so now the dove

Makes assignations with the olive tree,
Slurs with her voice the gestures of the time:
The day foundering, the dropping sun
Heavy, the wind a low portent of rain.

["Dictum: For a Masque of Deluge"]

It is for nothing that a troupe of days
Makes repeated and perpetual rummage
In the lavish vestry; or should sun and moon,
Finding mortality too mysterious,
Naked and with no guise but its own
—Unless one of immortal gesture come
And by a mask should show it probable—
Believe a man, but not believe his story?
Say the year is the year of the phoenix.
Now, even now, over the rock hill
The tropical, the lucid moon, turning
Her mortal guises in the eye of a man,
Creates the image in which the world is.

["East of the Sun and West of the Moon"]

What you remember saves you. To remember
Is not to rehearse, but to hear what never
Has fallen silent. So your learning is,
From the dead, order, and what sense of yourself
Is memorable, what passion may be heard
When there is nothing for you to say.

["Learning a Dead Language"]

When I return to Merwin's newest and most splendid volume, *The Shadow of Sirius,* I scarcely can link what I find to the apprentice bard:

The Laughing Thrush

O nameless joy of the morning

tumbling upward note by note out of the night

and the hush of the dark valley
and out of whatever has not been there

song unquestioning and unbounded
yes this is the place and the one time
in the whole of before and after
with all of memory waking into it

and the lost visages that hover
around the edge of sleep
constant and clear
and the words that lately have fallen silent
to surface among the phrases of some future
if there is a future

here is where they all sing the first daylight
whether or not there is anyone listening

It is not so much that the Eliot-Pound tradition is gone but that Merwin, perhaps with no conscious design, has gone back to *their* American poetic origin:
Whitman, celebrant of the hermit thrush in what I continue to regard as the
essential American poem, the "Lilacs" elegy for Lincoln, though Whitman
himself disliked that valuation, since he regarded all of *Leaves of Grass* from
"Song of Myself" on to his leavetakings as one vast poem of "these States." If
I now view Merwin also as one of Whitman's prodigals, I mean that, mediated
by Eliot and Pound, renegade sons of Walt, he has found his own way back to
origins. And that, applied to "Departure's Girl-Friend," is the path I now follow
into my favorite Merwin poem and its vistas.

In *The Mays of Ventadorn,* Merwin movingly relates his undergraduate pilgrimage to visit Pound at St. Elizabeths Hospital, in Washington, D.C., after
which he received postcards from the poet, one of them inscribed, "Read seeds
not twigs E.P." The image of the young Merwin moves me, though Pound is not
exactly an icon for my contemplation.

"Departure's Girl-Friend" is a dramatic monologue ultimately stemming
from the Eliot-Pound transformation of Tennyson and Browning, and it seems
to dissolve some of the distance between poet and speaker. We do not mistake
Browning for his Childe Roland or Tennyson for his Ulysses, but no one can
sever Eliot from Prufrock or Gerontion. Merwin is hardly departure's girl-
friend yet on a high level she speaks for him, or rather for his vocation as a poet.

To define that "high level" is to engage Merwin's transcendentalism, his version of the Native Strain emanating from Emerson, blooming in Whitman, and rejected by Eliot and his acolytes. Himself the son of a Presbyterian minister, Merwin in his poetry defines the gods as "what has failed to become of us." That is hardly Emerson's confident assertion that the poets are as liberating gods. Always just the other side of a visionary perspective, Merwin is a pure poet sustaining himself in a time that wants to turn all poets into prophets. His true mode is wisdom writing, not prophecy, and I go back to "Departure's Girl-Friend" to glean a wisdom he already manifested before he reached the middle of the journey.

To love departure more than arrival: Is that an unwisdom peculiarly American? Loneliness, a lioness of discontent, hides from her mirrored image, and sets out in darkness from the city "where nothing is moored." And yet it is her birthplace, even if she refuses to know that it is her city and to acknowledge that the boat is not hers:

> and I step once more
> Through a hoop of tears and walk on, holding this
> Buoy of flowers in front of my beauty,
> Wishing myself the good voyage.

"Buoy" and "beauty" play against one another, and the "leaves of the wreath" will constitute "a hoop of tears" as she walks on. And yet she is among the victors, not the defeated, a kind of Brunetto Latini to Merwin's Dante. If Merwin is Proteus, she is a wreath for the sea, abandoned by some but not all of its leaves.

The poem is phantasmagoria, more irrealistic than surrealist. Eliot's dreamlike reveries carry repressed traces of Whitman's "The Sleepers," and, possibly through Eliot, Walt is a live presence in "Departure's Girl-Friend." Who but Whitman is so prevalent at wishing himself the good voyage? If any American poet—setting Dickinson aside—is to touch the universal, she or he cannot go by a way in which there is no knowing but must know Whitman. It could be that Merwin has never written a poem with Whitman in his mind, but Walt is there nevertheless:

The River of Bees

> In a dream I returned to the river of bees
> Five orange trees by the bridge and
> Beside two mills my house
> Into whose courtyard a blind man followed

The goats and stood singing
Of what was older

Soon it will be fifteen years

He was old he will have fallen into his eyes

I took my eyes
A long way to the calendars
Room after room asking how shall I live

One of the ends is made of streets
One man processions carry through it
Empty bottles their
Image of hope
It was offered to me by name

Once once and once
In the same city I was born
Asking what shall I say

He will have fallen into his mouth
Men think they are better than grass

I will return to his voice rising like a forkful of hay

He was old he is not real nothing is real
Nor the noise of death drawing water

We are the echo of the future

On the door it says what to do to survive
But we were not born to survive
Only to live

This is one of the double handful of Merwin's poems that all my students come to possess: "The River of Bees" from *The Lice* (1967). I too have held it in my head since 1967, and it keeps changing for me. What does not change are the accents of American elegy, which Whitman captured forever.

Merwin himself returns to a prior dream, complete with the blind Homer singing and chanting the things that have become part of American poets after Whitman, "death and day" (Stevens). Of the grass the American bard Homerically chanted, "And now it seems to me the beautiful uncut hair of graves." The biblical "All flesh is grass" returns in Merwin also: "Men think they are better than grass." The tone and sentiment are neither of them Whitmanian, but the elegiac context necessarily suggests *Leaves of Grass*. Anything but a minimalist, the sublime Walt does share with Merwin a naturalist's concern for ecology, and the two write different forms of Angus Fletcher's environment-poem. *The Shadow of Sirius*, wonderful throughout, gives us what Merwin calls "A Momentary Creed":

> I believe in the ordinary day
> that is here at this moment and is me
>
> I do not see it going its own way
> but I never saw how it came to me
>
> it extends beyond whatever I may
> think I know and all that is real to me
>
> it is the present that it bears away
> where has it gone when it has gone from me
>
> there is no place I know outside today
> except for the unknown all around me
>
> the only presence that appears to stay
> everything that I call mine it lent me
>
> even the way that I believe the day
> for as long as it is here and is me

That is Whitman's creed, except that for him it was perpetual.

I have known Mark Strand for a half-century, and have read his poetry for some forty-five years. Like his major precursors, Walt Whitman and Wallace Stevens, Strand is a perpetual elegist of the self, not so much for himself as a person as for himself as a poet, which is the mode of "always living, always dying" he has learned from Whitman and from Stevens.

If I had to name Strand's most representative poems, they might be "The Story of Our Lives," "The Way It Is," "Elegy for My Father," and the long poem or Stevensian sequence *Dark Harbor*. I used to joke to Mark that his archetypal line was "The mirror was nothing without you," but as I have aged, I prefer a grand moment in the final canto of *Dark Harbor*, where someone speaks of poets wandering around who wished to be alive again and says, "They were ready to say the words they had been unable to say."

Even four decades back, I always read each new poem and volume by Mark Strand in the happy expectation that he would be ready to say the words he had been unable to say. Across the decades, it keeps puzzling me that really there are not any words he was ever unable to say. Though much sparser in output than Whitman, Stevens, and Ashbery, Strand has developed a versatility that can rival theirs.

The elegy for the self may be the most American of all poetic genres, because our two greatest makers always will be Walt Whitman and Emily Dickinson, and they were always at home in that mode. Like Ashbery, Strand is a legitimate descendant of grandfather Whitman and father Stevens. Is he perhaps too legitimate a descendant? Sometimes I think he is too good a son and wish he would be more Whitmanian instead.

Strand is always ahead of such wishes and published *Dark Harbor* in 1993, just before turning sixty, as his superb answer to a creative agon's maturation. A long poem of forty-eight pages in forty-five sections, *Dark Harbor* is Strand's ultimate self-elegy, in Whitman's mode, and his charming answer-by-incorporation to the Stevens of *The Auroras of Autumn* and "The Rock."

I start much farther back with Strand's quasi-chrestomathy *The Monument* (1978), whose fifty-two sections hint that this is his own "Song of Myself." Heaping together Octavio Paz, Miguel de Unamuno, Shakespeare, Sir Thomas Browne, Chekhov, Nietzsche, Robert Penn Warren, Whitman, Stevens, Juan Ramón Jiménez, Borges, Wordsworth, and others would seem to be acceptable only as a poet's notebook, yet Strand makes it work as a monument in the splendidly bizarre mode of Elizabeth Bishop's poem "The Monument." Addressing "you," his unborn translator, Strand bets this prose-poem on the future. Section 35 brazenly takes the title "Song of Myself":

> First silence, then some humming,
> then more silence, then nothing
> then more nothing, then silence,
> then more silence, then nothing.

Song of My Other Self: There is no other self.

The Wind's Song: Get out of my way.

The Sky's Song: You're less than a cloud.

The Tree's Song: You're less than a leaf.

The Sea's Song: You're a wave, less than a wave.

The Sun's Song: You're the moon's child.

The Moon's Song: You're no child of mine.

Whitman saved himself for poetry by splitting the self: Walt Whitman, one of the roughs, an American, and the real me or me myself. There is (in 1978) no real Mark, the wind does not inspirit, and the cloud, leaf, wave of Shelley's "Ode to the West Wind" all scorn the belated poet, disowned by the Sun his father and the Moon his mother. Writing in his Christological year, thirty-three, in section 30, Strand cites Mark's Gospel: "And what I say unto you, I say unto all, Watch!" It is also Elizabeth Bishop, inside her poem "The Monument," calling and calling: *Watch it closely.*

There are monuments and monuments, poets and poets, Shakespeare's "endless monument" and Sir Walter Ralegh's "the broken monuments of my great desires." What has to be the monument's monument is its last section, and that is Walt Whitman's:

. . . Oh, how do I bear to go on living! And how could I bear to die now!

O living always, always dying!
O the burials of me past and present,
O me while I stride ahead, material, visible, imperious as ever;
O me, what I was for years, now dead, (I lament not, I am content;)
O to disengage myself from those corpses of me, which I turn and look at where I
     cast them,
To pass on, (O living! always living!) and leave the corpses behind.

[*The Monument,* section 52]

But not all Whitman's; the outcry that precedes is Strand's.

Dark Harbor, fifteen years later, is Strand's capable figuration that, like Whitman, he disengages from his dead self-burials:

Of this one I love how beautiful echoed
Within the languorous length of his sentences,
Forming a pleasing pointless commotion;

Of another the figures pushing each other
Out of the way, the elaborate overcharged
Thought threatening always to fly apart,

Of another the high deliberate tone,
The diction tending toward falseness
But always falling perfectly short;

Of another the rush and vigor of observation,
The speed of disclosure, the aroused intelligence
Exerting itself, lifting the poem into prophecy;

Of this one the humor, the struggle to locate high art
Anywhere but expected, and to gild the mundane
With the force of the demonic or the angelic;

Of yet another the precision, the pursuit of rightness,
Balance, some ineffable decorum, the measured, circuitous
Stalking of the subject, turning surprise to revelation;

And that leaves this one on the side of his mountain,
Hunched over the page, thanking his loves for coming
And keeping him company all this time.

[*Dark Harbor,* canto XXVII]

Without consulting Strand I read the seven tercets as, in this order: Whitman, Stevens, Crane, Bishop, Marianne Moore, Eliot, and a reconciled Strand. As a literary critic, I am a kind of archaic survival, a dinosaur, and I particularly favor the brontosaurus, an amiable enough monster. I do not believe that poetry has anything to do with cultural politics. I ask of a poem three things: aesthetic splendor, cognitive power, and wisdom. I find all three in the work of Mark Strand.

One of Strand's unique achievements is to raise the self's poignant confrontation with mortality to an aesthetic dignity that astonishes me. His earlier volume, *Darker* (1970), moves upon the heights in its final poems, "Not Dying" and the longer "The Way It Is," the first work in which Strand ventures out from his eye's first circle toward a larger art. "Not Dying" opens in narcissistic desperation, and reaches no resolution, but its passion for survival is prodigiously convincing. "I am driven by innocence," the poet protests, even as, like a Beckett creature, he crawls from bed to chair and back again, until he finds the obduracy to proclaim a grotesque version of natural supernaturalism:

> I shall not die.
> The grave result
> and token of birth, my body
> remembers and holds fast.

"The Way It Is" takes its tone from Stevens at his darkest ("The world is ugly / And the people are sad") and quietly edges out a private phantasmagoria until this merges with the public phantasmagoria all of us now inhabit. The consequence is a poem more surprising and profound than Robert Lowell's justly celebrated "For the Union Dead," a juxtaposition made unavoidable by Strand's audacity in appropriating the same visionary area:

> I see myself in the park
> on horseback, surrounded by dark,
> leading the armies of peace.
> The iron legs of the horse do not bend.
>
> I drop the reins. Where will the turmoil end?
> Fleets of taxis stall
> in the fog, passengers fall
> asleep. Gas pours
>
> from a tricolored stack.
> Locking their doors,
> people from offices huddle together,
> telling the same story over and over.
>
> Everyone who has sold himself wants to buy himself back.
> Nothing is done. The night
> eats into their limbs
> like a blight.
>
> Everything dims.
> The future is not what it used to be.
> The graves are ready. The dead
> shall inherit the dead.

Strand's gift is harbored rather than sparse.

Dark Harbor, like some earlier poems by Strand, is an overt homage to Wallace Stevens. It is as though casting aside anxieties of influence. Strand wishes a reconcilement with his crucial precursor. The "Proem" sets forth vigorously: *"The burning / Will of weather, blowing overhead, would be his muse."* But, by canto IV, we all of us know we are in the world of Stevens:

> There is a certain triviality in living here,
> A lightness, a comic monotony that one tries
> To undermine with shows of energy, a devotion
>
> To the vagaries of desire, whereas over there
> Is a seriousness, a stiff, inflexible gloom
> That shrouds the disappearing soul, a weight
>
> That shames our lightness. Just look
> Across the river and you will discover
> How unworthy you are as you describe what you see,
>
> Which is bound by what is available.
> On the other side, no one is looking this way.
> They are committed to obstacles,
>
> To the textures and levels of darkness,
> To the tedious enactment of duration.
> And they labor not for bread or love
>
> But to perpetuate the balance between the past
> And the future. They are the future as it
> Extends itself, just as we are the past
>
> Coming to terms with itself. Which is why
> The napkins are pressed, and the cookies have come
> On time, and why the glass of milk, looking so chic
>
> In its whiteness, begs us to sip. None of this happens
> Over there. Relief from anything is seen
> As timid, a sign of shallowness or worse.

This is the voice of the master, particularly in "An Ordinary Evening in New Haven." Strand shrewdly undoes Stevens by the glass of milk, setting aside any more metaphysical concerns. An effort is made, for fifteen cantos, to domesti-

cate Stevens, but the great voice, of Stevens and Strand fused together, returns
in canto XVI:

> It is true, as someone has said, that in
> A world without heaven all is farewell.
> Whether you wave your hand or not,
>
> It is farewell, and if no tears come to your eyes
> It is still farewell, and if you pretend not to notice,
> Hating what passes, it is still farewell.
>
> Farewell no matter what. And the palms as they lean
> Over the green, bright lagoon, and the pelicans
> Diving, and the glistening bodies of bathers resting,
>
> Are stages in an ultimate stillness, and the movement
> Of sand, and of wind, and the secret moves of the body
> Are part of the same, a simplicity that turns being
>
> Into an occasion for mourning, or into an occasion
> Worth celebrating, for what else does one do,
> Feeling the weight of the pelicans' wings,
>
> The density of the palms' shadows, the cells that darken
> The backs of bathers? These are beyond the distortions
> Of chance, beyond the evasions of music. The end
>
> Is enacted again and again. And we feel it
> In the temptations of sleep, in the moon's ripening,
> In the wine as it waits in the glass.

It is Stevens who tells us that without heaven all farewells are final. What en-
chants me here are the Strandian variations on farewell. Waves and tears yield
to Stevensian palms, and to the pelicans of Florida, venereal soil. A greater
meditation, suitable to Strand and Stevens as seers of the weather, arrives in
canto XXIV:

> Now think of the weather and how it is rarely the same
> For any two people, how when it is small, precision is needed
> To say when it is really an aura or odor or even an air

Of certainty, or how, as the hours go by, it could be thought of
As large because of the number of people it touches.
Its strength is something else. tornados are small

But strong and cloudless summer days seem infinite
But tend to be weak since we don't mind being out in them.
Excuse me, is this the story of another exciting day,

The sort of thing that accompanies preparations for dinner?
Then what say we talk about the inaudible—the shape it assumes,
And what social implications it holds,

Or the somber flourishes of autumn—the bright
Or blighted leaves falling, the clicking of cold branches,
The new color of the sky, its random blue.

Is that final tercet Strand or Stevens? As the sequence strengthens, deliberate echoes of Ashbery, Paz, and Wordsworth are evoked by Strand, until he achieves a grand apotheosis in his final canto:

I am sure you would find it misty here,
With lots of stone cottages badly needing repair.
Groups of souls, wrapped in cloaks, sit in the fields

Or stroll the winding unpaved roads. They are polite,
And oblivious to their bodies, which the wind passes through,
Making a shushing sound. Not long ago,

I stopped to rest in a place where an especially
Thick mist swirled up from the river. Someone,
Who claimed to have known me years before,

Approached, saying there were many poets
Wandering around who wished to be alive again.
They were ready to say the words they had been unable to say—

Words whose absence had been the silence of love,
Of pain, and even of pleasure. Then he joined a small group,
Gathered beside a fire. I believe I recognized

Some of the faces, but as I approached they tucked
Their heads under their wings. I looked away to the hills
Above the river, where the golden lights of sunset

And sunrise are one and the same, and saw something flying
Back and forth, fluttering its wings. Then it stopped in midair.
It was an angel, one of the good ones, about to sing.

The aura is Dante's, and we are in a spooky place—paradise of poets or purgatory of poets. If one line above all others in *Dark Harbor* reverberates within me, it is still "They were ready to say the words they had been unable to say." The accent remains late Stevens, but with a difference that is Mark Strand's, an even more negative transcendence.

Charles Wright's own mode of negative transcendence Americanizes ancient Gnosticism more profoundly than I could have thought possible. Here are two lines from Wright's "Disjecta Membra" that encapsulate Valentinian gnosis.

> The restoration of the nature of the ones who are good
> Takes place in a time that never had a beginning.

Throughout his work, Wright increasingly composes one continuous long poem; his natural mode is the verse journal. The initial model by now is far away; I suspect Pound's *Pisan Cantos,* but no longer can find its echoes. Wright has the unique art of bringing up from their graves the mighty dead among the poets and performing this resurrection without self-consciousness. It is as though he knows he already is among his spiritual ancestors: Georg Trakl, Dino Campana, Franz Kafka, Paul Celan. His poets are part of his landscapes, which similarly are free of self-consciousness. I find this gift of Charles Wright's quite uncanny.

Having loved Hart Crane's poems since my early childhood, I am overcome by Wright's "Portrait of the Artist with Hart Crane":

> It's Venice, late August, outside after lunch, and Hart
> Is stubbing his cigarette butt in a wine glass,
> The look on his face pre-moistened and antiseptic,
> A little like death or a smooth cloud.
> The watery light of his future still clings in the pergola.

Crane never reached Venice, yet his presence in the arbor or pergola, where plants droop over trelliswork, is wholly natural, since the dead poets are so at home in Wright's vision. The greatest of American visionary poets, the High Romantic Crane carries in his expression the watery light of his Caribbean grave. Only a poet of Wright's contemplative mastery could give us something of Crane's immediacy in a spot he never reached. As Wright goes on to say, the subject of all poems is the clock, and one day more is one day less, since making a language where nothing stays is the poet's perpetual task and predicament.

In a later book, *Buffalo Yoga* (2004), Wright evokes Kafka:

> Kafka appears in a splotch of sunlight
> > beyond the creek's course,
> Ready, it seems, to step off the *via dolorosa* he's walked through the
> > dark forest.
> I offer him bread, I offer him wine and soft cheese,
> But he stands there, hands in his pockets,
> Shaking his head no, shaking his head,
> > unable, still,
> To speak or eat or to drink.
> Then raises his right hand and points to the lilacs,
> > smiles, and changes back into sunlight.

> ["Buffalo Yoga Coda II"]

Like the vision of Hart Crane, Kafka's appearance is both uncanny and canny, ordinary and outrageous. The lilacs, with Whitmanian appropriateness, intimate both ever returning spring, and the perpetual imminence of mourning, always caught in the country music of Wright's casually abrupt short lines, mixed into the rich texture of his longer thirteen-syllable lines. This is exquisitely right for Kafka, who was most himself in parables and fragments, like the extraordinary broken tale of the "Hunter Gracchus" that never ceases to haunt Wright.

It is not accidental that Wright is drawn to the great modern poets of hopeless and tragic yearning: the Orphic Dino Campana, the similarly driven mad John Clare and Georg Trakl, and the suicidal Paul Celan, ultimate victim of the Holocaust. There is a heroic pathos in Wright's poetry that is unique to him and yet affiliates him to the visionary company that Crane celebrated and then went out to meet through death by water.

Of the greatest American poets of the generation before Charles Wright, only John Ashbery remains; James Merrill and A. R. Ammons are gone. There is a quiet radiance in Wright's poetry that will prevail, an anti-self-consciousness that heals the mind's violence against itself. Wallace Stevens said that poetry was one of the enlargements of life. Charles Wright merits that judgment but something more as well. We all carry about with us the histories, shorter or longer, of our shadows. Poetry is not, cannot be therapy, but in a time when all spirituality is tainted by political exploitation, or by the depraved cultural politics of the academy and the media, a few poets can remind us of the possibility of a more authentic spirituality. Charles Wright preeminently is one of those poets.

CODA

A backward glance at these chapters reminds me of early reading experiences that occurred three-quarters of a century ago. An awkward boy, even then with a poor sense of balance, I hovered over Hart Crane's *Collected Poems* in the Melrose branch of the Bronx Public Library. I had opened by random at the "Atlantis" canto of *The Bridge* and was caught up in wonder at the sound and movement of the language. When I read *The Waste Land* soon after, the incantatory pitch again held me, yet I half apprehended that Crane was fighting off, as best he could, the spell of Eliot's music.

In January 1973 I received a postcard from Robert Penn Warren, kindly expressing his interest in my just-published *The Anxiety of Influence* and inviting me to lunch. We had been colleagues for many years but our few previous conversations had been difficult, as his friends were my enemies. After that we became friends and remained so until he died. We met weekly for lunch, spoke frequently on the phone, and corresponded, mostly about his poetry, which belatedly had moved away from Eliot into a voice decidedly Warren's. Inevitably we talked about his relation to Eliot, which had changed only with *Incarnations* (1968) and the long poem *Audubon: A Vision* (1969).

Warren remarked that my phrase "the anxiety of influence" was a metaphor for poetry itself, which is my starting point for this brief coda. Shakespeare's influence upon himself does not mark him as unique, and yet it mattered more than the combined effect of Marlowe, Ovid, Chaucer, and the English Bible.

Milton, Whitman, and Yeats did not creatively misread themselves so much as Milton misread Shakespeare, Whitman Emerson, and Yeats Shelley. Whitman's influence upon the world's poetry remains vast, while upon American making it is all but infinite. Only a few of the strongest—Robert Frost, Elizabeth Bishop, James Merrill—did not respond to him. Wallace Stevens, T. S. Eliot, and Hart Crane belong to a particular tradition in which form is almost totally unaffected by Whitman, but the inward motions of stance, trope, and self-awareness increasingly reveal their sonship to the American Homer.

Western poetry, perhaps unlike Eastern, is incurably agonistic. Homer's contest was with the poetry of the past, but after Homer all contended with him: Hesiod, Plato, Pindar, the Athenian tragedians, and the Latin latecomers. The Hebrew poetry of the Bible is more subtly agonistic, yet the contest between authority and inspiration remains prevalent. Dante triumphantly subsumed Vergil and the Latin Middle Ages, giving the West the only possible rival to Shakespeare.

When I began to formulate the image of anxiety of influence, I relied from the start on Lucretius, whose clinamen, "swerve," became my model for the rhetorical relation between earlier and later poets. That is why so much of this book is devoted to Lucretian poets: Shelley, Leopardi, Whitman, Stevens, and others. One could have added Robert Frost, perhaps the most Lucretian of all our poets.

Paul Valéry wisely said that no poem is ever finished but merely is abandoned. There is no way out of the labyrinth of literary influence once you reach the point where it starts reading you more fully than you can encompass other imaginations. That labyrinth is life itself. I cannot finish this book because I hope to go on reading and seeking the blessing of more life.

ACKNOWLEDGMENTS

I am grateful to my literary agents, Glen Hartley and Lynn Chu, who have sustained me since 1988. At Yale University Press my editor Alison MacKeen immensely aided me in realizing the shape of this book. My manuscript editor Susan Laity more than capably completed what Alison began. For many years now I have relied upon my friend and research assistant Brad Woodworth, without whom this book could not have been completed.

I express my deep appreciation for my publisher, John Donatich, who gave this book its title and subtitle, and whom I hope to keep as publisher for the remainder of all my days.

CREDITS

INDEX